EXAMPLES & EXPLANATIONS

Legal Writing

EDITORIAL ADVISORS

EXAMPLES & EXPLANATIONS

Legal Writing

FOURTH EDITION

Terrill Pollman
Emerita Professor of Law
William S. Boyd School of Law
University of Nevada, Las Vegas

Judith M. Stinson
Clinical Professor of Law Emerita
Sandra Day O'Connor College of Law
Arizona State University

To contact Customer Service, e-mail customer.service@aspenpublishing.com, call 1-800-950-5259, or mail correspondence to:

Aspen Publishing
Attn: Order Department
1 Wall Street
Burlington, MA 01803

Printed in the United States of America.

1 2 3 4 5 6 7 8 9 0

ISBN 978-1-5438-5875-4

Library of Congress Cataloging-in-Publication Data application is in process.

SUSTAINABLE FORESTRY INITIATIVE Certified Sourcing
www.forests.org
SFI-00756

About Aspen Publishing

Aspen Publishing is a leading provider of educational content and digital learning solutions to law schools in the U.S. and around the world. Aspen provides best-in-class solutions for legal education through authoritative textbooks, written by renowned authors, and breakthrough products such as Connected eBooks, Connected Quizzing, and PracticePerfect.

The Aspen Casebook Series (famously known among law faculty and students as the "red and black" casebooks) encompasses hundreds of highly regarded textbooks in more than eighty disciplines, from large enrollment courses, such as Torts and Contracts, to emerging electives, such as Sustainability and the Law of Policing. Study aids such as the *Examples & Explanations* and the *Emanuel Law Outlines* series, both highly popular collections, help law students master complex subject matter.

Major products, programs, and initiatives include:

- **Connected eBooks** are enhanced digital textbooks and study aids that come with a suite of online content and learning tools designed to maximize student success. Designed in collaboration with hundreds of faculty and students, the Connected eBook is a significant leap forward in the legal education learning tools available to students.

- **Connected Quizzing** is an easy-to-use formative assessment tool that tests law students' understanding and provides timely feedback to improve learning outcomes. Delivered through CasebookConnect.com, the learning platform already used by students to access their Aspen casebooks, Connected Quizzing is simple to implement and integrates seamlessly with law school course curricula.

- **PracticePerfect** is a visually engaging, interactive study aid to explain commonly encountered legal doctrines through easy-to-understand animated videos, illustrative examples, and numerous practice questions. Developed by a team of experts, PracticePerfect is the ideal study companion for today's law students.

- The **Aspen Learning Library** enables law schools to provide their students with access to the most popular study aids on the market across all of their courses. Available through an annual subscription, the online library consists of study aids in e-book, audio, and video formats with full text search, note-taking, and highlighting capabilities.

- Aspen's **Digital Bookshelf** is an institutional-level online education bookshelf, consolidating everything students and professors need to ensure success. This program ensures that every student has access to affordable course materials from day one.

- **Leading Edge** is a community centered on thinking differently about legal education and putting those thoughts into actionable strategies. At the core of the program is the Leading Edge Conference, an annual gathering of legal education thought leaders looking to pool ideas and identify promising directions of exploration.

To my family.
They have always been my anchor, my heart, and my joy.
—TP

And to my family—
by blood, by marriage, and by choice. I love you all.
—JMS

We also dedicate this book to the legal writing community,
whose members have sustained and nurtured us.

Contents

Acknowledgments

Terry Pollman thanks the William S. Boyd School of Law for its support of her and of legal writing at UNLV. She will always be grateful to her colleagues, her students, and especially to her coauthors for making it fun to work together..

Judy Stinson thanks Dayna Rauliuk for her insightful feedback making this fourth edition stronger, especially with the addition of a new common law problem. Thanks also to Matthew Lutz for being willing to share his memo on that problem.

We thank Richard Neumann for his substantial help in starting the project, and Elizabeth Pollman for her many important contributions to the first two editions. Thanks also to Linda Berger for writing a copyright and fair use problem that we adapted as an example that runs throughout the book, and the entire legal writing faculty at both ASU and UNLV. We know we are fortunate to be a part of the legal writing community, where so many great teaching ideas are so often and so generously shared. We hope that if we have forgotten to acknowledge an individual, you will understand that after years of teaching in such a generous community, we are sometimes no longer sure where each idea originated or how many wonderful colleagues have added to it.

PART I

Introduction

CHAPTER 1

How to Use This Book

Focus on the user and all else will follow.

—*Google slogan*

Google built a thriving business by making its products *useful* and *pleasingly easy to use*. We've tried to do something like that in writing this book.

Your memos and briefs will be more effective if you write them with the same goals in mind. Think about the reader's needs, just as Google has thought about yours. How can you make your memos and briefs *useful* to the reader? And how can you make them *pleasingly easy to use?* Your reader is your audience. In this book, for example, we've written in a more conversational tone than in a formal legal writing document because we think this will make it easier for you to read and use. When you can identify a specific reader—like your own legal writing professor—you'll need to pay attention, above all else, to that individual reader's priorities. This book explains what many professors typically consider to be effective writing, but you'll need to pay attention in class and ask questions in teacher–student conferences to tailor your document to the expectations of your audience—the reader who is also your professor. As with other books in the Examples & Explanations series, if we seem to be saying something different from what your professor says, your professor is right.

HOW THE BOOK IS ORGANIZED

The organization of this book generally follows the organization of typical first-year legal writing courses. Most courses first cover objective or predictive writing, asking students to write office memos, and then cover persuasive writing, asking students to write motions and briefs. We've also included a section on revising and rewriting because those skills are necessary to all good writing.

Most of this book's chapters are divided into four sections:

"What You Need to Know." The first section of each chapter explains, as simply as possible, the essentials about a part of the writing process. Writing is a complex art. Sometimes in our attempt to give you what you need quickly, we necessarily simplify some of the finer points. For the most part, we cover, at a basic level, the essentials—the things everyone in a legal writing course must master. We've tried to keep things as straightforward as possible, to make the material accessible and quick to digest. Later, as you mature as a lawyer and writer, you'll pick up more subtle nuances. Learning to write is a lifelong project.

"How to Do It." The next section provides a step-by-step process for accomplishing the writing task addressed in that chapter. Not everyone follows the same steps to accomplish a particular purpose, but we illustrate at least one way to think through the particular parts of your writing project.

"Examples" and "Explanations." A typical chapter includes examples that ask you to evaluate the effectiveness of a sample piece of writing. Examples are followed by explanations for you to check your work.

Throughout the book, most of our examples come from three hypothetical problems. The first involves a vehicular manslaughter prosecution in which the defendant used a cell phone while driving (Appendix A has the details). In the second hypothetical problem, a popular singer alleges a copyright violation by another singer, who might in turn raise an argument based on what copyright law calls the fair use defense (Appendix B has the details). The third hypothetical involves a claim of negligent infliction of emotional distress by a woman whose fiancé was seriously injured (Appendix C has the details). In many instances, you'll be able to follow the examples just by reading through the chapter in which they occur. But wherever you need more information or want to understand the example more fully, the facts and the relevant law are in the Appendices. In addition, some examples use fictional cases for illustrative purposes.

How you use these examples and explanations will determine how much value the book will hold for you.

"Checklists." A checklist at the end of each chapter will help you review the chapter's key points. You will find all of the checklists compiled in one place in Appendix D.

HOW TO USE EXAMPLES

Social scientists have studied how using examples helps you learn. Here are some of their findings.

Learning through examples can help you become a better writer. In law school, when you face a new writing assignment, you actually face two tasks. The first is to write a successful document for the assignment in your course. The second is to learn from the experience in a way that you can use in the future when you create new documents. Researchers have identified a problem with this process: the task of writing a new document takes up so much "cognitive load," or mental energy, that students have little left to spend on learning more generally from the experience. This research suggests there is great value in observing and thinking about writing when you're not also simultaneously tasked with creating a written document.

Passive observation helps little; students learn best from examples when they "self-explain" as they observe. The research makes clear that students can learn from examples, but it also shows that those who *actively engage* with the example learn much more than those who observe passively. As you work through the book, talk with yourself silently about what you see and the choices you make.

The best strategies for "self-explanation" include observation, evaluation, and reflection. We've designed the examples in this book to provide all three ways to improve learning from examples.

- **Step 1: Observe.** The step-by-step model in the "How to Do It" sections invites you to actively explain to yourself what you're *observing* as you work through the process. Check your work against our explanations of the steps.
- **Step 2: Evaluate.** It's especially important for you to *evaluate* your responses as you complete the questions in the "Examples" portions of each chapter.
- **Step 3: Reflect.** As you compare your "self-explanation" to the "Explanations" offered at the end of each chapter, *reflect* on the general rules you should learn from the chapter. This reflection will help when you next face the task of writing.

HOW TO USE THIS BOOK

If you're familiar with other books in the Examples & Explanations series, you'll notice that this book has many of the same features—most notably a series of examples to test your understanding of various concepts and explanations to help you understand the material more fully. Unlike some other E & E's, though, this book is focused on teaching a skill rather than doctrine. The chapters therefore include "How to Do It" sections that are not found in other E & E books. These sections will prepare you for the more familiar "Examples" and "Explanations" part of each chapter.

In addition, unlike other E & E's, some examples have more than one correct answer. In each chapter, we'll either ask you to figure out which is the "best" answer (sometimes there will only be one correct answer, but other times there will be a number of potentially good choices and you'll have to decide which answer is the strongest) or to identify all of the correct answers (and that could be one or more).

Legal writing professors sometimes hesitate to give students examples because occasionally students use them poorly. We stress two things:

- Please do *not* imitate one of our examples without thinking about whether it's appropriate to your assignment. It might work for your assignment . . . or it might not. Be thoughtful about whether and how you imitate examples.
- And please do not imitate an example just because it's in the book. Some of the examples illustrate ineffective writing and ask you to identify the mistakes in the example. Know what you're doing and why you're doing it.

By using the "self-explanation" technique as you work through the examples, you'll develop the ability to view your own work critically. You'll learn to articulate reasons for the choices you make in your writing, which will strengthen your writing and help you work as part of a team. Be as specific as you can during this self-explanation. For instance, "This way of structuring the Question Presented helps me present the crucial facts in a convincing way." Learning to examine your own writing critically and to reflect on your choices is essential to becoming an effective legal writer.

Two other learning techniques are worth considering as you use this book. The first is based on the research showing that retrieval through self-testing is a more effective learning technique than repetition. In other words, rather than just reading information over and over, your learning will be more effective and durable if you self-test by using the example questions as quizzes. You can also test yourself by creating your own quiz questions to test your learning.[1]

1. Terrill Pollman, Jeanne Frazier Price, & Linda L. Berger, Examples & Explanations: Legal Research 4-5 (2017).

The second technique suggests that "interleaving," or the practice of skipping around as you test yourself, rather than "massing" your practice into single-topic sessions where you simply and repeatedly read the same material, will improve your learning. Think of the times you have crammed for a test and then remembered nothing a few weeks later. Instead, while you are working on the example questions from one chapter, take the time to do a few questions from an earlier chapter.[2]

Although this book necessarily oversimplifies some of the finer points about legal writing, we hope that it helps you improve in the areas where you struggle. Remember that writing is an art. Formulas will help get you started and can definitely improve your final work product, but writing involves a lifelong learning process. Your dedication to the craft and willingness to continue observing, evaluating, and reflecting is what will make you a truly gifted legal writer.

Checklist

Chapter 1: How to Use This Book

✔	Write for your reader: your professor's advice trumps this book and you should always keep in mind who your audience is when writing.
✔	Observe, evaluate, and reflect as you work through this book.
✔	Actively engage with the examples by explaining to yourself why you made the choices you made.
✔	Think about whether the example fits your assignment before you imitate it.
✔	Practice "interleaving" by skipping around the text and returning to previous examples to improve your understanding.

You will find all of the chapter checklists compiled in Appendix D.

2. *Id.*

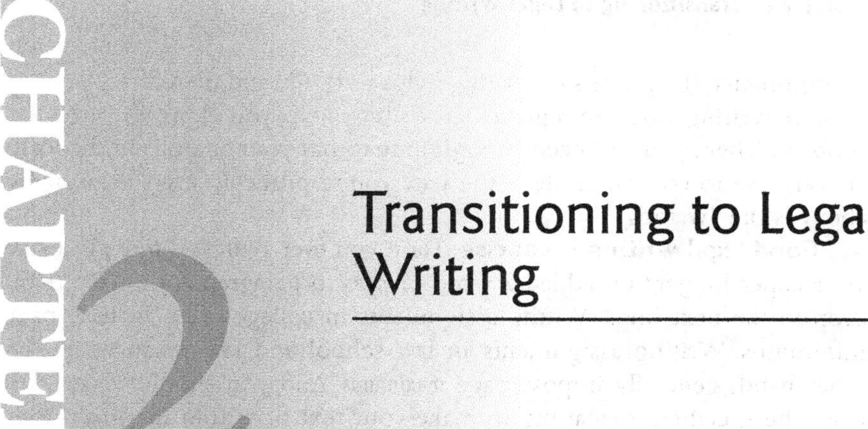

Transitioning to Legal Writing

The great skills you developed in your undergraduate studies will be helpful in law school, but often only after you internalize the conventions of legal writing. As you start, a few things will seem very different. For instance, you'll very likely need to study more. And the writing you'll do in law school (and law practice) differs in some respects from what you did in college. This chapter highlights a few of the differences between writing in college and writing in law school and provides some tips to succeed.

WHAT YOU NEED TO KNOW ABOUT TRANSITIONING TO LEGAL WRITING

Legal writing often takes more time than other kinds of writing you may have done before. It isn't just the actual act of writing that takes more time; the entire thought process is far more challenging and time-consuming for most students. Legal writing requires more than describing, summarizing, or categorizing; it also requires synthesizing, analyzing, and sometimes persuading. You'll get faster over time, but at first, this process will be surprisingly slow. In law school, writing will take longer than you expect.

Therefore, don't wait until the weekend before a memo or brief is due to start writing. Start early—much earlier than you're used to—so you'll have time to work through the analysis and refine your predictions or arguments. The process of writing helps us think, and therefore you need to start writing early enough to let writing help you think through the problem. Then, you still need enough time to put your analysis in the form lawyers use to communicate—the part you're probably used to thinking about as the "writing."

Good legal writing is concise. Have you ever switched fonts to make your paper longer? Or added a word or two to paragraphs to make them drop to the next line? Writing assignments in college often include page minimums. Writing assignments in law school and law practice, on the other hand, generally impose page *maximums*. And you should never vary from the specified formatting to make your text fit within the limit. Your goal is to make the paper as concise as you can and still say everything that needs to be said. This will take practice, but you'll get better at it just by recognizing that your goal isn't to make the document as long as possible. Chapter 31 explains how to write more concisely.

Legal readers expect your writing to be formal. In college, writers often have some flexibility with their tone. In law school and law practice, though, you'll almost always write in a formal tone. Avoid contractions, for example. (This book uses them a lot—but we aren't submitting this material to a judge, supervising attorney, or legal writing professor.) In addition, avoid the first person (I or we), even though the reader knows it's your analysis or argument. Use last names, don't omit articles (the, a, an), and otherwise think about making your writing more formal than your usual spoken tone.

Minimize the use of quotations, but quote key statutory language. Most of what you discuss in memos and briefs will be cases. Even though a court has some inherent credibility, don't quote its every word. Instead, determine what a particular case holds and express that holding in your own words. Of course, sometimes a court uses wonderfully helpful language. When that happens, quote it. And rules articulated by the highest court in a jurisdiction tend to be quoted more often than lower court pronouncements. But make that the exception when discussing cases.

When discussing statutes, quoting the relevant language is required. Statutory language is significant because the words the legislature chose affect the meaning of the law. But quote *only* the words that must be interpreted for your particular issue, not vast blocks of statutory language.

So remember: quote key statutory language, but generally paraphrase cases.

Avoid "elegant variation," unnecessary legalese, and other distracting stylistic choices. In college, students sometimes want their writing to sound "flowery" and interesting. They vary their use of terms to make it less monotonous or to sound smart. With legal writing, the subject matter is often complex and it's important to express your ideas as clearly and simply as possible.

Use terms of art—the key terms that the statute or cases use—repeatedly and consistently. Don't vary them just for the sake of breaking up the monotony. Similarly, avoid legalese *unless* it's one of those terms of art. In contrast to a "term of art," which has a specific legal meaning, "legalese" is just unnecessary gobbledygook. The movement to "Plain English" has caught on with force in legal writing, and most legal readers expect your writing to omit unnecessary legalese. It's also a good idea to avoid stylistic choices that might draw the reader's attention, like split infinitives ("to boldly go where no man has gone before"[1] —separating the "to go" with "boldly" in the middle). If the reader has to stop and wonder why you've written your document the way you have, chances are the reader isn't able to focus fully on your substance. And that means your writing isn't fully effective.

Use past tense to discuss the client's facts as well as the facts and holdings of other cases. But legal writers generally use present tense when stating a rule of law. For instance, "The court found the defendant had acted in self-defense when he punched the victim and held that he was therefore not guilty of assault. A defendant who uses force against another because he reasonably believes that the other person will imminently injure him acts in self-defense and does not commit assault." The first sentence discusses the case's facts and holding, and is therefore in past tense. The second sentence states the general rule of law, so present tense is used there.

Courts don't "feel," "think," or "believe." Courts "hold," "state," "find," "reason," "conclude," etc. Courts are institutions, not people. Accordingly, we refer to a court as "it" not "they." And so even though judges are people, we presume they act objectively. Discuss what the court reasoned rather than thought, what the court held rather than believed, and what the court found rather than felt.

HOW TO MAKE THE TRANSITION TO LEGAL WRITING

Using the cell phone manslaughter problem in Appendix A, we'll walk you through the process of using the tips from this chapter. If you haven't yet reviewed Appendix A, it would be helpful to review it now to get acquainted with the basic law and facts.

1. Some readers might recognize this line from the original *Star Trek* episodes.

PROBLEMS

Problem

Here is a quick overview of the cell phone manslaughter problem (for details, see Appendix A). Allison King used her wireless phone, without a hands-free device, while driving in dense fog on a winding road on the edge of an ocean cliff. King placed the call to warn her friends about the dangerous conditions, as they would be meeting later. While she was making the call, she hit and killed a bicyclist. The prosecution will attempt to convict King of vehicular manslaughter by showing that she drove while committing an illegal act (driving while using a wireless phone without a hands-free device) and with gross negligence. King will argue that her actions fit within the "emergency purposes" exception to the wireless phone prohibition; she will also argue that she did not act with gross negligence.

Step 1: Start working on your assignment immediately after you receive it, not days or weeks later. Because it will take longer to analyze—much less actually write—memos and briefs in law school, start early. Read the materials, think about them, and consider outlining your analysis. Chapter 7 explains how to organize that analysis.

Step 2: While writing, think about quoting key statutory language, being concise, and using a formal tone. Legal documents—even intra-office memos—are formal documents. It might sound stuffy at first, but you'll get used to the expected tone. Review good samples in your textbook or those provided by your professor to help get a feeling for what good legal writing "sounds" like.

Following these guidelines, you might transform this problematic statement of the rule:

> People are found guilty (convicted) of vehicular manslaughter when they kill another person unlawfully, and when they don't have malice when they commit the killing. Furthermore, this killing has to happen while the defendant is driving in the commission of an unlawful act, and that act can't be a felony, and the defendant has to have gross negligence. Cal. Penal Code § 192 (West 2022).

into this statement of the rule:

> Vehicular manslaughter is manslaughter—"the unlawful killing of a human being without malice"—that occurs when "driving a vehicle in the commission of an unlawful act, not amounting to felony, and with gross negligence." Cal. Penal Code § 192 (West 2022).

Note how much shorter the second rule statement is, and how it quotes the key phrases in the statute. The first rule statement includes some of that key language, but it doesn't use quotation marks—and that is problematic. Quote key statutory language, use quotation marks, and keep the rest of your writing formal and concise.

Step 3: Rewrite—again and again and again. In college, it might have been enough to write a paper in a single draft, proofread it, and turn it in. In law, you can't be an effective writer unless you go back to your draft many times, each time seeing it with fresh eyes and reorganizing it and rewriting paragraphs and sentences. It might take four or five drafts to write an effective memo or brief and several more drafts after that to write an excellent one. This will continue for the rest of your career.

Step 4: Review your writing to ensure you've used the appropriate writing style, tense, and word choice. Avoid distracting stylistic choices, like varying terms. Remember to use past tense for everything that already happened, but present tense for rules. Finally, keep in mind the role that judges play, and think about how you describe what it is they do.

Consider the problems in this paragraph:

> Allison King uses her cell phone for "emergency purposes" within the meaning of the statute when she calls her friends to warn them that the fog and low visibility make it dangerous for them to drive on Highway 1, the road she is driving on. Like the defendant in *Newton*, who calls his wife's obstetrician while driving to the hospital because his wife is in labor, King calls her friends to help protect them and others by trying to keep them off the aforementioned road. The *Newton* court felt that this reason was serious enough to be excusable. The same thing should happen in King's case.

With some rewriting, you might improve it like this:

> Here, King used her cell phone for "emergency purposes" when she called her friends to warn them of the dangerous driving conditions. Similar to the defendant in *Newton*, who called his wife's obstetrician while driving his wife to the hospital because she was in labor, King called her friends to protect them and others by keeping them off the road. The *Newton* court's holding that the call was made for emergency purposes suggests King's call was likely also made for emergency purposes.

The second paragraph is not only shorter, but it's also easier to understand.

EXAMPLES

Review the following examples. For each example, there may be more than one correct answer, but try to choose the *best* answer. Explain to yourself why you have chosen that answer. Then read the explanations in the last section of this chapter to check your work.

Example 2-1

This question uses the copyright and fair use problem, which you can find in Appendix B.

> Copyright protection includes an exception herewith for "fair use." The third factor of said exception concerns "the amount and substantiality of the portion used in relation to the copyrighted work as a whole." 17 U.S.C. § 107(3). In *Fisher v. Dees*, the court believed that "many parodies distributed commercially may be 'more in the nature of an editorial or social commentary than . . . an attempt to capitalize financially on the plaintiff's original work.' In such cases, of which this is one, the initial presumption need not be fatal to the defendant's cause. The defendant can rebut the presumption by convincing the court that the parody does not unfairly diminish the economic value of the original." 794 F.2d 432, 437 (9th Cir. 1986) (internal citations omitted). Similarly, in *Mattel, Inc. v. Walking Mountain Productions*, the court felt that we "assess the 'persuasiveness of a parodist's justification for the particular copying done,' recognizing that the 'extent of permissible copying varies with the purpose and character of the use.'" 353 F.3d 792, 803 (9th Cir. 2003) (citations omitted).

This is an . . .

A. effective paragraph because it sounds like it was written by a lawyer.
B. effective paragraph because it quotes the cases extensively.
C. effective paragraph because it avoids elegant variation.
D. ineffective paragraph.

Example 2-2

This question uses a hypothetical aggravated assault problem.

> Mark didn't commit assault, much less one that was "aggravated." True, he hits George with a pole, but George swings at him first. Plus, Mark thinks (and this seems reasonable) that George has a knife. Therefore, Mark's actions are in self defense, and he isn't guilty.

This is an . . .

- **A.** effective paragraph because it avoids legalese by being easy to read and not too stuffy.
- **B.** effective paragraph because it keeps the story active by using the present tense.
- **C.** effective paragraph because it is concise.
- **D.** ineffective paragraph.

EXAMPLES

Example 2-3

This question uses the cell phone manslaughter problem, which you can find in Appendix A.

> King is not likely to be found guilty of vehicular manslaughter in California. "Manslaughter is the unlawful killing of a human being without malice." Cal. Penal Code § 192 (West 2022). Vehicular manslaughter is manslaughter that occurs when "driving a vehicle in the commission of an unlawful act, not amounting to felony, and with gross negligence." Cal. Penal Code § 192(c)(1) (West 2022). There is no question that King's driving killed the bicyclist and that she acted without malice. She probably did not, however, commit an "unlawful act" or act with "gross negligence."

This is an . . .

- **A.** effective paragraph because it quotes only the necessary statutory language and uses proper tone and style.
- **B.** ineffective paragraph because the sentences are too short and choppy.
- **C.** ineffective paragraph because there are too many quotations.
- **D.** ineffective paragraph because it switches tenses too often, which is likely to confuse the reader.

EXAMPLES

Example 2-4

This question uses a hypothetical disorderly conduct problem.

> The defendant, who has been charged with disorderly conduct in violation of the statutes of New Mexico, Chapter 30, Article 20, Section 1, which requires that he was acting really loud or violent or using profanity, is not likely to be convicted but is more likely to be acquitted because he didn't really yell at the victim or swear at him, and he didn't hit him or do anything that seemed like he was going to go crazy or get really agitated. He was just talking to him, even though he used a voice louder than usual and that others could hear from a distance, but he wasn't really that mad and so it seems like he probably didn't do what the statute prohibits, being excessively noisy or profane or enraged, and even if he maybe did one of those things, I think a jury probably won't find him guilty.

This is an . . .

A. effective paragraph because it avoids quotations.
B. effective paragraph because it reinforces key points by repeating them while using different terminology to not bore the reader.
C. effective paragraph because it doesn't use legalese.
D. ineffective paragraph.

EXAMPLES

Example 2-5

This question uses the negligent infliction of emotional distress problem, which you can find in Appendix C.

> Poe likely cannot recover damages for negligent infliction of emotional distress as a bystander. A plaintiff will recover when: (1) the defendant's negligence injured or killed the victim; (2) the plaintiff had an "intimate familial relationship" with the victim; (3) the plaintiff directly observed or was "sensorially aware" of the accident and the victim's resulting injury; and (4) the plaintiff experienced severe emotional distress. *Dunphy v. Gregor*, 642 A.2d 372, 372 (N.F. 2013). Although three elements are probably met, Poe likely did not have an intimate familial relationship with Valenzuela.

This is an . . .

A. effective paragraph because it quotes the relevant statutory language.
B. effective paragraph because it is an example of good legal writing.
C. ineffective paragraph because it includes too much legalese.
D. ineffective paragraph because it is too formal and avoids contractions.

EXPLANATIONS

EXPLANATIONS

Explanation 2-1

A is wrong. The characteristics that make it "sound like it was written by a lawyer"—the legalese—actually make the paragraph ineffective. For instance, "herewith" is legalese and adds nothing to the substance of the sentence. Use plain English unless you're writing about a particular term of art. **B** is also wrong. Quote relevant statutory language, but quote sparingly from cases. The reader expects you to synthesize and summarize the material. These topics are covered in more detail in Chapters 8 and 9. **C** is not the best choice; although this paragraph avoids elegant variation, simply avoiding that one problem won't make an otherwise ineffective paragraph effective. **D** is the best answer. This paragraph is ineffective for the reasons A and B are wrong. In addition, the writing style is not concise and this paragraph refers to what a court "believed" and "felt," and those terms aren't used when describing a court's actions.

Explanation 2-2

A is wrong. Although avoiding legalese is good, legal writing uses a more formal, professional tone. For instance, use last names and avoid contractions. In addition, use terms of art—like "aggravated assault." **B** is also wrong. Using the active voice and following the traditional subject–verb–object sentence structure is generally easier for readers to follow. But that doesn't mean you shouldn't use past tense. Past tense (writing about things that happened in the past as if they already occurred) is different from passive voice, which often omits the subject or places the subject near the end of the sentence rather than at the beginning. The incident with the pole already happened, so describe it using the past tense. **C** is not the best choice. Although this paragraph is relatively short, it is too informal and the writing style is problematic. **D** is the best choice. For the reasons stated in A and B, this paragraph could be more effective.

Explanation 2-3

A is the best answer. This paragraph quotes the key statutory provisions. It also uses terms of art, like "unlawful act" and "gross negligence," consistently. The paragraph is easy to read and the writing style is not distracting. **B** is not the best answer because although the sentences are short, short sentences in the active voice often work best in legal writing. **C** is incorrect. Although you should rarely quote from cases, quoting key statutory language, as noted in A, is necessary. **D** is not the best choice. It is always important to avoid confusing your reader, but legal readers are trained to expect certain tenses for certain information. This paragraph properly uses past tense when stating the facts of King's case and present tense when stating rules of law. It also properly uses future tense in the first sentence when discussing what is likely to happen (the likely outcome of the case) in the future.

Explanation 2-4

A is incorrect because there is a statute involved in this problem. It's true that you shouldn't quote much from cases, but key statutory language needs to be quoted, even if it's just a few words. Here, the reader doesn't know what the statute actually prohibits, and this problem is made worse by the writer using a variety of terms to describe similar behavior in the same paragraph. **B** is wrong for some of the same reasons; terms of art—terms the legislature used when defining an offense, for example—need to be used consistently to avoid confusing the reader. Elegant variation isn't helpful in legal writing.

Furthermore, this two-sentence paragraph isn't concise. It's unnecessarily repetitive, and this is more likely to confuse the reader than help. **C** is also wrong. Terms of art are an exception to the general rule against using legalese. In addition, the writing style in this paragraph is too informal for legal writing and the writer should avoid the first person. **D** is the best answer. The paragraph is ineffective for the reasons stated in A, B, and C.

EXPLANATIONS

Explanation 2-5

A is incorrect because this problem does not involve a statute, so no statutory language is quoted. This is a common law problem (see Chapter 6). **B** is the best answer. This paragraph generally paraphrases cases, quoting only the key language—those "terms of art" (key terms that the cases use to define the applicable law). It is also relatively concise, considering the rule is somewhat lengthy. **C** is not the best choice. This paragraph is generally easy to understand and avoids legalese, using only the key terms of art. **D** is incorrect. Legal writing should be formal and avoid contractions.

Checklist

Chapter 2: Transitioning to Legal Writing

✔	Start working on your assignment early and plan for writing to take longer than usual and to work through many drafts.
✔	Be concise.
✔	Use a formal tone without first person or contractions but with last names and using articles.
✔	Quote key statutory language, but generally paraphrase cases.
✔	Avoid "elegant variation," unnecessary legalese, and other distracting stylistic choices.
✔	Use past tense to discuss the client's facts as well as the facts and holdings of other cases, but use present tense when stating a rule of law.
✔	A court doesn't "feel," "think," or "believe," and a court is an "it" not a "they."

You will find all of the chapter checklists compiled in Appendix D.

PART II

Objective Writing

CHAPTER 3

Overview: Office Memos

Your first major writing assignment might be an analysis that requires you to explicitly address both sides of an issue, like an office memo or part of one. This chapter provides an overview of the audience, purpose, and format of an office memo. It also discusses some helpful tips and some common pitfalls to avoid.

AUDIENCE AND PURPOSE OF AN OFFICE MEMO

An office memo analyzes a specific legal problem or question. Typically, an office memo is predictive—it answers a question about how the law would likely apply to a particular set of facts and predicts the outcome. For instance, a memo might address the question of whether under federal copyright law a court would likely conclude that a certain song that parodies another song falls within the fair use exception to copyright infringement.

The information in the office memo usually serves as a basis for deciding how to proceed in a case or situation—either to help with a client's planning decision (for instance, how to organize a business for certain tax consequences) or to help a lawyer make a strategic decision (for instance, whether filing a certain motion would likely be worthwhile). Typically, junior attorneys or summer clerks write office memos for more senior lawyers at a law firm or office, although sometimes clients or others also receive a copy.

A good memo fully and objectively evaluates each question presented without arguing for or against a certain outcome. The viewpoint is neutral. Your role as the writer is not to persuade the reader of any particular argument or result—only that your analysis is objective, thorough, and accurate. The reader wants to get as accurate a sense as possible of the facts, the law, and the likely outcome to make an informed decision about how to proceed. Assume that the reader hasn't read any of the legal authorities you discuss and doesn't know the relevant facts.

OFFICE MEMO FORMAT

Legal memos vary in their format. Some law firms or attorneys have a preferred format with specific section titles, ordering of sections, and the like. Sometimes preferences vary given the circumstances. For instance, if the requesting attorney wants to minimize the time spent on the memo and doesn't need a formal document for the client or file, she might ask for just an email with the key points of analysis and legal authorities. Sometimes attorneys prefer a more conventional, formal memo, such as when a copy of the memo is going to the client or when the memo addresses a question that arises frequently in similar cases.

Most legal writing courses require students to write a formal memo with the following components: Heading, Question Presented, Brief Answer, Facts, Discussion, and Conclusion. The heading, sometimes called the caption, is simply the top part of the memo with the "To," "From," "Date," and "Re" lines. Chapters 4 through 17 discuss the other memo components in more detail—and the skills you need to write them—and provide examples and explanations.

Once you learn how to write a good memo in the conventional, formal format, you can adjust the format as circumstances require in practice. If you're assigned a legal memo in your summer job, it's often wise to ask the requesting attorney if she wants a full formal memo or something more abbreviated and if a sample memo in the preferred format is available to use as a reference. And even if your assigning attorney requests an email response, you'll still use the basic format of a memo. Regardless of the format you use in practice, the legal research and analysis still needs to be thorough and accurate.

SOME TIPS FOR PLANNING YOUR TIME

Writing legal memos takes a lot more time than you might think. One of the most important things that you can do to ensure that your writing process goes smoothly and that your finished work product is good is to start on your assignment early.

You'll seldom write a memo from front to back. Although office memos typically follow a certain format (Heading, Question Presented, Brief Answer, Facts, Discussion, and Conclusion), there's no prescribed order for the actual writing of an office memo. Once you've researched the issue and read the sources, it's up to you whether to start by drafting the Heading and proceeding in order, or whether to start by drafting sections that are located further back in the memo.

Once you've got a working draft, make sure that the sections of the memo work together. For instance, you might write the Facts before the Discussion, but you'll need to edit the Facts afterward to ensure that all of the facts that you use in the Discussion are also included in the Facts. Writing is an iterative process.

Even if the assignment calls for a "first draft," don't hand in your *actual* first draft. Many professors will ask you to write the same memo or brief twice—once as a "first draft" and again as a "final draft." Between the two, the professor might give you feedback on the first draft to show you ways to improve your work in the final draft. Plan to revise your memo many times before handing it in, even as a first draft. After your professor provides feedback, revise several more times to produce the final draft. (Note that not all professors will ask you to turn in both a first draft and a final draft.)

Proofreading isn't the same thing as revising. Your revising process should be rigorous—read your document and ask yourself, for instance, whether it has all the required components in the proper order, whether each component accomplishes its purpose, whether you've excluded extraneous information that doesn't help answer the question presented, whether your organization is clear and logical, whether your analysis is thorough, and so on. After thoroughly revising the memo, proofread for more detailed, stylistic points such as a concise writing style, grammatical errors, typos, punctuation, proper citation, and so on. It will likely take several rounds to polish your document to meet the profession's high standards. The complaint we hear most often from practitioners is that students fail to polish their work until it is as perfect as they can make it.

SOME COMMON PITFALLS

Pitfall: Misinterpreting or misstating the applicable legal rules. You might be able to avoid this problem by reading the authorities carefully. Make sure to budget enough time to read them multiple times. If you're struggling with constructing a rule or explaining a rule, see Chapters 8 and 9.

Sometimes, students misinterpret the applicable legal rules because they don't yet understand weight of authority. To get additional practice with weight of authority concepts, see Chapter 4.

Pitfall: Organizing by authorities rather than substantive points. You'll need to synthesize the authorities rather than catalog them like a book report. For help with constructing a synthesized rule, see Chapter 8, and for help with organization, refer to Chapter 7. Once you have a good structure for organizing your analysis, use strong "roadmap" paragraphs and topic/thesis sentences to communicate that organization clearly to the reader. For more on these topics, see Chapters 13 and 30.

Pitfall: Using a persuasive, argumentative tone rather than an objective one. To avoid this, imagine how you'd feel if you make a recommendation and your employer relies on it to spend time and money on a case that turns out to be weaker than your memo said it was. You're not doing the requesting attorney or your client any favors by burying or ignoring a weakness in your client's case. You'll need to clearly state a likely conclusion, but be objective in how you reach and explain that conclusion.

Pitfall: Using a lot of waffling language. Edit out unnecessary waffling from your predictive analysis. For instance, words like "seems," "appears," "suggests," and "may" suggest the writer is hedging and lacks confidence in her analysis. Although no prediction is certain, aim to minimize the amount of waffling in your memo to the extent you can do so and maintain accuracy. It's generally okay to use words like "probably" and "likely" to express that you're making a prediction. Those usually aren't viewed as waffling.

Pitfall: Not thoroughly explaining all steps of the analytical process about how the law will likely apply to the facts. You probably need to be more explicit in explaining your analysis than you initially think. Some professors, much like your former math teachers, will tell you to "show your work." If you think your case is similar to a precedent, explain the similarities in detail. If you think the other party has a strong argument that the precedent is distinguishable, then you should likewise explain that in detail. Even if something seems clear to you, it might not be obvious to the reader, who might not have read or be as familiar with the legal authorities as you. Imagine yourself in the reader's shoes when deciding what to include and not include. It's important that your analysis doesn't jump to conclusions because the reader can't follow your thought process and, consequently, won't know whether she agrees with it. For practice with legal analysis, see Chapters 10, 11, and 12.

Checklist

Chapter 3: Overview: Office Memos

✔	Evaluate each question presented with objective, thorough, and accurate analysis.
✔	Determine if your audience wants a full formal memo and include the appropriate components (e.g., Heading, Question Presented, Brief Answer, Facts, Discussion, and Conclusion).
✔	Even if the assignment calls for handing in a "first draft," plan to revise your work so that you hand in the best draft you can.
✔	Budget time for reading the relevant authorities carefully.
✔	Avoid the pitfall of organizing by authorities rather than substantive points.
✔	Use an objective tone for memos, rather than a persuasive tone.
✔	Avoid waffling language to the extent you can while maintaining accuracy.
✔	Include thorough analysis regarding how the law will likely apply to the facts ("show your work").

You will find all of the chapter checklists compiled in Appendix D.

CHAPTER 4

Choosing Authority

It's the first day of class and it feels just like your fifth-grade civics lesson. "What are the three branches of government and how does each of them make law?" And you thought law school would be more sophisticated than this! But—regardless of whether beginning law students think this is just "background" material—understanding where law comes from and how much weight you give it is the key to legal analysis and organizing the documents you write.

In fact, social scientists have studied the differences in how practicing attorneys and new law students read cases. One of the key differences between the two is that practicing attorneys pay much more attention to where the law is from—the jurisdiction, the branch of government, and the level of the court within the jurisdiction.[1] This is different from the way students typically read cases in the casebooks used in many classes. In those law school classes, jurisdiction and court level matter little because casebook professors focus on broad legal principles or doctrines in the abstract. In your legal writing class, because you're working on a specific problem and using sources for a specific reason, you'll read cases the way you will read in practice.

1. Several authors have explored reading strategies for law students. *See, e.g.*, Dorothy H. Deegan, *Exploring Individual Differences Among Novices Reading in a Specific Domain: The Case of Law*, 30 READING RES. Q. 154, 161-62 (1995); Laurel Currie Oates, *Beating the Odds: Strategies of Law Students Admitted Through Alternative Admissions Programs*, 83 IOWA L. REV. 139 (1997); RUTH ANN MCKINNEY, READING LIKE A LAWYER: TIME-SAVING STRATEGIES FOR READING LAW LIKE AN EXPERT (2005); Leah M. Christensen, *Legal Reading and Success in Law School: An Empirical Study*, 30 SEATTLE L. REV. 605 (2007).

Terminology notes. "Mandatory authority" is also known as "binding authority." "Persuasive authority" is sometimes called "nonbinding authority."

WHAT YOU NEED TO KNOW ABOUT CHOOSING AUTHORITY

Sources from the relevant jurisdiction are most important, even if sources from another jurisdiction appear more on point. The United States contains multiple jurisdictions, including each state and the federal system.[2] The courts in each of those jurisdictions almost always rely on sources from their own jurisdiction.

"Primary sources" are more important and useful than "secondary sources" when writing practice documents. Primary sources are the texts produced by the three branches of government: statutes, treaties, case law, administrative regulations, and executive orders. The Constitution itself is also a primary source. Your professor might ask you to exclusively cite primary sources. Secondary sources, on the other hand, are texts about the law written by scholars or commercial companies, and may differ in how much weight they carry. Because they merely comment on or summarize the law, secondary sources are often not important enough to cite in practice documents like memos and briefs, although they're sometimes cited in cases of first impression.

Two hierarchies—the branch of government hierarchy and the case law hierarchy—govern your decision about which sources carry the most weight and which you'll cite first. You'll need to take both into account as you decide which sources to use and how to prioritize sources in your writing.

The branch of government hierarchy. This prioritizes the importance of various primary sources—which branch's law governs or trumps others. The Constitution's text trumps everything else. But after that, it's complicated because "judicial review" confers on courts the enormous power to decide whether statutes and regulations are constitutional. That's part of the "checks and balances" that make it impossible to say that the primary sources from one branch are always more important than another. But if the constitutionality of a statute or regulation is not at issue, then the following list shows

2. There are still more court systems if one includes the tribal court systems on Native American reservations across the country.

the priority that governs which sources to use and which to put first in your document:[3]

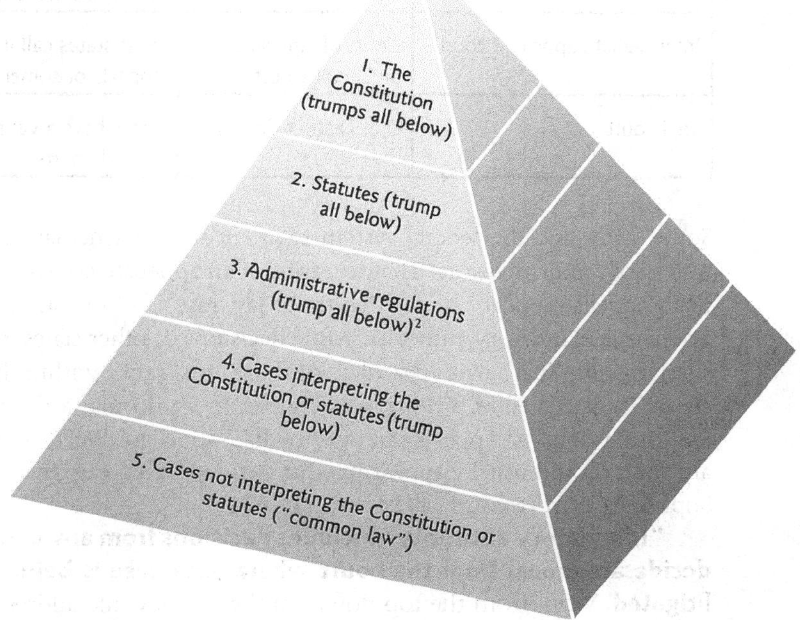
1. The Constitution (trumps all below)
2. Statutes (trump all below)
3. Administrative regulations (trump all below)2
4. Cases interpreting the Constitution or statutes (trump below)
5. Cases not interpreting the Constitution or statutes ("common law")

This means that if a statute is constitutional, it carries more weight than any of the cases interpreting the statute. Courts interpreting the statute are "bound by" or must follow the statute's text and you should set it out first in your writing, even before cases from the Supreme Court that interpret it.

The case law hierarchy. The case law hierarchy prioritizes cases within one jurisdiction. And recall from the first point above that a decision from a court within the jurisdiction where your assignment takes place is usually more important than any decision from a different jurisdiction. Here is the common pattern for weight of authority of the courts within one jurisdiction:

1. The court of last resort *(usually the "Supreme Court" of that jurisdiction)*[4]
2. An intermediate appellate court *(in most but not all states)*
3. Trial courts *(whose decisions are published in the federal system, but usually not in the state systems)*

3. There are exceptions to this generalization, however, especially with regard to when courts must defer to administrative regulations.

4. New York is one notable exception; the New York Supreme Court is not the court of last resort, but instead a trial court. In New York, the highest state court is the Court of Appeals.

Type of Court	Federal	State
Court of last resort	U.S. Supreme Court	Most states call it the (State Name) Supreme Court
Intermediate appellate court	Court of Appeals, or Circuit Court	Most states call it the Court of Appeals or something similar
Trial court	U.S. District Courts	States have a variety of names for trial courts

Some states and the federal system segment the intermediate appellate court into geographic divisions. The decisions of an appellate court—the "intermediate appellate court" or the "court of last resort"—in the state whose law governs is mandatory authority, while decisions of other states' courts are persuasive only.[5] That's true regardless of the courts' ranks within their respective states. Thus, if you're writing a memo set in California, a decision from the California Court of Appeals (an intermediate appellate court) is "more important" and should usually appear in your analysis *before* a case from the Michigan Supreme Court (a court of last resort).

"Mandatory authority" includes decisions from any court that might decide an appeal from the court where your case is being or would be litigated. Work from the top down on these lists while addressing authority in writing. Usually, you will address or summarize all mandatory authority. You'll put it first. Ignoring mandatory authority is a bad idea because courts must follow it. Further, no matter how similar the facts may be to a case from outside your jurisdiction, use cases within your jurisdiction before citing cases from outside your jurisdiction.

With case law, lower courts are bound only by a precedent case's holding. Anything unnecessary to the decision doesn't bind future courts (this is part of the doctrine of "stare decisis," the principle that judges respect prior decisions and are reluctant to overturn established legal doctrines). Judicial opinions often include statements that aren't necessary to the holding, such as "if the plaintiff had instead done X, then the situation might be different." Because the plaintiff didn't actually do X in the case before the court, the court's pronouncement about what the result would be in that circumstance isn't part of the holding. Those nonbinding statements are called "dicta" and even though they might carry some persuasive weight (especially if the dicta is from the Supreme Court), those statements are not binding on future courts.

The relationship between the federal system and the states' systems is a complex one, but except for constitutional issues or

5. Note that each state's rules about weight of authority are themselves a matter of law and they can vary by state.

"diversity jurisdiction,"[6] **usually the two systems operate separately.** These questions are more complicated than we can easily summarize here, but generally, if you're in federal court with a federal issue, you'll rarely cite to state law. If you're in state court on a state law question, you'll rarely cite to federal law. In state court, sometimes you'll get questions that implicate constitutional rights or federal statutes. For example, state law usually governs the crime of burglary, but a burglary trial in state court may need to address whether the defendant's federal constitutional rights regarding search and seizure were respected when the police gathered burglary evidence. In cases such as those, you'll cite federal law in state court.

The date of a source of law can also affect the weight of the authority. If two sources are of equal weight using the previous lists, the more recent source is usually more important. A more recent source may change the law and make an older source of questionable value. For example, the legislature may amend a statute and make earlier cases interpreting the statute irrelevant. Or a higher court may overturn or reverse earlier decisions, making them questionable sources.

HOW TO CHOOSE AUTHORITY

Using the copyright and fair use problem in Appendix B, we'll walk you through the process of choosing authority. If you haven't yet reviewed Appendix B, it would be helpful to review it now to get acquainted with the basic law and facts.

PROBLEMS

Problem

Here is a quick overview of the copyright and fair use problem (for details, see Appendix B). Page is suing Dash for violating the Copyright Act when Dash wrote a song based on Page's song (which in copyright terms is called the "original"), "Red, White, and Blue." Dash's song uses the structure and many lyrics of the original but changes the original song's political message. The music of the two songs is not at issue, only the lyrics. Page expects that Dash will argue that his song is a parody that falls under the fair use exception to the Copyright Act. The court will consider the relevant factors set out in the fair use statute, 17 U.S.C. § 107: whether the copy was transformative and

6. Diversity jurisdiction allows parties from different states to litigate a state law issue in federal court in a case when a substantial sum is at issue. You'll learn more about diversity jurisdiction in Civil Procedure.

targeted the original; whether it took more than necessary of the original; and whether it will interfere with the original's market.

Step 1: Make a list of all the available sources of law. Begin with statutes, as they will ultimately control if you have a relevant statute. With statutes, note the dates when the statute or amendments to the statute took effect, because cases interpreting the statute may be irrelevant if they were interpreting a different version of the statute. For cases, note the court that decided the case and when it was decided.

In the copyright and fair use problem, copyright is mentioned in the Constitution. But unless the Constitution's wording is at issue, do not write about the relevant constitutional provision. Appendix B includes several sources of law. Remember that Page, the plaintiff in our problem, is considering filing suit in a federal court in California, which is geographically part of the Ninth Circuit. For purposes of illustration, we'll add several sources to the list. Following are the available sources, in no particular order:

- *Fisher v. Dees*, 794 F.2d 432 (9th Cir. 1986) (this is a case from the Ninth Circuit, a federal intermediate appellate court)
- *Campbell v. Acuff-Rose Music, Inc.*, 510 U.S. 569 (1994) (this is a case from the U.S. Supreme Court)
- Barton Beebe, *An Empirical Study of U.S. Copyright Fair Use Opinions 1978-2005*, 156 U. Pa. L. Rev. 549 (2008) (this is a law review article from a prestigious journal)
- *Dr. Seuss Enters., L.P. v. Penguin Books USA, Inc.*, 109 F.3d 1394 (9th Cir. 1997) (this is a case from the Ninth Circuit, a federal intermediate appellate court)
- *Leibovitz v. Paramount Pictures Corp.*, 137 F.3d 109 (2d Cir. 1998) (this is a case from the Second Circuit, a federal intermediate appellate court)
- *Mattel, Inc. v. Walking Mountain Prods.*, 353 F.3d 792 (9th Cir. 2003) (this is a case from the Ninth Circuit, a federal intermediate appellate court)
- 17 U.S.C. § 106 (this is a federal statute on copyright)
- 17 U.S.C. § 107 (this is a federal statute on copyright)
- *Abilene Music, Inc. v. Sony Music Entm't, Inc.*, 320 F. Supp. 2d 84 (S.D.N.Y. 2003) (this is a case from a federal trial court in New York)

Step 2: Start with primary authority and apply the list of hierarchy of authority between primary authorities from different branches of the government. The list includes a federal statute, and its constitutionality is not at issue. That tells you where to start. The first source of law you'll mention in your memo will be the two provisions of the federal copyright statute, 17 U.S.C. §§ 106 and 107, which trump the case law that interprets these provisions. You'll start by setting out the parts of the statute that apply.

Step 3: Next look at the list of cases and apply the list of hierarchy of authority to those. Remember that cases from your own jurisdiction and any courts that are mandatory authority for it will be most important to the analysis. Your list has many federal cases and no state cases. If there were a state case on the list, you would probably put it last on your list of cases to use, or not use it at all, because it would not be mandatory authority on a federal issue like copyright. In the federal courts, the U.S. Supreme Court trumps all courts below. So use *Campbell* before the other cases. (But remember that before citing *Campbell*, you'll quote and cite the relevant portion of the statute.)

Next, after choosing any Supreme Court cases that apply, consider the fact that the plaintiff is considering bringing suit in a federal court in California, which is geographically in the Ninth Circuit. Cases from that circuit are mandatory primary authority and therefore will be more important to us than cases from other federal circuits. The Ninth Circuit cases are:

- *Fisher v. Dees*, 794 F.2d 432 (9th Cir. 1986).
- *Dr. Seuss Enters., L.P. v. Penguin Books USA, Inc.*, 109 F.3d 1394 (9th Cir. 1997).
- *Mattel, Inc. v. Walking Mountain Prods.*, 353 F.3d 792 (9th Cir. 2003).

Discuss these cases only after discussing the more highly ranked authority represented by the statute and *Campbell*. Deciding how to prioritize these cases can be complicated and there may be no clear answer. Here, the U.S. Supreme Court addressed fair use in detail in *Campbell*, and that case will trump or may have changed earlier law. *Campbell* was decided in 1994, so the *Seuss* case and the *Mattel* case are probably more important than *Fisher*, the other Ninth Circuit case on the list, because *Seuss* and *Mattel* were decided after *Campbell* and will take the Supreme Court's *Campbell* decision into account. Therefore, plan on using *Seuss* and *Mattel* instead of earlier cases in ordinary circumstances.

Step 4: After planning your analysis using mandatory primary authority, consider whether persuasive primary authority or secondary authority adds something important that is currently missing. Remember that primary authority—authority written by a governmental agency and regarded as "the law"—is usually more important than secondary authority—commentary written by a scholar or commercial company to explain the law. But primary authority, when it's not mandatory, is only persuasive. When you haven't found adequate mandatory authority to support your arguments, you may decide to use persuasive primary authority, usually cases from lower courts in your jurisdiction or cases and statutes from other jurisdictions. When you use persuasive primary authority, use it after you've addressed the mandatory authority from your jurisdiction.

Cases from the nonbinding federal intermediate appellate courts (in our example, those other than the Ninth Circuit) will be more important than cases from the federal trial courts. If you have enough cases from your own jurisdiction to present a good picture of the law and address most of the issues in your analysis, you might decide to ignore other circuits. In contrast, if you have scant authority from the higher courts in your jurisdiction, you'll likely want to use out-of-jurisdiction cases to fill out your analysis. But either way, you'll usually address those cases *after* you've addressed mandatory authority.

Also, consider whether the cases from the trial level federal courts will help you. Often the lower courts will be the place to look for fact-based reasoning that will fill in the gaps left by higher courts. Sometimes that's very useful. But usually you'll discuss such decisions *after* you've addressed mandatory authority.

In addition, although secondary authority can help you find mandatory primary authority and understand an issue, it rarely adds something important that you can't find in your primary sources, which have precedential value. In fact, some legal writing professors discourage citing secondary authority in memos and briefs for this reason. Here, the law review article is helpful as background reading for the writer, but it's not worth citing in your writing because it likely would not carry weight with a court. Occasionally, a secondary authority is such a well-known, respected text that jurists consider it influential, such as the Restatements of the Law.

Step 5: Using the priority of authority you've established for the section, you can start writing. Most sections of your memo on the copyright and fair use problem will start by quoting the relevant part of the copyright statute. Then you'll need to formulate a rule that explains how the cases have interpreted the statute on the particular issue this section addresses. (For help with that see Chapter 8 on Constructing a Rule.) You'll use the U.S. Supreme Court case, *Campbell,* if it's helpful to this particular issue. Next explain the law the Ninth Circuit has applied to this issue, focusing on the post-*Campbell* cases from the Ninth Circuit when you can. That may be all you need to do. But if you feel the need to give the reader a more complete picture, you might turn to pre-*Campbell* Ninth Circuit cases, other circuits, or to trial-level opinions on your issue. And by now you have a pretty good handle on using weight of authority to help decide how to write strong analysis and how to organize the section of your memo where you describe the law.

Putting all these steps together, your hierarchy of authority might look like this:

- 17 U.S.C. § 106
- 17 U.S.C. § 107
- *Campbell v. Acuff-Rose Music, Inc.*, 510 U.S. 569 (1994)
- *Mattel, Inc. v. Walking Mountain Prods.*, 353 F.3d 792 (9th Cir. 2003)
- *Dr. Seuss Enters., L.P. v. Penguin Books USA, Inc.*, 109 F.3d 1394 (9th Cir. 1997)

You might also use—depending, of course, on your particular facts:

- *Fisher v. Dees*, 794 F.2d 432 (9th Cir. 1986)
- *Leibovitz v. Paramount Pictures Corp.*, 137 F.3d 109 (2d Cir. 1998)
- *Abilene Music, Inc. v. Sony Music Entm't, Inc.*, 320 F. Supp. 2d 84 (S.D.N.Y. 2003)
- Barton Beebe, *An Empirical Study of U.S. Copyright Fair Use Opinions 1978-2005*, 156 U. PA. L. REV. 549 (2008) (you'd likely use this source only if you had a case of first impression and the article argued in favor of your position)

EXAMPLES

Review the following examples. For some examples there may be more than one correct answer. Explain to yourself why you have chosen that answer or those answers. Then read the explanations in the last section of this chapter to check your work.

EXAMPLES

Example 4-1

This question uses a hypothetical adverse possession problem.

You're writing a memo on a state law question involving Ohio property law. The issue involves adverse possession and Ohio has a statute on point. Under the statute, adverse possession occurs when a landowner fails to prevent others from using his land. In that circumstance, the original owner loses title and the adverse possessor(s) become the lawful property owner. The constitutionality of Ohio's adverse possession statute is not at issue, which means this problem involves just state law.

Consider the following sources and decide which sources would appear before others in your memo. Then answer the question that follows.

- A 1999 case on adverse possession from the intermediate appellate court in Ohio with similar facts to yours
- A 2005 U.S. Supreme Court "takings" case on when the government can take land from private citizens for governmental purposes under the Fifth Amendment of the U.S. Constitution
- A 2009 case on adverse possession from the Illinois Supreme Court with similar facts to yours
- The most recent Ohio adverse possession statute
- A 2008 case from the Ohio Supreme Court on a procedural issue but with similar facts to yours

- A 2001 law review article from the *Ohio State Law Journal* on adverse possession
- A 1975 case on adverse possession from the Ohio Supreme Court

The *best way to prioritize* the sources listed is to start with these two authorities:

A. The U.S. Supreme Court case, and then follow with the 1975 Ohio Supreme Court case.
B. The Ohio adverse possession statute and then use the most recent Ohio case on adverse possession (the 1999 case from an Ohio intermediate appellate court with facts similar to yours).
C. The Ohio adverse possession statute and then use the 1975 Ohio Supreme Court case on adverse possession.
D. The Ohio adverse possession statute and then move to the most recent Ohio Supreme Court case (the 2008 Ohio Supreme Court case with similar facts but on a procedural issue).

EXAMPLES

Example 4-2

This question uses the hypothetical adverse possession problem used in Example 4-1.

Which of these statements reflect sound decisions about choosing sources to include in your memo for the previous problem?

A. Use every source listed from Ohio.
B. Use the Illinois Supreme Court case, but only if it adds something my analysis needs and if the case was based on an Illinois statute similar to the Ohio statute.
C. Include the U.S. Supreme Court case because everyone must follow the U.S. Supreme Court; even though takings and adverse possession are different claims, both are about taking property from private owners without paying for it.
D. Do not use the *Ohio State Law Journal* article.

EXAMPLES

Example 4-3

This question uses a hypothetical employment discrimination problem.

You're writing a brief that addresses the federal question of whether an employer in Boston, Massachusetts, has violated the Civil Rights Act of 1964 (42 U.S.C. § 2000 et seq.) by discriminating in hiring on the basis of race. The constitutionality of the act is not at issue. You're in the First Circuit, a federal intermediate appellate court. Consider the following sources and decide which sources would appear before others in your memo. Then answer the question that follows.

- A 2011 newspaper article on unemployment that states there are 500 qualified applicants for every position open in Massachusetts
- A 2010 case with similar facts and on the same issue from the Third Circuit
- Title VII of the Civil Rights Act, the applicable provision from the U.S. Code (the federal statute)
- A 2001 federal district court (trial level) case from Massachusetts with somewhat similar facts
- A 1993 U.S. Supreme Court case that sets out the test for the relevant provision of Title VII
- A 2007 Massachusetts Supreme Court case that interprets the Massachusetts state statute on employment discrimination
- A 1995 First Circuit case that applies the test set out in the U.S. Supreme Court case above
- A 2004 First Circuit case that applies the test set out in the U.S. Supreme Court case above and adds a test to be applied in the First Circuit

Which answer *best identifies* which sources you would most likely use in your memo and *best prioritizes* those sources from the most weight to the least weight?

A. Title VII of the Civil Rights Act; the 1993 U.S. Supreme Court case; the 2004 First Circuit case. I might also use the 1995 First Circuit case; the 2010 Third Circuit case; and the 2001 federal trial court case from Massachusetts. I would not use the Massachusetts Supreme Court case or the newspaper article.

B. The U.S. Supreme Court case; Title VII of the Civil Rights Act; the 2007 Massachusetts Supreme Court case; the 2004 First Circuit case. I might also use the 1995 First Circuit case; the 2001 federal district court case from Massachusetts; the 2010 Third Circuit case; and the newspaper article.

C. Title VII of the Civil Rights Act; the 1993 U.S. Supreme Court case; the 1995 First Circuit case; the 2004 First Circuit case; the Massachusetts Supreme Court case; the 2010 Third Circuit case; the 2001 federal trial court case from Massachusetts; the newspaper article.

D. The 1993 U.S. Supreme Court case; Title VII of the Civil Rights Act; the 2004 First Circuit case; the 1995 First Circuit case; the 2010 federal trial court case. I might also use the 2010 Third Circuit case and the Massachusetts Supreme Court case. I would not use the newspaper article.

EXAMPLES

Example 4-4

Read the following statements and decide whether each makes a correct statement about using sources of law in a document.

A. If you get all the sources into the document, it really doesn't matter what order you put them in. Choose the cases you like best first.
B. Use primary sources when you can to support your arguments or analysis.
C. The exact order sources should appear in your document is always clear.
D. It's not unusual for a document to contain only federal sources or only state sources.

EXAMPLES

Example 4-5

This question uses a hypothetical gift in contemplation of marriage problem.

In the following excerpt, consider how the author uses authority. The excerpt comes from the beginning of a memo section that explains California law concerning "gifts in contemplation of marriage." To identify the court to which the author is citing, you need to know that "Cal." in the date parenthetical indicates the case is from the California Supreme Court and "Ct. App." in that parenthetical indicates a case is from a state appellate court in California. Decide whether the statements that follow the example are correct.

> According to judicial interpretation of the California "Gifts in Contemplation of Marriage" statute, there must be (1) a conditional statement (2) implied to the donee (3) during the transfer of the conditional gift. When determining whether a gift is conditional or not, courts in this jurisdiction search for unambiguous indicators of a condition.
>
> For example, the court found that although a donor believed that the donee had accepted his marriage proposal, her true intentions were otherwise. *Steinback v. Halsey*, 115 Cal. Rptr. 2d 213, 255 (Ct. App. 1978). In that case, the court found the donee could retain some gifts because they were not made in contemplation of marriage. The *Steinback* donee retained gifts of perfume, luggage, clothing, and money, even though the court found her at fault for the breach of marriage promise. Similarly, in *Simon*, the donor's parents were present at the moment of the marriage proposal and on that occasion gave the donee a wristwatch with the explanation that "this is from dad and I." *Simon v. Marks*, 634 P.2d 259, 262 (Cal. 1969). The California Supreme Court in that case found that the words uttered during the transfer of the wrist watch were not conditional and therefore the wrist watch was a gift not in contemplation of marriage.

A problem (or problems) with this excerpt is that:

A. It doesn't quote and cite the statute it mentions.
B. All the cases it cites are from California.
C. It cites no authority for the statements it makes in the first paragraph.
D. It cites to intermediate appellate courts before it cites to the California Supreme Court, which is stronger authority.

EXAMPLES

Example 4-6

This question uses the negligent infliction of emotional distress problem, which you can find in Appendix C. The incident occurred in a fictional jurisdiction, New Fornia, and there is no statute on point. One key question in the case is whether the engaged plaintiff/bystander and the victim had an "intimate, familial relationship." Consider the following sources and decide which sources would appear before others in your memo. Then answer the question that follows.

- A 2020 encyclopedia entry on New Fornia claims for negligent infliction of emotional distress by bystanders
- A 2018 case from the Supreme Court of New Hampshire explaining why intimate, familial relationships should be broadly construed in the context of negligent infliction of emotional distress claims
- A 2013 case from the Supreme Court of New Fornia that lays out the elements required to prove negligent infliction of emotional distress by a bystander and describes the factors courts should consider when determining whether the plaintiff and victim had an intimate, familial relationship
- A 2014 case from the Supreme Court of New Fornia holding that fiancés have an intimate, familial relationship when interpreting New Fornia's domestic violence statute
- A 2017 case from the New Fornia Appellate Court holding that the plaintiff and victim did not have an intimate, familial relationship and therefore the plaintiff could not prevail on a claim of negligent infliction of emotional distress by a bystander

Which answer *best identifies* two sources you would be sure to discuss in your memo?

A. The 2014 and 2013 cases from the Supreme Court of New Fornia.
B. The 2014 case from the Supreme Court of New Fornia and the 2018 case from the Supreme Court of New Hampshire.

C. The 2017 case from the New Fornia Appellate Court and the 2020 encyclopedia entry on New Fornia claims for negligent infliction of emotional distress by bystanders.

D. The 2013 case from the Supreme Court of New Fornia and the 2017 case from the New Fornia Appellate Court.

EXPLANATIONS

Explanation 4-1

A is an easy mistake to make because most people think of the U.S. Supreme Court as the most powerful decision maker about the law. But here, the Supreme Court addresses a federal constitutional issue—takings—that has nothing to do with Ohio adverse possession law. This is a state law question and federal cases aren't likely to help. **B** is also wrong. Although it's important to start with the statute, and the factually similar case from an Ohio appellate court is a good case to use, you would most likely address the Ohio Supreme Court case before moving to the case from the Ohio intermediate appellate court. **C** is correct. The constitutionality of the Ohio adverse possession statute is not at issue, and thus the Ohio courts are bound by the statute's text. You'll start your analysis by quoting the state statute. Then you'll move to the highest court interpreting the statute, the Ohio Supreme Court case that addresses adverse possession specifically. This is true even though the case is old. In addition, you might then use the case from the Ohio intermediate appellate court. **D** is not the *best* way to prioritize the sources because even though the 2008 Ohio Supreme Court case has similar facts and is much more recent than the 1975 case, the 2008 case was decided on a different issue and is not really relevant to your analysis.

Explanation 4-2

A is incorrect because although you want to concentrate on Ohio sources, your list includes Ohio sources that you would probably not use. The secondary source might be useful for you to read, but you probably wouldn't cite it. **B** is correct and illustrates the factors to consider when deciding to use a case from another jurisdiction. You probably have adequate Ohio law to write your analysis here and you're not likely to cite the Illinois case, but if it was based on a similar statute and added something to the analysis, you could use the Illinois case. **C** is incorrect. One of the important lessons of the first-year legal writing course is to keep the analysis for each type of claim separate. The U.S. Supreme Court has written much about "takings," but that is a completely different cause of action than adverse possession, which is usually a state law issue. The U.S. Supreme Court case is irrelevant. **D** is also correct. Most professors believe it's efficient to use secondary sources to educate yourself about the law and to use the article's footnotes to find primary sources. They would not, however, be particularly impressed if you were to cite to a law review article instead of primary mandatory authority.

Explanation 4-3

A is correct because this list *best identifies* the sources you would use and *best prioritizes* those sources. This question includes some tough judgment calls, but this answer starts with the text that binds the courts—the federal statute—and moves to the highest court in the federal system interpreting it, the U.S. Supreme Court. Because both of the First Circuit cases set out the test for courts in the First Circuit to follow, most writers would choose the most recent First Circuit case next. These three binding sources are essential, but note that the First Circuit case comes after the statute and the U.S. Supreme Court case. The next group—cases you might use—starts with the older First Circuit case. If that case was very widely cited or its facts were closer to your case than the more recent First Circuit case, this case would be more important to include and might make the list of "essential" sources. You would then move to persuasive sources. Here the two most persuasive, because they have similar facts and are both from federal courts, are the Third Circuit case and the district court case. The Third Circuit case is usually considered more important than a district court case, even if the district is geographically within the same circuit as your problem. So the level of court within the federal system generally trumps both geographic location and date. Finally, most writers would not choose to go outside the law from the federal system to use the state court decision that is based on a different statute. Similarly, most writers would ignore newspaper articles, regardless of their relevancy. **B** mistakenly puts the U.S. Supreme Court case before the federal statute that binds that Court. It also places the Massachusetts Supreme Court case in a position of importance. Remember that usually on federal issues you will not use state law cases. **C** again incorrectly uses the Massachusetts Supreme Court case and places it before other important federal system decisions. Finally, **D** is incorrect because it starts with a case, albeit an important one, before the statute.

Explanation 4-4

A is incorrect because the point of learning how legal readers weigh sources of law is to use that knowledge to prioritize authorities in your writing. Answer **B** is correct. Good legal writers almost always use secondary sources, if at all, after they have addressed primary authority. Remember, some legal writing professors ask first-year students not to cite secondary authority at all. **C** is incorrect. Although the rules you've learned about weight of authority will guide you while deciding which sources to use and how to prioritize them, using authority is not an exact science. Sometimes authorities are close in weight, or you have other good reasons for choosing one authority over another. Those reasons might include unusual facts in your case or knowing your audience's specific preferences. **D** is also correct. If you're writing about a federal issue, it's not unusual for *all* the sources you use to be federal sources. Similarly, it would be typical for a document addressing a state law issue to contain only state law sources.

EXPLANATIONS

Explanation 4-5

A is correct. Generally speaking, start with your highest authority, and in this case that's the statute. Additionally, usually you'll quote the relevant part of the statute. With cases, on the other hand, you will most often paraphrase. **B** is incorrect. When you have enough case law to present a convincing analysis, as you appear to here, there's no need to go outside your jurisdiction. **C** is correct. This chapter explains how important it is for the reader to know how much weight to give a statement about the law. If you don't provide a cite the reader will not know where the assertion comes from or how much deference to give to the assertion. **D** is also correct. Although occasionally there might be a good reason to deviate from ordering authority strictly according to weight, here there's no reason to explain what the lower courts did before explaining how the California Supreme Court resolved your issue.

EXPLANATIONS

Explanation 4-6

A is incorrect. Even though the New Fornia Supreme Court is the highest court in New Fornia and both cases address "intimate, familial relationships," the 2014 case did not rule on how that term of art should be interpreted in the context of negligent infliction of emotional distress claims. That court was interpreting New Fornia's domestic violence statute; that statute may have separate definitions and different requirements. **B** is incorrect. Although you would use the 2013 New Fornia Supreme Court case, the 2018 New Hampshire case won't be very helpful because it's from a different jurisdiction. This is true even though the decision deals with the same issue, is recent, and is by the highest court in New Hampshire. You might decide the policy argument is helpful, but the New Hampshire case should not be one of the two cases you ensure is in your memo. **C** is incorrect. The encyclopedia entry may help you understand the issue, but you would generally not discuss or cite it in your memo. **D** is correct. The two New Fornia cases with holdings on the exact issue your memo addresses should be discussed, as they are both mandatory authority.

Checklist

Chapter 4: Choosing Authority

✔	Make a list of all your research and organize the sources according to weight of authority principles, starting with rules from governing statutes and regulations and then moving to cases.
✔	Plan to use mandatory authority before persuasive authority.
✔	Plan to use primary sources before secondary sources (use secondary sources to inform yourself, but they are often not important enough to cite).
✔	If your case is governed by a statute, start the discussion by quoting its relevant parts.

You will find all of the chapter checklists compiled in Appendix D.

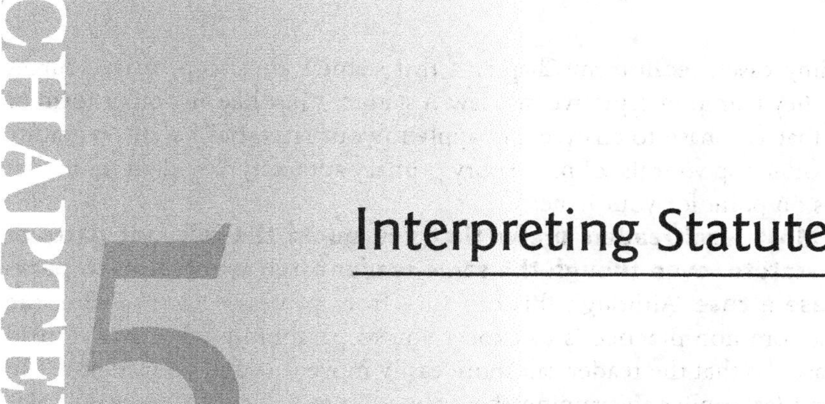

Interpreting Statutes

Is your first reaction when you see a statute quoted in a case or a casebook to skip it? If it is, you're like many readers. "After all," some readers rationalize, "the case will tell me about the important language. I don't need to parse it all out for myself." The trouble with that reaction is that learning to read statutes closely and to make arguments about them is one of the most important skills you'll learn in law school.

Terminology notes. Some professors and textbooks speak of the "rules of statutory interpretation." Others talk about "canons of construction." They mean the same thing. In addition, when talking about statutes, the terms "plain meaning" and "plain language" are used interchangeably.

WHAT YOU NEED TO KNOW ABOUT INTERPRETING STATUTES

Statutes require close reading. Outlining a statute to understand what the statute requires a party to prove often helps you understand what you're reading. Assume every word in the statute is there for a reason. Pay close attention to words like "and," "or," "except," "either," "unless," and "all." Once you've figured out what the statute requires a party to prove, then you'll know whether and how it applies to your problem.

A statute is often the most significant primary source for a particular legal issue. Although you'll spend most of your time in law school reading cases, recall from Chapter 4 that statutes are also primary sources and they trump interpretive case law. A statute is just like any other form of law that you have to analyze and apply to your facts, but because a statute will often top your list of mandatory primary authority, you'll set it out first if it's on point for your issue.

Most legal readers prefer that you quote the relevant parts of the statute, even though the same reader often wants you to paraphrase a case. Although this can vary from professor to professor, the most common practice is to expect you to paraphrase what you've read in cases so that the reader can more easily move through your memo. The same idea applies to pruning the statute down to its most relevant parts by using ellipses or partial quotes. But because lawyers pay such close attention to the actual text of the statute, you'll want to quote those relevant sections. Paraphrase to explain a case's reasoning. Quote a statute's relevant words.

Statutory arguments are usually ordered according to the rules of statutory construction, also known as the canons of construction. The rules on how to interpret statutes are largely common to all jurisdictions. You'll find them in the cases from your jurisdiction. And like any other authority, you'll look for your jurisdiction's highest court's rules on how to interpret statutes on a particular legal issue.

There are too many canons to list, but here are a few examples:

- A statute should be read as a harmonious whole with its separate parts being interpreted in a manner that furthers the statutory purpose.
- All words in a statute should be given effect.
- A term used more than once in a statute should be given the same meaning throughout.

The canons are not always respected. In fact, scholars have sometimes criticized them for directing courts to treat statutes in inconsistent ways. Nevertheless, courts often use the canons in interpreting statutes.

One of the canons that courts most often honor is: "If the meaning of the statute is clear and unambiguous, the court will apply the plain meaning to the facts and look no farther." Thus, if the statutory language has only one meaning and is not ambiguous on its face, most lawyers will order statutory arguments in this way:

- First, analyze based on the "plain meaning" of the statute, including definitions or statements of purpose.
- Next, if the plain meaning of the statute doesn't favor your client, then you'll want the court to look beyond it. Your job will be to explain why the statute may have more than one meaning and thus is

ambiguous, which allows the court to look to courts' interpretations and legislative intent. Or to turn to other canons of construction that may apply.

- If one side can show the plain meaning of the statute is ambiguous, then both sides will look to cases interpreting the statute or cases interpreting similar statutes. Choose cases following the rules about weight of authority. (See Chapter 4.)
- Next, if the above is still insufficient, consider turning to the statute's legislative history.
- Finally, if none of the above helps much, consider citing secondary authority like law reviews or treatises to support your analysis about the statute.

HOW TO INTERPRET STATUTES

Using the cell phone manslaughter problem in Appendix A, we'll walk you through the process of developing statutory arguments.

PROBLEMS

Problem

Here is a quick overview of the cell phone manslaughter problem (for details see Appendix A). Allison King used her wireless phone, without a hands-free device, while driving in dense fog on a winding road on the edge of an ocean cliff. King placed the call to warn her friends about the dangerous conditions, as they would be meeting later. While she was making the call, she hit and killed a bicyclist. The prosecution will attempt to convict King of vehicular manslaughter by showing that she drove while committing an illegal act (driving while using a wireless phone without a hands-free device) and with gross negligence. King will argue that her actions fit within the "emergency purposes" exception to the wireless phone prohibition. She will also argue that she did not act with gross negligence.

Step 1: Read the statute closely, and decide which parts are most relevant for your problem by outlining a rule. As you read, ask yourself whether a change in your facts would make a difference to how this part of the statute would apply. If it would, then it's an important part of the statute for your problem.

Here is the first part of the statute:

> **Cal. Penal Code § 192. Manslaughter; voluntary, involuntary, and vehicular**
> Manslaughter is the unlawful killing of a human being without malice. It is of three kinds:
> (a) Voluntary—upon a sudden quarrel or heat of passion.
> (b) Involuntary—in the commission of an unlawful act, not amounting to felony; or in the commission of a lawful act which might produce death, in an unlawful manner, or without due caution and circumspection. This subdivision shall not apply to acts committed in the driving of a vehicle.
> (c) Vehicular—
> (1) Except as provided in subdivision (a) of Section 191.5, driving a vehicle in the commission of an unlawful act, not amounting to felony, and with gross negligence; or driving a vehicle in the commission of a lawful act which might produce death, in an unlawful manner, and with gross negligence.

This part will often be pretty easy. The state doesn't have to prove malice. There are three kinds of manslaughter and to determine which part or parts apply, consider the facts, loosely interpreted. Your client was driving a car, suggesting that subsection (c) is the applicable part. First, you'd need to check to make sure the exception in Section 191.5(a) doesn't apply. Here, you'd see that section involves intoxication and doesn't apply to King's facts so it can be ignored. The state has to prove your client was driving a vehicle with gross negligence *and* either committing an unlawful act that is not a felony *or* a lawful act that might produce death in an unlawful manner.

So, your outline looks like this so far:

The state must prove that:
(1) King was driving with gross negligence
AND
(2) committing either:
(a) an unlawful act
OR
(b) a lawful act that might produce death in an unlawful manner.
(Note to self: The state does NOT have to prove malice and the unlawful act can't be a felony.)

You now know that the state has two ways of convicting King. One way is to show that (1) she was driving with gross negligence and (2)(a) committing an unlawful act. The other is to show that (1) she was driving with gross negligence and (2)(b) committing a lawful act that might produce death in an unlawful manner. You consider our facts and decide that provision (2)(b) is unlikely to apply because the courts have never applied it in circumstances remotely similar to our case.

That leaves us with one way the state might convict King—if she was acting with gross negligence and she committed an unlawful act. The task at this stage is to figure out if King was committing an unlawful act. Your research locates a statute concerning using a wireless telephone. These are the words of that statute:

> **Cal. Vehicle Code § 23123. Driving motor vehicle while using wireless telephone; penalty; exceptions**
>
> (a) A person shall not drive a motor vehicle while using a wireless telephone unless that telephone is specifically designed and configured to allow hands-free listening and talking, and is used in that manner while driving.
>
> (b) A violation of this section is an infraction punishable by a base fine of twenty dollars ($20) for a first offense and fifty dollars ($50) for each subsequent offense.
>
> (c) This section does not apply to a person using a wireless telephone for emergency purposes, including, but not limited to, an emergency call to a law enforcement agency, health care provider, fire department, or other emergency services agency or entity.

Let's outline and analyze this statute.

a. A person can use hands-free technology. (It appears that King may have violated this statute because she wasn't using her cell phone in a hands-free way. You should continue reading and outlining the statute.)

b. The punishment scheme. (We're unconcerned with this so far because at this point you're most concerned with determining whether King was driving while committing an unlawful act by making a cell phone call without a hands-free device.)

c. King will be excused for using the cell phone if she was making the call for "emergency purposes." The statute does not define when a call is for emergency purposes, but the legislature did provide this list of calls that would be considered as emergency calls (and others could qualify):

1. A law enforcement agency
2. A health care provider
3. A fire department
4. Another emergency services agency

Adding this to the manslaughter statute (for more on synthesizing rules from two or more sources, see Chapter 8), at this stage you know the state must prove that:

(1) King was driving with gross negligence
AND

(2) (a) she was committing an unlawful act by using a wireless telephone without hands-free technology while driving and not meeting the "emergency purposes" exception.

The state can show King was driving and that she was using her cell phone without a hands-free device. This means your reading of the relevant part of the statute boils down to two questions:

1. Can the state show she was grossly negligent?
   AND
2. Can the state show her call was NOT for "emergency purposes"?

Step 2: Quote the relevant parts of the statute. You'll need to address two issues that grow out of the statute. So first, you'll quote the parts of the statute that set up both issues early in the memo's Discussion section (for more on organizing the Discussion section, see Chapter 7). Later in the Discussion section (at the beginning of each subsection) you'll quote the relevant parts of the statute for that particular section and, after quoting the statute's language, discuss any cases that illuminate that part of the statute.

Step 3: Analyze how the statute applies to our facts. Take a look at the order of arguments that lawyers usually follow when they make arguments about statutes and consider how they apply here. First come the "plain meaning" arguments. Here, the first issue is whether the exception to the prohibition against driving while using a wireless telephone applies to King because her call was for "emergency purposes."

King might make this plain meaning argument:

> Allison King was not committing an "unlawful act" when she used her wireless telephone without a hands-free device because she falls under the plain language of the exception that allows her to make calls for "emergency purposes." The situation was an emergency because it was necessary for her to call her friends to prevent them from entering dangerous driving conditions. Under the plain meaning of the statute, she was not driving unlawfully.

The state, in contrast, can argue:

> Allison King does not fall under the plain meaning of the exception to the statute that allows calls for "emergency purposes" because the plain language of the statute includes a list of circumstances that all involve calling an institution involved with public safety or health. Under the statute's plain language, calling one's friends is not an "emergency."

Next both sides might argue why, even if they don't prevail under the plain meaning, the statute is ambiguous. Then, each side will turn to cases for support.

King: Further, even if this court decides that the plain meaning of the statute does not include King's emergency, the language of the statute is ambiguous because it does not limit the "emergency purposes" exception to the calls included in the statute's list. In an emergency, imminent danger is present. *People v. Harris*, 89 Cal. Rptr. 3d 904, 906 (Ct. App. 2009). (The argument would continue from here, using fact-based or analogical analysis.)

State: Alternatively, the plain meaning of the statute is ambiguous because the courts have been left to define the meaning of "emergency." Thus, the court may turn to case law such as *People v. Harris* and *People v. Tompkins* for guidance about when an emergency exists. (The argument would continue from here, using fact-based or analogical analysis.)

Although many statutes lend themselves to plain meaning arguments, no strict rule requires lawyers to make this sort of argument. For instance, where courts have developed a lot of case law interpreting a statute, lawyers will typically start with arguments based on that case law rather than on the plain language of the statute.

When the statute's language isn't clear and case law is not dispositive, sometimes the legislature's intent when passing the bill sheds light on how a statute should be interpreted. Secondary authority might also help in these cases to support an argument for your client. But those types of arguments are generally made only when the statute's terms are ambiguous and no cases resolve the ambiguity.

EXAMPLES

Review the following examples. For each example, there may be more than one correct answer. Explain to yourself why you have chosen that answer or those answers. Then read the explanations in the last section of this chapter to check your work.

Example 5-1

This question uses a hypothetical Title IX problem.

Title IX of the Education Amendments of 1972 provides that "no person in the United States shall, on the basis of sex, be excluded from participation in, be denied the benefits of, or be subjected to discrimination under any education program or activity receiving federal financial assistance." Teenagers at Smithtown High School are bullying a team member, Jason Johnson, because he is gay. We know that Jason is a "person." Which of the following outlines shows what else the statute requires Jason to prove?

A. Jason must prove:

1. he was excluded from an education program

   AND

2. the education program was receiving federal financial assistance

B. Jason must prove:

1. one of the following occurred:
   a. he was effectively excluded from participation in an education program or activity on the basis of sex; or
   b. he was effectively denied the benefits of an education program or activity on the basis of sex; or
   c. he was effectively subjected to discrimination under an education program or activity on the basis of sex,

   AND

2. one of the following is true:
   a. the education program received federal financial assistance; or
   b. the education activity received federal financial assistance.

C. Jason must prove:

1. on the basis of sex one of the following is true:
   a. he was excluded from participation in an education program or activity; or
   b. he was denied the benefits of an education program or activity; or
   c. he was subjected to discrimination under an education program or activity,

   AND

2. one of the following is true:
   a. the education program received federal financial assistance; or
   b. the education activity received federal financial assistance.

D. Jason must prove:

1. because of his sexual orientation the school:
   a. excluded him from participation in an education program or activity; or
   b. denied him the benefits of an education program or activity; or
   c. subjected him to discrimination under an education program or activity,

   AND

2. either:
   a. the education program received federal financial assistance; or
   b. the education activity received federal financial assistance.

EXAMPLES

Example 5-2

This question uses the hypothetical Title IX problem used in Example 5-1.

You represent the gay teenager, Jason Johnson, suing the school district under Title IX, the statute you outlined in Example 5-1. Review the following arguments and decide which ones would be effective.

A. Argue that under the plain meaning of Title IX, Jason Johnson suffered discrimination "based on sex" because his teammates bullied him because of his sexual orientation.
B. Argue that even if the statute does not mention sexual orientation, and no case law expands the word "sex" to include sexual orientation, Congress meant to include it because the statute uses the word "sex."
C. Analogize to a Title VII case from the U.S. Supreme Court that held that bullying someone based on his sexual orientation is discrimination "based on sex."
D. Argue that if the statute is ambiguous, another canon applies that requires the court to interpret various provisions of the federal code in harmony with each other.

EXAMPLES

Example 5-3

This question uses a hypothetical arson problem.

New Mexico's negligent arson statute provides that negligent arson "consists of a person recklessly starting a fire or causing an explosion, whether on the person's property or the property of another person, and thereby directly causing the death or bodily injury of another person; or damaging or destroying a building or occupied structure of another person." Jessie Thomas threw a lit firecracker into a phone booth in Albuquerque, which cracked the glass of the phone booth.

To convict Jessie of negligent arson, what must the prosecutor prove?

A. The prosecutor must prove that Jessie:
1. whether on a person's property or the property of another a person:
   a. recklessly started a fire; or
   b. recklessly caused an explosion,

AND

2. directly caused:
   a. the death of another person; or
   b. the bodily injury of another person; or
   c. damage to another person's building or occupied structure; or
   d. destruction to another person's building or occupied structure.

B. The prosecutor must prove that Jessie recklessly caused an explosion and damaged a building of another person.

C. The prosecutor must prove that Jessie:
1. either:
   a. on the person's property; or
   b. on the property of another a person,

AND
2. either:
   a. recklessly started a fire; or
   b. recklessly caused an explosion,

AND
3. either:
   a. directly caused the death of another person or the bodily injury of another person; or
   b. damaged a building or an occupied structure of another person.

D. The prosecutor must prove that Jessie was on another person's property and recklessly caused another person's death.

EXAMPLES

Example 5-4

This question uses the hypothetical arson problem used in Example 5-3.

Jessie Thomas threw a lit firecracker into a phone booth in Albuquerque, which cracked the glass of the phone booth. You're the prosecutor. Assume that you have set out the rule by quoting the relevant parts of the negligent arson statute. You're writing a section on "damaging or destroying a building or occupied structure of another person," and have explained the law by describing mandatory authority that illustrates its application.

As you begin to apply the statute, you would start . . .

A. with a plain meaning argument because the statute is clear that it applies to buildings and all structures.

B. with a plain meaning argument because the word "building" normally has one meaning.

C. by arguing the legislature intended to include telephone booths because they are buildings.

D. by making arguments either using other canons of construction to clarify what the New Mexico Legislature intended when it wrote the statute or by making analogies to other cases about what "building" means.

EXPLANATIONS

Explanation 5-1

A is incorrect because it's incomplete. This outline identifies one way the teenager could prove his claim, but it leaves out "on the basis of sex" and "or activity," both important parts of the statute. Every word counts! **B** is also incorrect. It identifies most of the elements of the statute, but it adds the word "effectively" to the statute. Although the case law interpreting the statute may add this concept, when working with statutes you can neither add nor subtract words from the statute. Lawyers will want to see the exact words of the statute. **C** is correct because it illustrates one good way to outline the statute. You can easily see what the teenager has to prove. **D** is incorrect because, like B, it adds a concept to the statute—"sexual orientation" instead of "sex."

Explanation 5-2

A is correct. Lawyers often make arguments based on the plain meaning of the statute. The U.S. Supreme Court has held that if the language is clear and admits only one meaning, the Court will look no farther. **B** is incorrect. Most lawyers would reject that argument as too weak and unsupported to include in your analysis. Generally speaking, your analysis will focus on arguments each side can support with a cite to authority. **C** is correct. Analogizing to mandatory authority addressing a similarly worded statute is an argument most lawyers would be happy to make. **D** is also correct. There are many canons of construction and finding another that suggests that the court should interpret the statute in a way that is useful to your case is a good option.

Explanation 5-3

A is correct in that it's one of the possible ways you could outline the statute to figure out what the prosecutor has to prove. There isn't just one right way to outline the statute; the important thing is that you can see at a glance exactly what a prosecutor must prove. In the process of outlining, it's especially important to pay attention to modifiers and to discover whether the statute is ambiguous. **B** is also a correct answer although it's very brief and may be only one way of many that the prosecutor might bring his case. **C** is yet another correct answer because it's another way one might outline the statute without leaving out any relevant part. **D** is wrong. It not only leaves out relevant elements of the statute, but also chooses to include parts of the statute that don't apply to the facts.

Explanation 5-4

A is incorrect. The statutory language specifically limits its applicability to buildings and *occupied* structures, not buildings and *all* structures. Although the facts might support a plain meaning argument that the telephone booth is a "building," the phrase "occupied structure" probably doesn't apply to these facts. **B** is a correct answer, although if your research had revealed many cases interpreting the word "building," you would no longer make the plain meaning argument. **C** is incorrect. Generally, make a legislative intent argument only after you've argued the plain meaning or the case law interpreting the statute. **D** could be correct under certain circumstances. If your research had established that the word "building" is susceptible to several meanings, you would not make a plain meaning argument, but would instead start by making arguments referring to the cases that interpret the word. Or perhaps your research has disclosed other canons of construction that courts typically apply in a case like yours. In that case, you might make arguments with another canon.

Checklist

Chapter 5: Interpreting Statutes

✔	Closely read the statute to figure out exactly what parts are relevant for the problem at hand.
✔	Quote the relevant parts of the statute early in the memo's Discussion section or the brief's Argument section.
✔	Notice whether any canons or rules of construction apply.
✔	Discuss the cases interpreting the statute and use weight of authority to order those cases.
✔	If a plain language argument applies, analyze or make it first.

You will find all of the chapter checklists compiled in Appendix D.

CHAPTER 6

Interpreting the Common Law

Luckily, analyzing common law is not very different from the analysis we just looked at in Chapter 5 when we were applying case law that interprets a statute. In both scenarios, you find the rule and outline it. Then you apply precedent to your assignment's facts. "Common law" is the law judges make in the absence of a governing statute. Reading cases may seem easier than reading statutes because judges write in full sentences and paragraphs and often use familiar terms. The structure and language used by legislatures when drafting statutes, on the other hand, can seem more complicated. But reading cases and identifying an opinion's key information takes practice, which we'll work on below.

Terminology notes. Terminology can be hard to follow when we talk about how the common law developed. By its very nature, the common law is rooted in history, so the language can feel old and strange to us. *Stare decisis* (translated literally from Latin) means "to stand by things decided." This doctrine requires courts to follow previous judgments when deciding similar cases, whether interpreting a statute or deciding a case without a governing statute. Lawyers contrast common law jurisdictions that rely on *stare decisis* with civil law jurisdictions, where courts approach each case by applying anew the language of the enacted law—statutes—to each case that arises. Most countries that were once a part of the British Empire follow *stare decisis* and are common law jurisdictions. Much of the rest of the world are civil law jurisdictions.

WHAT YOU NEED TO KNOW ABOUT ANALYZING A PROBLEM WHERE NO STATUTE APPLIES

When we talk about a "common law jurisdiction," we mean that precedent plays the key role in analysis. Whether the issue you are writing about is governed by a statute or by rules judges make in the absence of a statute, remember that in a common law jurisdiction, you will use precedent that has applied and interpreted the applicable rule to analyze your issue. And all the rules about hierarchy of authority that we learned in Chapter 4 will apply. You'll look to the decisions from the jurisdiction's highest available court to form and apply your rule.

When no statute governs, you'll look to the jurisdiction's caselaw to construct a rule. Sometimes this is easy because the jurisdiction's highest court has set out the applicable rule very clearly. Other times, you'll need to synthesize several cases to construct the current rule. (For more on constructing a rule, see Chapter 8.) With common law problems as opposed to statutory problems, you're much more likely to need to synthesize a number of authorities to identify the rule. Statutes are—by their nature—intended to be clear rule statements. The words the legislature used are significant. They *are* the rule. Judicial opinions, on the other hand, are intended to resolve disputes between the parties. In that process, judges use, and often state, rules. But sometimes they don't clearly state the rule they are using to resolve the dispute. And it's not unheard of for courts to misstate or misapply a rule. Hence, you often need to consider several cases to deduce a rule.

With each case, you'll need to identify the relevant facts, issue, holding (including the outcome of the case), and rationale in order to deduce the rule. You should have experience identifying these key case components by briefing cases for your other courses, but we'll review that process in this chapter. With facts, include only those facts that could impact the outcome of the case, plus the procedural facts, meaning the judicial process that came before the opinion you are reading. The issue should be the narrow question the court addressed to resolve the dispute, and the holding is the court's response to that issue. In contrast to statutes, with case law the words a court used have no independent significance. What the court did—in the context of the specific issue the court was addressing and the underlying facts—is significant. And in terms of holdings, just like with rules, sometimes a judge will specifically state it, sometimes a judge won't state it, and sometimes a judge will misstate it. Hence, your job is to focus on what the court *did* (as opposed to focusing on what a legislature *said*). Include the outcome of the case—summary judgment for the defendant was affirmed, for example—to ensure you are accurately identifying the holding. The reasons the court articulated in reaching its decision can also help identify the rule and its parameters.

When formulating the common law rule, it's especially important to distinguish between holding and dicta. Remember that even when courts state a rule, that statement isn't always the rule the court actually applied. Judges can say anything they want. But courts are only bound, under *stare decisis*, to follow the *holding* of a higher court—not dicta. Holdings are the courts' conclusions after applying the law to the relevant facts. Dicta are those statements and asides that aren't necessary for the court's specific ruling. (For more on dicta versus holding, see Chapter 4.) Judges often make extraneous comments that go beyond the specific issue and facts before the court, such as "if the defendant had slowed down after seeing the plaintiff, even if her car hit him, she would not be negligent." Those statements are dicta. Dicta is never binding. It can sometimes be persuasive, but it's important to distinguish case holdings from dicta in order to accurately state the controlling rule and to predict the result in your case.

The common law evolves—and that means you need to look at the most recent cases on point in the controlling jurisdiction to form a rule. Don't assume that when you find one case that sets out a rule that you have the rule the courts will apply in your jurisdiction. You need to examine the most recent formulation of the rule from the highest available courts in your jurisdiction.

As noted above, you may need to create a synthesized rule; this often happens when a subsequent case extends the rule or adds something new to the rule. And you'll also need to consider the facts in the case in which the court set out the rule, because the facts may change how far the courts will go in applying the rule. Thus, the facts of previous cases may limit your application of the rule. This is true whether you are analyzing a problem in the absence of a statute or whether you are looking at cases to interpret part of a statute.

Statutory law often codifies common law; at other times, statutory law attempts to negate common law. In early American history, most of the law was common law. But as time moves on and legislatures of all sorts stay busy, much of the common law has been codified in statutes. Most lawmakers look to what the courts have already accepted as a good rule when they write statutes. Uniform codes, such as the Uniform Commercial Code and the Model Penal Code, are codes that judges and scholars have written to serve as models for legislatures codifying the rules in a jurisdiction in a particular subject area. The Restatement is particularly influential in many courts; it "restates" the common law as if it were a statute. Thus, the common law has shaped many statutes.

But sometimes, legislatures react negatively to a common law development. When that happens, the legislature has the power to *change* the law by enacting a statute with a different rule. The later-enacted statute would control over earlier, conflicting common law. Once the legislature has spoken on a topic by enacting a statute, a judge's only power is to interpret that statute. The judge is not free to create her own common law rule.

And sometimes common law relies on statutes from other jurisdictions or on a statute within the same jurisdiction on a related, but not identical, area of the law. In this way, the relationship between statutory and common law is somewhat reciprocal.

Although we try to avoid stringing together quotes from cases to form an analysis, if there is a generally accepted common law rule in your jurisdiction, it's often good practice to quote it. The general principle of quoting from statutes and paraphrasing from cases has limits; when a common law rule is set out simply and consistently in a jurisdiction, it's fine to quote it.

HOW TO ANALYZE A COMMON LAW PROBLEM

Using the negligent infliction of emotional distress problem in Appendix C, we'll walk you through the process of developing a rule and arguments in a common law assignment.

PROBLEMS

Problem

Here is a quick overview of the negligent infliction of emotional distress problem, which you can find in Appendix C. Jane Poe was gardening and listening to music on her earbuds when she heard a sound and turned to see a lawnmower coming toward her. She was able to jump out of the way and then saw that a car driven by Dan Defoe had hit her fiancé, John Valenzuela. Valenzuela was lying motionless, barely breathing and covered in blood. Poe and Valenzuela were recently engaged and planned to marry within two years. They spent most nights together and planned to live together within the next few months. They had purchased a car together but most of their finances were separate. After the accident, Poe suffered anxiety attacks and was under the care of a psychiatrist who prescribed medication. Poe wishes to sue Defoe for negligent infliction of emotional distress as a bystander who witnessed her fiancé's injuries. Your supervisor has asked you assume that Poe can prove Defoe's negligence and Poe's severe emotional distress as a result of negligence. The elements at issue will be whether Poe "directly observed the accident and resulting injury" and whether Poe's relationship with Valenzuela was an "intimate, familial relationship." (Note: the caselaw for this problem is based on a series of cases from New Jersey, with modifications for educational purposes. This problem takes place in the fictional jurisdiction of New Fornia.)

Step 1: If your research reveals that no statute applies, read the cases most relevant to your problem and summarize, for each case, the facts, issue, holding (including the outcome), and rationale. In our fictional jurisdiction we find five cases that apply. Although you should read them in full in Appendix C, here is a thumbnail sketch of the five, noting the date and the level of the court in each case:

Case 1: *Portee v. Jaffee*, Supreme Court of New Fornia, 1980. The court decided that a bystander could sue for negligent infliction of emotional distress and adopted a four-part test, citing with approval a prominent California case, *Dillon v. Legg*. To prove negligent infliction of emotional distress, a bystander plaintiff must show the death or serious physical injury of another caused by the defendant's negligence; a marital or close blood relationship between the plaintiff and the injured person; the plaintiff directly observed the death or injury at the scene where it occurred; and the plaintiff suffered severe emotional distress as a result. In *Portee*, a mother watched her child suffer a slow and terrible death after becoming trapped in an elevator. The court held the plaintiff could proceed and reversed the trial court's dismissal of her claim.

Case 2: *Dunphy v. Gregor*, Supreme Court of New Fornia, 2013. The court restated the four-element rule from *Portee*, but expanded the "relationship" element beyond spouses and those with a close blood relationship. The plaintiff in *Dunphy* met three of the elements, but she was not married to the victim and was not a close blood relative of the victim, who was killed when the defendant's car struck him. The *Dunphy* court, relying on the prevalence of cohabitating couples in today's society, held that an "intimate, familial relationship" could suffice even if the plaintiff and victim were not married. In determining whether a relationship was an intimate, familial relationship, the court considered the following factors: "the duration of the relationship; the type of relationship (dating, engaged, cohabitating, etc.); the degree of financial intermingling; and the extent and quality of shared experiences." The plaintiff and victim in *Dunphy* were engaged, had been dating for seven years and cohabiting for over two years, had joint bank accounts, had purchased a car together, and had life insurance policies naming each other as beneficiaries. The victim had introduced the plaintiff as his wife. The court held this relationship was sufficient to maintain a claim for negligent infliction of emotional distress by a bystander and affirmed a jury verdict for the plaintiff.

Case 3: *Ortiz v. JDP Builders, Inc.*, Supreme Court of New Fornia, 2015. The court restated the *Dunphy* rule, and then expanded the "direct observation" requirement to include being "sensorially aware" of the injury or death. The defendant conceded every element except whether the plaintiff directly observed the victim's death or injury. In *Ortiz*, a mother was separated from her young daughter while trying to escape a burning house and save all three of her children from the fire. She watched the fire consume her house and realized her young daughter was trapped inside, even though she could not directly see her burning to death. The court held this element was met because the plaintiff was "sensorially aware" of her daughter burning to death and affirmed a jury verdict for the plaintiff.

Case 4: *Miller v. Davidson*, Superior Court of New Fornia, Appellate Division, 2017. The *Miller* court relied on the four-part *Dunphy* test and added the modification from *Ortiz* to permit recovery when a plaintiff was "sensorially aware" of the injury or death. At trial, the defendant prevailed on summary judgment for two reasons: the plaintiff and the victim did not have an intimate, familial relationship, and the court found the plaintiff did not directly observe the victim's death or serious injury. The plaintiff appealed. In *Miller*, the plaintiff was at a circus with her boyfriend. She was on the phone facing away from the ring when a leopard attacked her boyfriend; after her call, she realized something was wrong and ran toward him, but he had already bled to death. On the first issue, the *Miller* court cited the *Dunphy* factors used to determine when a plaintiff's relationship with the injured party meets the intimate, familial relationship element. In *Miller*, the plaintiff and her boyfriend had been dating for three years but did not live together; they were not engaged; and their finances were generally separate. They did stay over in each other's apartments two or three times a week and they shared a bank account to pay for entertainment. The court held the plaintiff and the victim did not have an intimate, familial relationship, and hence, summary judgment was proper. On the second issue, the court held that because she was unaware of the mauling until after her boyfriend had bled to death, the plaintiff did not directly observe, nor was she sensorially aware, of the attack and her boyfriend's death at the time of the incident. The court upheld the summary judgment dismissal on this basis as well.

Case 5: *Vargas v. Quinones*, Superior Court of New Fornia, Appellate Division, 2018. In *Vargas*, the only issue was whether the plaintiff had directly observed the death or injury at the scene of an accident. The court applied *Dunphy's* requirement that the plaintiff be a witness at the scene of the accident as well as the "sensorially aware" exception created by the *Ortiz* court. In *Vargas*, the plaintiff was at home when he learned that his pregnant wife had been in a car accident and an ambulance had arrived to take her to the hospital. Vargas witnessed his wife in the ambulance and followed her to the hospital, where he learned that the fetus had died in utero. The court held that because the plaintiff was not at the scene of the accident when it occurred and therefore could not see or hear the accident, he did not directly observe and was not sensorially aware of the resulting death. The court upheld the trial court's dismissal of the plaintiff's claim.

We might draft a chart, like the one below, to summarize all five cases, using "P" to represent the plaintiff, "D" to represent the defendant, and "V" to represent the victim:

Case (with court/year)	Facts	Issue(s)	Holding(s)/ Outcome	Rationale
Portee v. Jaffee (N.F. 1980)	Child/V trapped by elevator Mom/P watched child's slow, painful death Procedure: trial court dismissed P's claim	Can a bystander sue for negligent infliction of emotional distress?	Yes. Reversed trial court's dismissal.	Must show D caused death/serious physical injury to V; P & V had a "marital or close blood relationship"; P "directly observed" death/injury at scene; and P "suffered severe emotional distress."
Dunphy v. Gregor (N.F. 2013)	P watched V, her fiancé, be hit and killed by a car Although not married or blood related, P & V dated 7 years, lived together for 2 years, and had joint bank accounts, a joint vehicle, and life insurance policies for each other. V introduced P as his wife Procedure: at trial, jury ruled for P	Can a P & V meet the relationship requirement when they are not married or related but have an "intimate, familial relationship"?	Yes. Affirmed jury verdict for P.	P & V's relationship was foreseeable and the functional equivalent of marriage, so that element should be expanded. Courts should consider four factors in deciding if the relationship suffices: "the duration of the relationship; the type of relationship (dating, engaged, cohabitating, etc.); the degree of financial intermingling; and the extent and quality of shared experiences."
Ortiz v. JDP Builders, Inc. (N.F. 2015)	A mother, P, watched her house burn down while her young daughter, V, was trapped inside. P could not actually see the V burning to death. D conceded every element except "direct observation" of the injury or death. Procedure: at trial, jury ruled for P	Is the observation requirement met when the P cannot directly see the V being killed, but instead is "sensorially aware" of the injury/death as she watches her house burn down, knowing the V is inside?	Yes. Affirmed jury verdict for P.	Fire and smoke can prohibit direct observation, but P was at the scene and aware her daughter was burning to death. The "direct observation" requirement is expanded to include being "sensorially aware" of V's injury or death.

Case (with court/year)	Facts	Issue(s)	Holding(s)/ Outcome	Rationale
Miller v. Davidson (N.F. App. 2017)	P & V, her boyfriend, went to a circus P was on a phone call not watching the ring when a leopard attacked and killed V; P ran to V, but he had already bled to death P & V dated 3 years, did not live together, were not engaged, and had separate finances other than one account to pay for entertainment P & V stayed at each other's apartments 2-3 times a week Procedure: summary judgment granted for D because P & V did not have an "intimate, familial relationship," and because P did not directly observe V's death	1) Do P & V have an "intimate, familial relationship" after dating 3 years, are not engaged, have only one intermingled bank account, and spend 2-3 nights a week together? 2) Does P meet the observation/ sensorial awareness requirement when she was on her phone and did not see V being killed, even though she was in the same physical location?	1) No. 2) No. Affirmed the trial court's grant of summary judgment to D for both reasons.	On balance, the factors did not show P & V had an intimate, familial relationship. P was unaware V had been mauled until after V bled to death, so she did not directly observe and was not sensorially aware of the injury/death at the time.
Vargas v. Quinones (N.F. App. 2018)	P was at home when V, his pregnant wife, was in a car accident P saw V in the ambulance At the hospital, P learned the fetus had died in utero Procedure: trial court dismissed P's claim	Did P directly observe or was he sensorially aware of the death/ injury at the scene when he was not present at V's accident and did not observe the baby dying?	No. Affirmed dismissal of P's claim.	Because P was not at the scene of the accident when it occurred, he could not see or hear the accident so he did not "directly observe" and was not "sensorially aware" of the resulting death.

Step 2: Using those cases, outline a rule. Upon reading the cases, you notice that the rule evolves some over time, especially with regard to two of the elements. And a different element may be at issue in the different cases. Here is an outline of the rule from these cases:

To prove negligent infliction of emotional distress as a bystander, a plaintiff must prove:

(1) the defendant's negligence caused:
  (a) the death
    OR
  (b) serious physical injury of another
  AND
(2) the plaintiff and victim shared:
  (a) a marital
    OR
  (b) close blood relation
    OR
  (c) an intimate, familial relationship
  AND
(3) (a) the plaintiff directly observed the death or injury at the scene where it occurredOR
  (b) the plaintiff was sensorially aware of the death or injury at the scene where it occurred
  AND
(4) the plaintiff suffered severe emotional distress as a result.

Step 3: State the common law rule from the cases. If you have a complete rule from the courts and don't need to synthesize to arrive at a rule, quote the rule using the most recent case from the highest court as authority. Sometimes there is a landmark case that adopts a rule and it has not changed subsequently. It's often a good idea to cite the landmark case that most subsequent cases cite.

If you need to synthesize the rule, you'll need to set out the complete rule and to cite more than one case for that rule. In a synthesized rule, you shouldn't take an historical approach. You don't need to show how the rule evolved. It's most often enough to just set out the rule you synthesized and cite to the cases you used.

Here, the cases consistently use the same rule, with additions over time to the second and third element from *Dunphy* and *Ortiz*: To prove negligent infliction of emotional distress as a bystander, a plaintiff must show: "(1) the death or serious physical injury of another caused by defendant's negligence; (2) a marital or close blood relationship," or an "intimate, familial relationship," between the plaintiff and the victim; "(3) the plaintiff's direct observation" or "sensorial awareness" of the "death or injury at the scene of the accident; and (4) resulting severe emotional distress in the plaintiff."

You would generally cite the most recent Supreme Court case, Ortiz; you may also cite the landmark case that most other cases cite, Dunphy. When stating the rule, you wouldn't cite a lower court case because we have a case from the state Supreme Court—even if the facts of that lower court case were more similar to ours. (You will, though, rely on those other cases when applying the rule, which is discussed in Chapters 10, 11, and 12.) You would cite the highest judicial authority in the jurisdiction. You can quote a rule that you haven't had to synthesize, so we would quote our rule here.

Step 4: Analyze how the common law rule applies to our facts. When we outline our rule, we see that plaintiffs must prove four elements. All must be present, so we would call them elements.

Your assigning partner has asked you to address only elements 2 (the relationship between the injured person and the plaintiff) and 3 (whether the plaintiff directly observed or was sensorially aware of the injury at the scene where it occurred). You'll write a section of your analysis on each element. Thus, you'll examine whether the relationship between Poe and Valenzuela is close enough to be characterized as marital, close blood relatives, or an intimate, familial relationship. You know they are not married or close blood relatives, so you will focus on whether they had an "intimate, familial relationship." And you will further examine whether Poe "directly observed" or was "sensorially aware" of the injury when she turned her head moments after the accident occurred.

As you read the cases, you will see that some cases will help you with one of the elements, and some may help with others. Sometimes a precedent will help you argue both. You'll generally address all the governing law that addresses each particular issue. The important point is to structure your analysis around the *issues* rather than the authorities (here, cases). It may help to outline each element and note which case or cases address that issue.

Here, for the issue addressing the nature of the relationship, the Dunphy court supplied a new rule providing factors for the court to weigh: "the duration of the relationship; the type of relationship (dating, engaged, cohabitating, etc.); the degree of financial intermingling; and the extent and quality of shared experiences." You would use these factors as the rule in the section of the paper addressing that element. You'll learn more about this in Chapters 9-12, but most likely you would compare Poe's facts with the facts in Dunphy and Miller.

Similarly, you would fashion a rule from Ortiz, Vargas, and Miller about what it means to "directly observe" or be "sensorially aware" of the injury. You'd then likely compare Poe's facts with the facts in Portee (or Dunphy), Ortiz, Miller, and Vargas.

EXAMPLES

Review the following examples. For each example, there may be more than one correct answer. Explain to yourself why you have chosen that answer or those answers. Then read the explanations in the last section of this chapter to check your work.

Example 6-1

Which of the following statements are true?

A. There are no differences between a common law problem and a statutory problem.
B. With statutory problems, all you need to do is read the statute, and with common law problems, you need to read cases.
C. With both common law problems and statutory problems, you need to construct a rule and consider the impact of precedent cases.
D. Analyzing common law is similar to analyzing case law that interprets statute: you find and outline the rule, and then you apply precedent to your assignment's facts.

The next four questions use a hypothetical common law interference with contractual relations problem.

Example 6-2

Below are four relevant cases, all from the controlling jurisdiction's highest court. In these short cases, the plaintiff's name starts with P, the defendant's name starts with D, and any relevant third party starts with T. Furthermore, other claims may exist between the plaintiff and defendant; this problem focuses only on the common law "interference with contractual relations" claim (as opposed, for example, to a breach of contract claim).

Patel v. Dutton (2013): Dutton agreed, in a contract with Patel, to buy 1,000 widgets within three months. Dutton became angry with Patel over a separate matter and refused to purchase the widgets. Patel sued Dutton for interference with contractual relations and alleged his interference was intentional. Dutton agreed his conduct was intentional, but moved for summary judgment. The trial court granted Dutton's motion and dismissed the case. This appellate court affirms.

Peterson v. Dragic (2015): Thompson agreed, in a contract with Peterson, to buy 1,000 widgets within three months. Thompson was ready to purchase the widgets, but Dragic accidentally started a fire that burned Thomson's shop; Thompson had to close his business and did not buy Peterson's widgets.

Peterson sued Dragic for interference with contractual relations. Dragic moved for summary judgment. The trial court granted Dragic's motion and dismissed the case. If Thompson refused to perform because Dragic had instead disabled Thompson's truck so he could not pick up the widgets, this court would rule differently. Dragic did not intentionally cause Thompson to breach the contract, and this appellate court therefore affirms the trial court's dismissal.

Proctor v. Dilo (2016): Talbot agreed, in a contract with Proctor, to buy 1,000 widgets within three months. Talbot was ready to purchase the widgets. Dilo, who was angry with Proctor over a separate matter, told Talbot that Proctor's widgets were inferior and convinced Talbot to buy his widgets from a different seller. Proctor sued Dilo for interference with contractual relations. At trial, Proctor prevailed. This appellate court affirms the jury's verdict.

Proud v. Dinger (2019): Dinger agreed, in a contract with Proud, to buy 1,000 widgets within three months. Dinger was prepared to comply with the contract but his shop was destroyed in a fire, rendering him unable to buy Proud's widgets. Proud sued Dinger for interference with contractual relations. Dinger moved for summary judgment. The trial court granted Dinger's motion and dismissed the case, and this appellate court affirms.

Which of the following statements are true?

A. You need to read the most recent case, *Proud v. Dinger*, closely but can skim the earlier cases because the most recent common law case will always have the current, controlling rule.

B. These cases need to be synthesized in order to create a clear rule.

C. The most helpful way to analyze this problem is to describe each case's facts and outcome and let the reader deduce the rule.

D. You need to read the case where the plaintiff prevailed, *Proctor v. Dilo*, closely but can skim the other cases because you are unlikely to learn more about the rule when the plaintiff loses.

Example 6-3

This Example uses the first case in Example 6-2, *Patel v. Dutton*. In the case reproduced below, identify the underlying facts.

Patel v. Dutton (2013): Dutton agreed, in a contract with Patel, to buy 1,000 widgets within three months. Dutton became angry with Patel over a separate matter and refused to purchase the widgets. Patel sued Dutton for interference with contractual relations and alleged his interference was intentional. Dutton agreed his conduct was intentional, but moved for summary judgment. The trial court granted Dutton's motion and dismissed the case. This appellate court affirms.

Example 6-4

This Example uses the second case in Example 6-2, *Peterson v. Dragic*. In the case reproduced below, identify any dicta.

> *Peterson v. Dragic* (2015): Thompson agreed, in a contract with Peterson, to buy 1,000 widgets within three months. Thompson was ready to purchase the widgets, but Dragic accidentally started a fire that burned Thomson's shop; Thompson had to close his business and did not buy Peterson's widgets. Peterson sued Dragic for interference with contractual relations. Dragic moved for summary judgment. The trial court granted Dragic's motion and dismissed the case. If Thompson refused to perform because Dragic had instead disabled Thompson's truck so he could not pick up the widgets, this court would rule differently. Dragic did not intentionally cause Thompson to breach the contract, and this appellate court therefore affirms the trial court's dismissal.

Example 6-5

Using the four cases in Example 6-2, you could deduce the following synthesized rule:

A. A party is liable for interference with contractual relations when she intentionally interferes with a contract and is not a party to the contract.

B. A party is not liable for interference with contractual relations when she accidentally starts a fire.

C. A party is liable for interference with contractual relations when she is not a party to the contract and she intentionally keeps a third party from performing under the contract.

D. A party is liable for interference with contractual relations when she breaks her promise and does not fulfill her contractual obligations.

EXPLANATIONS

Explanation 6-1

A is incorrect. The specific language used in a statute is significant, but with case law, the words used are much less important. With cases, what the court did is important—the *holding* is what matters, even if that is not explicitly stated. In addition, you're more likely to have to synthesize case law to deduce a rule. **B** is also incorrect. You'll almost always have to read cases even when a statute applies, because judges interpret statutory language. Those judicial decisions, if from a higher court within your jurisdiction (for more on choosing authority, see Chapter 4), are binding precedent and become part of the rule. **C** is correct. It's rare to find a statute with no interpretive case law. Because we operate in a common law jurisdiction, those interpretive cases become part of the law. **D** is also correct. The analytical process is the same for cases that interpret a statute and for common law cases.

EXPLANATIONS

Explanation 6-2

A is incorrect. You should always read every relevant case closely. It's true that the common law evolves, so you can't be confident you have the complete rule without checking the most recent case in your jurisdiction. But that case won't necessarily state the complete rule. Use your judgment to figure out which cases are most helpful, taking care to review recent cases on your issue. **B** is correct. These cases don't state a clear rule. You need to read and analyze all of them to deduce the controlling common law rule. **C** is incorrect. The reader will want assurances that the rule you state is the actual rule, but rule explanation (see Chapter 9) is what convinces a reader your rule formulation is accurate. The reader is paying you, the writer, to do the heavy lifting and figure out and state simply the controlling rule. **D** is incorrect; you need to read each relevant case closely, regardless of the outcome. To synthesize a rule, you need to understand when the test is—and is not—met. Hence, cases where the plaintiff lost are helpful. Furthermore, by only skimming the most recent case, *Proud v. Dinger*, you could miss a significant development in the law.

EXPLANATIONS

Explanation 6-3

Patel v. Dutton (2013): **Dutton agreed, in a contract with Patel, to buy 1,000 widgets within three months. Dutton became angry with Patel over a separate matter and refused to purchase the widgets.** Patel sued Dutton for interference with contractual relations and alleged his interference was intentional. **Dutton agreed his conduct was intentional**, but moved for summary judgment. The trial court granted Dutton's motion and dismissed the case. This appellate court affirms.

The underlying facts are in bold. Note how one of the facts is stated below the court's factual summary, as part of the procedural history of the case. Although judges usually state all of the facts early in their opinions, relevant facts can appear anywhere.

Although the question only asked about underlying facts, the other key components are:

- procedural facts: Patel sued Dutton, Dutton moved for summary judgment, and the trial court granted Dutton's motion and dismissed the case.

- issue: it isn't explicitly stated, but you can infer the appellate court had to decide whether the defendant's conduct constituted interference with contractual relations when the plaintiff and defendant were parties to the contract and the defendant intentionally refused to perform. You can infer that because the appellate court could not decide whether the trial court's ruling was correct without answering that question and considering those facts.
- holding: no—this conduct does not meet the test for interference with contractual relations.
- outcome: the appellate court affirmed summary judgment for the defendant.

This case is so short it does not include any rationale, but courts often do explain their reasoning.

EXPLANATIONS

Explanation 6-4

Peterson v. Dragic (2015): Thompson agreed, in a contract with Peterson, to buy 1,000 widgets within three months. Thompson was ready to purchase the widgets, but Dragic accidentally started a fire that burned Thomson's shop; Thompson had to close his business and did not buy Peterson's widgets. Peterson sued Dragic for interference with contractual relations. Dragic moved for summary judgment. The trial court granted Dragic's motion and dismissed the case. **If Thompson refused to perform because Dragic had instead disabled Thompson's truck so he could not pick up the widgets, this court would rule differently.** Dragic did not intentionally cause Thompson to breach the contract, and this appellate court therefore affirms the trial court's dismissal.

The statement in bold is dicta. The appellate court was not presented with a case where Dragic had intentionally disabled Thompson's truck to keep him from complying with the contract. These comments are not necessary to the outcome and are not binding on future courts.

EXPLANATIONS

Explanation 6-5

A is correct. No court explicitly states this rule, so you have to deduce the rule based on the outcome of several cases. Looking at the four cases together, you can conclude that two facts seem to affect liability for interference with contractual relations: 1) whether the defendant's interference with the contract was intentional; and 2) whether the defendant was an actual party to the contract. (Recall that other causes of action may be available to the wronged plaintiff, such as breach of contract when the defendant is a party to the contract.) Using a chart to highlight the key facts and outcome from each of the cases can often help synthesize a complete rule from a number of cases. A chart for these four cases might look like this:

Case (Year)	Intentional?	Party to the Contract?	Outcome
Patel v. Dutton (2013)	Yes	Yes	**P loses**
Peterson v. Dragic (2015)	No	No	**P loses**
Proctor v. Dilo (2016)	Yes	No	**P wins**
Proud v. Dinger (2019)	No	Yes	**P loses**

Reviewing this chart, you can deduce that a defendant is only liable when he intentionally interferes with a contract *and* he is not a party to that contract. For more on rule synthesis, see Chapter 8. **B** is incorrect. This rule formulation only addresses one of the two necessary elements. Furthermore, it is so specific—"when she accidentally sets a fire"—that it fails to account for any other unintentional interference. **C** is correct. Using the chart above, we have identified the two key elements. You generally can state them in either order. **D** is incorrect. This may create liability for breach of contract, but to be liable for interference with contractual relations, the defendant cannot be a party to the contract.

Checklist

Chapter 6: Interpreting the Common Law

✔	Use precedent that has applied and interpreted the applicable rule—whether that comes from common law or a statute—to analyze your issue.
✔	For each case, identify the relevant facts, issue, holding (including the outcome), and rationale so you can deduce the rule.
✔	Pay special attention to the *most recent* formulation of the rule from the highest court or courts because the common law evolves.
✔	Make sure to rely on holdings rather than dicta.
✔	Outline the complete, synthesized rule, and using a chart for the key case facts and outcomes might help.
✔	Articulate the current, complete, synthesized rule.

You will find all of the chapter checklists compiled in Appendix D.

CHAPTER 7

Organizing the Discussion

How should the Discussion section of your memo be organized? You might wonder whether the organization really matters much. The short answer is, "Yes, it does." Professor Sheila Simon's lasagna metaphor demonstrates why. Lots of people like lasagna, and some don't. But we all expect it to be layered a certain way and to look "right." We expect meat (or vegetables), cheese, pasta, and sauce—and even though it's all in one casserole, we can still see (and taste) the distinct layers. Now imagine that the chef put the lasagna in a blender. Would we still like it? Probably not as well, even though all the parts are there. Somehow, the organization matters. The same is true for the Discussion section of a legal memo: the organization matters. Your reader expects the parts to be in a certain order, and she likely will be unhappy or confused if her expectations are not met.

Terminology notes. Professors and textbooks use a variety of acronyms, most often a variation on the term "IRAC," to describe the organizational framework for legal analysis. Regardless of the label, it's likely that the framework being discussed has the same components we describe in this chapter.

WHAT YOU NEED TO KNOW ABOUT ORGANIZING THE DISCUSSION

The pattern of organization known as "IRAC" reflects the way legal readers *think through* an issue. First, the reader will want to know what is at issue. Next the reader will need to know the legal rules that apply to the issue as well as how courts have applied those rules in the past. Then, the reader will expect to see how the rules likely apply to the new facts at hand. Finally, the reader will expect to see the conclusion that you have drawn from your analysis. Use IRAC to *plan* your work before you write, but the organization you actually write with will be slightly different, as we'll explain in a moment.

Although formulaic, IRAC (and each of its variations) is simply the structure of deductive reasoning. The IRAC letters stand for these parts:

I = issue
R = rule
A = application/analysis
C = conclusion

We'll go through each component in more detail in this chapter, with one modification (discussed in the next few paragraphs). And as this analytical structure implies, you'll organize your Discussion section around the issues rather than around the relevant authorities.

In a memo's Discussion section, use a variation on IRAC that begins with the conclusion you reach rather than a statement of the issue. Various terms are used in textbooks to express this structure, but they are all getting at this same basic idea. For example, your textbook might refer to CRAC, CREAC, CRuPAC, the organizational paradigm, or some other version of the IRAC structure that begins with a conclusion. The differences between these terms are simply in the letters they use to describe how you will state the rule and then explain or prove it, a topic that is introduced below and discussed in detail in Chapter 9. The following chart summarizes what these acronyms represent.

IRAC	CRAC	CREAC	CRuPAC
Issue	Conclusion	Conclusion	Conclusion
Rule	Rule	Rule	Rule
		Explanation	Proof
Application/ Analysis	Application/ Analysis	Application/ Analysis	Application/ Analysis
Conclusion	Conclusion	Conclusion	Conclusion

In this chapter, we use the acronym CRAC, but as noted CREAC and CRuPAC are conceptually the same. When discussing organization with your professor, it's a good idea to use the term your textbook or professor uses.

The "conclusion" is the answer to the legal question—the issue—your memo addresses. In undergraduate writing you may have called it a thesis statement. It's the decision you think the court will make on this particular issue or sub-issue that you will support in the analysis that follows. Why were you asked to write this memo? What problem does your client have? For instance, if you were writing a memo that addressed whether the court had personal jurisdiction over the defendant as well as whether the defendant was negligent, the conclusion on the first issue might be expressed this way: "The court likely has personal jurisdiction over the defendant." The conclusion on the second issue might be "The defendant was likely negligent." Notice how these conclusions are short; keep them to one short phrase or sentence, depending on your reader's expectations. You'll be able to express the conclusion more clearly after you've completed the analysis, so don't feel as though you have to draft a perfect conclusion for each issue at the beginning of the writing process. You can always go back and perfect your conclusions as you complete the Discussion section.

The "rule" is the law the decision maker will use to resolve your issue. The rule can come from any type of authority—a constitution, a statute, an administrative regulation, or case law—or from some combination of them. If the rule comes from one source, your task is to articulate that rule and, if applicable, to break it into its parts, which are often elements or factors. For instance, if the issue is whether the statute of limitations has run in a negligence suit, the rule might be a state statute providing that all negligence suits must be filed within two years of the underlying incident giving rise to the claim. When the rule comes from more than one source, you need to synthesize a rule for the reader, as explained in Chapter 8. But most often the "rule" section of CRAC will be more than one or two sentences that set out the rule. To support the rule in your writing, in addition to a citation to the source for the rule, you will include a discussion of the authorities that create and illustrate the rule—often referred to as rule explanation or rule proof. For more on rule explanation and rule proof, see Chapter 9.

The "application/analysis" is where you apply the legal rule identified previously to the facts of your client's case. Notice this component is called both "application" and "analysis." Be sure to include counterarguments, and don't think of this step as simply mechanical. Organizationally, you'll generally want to group your arguments together. Then, identify and explain the strongest counterarguments and respond to those counterarguments so the reader can weigh each side easily. The application/analysis is where you express your thought process and show your reader how the law and the facts fit together. In that sense, the application/analysis is a lot like eighth-grade math. In math courses, even if you got the correct answer, you didn't get all the credit unless you "showed your work." In memo writing, the application/analysis section is where you "show your work"—and if you've done that well, the reader can reach her own conclusion and have confidence in your work product even if she disagrees with your conclusion. For more on application/analysis, see Chapters 10 through 12 on Fact-Based Analysis, Analogical Analysis, and Policy Analysis.

The final "conclusion" is where you briefly state the conclusion to your analysis on the issue. The conclusion should be explicit. You can hedge—"likely" and "probably" are fair game if it really is a close call—but you shouldn't just say "maybe." You were asked to write the memo because the reader wants your legal analysis, not to have to figure it all out for himself. The conclusion can usually be short, and is often a single sentence. It needs to be consistent with the answer you provide in the memo's Brief Answer section, but it can usually be much shorter. And it also has to be consistent with the conclusion you state at the beginning of the discussion of that issue.

If the memo addresses only one issue or sub-issue, though, many writers skip the final "conclusion" within the Discussion section's CRAC. Instead, they save that summation for the final Conclusion section of the memo, because it follows immediately after the Discussion section. For more on writing the Conclusion section, see Chapter 17.

You should have one CRAC for each issue the memo addresses and one CRAC for each sub-issue within each issue. It is much easier to follow one discussion at a time than to have a number of issues all mixed up together. So keep each issue separate, and analyze each issue in successive CRACs. If you have two issues, your Discussion section should have two CRACs, one after the other. This structure is much more effective than lumping the conclusions on the two issues together, then the two rules, then the two applications, and then both final conclusions. These two structures, in an outline format, would look like this:

<u>EFFECTIVE</u> ORGANIZATION FOR 2-ISSUE DISCUSSION

DISCUSSION

Umbrella/roadmap section

<u>Issue 1</u>
C for issue 1
R for issue 1
A for issue 1
C for issue 1

<u>Issue 2</u>
C for issue 2
R for issue 2
A for issue 2
C for issue 2

<u>INEFFECTIVE</u> ORGANIZATION FOR 2-ISSUE DISCUSSION

DISCUSSION

Umbrella/roadmap section

C for issue 1
C for issue 2
R for issue 1
R for issue 2
A for issue 1
A for issue 2
C for issue 1
C for issue 2

Use headings to help your reader know when you begin a new issue or a new sub-issue. Each issue—each CRAC—should have its own subheading within the Discussion section (unless the memo is extremely short, but even then headings are often helpful). Your professor may prefer headings that are complete sentences that function as a conclusion, or simplified one- or two-word headings. Often you can use formatting options like bold or italics or initial capital letters to let your readers know at a glance whether they are reading issues or sub-issues. Use the formatting options your professor prefers.

When you're addressing more than one issue, you usually want a roadmap in the introduction or umbrella section to let the reader know there are a number of issues and to show how they relate to each other. If you have questions about how to write an umbrella section, see Chapter 13.

Sub-issues are usually organized into mini-CRACs within the main CRAC. Sub-issues are, after all, issues. They are just issues that fall under the umbrella of a larger issue. So you'll have a main CRAC to address the main issue, but you'll also organize the discussion of the sub-issues into mini-CRACs. How do you know whether you have sub-issues? If you have more than one contested factor or element of a rule, you generally have sub-issues that need their own mini-CRACs. As with main issues, you generally will use headings to introduce the sub-issues (hence, the mini-CRACs).

These mini-CRACs fit in the "application/analysis" section of the main CRAC. Because they flow from the contested factors or elements—which are part of the "rule"—they have to come in a part of the Discussion section that comes after the rule. That part is the application/analysis section, and the sub-issues follow each other the same way main CRACs would.

	DISCUSSION	
C	(conclusion on the main issue)	
R	(main rule)	
A	(umbrella paragraph identifying the sub-issues)	
	Sub-issue 1:	c
		r
		a
		c
	Sub-issue 2:	c
		r
		a
		c
C	(main conclusion)	

HOW TO ORGANIZE THE DISCUSSION

Using the cell phone manslaughter problem in Appendix A, we'll walk you through the process of organizing the Discussion.

PROBLEMS

Problem

Here is a quick overview of the cell phone manslaughter problem (for details, see Appendix A). Allison King used her wireless phone, without a hands-free device, while driving in dense fog on a winding road on the edge of an ocean cliff. King placed the call to warn her friends about the dangerous conditions, as they would be meeting later. While she was making the call, she hit and killed a bicyclist. The prosecution will attempt to convict King of vehicular manslaughter by showing that she drove while committing an illegal act (driving while using a wireless phone without a hands-free device) and with gross negligence. King will argue that her actions fit within the "emergency purposes" exception to the wireless phone prohibition. She will also argue that she did not act with gross negligence.

Step 1: Articulate the conclusion on your issue, because the reader wants to know that first. Even if the conclusion was not clear to you when you started your memo, making the conclusion clear to the reader from the outset will make it much easier to follow your analysis. The conclusion can be as brief as a heading, such as: *The State Can Likely Prove that King Committed Vehicular Manslaughter*. Most readers will think that more than this sentence heading is too much detail for this introductory conclusion. And some readers will expect just the issue here, rather than the conclusion. In those instances, the phrase *Vehicular Manslaughter* would suffice. But absent a reason to think your particular reader expects that you simply state the issue, you are usually safest to start with your conclusion on that issue.

Furthermore, if you have more than one main issue, number them and keep the numbering in the Discussion section consistent with what you've used in the Questions Presented and Brief Answers. If you had two issues in the Questions Presented and labeled them "I" and "II," do the same thing with the conclusions on those CRACs in the Discussion section—and keep them in the same order. That way, if readers want to follow the discussion on one of the issues, they can find it easily.

Step 2: Next, the reader needs to know the rule. Rules come from a variety of sources. Frequently, you have to synthesize the rule from more than one source. Sometimes, this can be a complicated process. (For more on putting together a rule, see Chapter 8.) State the rule as clearly and accurately as possible, breaking it into parts such as elements or factors when possible and using the terms of art the legislature or courts use. The rule will also include—either explicitly (under the structures of CREAC or CRuPAC) or implicitly under CRAC—an explanation or proof of the rule. Rule explanation/proof consists of the citations to the source(s) for the rule and a discussion of the authorities that support the rule, including alternative formulations of the rule. (For more on rule explanation/proof, see Chapter 9.)

For the cell phone manslaughter problem, the main rule might be stated as follows:

> "Manslaughter is the unlawful killing of a human being without malice." Cal. Penal Code § 192 (West 2022). Vehicular manslaughter is manslaughter that occurs when "driving a vehicle in the commission of an unlawful act, not amounting to felony, and with gross negligence." Cal. Penal Code § 192(c)(1) (West 2022).

From this rule, we can deduce four elements necessary to prove vehicular manslaughter in California:

1. the unlawful killing of a human being without malice;
2. while driving a vehicle;
3. committing an unlawful act that is not a felony; and
4. with gross negligence.

The analysis for each element, if in dispute, would form a mini-CRAC within the Discussion. In the problem, it is clear the bike rider died, and King didn't know him or hold any malice toward him, so the first element is not contested. It is also clear King was driving a vehicle—her car—so the second element is also not contested. You'd point these facts out and demonstrate, not simply assert, that the first two elements were met. But because you could accomplish that in a few short sentences, you do not need mini-CRACs with complete headings for these uncontested elements. You could discuss those in the introduction/umbrella section or address them very briefly at the beginning of the application.

The third and fourth elements, though, are contested, so you'd address those two elements in mini-CRACs, under the "A," within the main CRAC of "vehicular manslaughter." Thus, the organization for the cell phone manslaughter problem *so far* would look like this:

DISCUSSION

Conclusion: King Is Likely Guilty of Vehicular Manslaughter

Rule/Rule Explanation: Quote the relevant parts of the vehicular manslaughter statute; cite that statute; then state that the first two elements are not at issue, leaving two sub-issues: committing an unlawful act not a felony while driving and gross negligence.

Application/Analysis: Mini-CRACs fit here:

> **Sub-issue 1 Conclusion:** King likely committed an unlawful act that was not a felony.
>
> **Sub-issue 1 Rule:** It is unlawful to "drive a motor vehicle while using a wireless telephone" without "hands-free listening and talking" unless for "emergency purposes."
>
> **Sub-issue 1 Rule Explanation or Rule Proof:** Cite this statute and use case law to explain and illustrate the rule regarding using a cell phone without hands-free technology while driving and what constitutes emergency purposes.
>
> **Sub-issue 2 Conclusion:** King likely acted with gross negligence.
>
> **Sub-issue 2 Rule:** Gross negligence is . . .
>
> **Sub-issue 2 Rule Explanation or Rule Proof:** Use case law to describe and illustrate what constitutes gross negligence.

Step 3: Next, the reader needs to know how the rule applies to the facts—the "application/analysis." As always, try to help the reader as much as possible. Starting the application/analysis section with a transition like "here" or "in our case" tells the reader you're moving from the rule section to your facts.

What facts do you include in your analysis? Include any fact that is relevant, meaning it could—at least potentially—affect the outcome. Even if you thought about a fact and ultimately decided it would not change the result, you should still address that fact in the application/analysis. The reader may wonder about the same fact, and if you haven't explained why it doesn't change the result, the reader may have less confidence in your final conclusion. You can't completely know which facts are relevant until you understand the law, and additional facts themselves can make a fact relevant that might otherwise be insignificant. But if you think the reader might wonder about a fact, you should include it in your analysis. If the parties' dispute primarily concerns how the law applies to the facts at hand, then the application/analysis portion of the memo—the "A"—will likely be the longest bit of the Discussion.

In our cell phone manslaughter problem, we would address the sub-issue created by the fourth element of the main rule: whether King acted with "gross negligence." Imagine that you formulated your basic gross negligence rule as follows (which would be followed with an explanation of more detail and facts from the relevant cases):

> "'Gross negligence' is the exercise of so slight a degree of care as to raise a presumption of conscious indifference to the consequences." *People v. Harris*, 89 Cal. Rptr. 3d 904, 906 (Ct. App. 2009). Courts apply the standard objectively. *Id.* If a "reasonable person in the defendant's position would have been aware of the risk involved," the law presumes the defendant was aware of the risk and he acted with gross negligence, even if he in fact was unaware of the risk. *Id.* Gross negligence depends on the circumstances of each case. *People v. Newton*, 104 Cal. Rptr. 3d 138, 141 (Ct. App. 2010). However, at least one California court held that, as a general matter, a defendant "knew or should have known that using his cell phone while driving was endangering the lives of others." *People v. Tompkins*, 104 Cal. Rptr. 3d 131, 134 (Ct. App. 2010).

Once you understand the rule and the relevant cases, you'd likely conclude that the following facts are relevant to the gross negligence sub-issue:

- King dialed her cell phone while driving.
- The road was a winding two-lane road.
- The road was on the edge of a cliff with the sea below.
- There was dense fog, described as "near whiteout conditions."
- Driving conditions were even more hazardous than usual.
- King was driving slowly.

If, on the other hand, the issue you were concerned with was whether King was entitled to the "emergency purposes" defense, which is a sub-issue under the third element—committing an act that is not a felony (driving while talking on her cell phone)—the relevant facts might include these:

- The road offers very few places to pull over.
- King was concerned for the safety of several friends and others on the road.
- King planned to warn her friends to refrain from driving until road conditions improved and it was safer.

Notice how the relevant facts change depending on the issue; the facts necessary to resolve the "gross negligence" element are different from the facts necessary to resolve the "emergency purposes" defense.

Once you've determined which facts are relevant, your task in this part is to connect those facts to the rule. In King's case, you could directly apply the statutory test to her facts (Fact-Based Analysis, explained in Chapter 10), you could compare and contrast—in legal writing terms "analogize" and "distinguish"—your facts with the facts in the precedent cases (Analogical Analysis, explained in Chapter 11), or you could discuss how policy rationales support a particular outcome (Policy Analysis, explained in Chapter 12)—or use some combination of these analytical tools.

Step 4: Finally, remind the reader of your conclusion. You began by stating your conclusion. And after reading the rule and application/analysis, the conclusion ought to be obvious. But you still need to explicitly restate it. Do so at the end, usually in just a sentence at the end of the application section. And just as signal words help in the application/analysis section, signaling this conclusion with words like "therefore" or "in conclusion" makes your organization easier for the reader to follow. Few legal questions are a slam dunk, so don't be afraid to qualify your predictions with "probably" or "likely."

The only time readers might not expect this final conclusion is in a single-issue memo with no sub-issues; that's because the next section is the memo's Conclusion section, which would be identical to the CRAC's conclusion. Any other time, be sure to explicitly conclude at the end of each CRAC.

Using these principles, here is an outline of one way to effectively organize the Discussion section for the cell phone manslaughter problem:

DISCUSSION

Conclusion: King Is Likely Guilty of Vehicular Manslaughter

Rule/Rule Explanation: Quote the relevant parts of the vehicular manslaughter statute; cite that statute; then state the first two elements are not at issue, leaving two sub-issues: committing an unlawful act not a felony while driving and gross negligence.

Application/Analysis:

(heading for sub-issue one) Unlawful Act

> **Sub-issue 1 Conclusion:** King likely committed an unlawful act that was not a felony.
>
> **Sub-issue 1 Rule:** It is unlawful to "drive a motor vehicle while using a wireless telephone" without "hands-free listening and talking" unless for "emergency purposes."
>
> **Sub-issue 1 Rule Explanation or Rule Proof: Cite this statute and** use case law to explain and illustrate the rule regarding using a cell phone without hands-free technology while driving and what constitutes emergency purposes.
>
> **Sub-issue 1 Application/Analysis:** Apply the law to our facts, making fact-based arguments and analogizing and distinguishing precedent.
>
> **Sub-issue 1 Conclusion:** King likely committed an unlawful act that was not a felony.

(heading for sub-issue two) Gross Negligence

Sub-issue 2 Conclusion: King likely acted with gross negligence.

Sub-issue 2 Rule: Gross negligence is . . .

Sub-issue 2 Rule Explanation or Rule Proof: Use case law to describe and illustrate what constitutes gross negligence.

Sub-issue 2 Application/Analysis: Apply the law to our facts, making fact-based arguments and analogizing and distinguishing precedent.

Sub-issue 2 Conclusion: King likely acted with gross negligence.

You would go on to write a Conclusion section for the entire memo. (See Chapter 17.)

If your problem has multiple issues (as opposed to a single issue problem with multiple sub-issues, like the cell phone manslaughter problem), you'll need one main CRAC for each independent issue. Imagine a case where there were two main issues: first, whether the suit violates the Statute of Limitations (meaning it wasn't filed timely) and second, whether the Defendant committed a civil battery upon the Plaintiff despite the Defendant's intent to hit his dog, not the Plaintiff. Each of these main issues would be organized by a main CRAC, and any sub-issues (as depicted below, the battery issue has sub-issues) would be organized into mini-CRACs. The outline below shows how you might effectively outline the Discussion section of that memo:

DISCUSSION

Umbrella/roadmap section	
C	I. The Statute of Limitations Is Not Likely a Bar.
R	Rule for statute of limitations
	Rule explanation/proof for statute of limitations
A	Application/analysis for statute of limitations
C	Conclusion for statute of limitations
C	II. Liability for Civil Battery Is Unlikely.
R	Rule for civil battery: occurs when the defendant (1) causes a harmful or offensive contact with the plaintiff, and the defendant (2) intends to cause harmful or offensive contact with the plaintiff or a third person.
	Rule explanation/proof for civil battery
A (mini-CRACs for sub-issues 1 and 2)	1. Likely Intent to Cause a Harmful/Offensive Contact
	Rule for harmful/offensive contact
	Rule explanation/proof for harmful/offensive contact
	Application/analysis for harmful/offensive contact
	Conclusion for harmful/offensive contact
	2. Likely No Intent Regarding a "Third Person"
	Rule for third person
	Rule explanation/proof for third person
	Application/analysis for third person
	Conclusion for third person
C	Conclusion for civil battery

EXAMPLES

Review the following examples. For each example, there may be more than one correct answer, but try to choose the *best* answer. Explain to yourself why you have chosen that answer. Then read the explanations in the last section of this chapter to check your work.

Note. As with many of the illustrations provided in this chapter, these examples are in bullet format so you can quickly see the organizational structure rather than the details within each component.

EXAMPLES

Example 7-1

This question uses the negligent infliction of emotional distress problem, which you can find in Appendix C.

DISCUSSION

- To recover for negligent infliction of emotional distress as a bystander, a plaintiff must prove four elements:
  1) the defendant's negligence caused the victim's injury or death;
  2) the plaintiff had a marital or close blood relation, or an "intimate, familial relationship," with the victim;
  3) the plaintiff directly observed or was "sensorially aware" of the accident and the victim's resulting injury; and
  4) the plaintiff experienced severe emotional distress.
- Cite *Ortiz v. JDP Builders, Inc.*, the most recent New Fornia Supreme Court case, which uses those four elements and discuss that case's facts, issue, and holding.
- Umbrella/roadmap for the application section: this memo assumes the first two elements, and briefly explain the facts suggesting each element is met. This discussion therefore focuses on whether Poe and her fiancé had an "intimate, familial relationship" and whether Poe directly observed or was sensorially aware of the accident and her fiancé's resulting injury.
- Include mini-CRACs for all four elements.
- Poe will therefore likely succeed on her claim of negligent infliction of emotional distress as a bystander.

This is an . . .

A. effective organization for the memo's Discussion section because it states a clear rule and then proves that rule.
B. effective organization for the memo's Discussion section because it includes mini-CRACs for all of the sub-issues.
C. ineffective organization for the memo's Discussion section because it includes an umbrella/roadmap within the application section of the main CRAC.
D. ineffective organization for the memo's Discussion section because it starts with the main rule and omits the initial conclusion (the first "C" in CRAC).

EXAMPLES

Example 7-2

This question uses the cell phone manslaughter problem, which you can find in Appendix A.

DISCUSSION

- Vehicular Manslaughter Is Likely.
- Quote and cite the vehicular manslaughter statute and the statute on driving while using a cell phone.
- *Harris*—arguably similar (a reasonable person would realize making a cell phone call while driving, especially with road conditions King faced, was dangerous), so probably gross negligence, but probably more of an emergency, so maybe not an unlawful act.
- *Tompkins*—arguably similar (a reasonable person would realize making a cell phone call while driving, especially with road conditions King faced, was dangerous), so probably gross negligence, and probably similar regarding whether an emergency, so likely an unlawful act.
- *Newton*—arguably distinguishable on gross negligence because the circumstances weren't as extreme; similarly, arguably not as strong in terms of an emergency, so likely an unlawful act.
- It is therefore likely King committed vehicular manslaughter.

This is an . . .

A. effective organization for the memo's Discussion section because the conclusion on the main issue is clearly identified, all of the relevant authorities are analogized or distinguished from your case, and it ends with the conclusion.

B. effective organization for the main issue of vehicular manslaughter because it includes all the components of deductive reasoning.
C. ineffective organization for the memo's Discussion section because it's organized around the authorities rather than the issues.
D. ineffective organization for the main issue but an effective organization of the two sub-issues.

EXAMPLES

Example 7-3

This question uses the cell phone manslaughter problem, which you can find in Appendix A.

DISCUSSION

- King Did Not Likely Commit an "Unlawful Act."
- King's case is like *Newton*, where the call to the obstetrician satisfied the "emergency purposes" exemption, and not like *Harris* or *Tompkins*.
- Although cell phone calls while driving are generally prohibited, that prohibition "does not apply to a person using a wireless telephone for emergency purposes." Cal. Vehicle Code § 23123 (West 2022).
- King probably did not commit an unlawful act by talking on her cell phone while driving because she likely made the call for "emergency purposes."

This is an . . .

A. effective organization for the "unlawful act" sub-issue because it follows the CRAC format.
B. effective organization for the "unlawful act" sub-issue because it includes all of the components necessary to answer the legal issue.
C. ineffective organization for the "unlawful act" sub-issue because although it includes the sub-rule for unlawful act, it does not quote the main rule governing vehicular manslaughter.
D. ineffective organization for the "unlawful act" sub-issue because the rule should come before the application/analysis.

EXAMPLES

Example 7-4

This question uses the cell phone manslaughter problem, which you can find in Appendix A.

DISCUSSION

- "No Gross Negligence"
- "[T]he exercise of so slight a degree of care as to raise a presumption of conscious indifference to the consequences"
- Discuss cases that consider gross negligence
- Analogize/distinguish King's facts with case facts

This is an . . .

A. effective organization for the "gross negligence" sub-issue because it includes the conclusion, rule, and application/analysis in order.
B. effective organization for the "gross negligence" sub-issue because a final conclusion is not necessary for a sub-issue; the conclusion can be included in the overall Conclusion section of the memo.
C. effective organization for the "gross negligence" sub-issue because it includes all of the components of deductive reasoning.
D. incomplete organization for the "gross negligence" sub-issue because it omits the final conclusion.

EXAMPLES

Example 7-5

This question uses the cell phone manslaughter problem, which you can find in Appendix A.

DISCUSSION

- Conclusion = King Is Likely Guilty of Vehicular Manslaughter.
- Rule = quote and cite Cal. Penal Code § 192(c)(1) (West 2022); elements =
  1) the unlawful killing of a human being;
  2) while driving a vehicle;
  3) committing an unlawful act that is not a felony; and
  4) with gross negligence.
- Application/Analysis = first two elements met (briefly explain why); final two elements contested (mini-CRACs)

  A. c = King Likely Committed an Unlawful Act.
  r = quote/cite Cal. Vehicle Code § 23123 (West 2022). Statute has an exception when call is for "emergency purposes." Discuss cases (*Harris, Tompkins, Newton*) with regard to the "emergency" element—facts, issue, holding.

a = analogize/distinguish King's facts from facts in each of the cases on this issue.

c = King's call likely not made for a "emergency purposes" so she likely violated the statute, committing an unlawful act.

B. c = King Likely Acted with Gross Negligence.

r = synthesized rule from the cases (good language in *Harris*). Then discuss cases on the gross negligence issue—facts, issue, holding.

a = analogize/distinguish King's facts from facts in each of the cases on this issue.

c = King likely acted with gross negligence.

- Conclusion = because all four elements are met, including unlawful act (because probably not an "emergency purpose") and gross negligence, King is likely guilty of vehicular manslaughter.

This is an . . .

A. effective organization for the Discussion section because it follows the CRAC format, including using mini-CRACs for the sub-issues.

B. effective organization because the reader can logically follow the discussion, even though it does not technically follow the CRAC format.

C. ineffective organization because the application/analysis section is too long.

D. ineffective organization because the sub-issues can be better addressed together rather than separating them.

EXPLANATIONS

Explanation 7-1

A is not the best answer. Even though this example states and proves a clear rule, that is not enough for the overall organization of the Discussion section to be effective. This example is missing a key component of CRAC—the initial conclusion. In addition, mini-CRACs are not necessary for elements that you're instructed to assume. **B** is incorrect. When you are instructed to assume issues, your memo shouldn't include CRACs (or mini-CRACs, if they are sub-issues) on those issues. Use the umbrella/roadmap to explain to the reader why they are not fully discussed and move on to the contested issues (or sub-issues). **C** is also not the best answer. Although this organization appropriately includes an umbrella/roadmap, that alone is not enough to make the overall organization effective, as explained in answer A above. **D** is the correct answer for the reason stated in A.

Explanation 7-2

A is incorrect. Although the conclusion on the main issue is articulated, it anticipates analogizing and distinguishing the relevant authorities, and it ends with the conclusion, this organization is ineffective. This outline organizes the Discussion around the relevant cases rather than the better approach of organizing by the issues—which in this case are (1) whether King committed an unlawful act and (2) whether she acted with gross negligence. **B** is not the best answer. Simply including all the components of deductive reasoning does not ensure they are organized effectively. **C** is the best answer. As noted in A, this outline is organized by the cases rather than the better approach of organizing by relevant sub-issues. In CRAC terms, the organization of this outline would be difficult for a reader to follow: C*R*A*R*A*R*A*C. When analysis is organized by cases instead of sub-issues, the reader has to jump back and forth to figure out the synthesized rule and analysis for each sub-issue instead of having the writer do that work for the reader. ***D*** is wrong. The sub-issues should be divided into mini-CRACs allowing the reader to follow the analytical process for each sub-issue independently. Mixing them together will only confuse the reader.

Explanation 7-3

A is incorrect. This outline starts with the conclusion on the sub-issue and ends with the conclusion, as the CRAC structure suggests. But the application/analysis section should not come before the rule, and in this example, the writer has started analogizing and distinguishing cases before telling the reader about the governing statute, which creates the rule, or the cases that interpret that statute. This structure is ineffective because the reader expects to read about the legal rule before reading your analysis of how that rule applies to the facts at hand. Keep the rule and application separate from each other and state the rule before applying it. **B** is not the best answer. Even when all of the components of CRAC are present, their order matters, and here, the order is ineffective for the reasons noted in A. Furthermore, the cases should be discussed before they are applied to your case. **C** is incorrect. The organization is ineffective for the reasons noted in A. In addition, within a mini-CRAC, readers seldom expect the main rule to be quoted again. Remember that this section is just one part of a larger Discussion section: The main CRAC would cover the vehicular manslaughter requirements and quote the relevant portions of the statute. Within a mini-CRAC, the reader only needs to understand the answer to that smaller question. Hence, the main rule might (or might not) be referred to, but is usually not quoted even when it's included. **D** is the best answer for the reasons stated in A, B, and C.

Explanation 7-4

A is not the best answer. Although the sub-issue outline does include the conclusion, rule, and application in order, it has no final conclusion. Instead, it ends with the application/analysis. The reader expects an explicit conclusion at the end of the analysis for a sub-issue—even if it's a close case, even if it follows logically from the application/analysis section, even if the reader can figure out how you would have concluded, and even though you have already stated your ultimate conclusion in the heading. **B** is incorrect. Although it's true that some writers omit the final "C" within a Discussion section's CRAC because the memo's Conclusion section will immediately follow the Discussion, that should only be the case when you are writing a single-issue memo. An explicit conclusion at the end of each mini-CRAC is necessary for sub-issues. **C** is not the best answer for the reasons listed in A. Although the rule and the rule explanation are explicitly broken apart in this outline, the final conclusion is missing. **D** is the best answer for the reasons stated in A, B, and C.

Explanation 7-5

A is the best answer. This example follows the CRAC format well. It is organized around issues rather than authorities and the sub-issues are addressed in separate mini-CRACs. The headings are logical—labeling the sub-issues "A" and "B" helps keep them separate—and the sub-issues are properly within the application/analysis section of the main CRAC. **B** is not the best answer. It is important to think about whether the reader can logically follow the discussion, but that is most likely to happen when the writer follows the CRAC format—which this example does. **C** is incorrect. When a memo addresses sub-issues, the application/analysis section will likely be relatively long. That section includes the mini-CRACs for the sub-issues, so it's often the longest part of a memo with sub-issues. **D** is also incorrect. Combining sub-issues will make the memo harder, not easier, to follow. They have separate rules and the facts relevant to each sub-issue vary. Therefore, breaking them apart, as done in this example, into separate mini-CRACs is generally the most effective organization for sub-issues.

Checklist

Chapter 7: Organizing the Discussion

✔	Use IRAC, CRAC, or the organizational paradigm that your professor uses to organize each issue and sub-issue in the assignment.
✔	Start and end each CRAC with a conclusion statement for that issue or sub-issue, generally signaling this with a heading at the beginning of each issue or sub-issue.
✔	State the rule for that issue or sub-issue.
✔	Explain the rule with citations to authority and a discussion of the facts, outcomes, and rationales in the precedent cases for that issue or sub-issue.
✔	Apply the law in the rule and rule explanation to your assignment facts for each issue or sub-issue.

You will find all of the chapter checklists compiled in Appendix D.

CHAPTER 8

Constructing a Rule

In law, what is a rule? You know about lots of rules from daily life—such as "No trespassing," "No parking here between 8 am and 6 pm," and "All drivers must wear seatbelts." In the context of law, a rule is a principle that governs actions. It can also be thought of as the legal test that a court applies to resolve an issue.

Understanding the applicable rule is important. It's a foundational building block for an office memo's legal analysis and the argument in a persuasive brief. Indeed, one of the first things a reader wants to know is what rule will apply to your set of facts. This chapter explains how to identify the rule that a court applies in a case and how to synthesize multiple cases or sources of law to determine the governing rule of law.

Terminology notes. This interpretive process of reading and understanding how various sources of applicable law work together is what we mean by "rule synthesis" or "constructing" a rule.

WHAT YOU NEED TO KNOW ABOUT CONSTRUCTING A RULE

In law, you'll see common rule types and structures over and over again. A rule can require action (e.g., "shall," "must"), prohibit action (e.g., "shall not," "is prohibited"), authorize action (e.g., "may," "at its discretion"), or declare something to be true (e.g., "Any person who . . . is guilty of . . ."). And rules can be structured in various ways, for instance requiring that certain elements be met or listing factors for a court to consider in making a determination. Don't worry about memorizing these rule structures or their names. But it might be helpful to know as you're reading authorities such as statutes and case law that there are common rule structures. Pay attention to words like "and," "or," and "must" that will help you understand how a rule works. Also, the rule structure will guide your large-scale organization choices, as you learned in Chapter 7.

Here are some common rule structures and an idea of how they might appear:

A *conjunctive test* (also known as an *elements test*): a rule that has a list of required elements.
X results if these elements are met: 1, 2, *and* 3.

A *disjunctive test*: a rule that is structured by an "either/or" test.
X results if either A *or* B is met.

A *defeasible rule*: a rule with an exception or exceptions.
X results where . . . *unless* . . . occurs or exists.

A *factors test*: a rule that provides multiple factors or criteria for determining whether a certain standard is met.
To determine whether X results, *consider* A, B, C, and D.

A *balancing test*: a rule that weighs various considerations against each other, often using factors to measure the considerations.
X results where A *outweighs* B.

Sometimes a rule will have more than one of these structures, in a nested fashion. For instance, a rule might be a conjunctive test with a list of required elements, and one of the elements might use a factors test for determining whether it's met.

X results if these elements are met:
1. –,
2. –, and
3. –. To determine whether element 3 is met, consider the following factors:
A,
B,
C, and
D.

When you have a single relevant opinion, understanding the rule is simply a matter of reading and analyzing the opinion to figure out the legal test the court applied and how it works. You've probably done this when briefing a case. Note that the rule is different than the case holding. The rule is the legal test that the court applied to resolve the issue. The holding is the court's conclusion after applying that rule to the specific facts of the case. When you're looking for the rule, you're looking to find out what test a court would likely apply to the next case that comes along after the one you're reading.

To figure out what the rule means and how it works, first break the rule down into its parts and diagram or outline it (i.e., list and number the elements or factors in the test).

Pay careful attention to the opinion itself, for example noting whether the rule's language uses words like "must," which suggests a mandatory rule, or "may," which suggests a discretionary rule. Also pay attention to how the case defines the element or factors, how many factors or elements are in the rule, whether a piece of the analysis is an exception, and so on. Once you've diagrammed the rule into its parts, examine each part separately and figure out its meaning. Then put the rule back together in your mind by mentally walking yourself through how it works, or by jotting it down as a flowchart and running through how the rule would apply to a hypothetical set of facts.

When you have more than one relevant opinion or source of law, you've got to synthesize them to construct the rule. Synthesis means a conceptual combining of several cases or sources of law into a statement of a legal rule. To do this, first read each authority, and then figure out how they fit together. In this analytical step, abstract a rule that explains all authorities together and forms the legal test that a court looking to those authorities would apply.

Synthesizing authorities doesn't mean creating a catalog in which you describe them one after another. For instance, you aren't synthesizing authorities if you simply say, "Section 123 of the ABC Act provides: . . . . In *Jones*, the court held . . . . In *Woods*, the court held . . . . In *Meyers*, the court held . . . ." That sounds like a list of holdings rather than a rule. Instead, to synthesize authorities you must analyze what they have in common and consider how they relate to each other. Once you've done that, you're ready to state what rule those authorities stand for together—the rule that will be applied to the next case that comes along. This requires reading authorities carefully, including reading cases actively and grappling with which facts were important to the result, what the result was, the court's reasoning for reaching that result, and how those aspects of the case compare and relate to the other cases. Sometimes it helps to create a chart or take notes. We'll explain how to do this for one of the examples that follows. You'll also need to consider the weight of authority and the dates of the cases. Sometimes not all of the cases are binding authority, or you may find two seemingly conflicting cases but one is more recent and may have implicitly overruled the earlier case.

This is usually a process of inductive reasoning, as you'll work with the details of the authorities until you see the larger common threads that create a synthesized rule. Sometimes you'll find that a recent decision from a binding court in your jurisdiction has explicitly stated a synthesized legal rule. In that instance, you can just restate that rule if it applies. More often, you have to do the analytical work of figuring out how the authorities fit together to create the governing law.

When you move from figuring out the legal rule to writing about it, you'll want to start by writing about the synthesized rule rather than focusing on the individual authorities. This is the opposite of the inductive reasoning that you did when figuring out how to synthesize the rule. When writing, start by stating your broader synthesis and then explain that rule with narrower detail from the authorities, usually precedent cases. This gives the reader what she wants: a statement of the rule and some explanation of what the rule means and how it works by using explanatory detail from the precedent cases that you used to construct the rule. The next chapter addresses this in more detail.

When the relevant cases don't explicitly state a rule, constructing the rule is a subjective, analytical process. Keep in mind that constructing the rule is more a craft than a science and it's often possible to construct the rule in slightly varying yet still accurate ways. The rule can be formulated narrowly or broadly. You'll want to be aware of this choice and align it with the purpose of your writing, whether that's objective analysis or persuasive argument. For instance, a plaintiff might argue that the court should interpret some case law broadly, to apply to the defendant, while the defendant might argue that the court should construe the case law as setting out a narrow rule that applied to the facts in the precedent case but not to the defendant at hand. In an objective office memo, you'd want to construct the rule neutrally: in the way you think a court would likely view it.

HOW TO CONSTRUCT A RULE

Using the copyright and fair use problem in Appendix B, we'll walk you through the process of constructing a rule.

PROBLEMS

Problem

Here is a quick overview of the copyright and fair use problem (for details, see Appendix B). Page is suing Dash for violating the Copyright Act when Dash wrote a song based on Page's song (which in copyright terms is called the "original"), "Red, White, and Blue." Dash's song uses the structure and many lyrics of the original but changes the original song's political message. The music of the two songs is not at issue, only the lyrics. Page expects that Dash will argue that his song is a parody that falls under the fair use exception to the Copyright Act. The court will consider the relevant factors set out in the fair use statute, 17 U.S.C. § 107: whether the copy was transformative and targeted the original; whether it took more than necessary of the original; and whether it will interfere with the original's market.

A preliminary note. This process can be hard. Learning to read and understand law, particularly when you've got many authorities, requires some intellectual heavy lifting. Sometimes you have to read the authorities multiple times, consult legal dictionaries or other resources, and work through the details of the law like a puzzle. And there isn't a trick that always works for this analytical process. Sometimes it helps to make a chart of the cases. Sometimes you'll find a recent case that provides a thorough, comprehensive statement and explanation of the synthesized rule. Other times you need to slog through the authorities, closely reading them in search of a pattern or way of understanding them as a synthesized rule or finding gaps in the law.

Step 1: Identify the relevant authorities. This usually requires legal research. For your legal writing class, sometimes your professor may provide authorities to use for your assignment.

Assume that you're working on the copyright and fair use problem and have the authorities in Appendix B: federal copyright statutes regarding exclusive rights in copyrighted works and a "fair use" limitation to those exclusive rights, 17 U.S.C. §§ 106 & 107, and case law interpreting those sections. The case law includes *Campbell v. Acuff-Rose Music, Inc.*, 510 U.S. 569 (1994), *Dr. Seuss Enterprises, L.P. v. Penguin Books USA, Inc.*, 109 F.3d 1394 (9th Cir. 1997), and *Mattel, Inc. v. Walking Mountain Productions*, 353 F.3d 792 (9th Cir. 2003).

At this point you might mentally order these in terms of their weight of authority: the federal statutes trump the case law interpreting them and the U.S. Supreme Court case trumps the Ninth Circuit cases. If you need a refresher on the basic concepts of weight of authority, see Chapter 4.

Step 2: Read the authorities and try to figure out how they relate to each other in terms of a legal rule. Look for the legal test set out in each of the authorities and then see how each compares with the others. Carefully read language that states a legal test, noting words like "must" or "shall," suggesting a mandatory rule, or "may," suggesting a discretionary rule. Also note the structure of the rule, how the case defines the elements or factors or if the rule requires a balancing test, what connectors are present (and/or), and whether there are exceptions to the rule.

In the copyright and fair use problem, you're trying to figure out the rule that would determine whether Dash infringed Page's copyrighted lyrics and whether Dash has a viable defense. Start with the statutory authority in Appendix B. Section 106 provides that the owner of a copyright has certain exclusive rights. And § 107 sets out a limitation on the exclusive rights, called "fair use." It provides that "fair use of a copyrighted work . . . for purposes such as criticism, comment, news reporting . . . is not an infringement of a copyright." This language sounds like a defense to copyright infringement. If the use is a "fair use" then there's no copyright infringement.

How do you know if a use is a "fair use"? The next line of the statute tells us: "In determining whether the use made of a work in any particular case is a fair use the factors to be considered shall include . . ." and then lists four factors. Notice that the statute calls the four items "factors" and notes that they "shall" "be considered." This tells us that they're not required elements that all have to be met, but that a court must consider these four factors in making its decision about fair use. You might wonder at this point how to interpret those factors and how courts have decided the case when some of the factors weigh against fair use. Look to the case law to better understand this statutory rule.

It often makes sense to read the case law by starting with the most recent binding authority, which for the copyright and fair use problem is *Mattel, Inc. v. Walking Mountain Productions*, 353 F.3d 792 (9th Cir. 2003), or with the case from the highest authority, which is *Campbell v. Acuff-Rose Music, Inc.*, 510 U.S. 569 (1994). From these cases, a picture starts to emerge about how courts interpret the four-factor fair use test. This leads us to our next step.

Step 3: Fully synthesize the authorities to determine the specific rule of law. After you've gotten a basic sense of how the authorities relate to each other with respect to a legal rule, you need a more specific understanding. This usually requires fully synthesizing the case law at a detailed level. As noted previously, there's no special trick for this. You've got to closely read the authorities in search of a pattern or way of understanding them as a synthesized rule.

Continuing on with the sample of our copyright and fair use problem, you need to synthesize the case law to figure out how courts have interpreted the four statutory factors for fair use and applied these factors in precedent cases. Start by reading *Campbell* because it's the only Supreme Court case in our set of authorities and thus carries the greatest weight of authority. We are reading closely and pulling out what looks like important information about how the Supreme Court interprets the statutory factors as a legal test.

Imagine that you take the following notes on *Campbell*. You could put them in a chart format or just jot them down. Do whatever works best for you to process the information.

	17 U.S.C. § 107 (the fair use statute)	***Campbell v. Acuff-Rose Music, Inc.*, 510 U.S. 569 (1994)**
General	"In determining whether the use made of a work in any particular case is a fair use the factors to be considered shall include — [the statutory factors]"	To determine whether an alleged infringing act falls within the fair use exception, courts engage in a case-by-case analysis and do not treat the four statutory factors in isolation, rather the "results [are] weighed together, in light of the purposes of copyright."
First Fair Use Factor	"the purpose and character of the use, including whether such use is of a commercial nature or is for nonprofit educational purposes"	The inquiry here is "whether and to what extent the new work is 'transformative.'" A "transformative use is not absolutely necessary for a finding of fair use, [but] the goal of copyright, [is] to promote science and the arts . . ." Parody has transformative value when it has "critical bearing on the substance or style of the original composition" and its "parodic character may reasonably be perceived."
Second Fair Use Factor	"the nature of the copyrighted work"	This factor is not likely to help make the fair use determination in cases involving parodies "since parodies almost invariably copy publicly known, expressive works."
Third Fair Use Factor	"the amount and substantiality of the portion used in relation to the copyrighted work as a whole"	Courts consider whether "the amount and substantiality of the portion used in relation to the copyrighted work as a whole . . . [is] reasonable in relation to the purpose of the copying." "[T]he extent of permissible copying varies with the purpose and character of the use." A parody "must be able to 'conjure up' at least enough of the original to make the object of its critical wit recognizable," but "how much more is reasonable will depend . . . on the extent to which the song's overriding purpose and character is to parody the original or, in contrast, the likelihood that the parody may serve as a market substitute for the original."
Fourth Fair Use Factor	"the effect of the use upon the potential market for or value of the copyrighted work"	Courts must consider "the extent of market harm caused by the particular actions of the alleged infringer" and "whether unrestricted widespread conduct of the sort engaged in by the defendant . . . would result in a substantially adverse impact on the potential market for the original."

You might also take notes on the key facts of *Campbell* and how the Court applied the test to those facts. Next, you might read *Mattel*, the most recent Ninth Circuit case in our set of authorities. You'd read it with a critical eye toward reconciling it with *Campbell*. Does it add or change anything in the rule?

Comparing *Mattel* to *Campbell*, the general rule about applying the statutory factors appears the same. The *Mattel* court in fact cited *Campbell* in explaining the case-by-case analysis that uses a "flexible balancing" of the statutory factors. And the *Mattel* court seems to explain each of the statutory factors in the same way, often quoting and citing *Campbell*. If you were to add a column for *Mattel* in our chart, you wouldn't have much to say other than that it basically said the same thing about the factors as *Campbell*.

Before finalizing our understanding of the synthesized rule, you'd want to carefully read the rest of *Mattel* to see whether the *Mattel* court did anything notable in applying the test set out in *Campbell*. You'd also want to read the rest of our authorities, bearing in mind the weight of those authorities. After doing that, you'd find that *Campbell* set out the rule regarding the fair use statutory factors and that the Ninth Circuit has followed it. Therefore, the Supreme Court's statement of the rule in *Campbell*, as reflected in our chart, represents a view of the synthesized rule. The next chapter addresses how to turn your rule construction into a written rule statement and explanation for the Discussion section of your office memo.

EXAMPLES

Review the following examples. For each example, there may be more than one correct answer, but try to choose the *best* answer. Explain to yourself why you have chosen that answer. Then read the explanations in the last section of this chapter to check your work.

Example 8-1

This question uses the cell phone manslaughter problem, which you can find in Appendix A.

Read the following three statutory sections for the hypothetical cell phone problem: California Penal Code §§ 192 and 191.5 and California Vehicle Code § 23123.

Cal. Penal Code § 192. Manslaughter; voluntary, involuntary, and vehicular

Manslaughter is the unlawful killing of a human being without malice. It is of three kinds:

(a) Voluntary—upon a sudden quarrel or heat of passion.

(b) Involuntary—in the commission of an unlawful act, not amounting to felony; or in the commission of a lawful act which might produce death, in an unlawful manner, or without due caution and circumspection. This subdivision shall not apply to acts committed in the driving of a vehicle.

(c) Vehicular —

(1) Except as provided in subdivision (a) of Section 191.5, driving a vehicle in the commission of an unlawful act, not amounting to felony, and with gross negligence; or driving a vehicle in the commission of a lawful act which might produce death, in an unlawful manner, and with gross negligence.

Cal. Penal Code § 191.5. Gross vehicular manslaughter while intoxicated

(a) Gross vehicular manslaughter while intoxicated is the unlawful killing of a human being without malice aforethought, in the driving of a vehicle, where the driving was in violation of Section 23140, 23152, or 23153 of the Vehicle Code, and the killing was either the proximate result of the commission of an unlawful act, not amounting to a felony, and with gross negligence, or the proximate result of the commission of a lawful act that might produce death, in an unlawful manner, and with gross negligence.

Cal. Vehicle Code § 23123. Driving motor vehicle while using wireless telephone; penalty; exceptions

(a) A person shall not drive a motor vehicle while using a wireless telephone unless that telephone is specifically designed and configured to allow hands-free listening and talking, and is used in that manner while driving.

(b) A violation of this section is an infraction punishable by a base fine of twenty dollars ($20) for a first offense and fifty dollars ($50) for each subsequent offense.

(c) This section does not apply to a person using a wireless telephone for emergency purposes, including, but not limited to, an emergency call to a law enforcement agency, health care provider, fire department, or other emergency services agency or entity.

Synthesize these into a rule that would apply to Allison King. She has been charged with vehicular manslaughter after hitting and killing a cyclist while driving in the fog on a highway located on a narrow, winding cliff. When she hit the cyclist, she was making a cell phone call, without a hands-free device, to warn a friend of the hazardous conditions. Which of the following choices best synthesizes the statutory sections for our own analytical purposes (although not necessarily phrased in the exact language you would use when drafting a memo or brief)?

A. A person commits vehicular manslaughter by unlawfully killing a human being while driving a vehicle with gross negligence and using a wireless telephone, unless the telephone was used "hands-free" or for "emergency purposes."

B. Vehicular manslaughter is "the unlawful killing of a human being without malice." There are three kinds: voluntary, involuntary, and vehicular. The California Penal Code has a separate section for gross vehicular manslaughter while intoxicated. That is one type of vehicular manslaughter. It would also be vehicular manslaughter if the person were driving "in the commission of an unlawful act" that was not a felony and with gross negligence or if driving "in the commission of a lawful act which might produce death, in an unlawful manner," and with gross negligence. One unlawful act would be driving while using a wireless telephone unless used in a "hands-free" manner or for "emergency purposes."

C. It is vehicular manslaughter when someone kills someone else while driving and using their cell phone, unless used "hands-free" or for "emergency purposes."

D. A person commits vehicular manslaughter by driving a vehicle with gross negligence and using a wireless telephone, unless used "hands-free" or for "emergency purposes."

EXAMPLES

Example 8-2

This question uses the cell phone manslaughter problem, which you can find in Appendix A.

After reading the statutory sections in Example 8-1, you understand the statutory rule that a court would apply to King. The statute doesn't, however, explain what constitutes "gross negligence" or what qualifies as using a cell phone for "emergency purposes." (The statute provides that "emergency purposes, includ[es], but [is] not limited to, an emergency call to a law enforcement agency, health care provider, fire department, or other emergency services agency or entity." So you know the listed instances would qualify, but because the list isn't exclusive, you don't know what else would qualify as an "emergency purpose.")

You'd look to case law to understand these terms better. Read these summaries of the following three cases: *People v. Harris*, *People v. Tompkins*, and *People v. Newton*.

Case 1: *People v. Harris*, 89 Cal. Rptr. 3d 904 (Ct. App. 2009)

Harris was driving his car in the middle of the day, in clear conditions, at approximately the speed limit, 45 mph. The vehicle in front of Harris, which was driven by Colter, stopped. Colter was preparing to turn right but a pedestrian was crossing in the crosswalk. Harris was talking on his cell phone, and his phone was not configured for "hands-free" listening and talking. Harris struck the back of Colter's car and Colter was killed. Harris did not apply his brakes until his car was only three feet from Colter's vehicle. Harris was convicted of vehicular manslaughter under Cal. Penal Code § 192(c)(1) (West 2008), and he now appeals that conviction.

Harris was on his way to a wedding where he was the best man. At the time of the accident, Harris was talking to a friend in the wedding party to inform him that he would be late. Harris contends that his conviction should be reversed because his actions met the "emergency purposes" exception to California's prohibition on driving a motor vehicle while using a wireless telephone and because he did not act with "gross negligence" as required by California's vehicular manslaughter statute. For the following reasons, we affirm.

First, we hold that calling to inform a wedding party that the best man would be late does not meet the "emergency purposes" exception within Cal. Vehicle Code § 23123(c) (West Supp. 2008). The statute includes examples of the types of calls that the legislature considered as emergencies, including calls to law enforcement agencies, health care providers, fire departments, and other emergency services providers. Even though the bride and groom might think of their wedding as the most significant moment in their lives, being late for that event, even for the best man, is not a true "emergency" as contemplated by the statute. Furthermore, Harris' contention that pulling over to call would make him even later does not elevate the nature of the call to emergency status. If it did, every call made to inform someone that the caller was late would qualify as an "emergency," and that is clearly beyond the scope of the statute's exception.

Second, as for whether Harris acted with "gross negligence" under Cal. Penal Code § 192(c)(1) (West 2008), a reasonable person in Harris' position would have realized the risk involved in making the phone call while driving. "Gross negligence" is the exercise of so slight a degree of care as to raise a presumption of conscious indifference to the consequences. The test is objective: whether a reasonable person in the defendant's position would have been aware of the risk involved. If a *reasonable person* in the defendant's position would have been aware of the risk involved, then the defendant is presumed to have had such an awareness. The defendant's *lack* of such awareness does not preclude a finding of gross negligence if a reasonable person would have been so aware.

The fact that Harris was from Nevada and that the state of Nevada allows drivers to use cell phones while driving does not mitigate the risk. Harris' subjective belief in the safety of his act does not mitigate the fact that he should have known the danger involved.

For the foregoing reasons, we affirm Harris' vehicular manslaughter conviction.

Case 2: *People v. Tompkins*, 104 Cal. Rptr. 3d 131 (Ct. App. 2010)

Tompkins was convicted of vehicular manslaughter for causing the death of Jordan Smith while driving and simultaneously talking on his cell phone. To be guilty of vehicular manslaughter the state must show the defendant was "driving a vehicle in the commission of an unlawful act, not amounting to felony, and with gross negligence." Cal. Penal Code § 192(c)(1) (West 2008). In this case, the unlawful act was the violation of Cal. Vehicle Code § 23123(a) (West Supp. 2008), driving "a motor vehicle while using a wireless telephone" that is not "configured to allow hands-free listening and talking."

It is undisputed that Tompkins was driving and simultaneously using his cell phone without a hands-free device when he struck and killed Smith. Tompkins contends, however, that he did not act with "gross negligence" as required by the vehicular manslaughter statute, Cal. Penal Code § 192(c), and that the exception in the vehicle code that permits using a cell phone in case of an emergency under Cal. Vehicle Code § 23123(c) applies.

Tompkins was driving from San Francisco to Los Angeles when he learned from a radio newscast that an earthquake measuring 6.9 on the Richter scale had struck the Bay Area. At the time he heard the broadcast, which was about 9 p.m., Tompkins was driving south on Interstate 5 just past exit 263 near Buttonwillow. He called home to reassure himself that his wife and children were safe. As Tompkins was dialing, he failed to notice a piece of tire in the road. When he looked up, he swerved to avoid the obstacle and his vehicle struck the side of a motorcycle being driven by Mr. Smith. Smith was thrown from the motorcycle and died immediately.

Tompkins' first claim, that he did not act with "gross negligence," is without merit. Cal. Penal Code § 192(c). "Gross negligence" is determined using an objective test; if a reasonable person in the defendant's position would have been aware of the risk involved in his behavior, then the defendant is considered to have acted with gross negligence. Under the circumstances presented in this case, driving at night on a freeway at high speeds where debris is occasionally left and other drivers are often present, Tompkins either knew or should have known that using his cell phone while driving was endangering the lives of others.

We also hold that under these facts, Tompkins does not meet the "emergency purposes" exception. Cal. Vehicle Code § 23123(a). "Emergency" implies imminent danger. It implies the need to react quickly to avoid harm, such as when there is a fire or when being attacked at a stop light by a potential car-jacker. Those are emergencies, and calls made to prevent that imminent danger are calls made for "emergency purposes." But the earthquake in this case had already happened in northern California, and any danger to either Mr. Tompkins or his family had passed before the time of Tompkins' phone call. It is understandable that a husband and father would want to reassure himself that his family was safe. But the law requires that to do so, he not endanger the lives of others. He could have waited until it was safe to pull over or exit the freeway and make his call then. The situation was no longer an emergency and his call was not for "emergency purposes" as required by the statute's exception.

Therefore, we affirm the trial court's decision finding the defendant guilty of vehicular manslaughter.

Case 3: People v. Newton, 104 Cal. Rptr. 3d 138 (Ct. App. 2010)

Roger Newton was driving to the mall just outside of San Bernardino, California. He was driving the speed limit, 40 mph, and road conditions were normal. Newton was accompanied by his wife, Annette, who was seven months pregnant. Annette Newton had experienced several problems in the pregnancy, but had been free of problems for the previous three weeks. Suddenly, Mrs. Newton moaned in pain and announced she could "feel the baby coming."

Mr. Newton immediately altered his course to head to St. Thomas Hospital in San Bernardino, which was approximately 15 minutes away and where the couple had been taking birthing classes. He also used his wireless telephone to call Mrs. Newton's obstetrician, hoping the doctor would meet the couple at the hospital. While on the phone, Newton did not see Julie Wolfe, who was jogging on the side of the road. The Newtons' car struck Ms. Wolfe and she died from injuries suffered in the accident. The Newtons' baby was born at the site of the accident.

Roger Newton was charged with vehicular manslaughter under Cal. Penal Code § 192(c) and convicted. At trial, Newton made two claims; first, he argued that calling his wife's doctor was a call made for "emergency purposes," and hence, he was entitled to the exception in the statute that generally prohibits making wireless telephone calls while driving. Second, Newton argued that under the circumstances, it was impossible for him to be aware of any risks inherent in his actions because of the urgency of his wife's medical condition. The trial court rejected both arguments. On Newton's first claim, the court stated that he could have pulled over to make the call and although the statute contemplates calls for emergency medical help, Newton was not calling doctors to the scene of an emergency. The trial court also noted that there would be doctors at the hospital when the couple arrived. On his second claim, the court relied on *People v. Harris* to conclude that "a reasonable person in [his] position would have realized the risk involved in making the phone call while driving." *People v. Harris*, 89 Cal. Rptr. 3d 904, 908 (Ct. App. 2009). Newton appeals his conviction.

We hold that Newton's call meets the statute's "emergency purposes" exception. Cal. Vehicle Code § 23123(c) (West Supp. 2008). The trial court concluded that Newton could have pulled over to call the doctor, but that reasoning fails to acknowledge the severity of the situation: Newton's wife was in labor and it was two months before her due date. She had already experienced difficulties in the pregnancy, and Newton was no doubt aware of the dangers to his wife and child of any delivery, much less an early one.

Furthermore, even though the call was not made to the scene of the emergency, the call was made *in* an emergency and to *address* that emergency—his wife and child were far more likely to survive if Newton drove to the hospital and met his wife's obstetrician there than if he waited where he was for an ambulance and an EMT to deliver the baby roadside. This life-and-death situation is the epitome of an emergency. And even though there would be doctors at the hospital when the couple arrived, Newton's wife's obstetrician was familiar with her medical history and would be best equipped to deliver the baby safely.

A genuine emergency existed and a reasonable person in Newton's shoes would have wanted the physician most familiar with his wife's pregnancy to meet the couple at the hospital. Under all these circumstances, the wireless telephone call in this case qualifies as a call for "emergency purposes." In addition, "gross negligence" depends on the nature of the circumstances and was not present here. This court has defined "gross negligence" as "the exercise of so slight a degree of care as to raise a presumption of conscious indifference to the consequences." *People v. Harris*, 89 Cal. Rptr. 3d 904, 906 (Ct. App. 2009). It is an objective test, but the test is not whether any person would be aware of the risks of making a cell phone call while driving under any circumstances—the test is whether "a reasonable person *in the defendant's position* would have been aware of the risk involved." *Id.* (emphasis added). A reasonable person in the Defendant's position would not likely have been aware of the risks of making such a call because of the emergency he was trying to address. The cell phone call, even though made while driving, was in this case the lesser of two evils and this court could not have expected Mr. Newton to appreciate the risks inherent in making that call.

This case also differs substantially from the other case on this issue that we decide today, *People v. Tompkins*. There, we held that "[u]nder the circumstances presented in this case, driving on a freeway at high speeds where debris is occasionally left and other drivers are often present, Tompkins either knew or should have known that using his cell phone while driving was endangering the lives of others." *People v. Tompkins*, 104 Cal. Rptr. 3d 131, 134 (Ct. App. 2010). Tompkins was not facing an emergency, and he was driving on a freeway at high speeds with other vehicles, including a motorcycle, nearby. Newton was making the best decision he could under difficult and obviously emotional circumstances. He had to act quickly and this court finds that in doing so, he did not act with gross negligence.

We therefore reverse Newton's vehicular manslaughter conviction.

Synthesize these cases into a rule explaining what constitutes "gross negligence." (The next example asks you to synthesize a rule about "emergency purposes.") Which of the following choices best synthesizes the case law on the rule for gross negligence?

A. Gross negligence depends on the defendant's belief about the danger involved and awareness of the risk of driving while talking on a cell phone.

B. It is grossly negligent to drive and make a phone call to check on your family after an emergency or to tell a wedding party that the best man will be late because driving while talking on a cell phone endangers the lives of others.

C. The test for gross negligence is objective: whether a reasonable person in the defendant's circumstances would have realized the risk involved and refrained from doing the act.

D. It is grossly negligent to drive and make a phone call that is not for emergency purposes.

EXAMPLES

Example 8-3

This question uses the cell phone manslaughter problem, which you can find in Appendix A.

Continuing from Example 8-2, which of the following best synthesizes the case law on the rule for using a cell phone for "emergency purposes"?

A. Calling a wife's obstetrician when she goes into early labor and has pregnancy difficulties constitutes using a cell phone for emergency purposes.

B. The "emergency purposes" exception permits using a phone to deal with urgent circumstances.

C. A genuine emergency exists when a passenger goes into early labor, but not when a best man is late for a wedding or an earthquake has already occurred and a family member calls to check on his family.

D. A call is for "emergency purposes" if to an emergency services agency, to someone who is in imminent danger, or from someone who is in imminent danger to someone who is specially suited to assist the caller.

EXAMPLES

Example 8-4

This question uses the copyright and fair use problem, which you can find in Appendix B.

Read the following excerpts.

17 U.S.C. § 107. Limitations on exclusive rights: fair use.
In determining whether the use made of a work in any particular case is a fair use the factors to be considered shall include: (1) the purpose and character of the use, including whether such use is of a commercial nature or is for nonprofit educational purposes. . . [.]

***Campbell v. Acuff-Rose Music, Inc.*, 510 U.S. 569, 578-79 (1994) (internal citations omitted)**
"The first factor [in a fair use inquiry is] 'the purpose and character of the use.' . . . question is whether the new work 'merely supersede[s] the objects' of the original creation, or instead 'adds something new, with a further purpose or different character, altering the first with new expression, meaning, or message; it asks, in other words, whether and to what extent the new work is 'transformative.' Such transformative use is not absolutely necessary for a finding of fair use, but the goal of copyright . . . is generally furthered by the creation of transformative works."

***Mattel Inc. v. Walking Mountain Prods.*, 353 F.3d 792, 800-01 (9th Cir. 2003) (internal citations omitted)**
"The first factor [in the fair use inquiry] asks 'to what extent the new work is transformative.' . . . Parodic works, like other works that comment and criticize, are by their nature often sufficiently transformative to fit clearly under the fair use exception. . . . '[I]n parody, as in news reporting, context is everything.' "

Which one of the choices below is the best construction of a rule statement for the first "fair use" factor?

A. All parodies are considered "fair use."
B. In assessing whether a parodic work is "transformative" for the first fair use factor, a court should consider the context of the work itself and analyze if the work presents a new meaning or message that is different from that of the original.
C. Even if a work is not transformative, a court may still find that it is fair use.
D. A party must prove that a work is a parody to establish it is "fair use."

EXPLANATIONS

EXPLANATIONS

Explanation 8-1

A is the best answer. This nicely synthesizes the statutory rule that would apply to Allison King. Remember, at this point, you're just working on the analysis you'd want to figure out before writing. When writing your memo or brief you'd quote more of the key statutory language, but at this stage you're just trying to figure out a synthesized rule and how it works. The prosecution would have to show that she killed someone while driving a car, that she was driving with gross negligence, that she was using a cell phone that she hadn't configured and used in the "hands-free" mode, and that she hadn't been using the phone for emergency purposes. Since you know that she was driving a vehicle and she hit and killed the cyclist when using a cell phone held up to her ear, the issues will be whether she was driving with "gross negligence" and whether calling her friend to warn her of the hazardous driving conditions was an "emergency purpose." **B** is not the best choice. It reflects correct analytical steps, but because it's not fully synthesized into the specific rule that would apply to King this isn't the best choice. **C** is incorrect because it omits the gross negligence requirement. Synthesizing authorities can be like working a puzzle. Be careful not to leave out an important piece. **D** is incorrect because it omits the part of the rule about killing a human being. It's not vehicular manslaughter unless there's an "unlawful killing of a human being without malice."

Explanation 8-2

Now that you're synthesizing the rule from multiple cases interpreting gross negligence (and "emergency purposes" in the next example), it'd be a good idea to make a chart, outline, or some other kind of diagram or notes to help us puzzle this out. Here's what one might look like for this problem:

	Key Facts	Using Cell Phone for "Emergency Purposes"?	Gross Negligence?	Result: Vehicular Man-slaughter?
People v. Harris	Harris hit and killed Colter when Colter had on his turn signal but had to stop for a pedestrian in the crosswalk. Harris didn't apply his brakes until his car was only 3 feet from Colter's car. Harris was talking on a cell phone (without a "hands-free" device) to inform a wedding party that he, the best man, was late.	No. Calling to tell a wedding party that the best man will be late is not an emergency.	Yes. A reasonable person in Harris' position would've realized the risk involved.	Yes.
People v. Tompkins	Tompkins killed someone while driving. He was on his cell phone without a "hands-free" device, driving from San Francisco to Los Angeles, calling home to assure himself that his wife and children were safe after a 6.9 earthquake had struck the San Francisco Bay Area.	No. There was no imminent danger to Tompkins or his family at the time of his phone call.	Yes. Tompkins knew or should have known the risk involved.	Yes.

	Key Facts	Using Cell Phone for "Emergency Purposes"?	Gross Negligence?	Result: Vehicular Man-slaughter?
People v. Newton	Newton's pregnant wife started to go into early labor and Newton used his cell phone while driving to call his wife's obstetrician, who had helped with earlier difficulties in the pregnancy. Newton struck and killed a jogger on the side of the road while on the phone.	Yes. A genuine emergency existed on these facts.	No. A reasonable person in those circumstances would have wanted the obstetrician familiar with the wife's pregnancy to meet them at the hospital.	No.

This chart helps us sort out the rule on what gross negligence means. To make it, just list the case names down the left and then across the top write "key facts," whatever elements, factors, or considerations the courts analyze, and the result on the ultimate issue (here, vehicular manslaughter). After a preliminary first or second read of the cases, you'll fill in the chart by consulting each case again. Charts like these are often helpful when you've got fact-intensive precedents and several factors or considerations the courts analyze.

Looking at this completed chart, and reflecting on the cases you read, you see that courts use an objective test for gross negligence that asks what a reasonable person would have done in the defendant's circumstances. ***A*** is therefore wrong. The test doesn't consider what the defendant thought; it considers whether a *reasonable person* in the same circumstances would've been aware of the risk involved. **B** is a good start on the rule synthesis, but it's not the best choice because it focuses on the details of the cases like a catalog instead of focusing on the more general rule that the cases provide. **C** is the best answer. This choice reflects what the gross negligence column on our chart reflects, which is that all of the case law provides an objective test for gross negligence. **D** is not the best choice. Looking at our completed chart, and reflecting on the cases you read, it indeed seems that there's a relationship between gross negligence and whether the person's phone call was for emergency purposes. In both cases where the courts found vehicular manslaughter, the courts concluded the defendant had acted with gross negligence and made a phone call that was not for emergency purposes. C is a better choice than D, however, because the question asks for the best synthesis of the case law on the rule for gross negligence, which the cases interpret as C expresses.

Explanation 8-3

A is not the best choice. It's a good summary of facts that a court held constituted "emergency purposes," and it provides good explanation of the rule, which the next chapter discusses. But it's not the best choice of a synthesized rule because it simply asserts the result in one of the relevant cases. **B** is also not the best choice. The first part of the sentence "The 'emergency purposes' exception permits using a phone to . . ." is off to a great start. It's phrased like a synthesized rule. But the end of the sentence "to deal with urgent circumstances" doesn't tell the reader anything about the rule from the case law. Unlike A, choice B moved in the right direction of abstracting a rule from the multiple relevant cases, but it went too far into abstraction. "Urgent circumstances" doesn't tell the reader much more than "emergency purposes" itself, and so B is not the best answer. **C** is also not the best choice. It's a good summary of facts and it provides a good explanation of the rule. But it's not the best choice of a synthesized rule because it's focused more on the results in particular precedent cases and not phrased as a synthesized rule that would apply to the next case that comes along. **D** is the best choice of a synthesized rule on what constitutes "emergency purposes." It accurately reflects the case law, meshes the statutory example of a call to an emergency services agency, and is phrased as a rule that would apply to the next case that comes along. If you were stating and explaining the rule in the Discussion section of a memo or brief, it'd be good to explain this rule with key facts from the precedent cases. C does a nice job of this and would follow well after D. The next chapter covers the topic of writing your rule construction.

Explanation 8-4

A is incorrect. The case law indicates that parodies are often transformative, which meets the first factor, but this rule statement should address only the first factor, not the ultimate conclusion of "fair use" more generally. Furthermore, just because one factor is met, a work isn't necessarily fair use—all of the factors have to be considered together to make that final determination. **B** is correct. This statement synthesizes the court's main considerations for the first factor when dealing with a parodic work in a "fair use" case. **C** is incorrect. Although it presents a true statement related to the first factor of fair use, it cannot be considered a complete rule statement. **D** is incorrect; a work does not have to be a parody (although parodies are often transformative) to be considered "fair use." Furthermore, this rule statement does not state the pertinent part of the rule for the first factor: whether a work is transformative.

Checklist

Chapter 8: Constructing a Rule

✔	Pay attention to rule construction: whether the rule is structured as a conjunctive, disjunctive, defeasible, factors, or balancing test.
✔	Decide whether the rule is completely stated in one source or whether you need to synthesize multiple sources to state the rule.
✔	If you need to synthesize multiple sources, identify the relevant authorities and think about how they relate to each other in terms of weight of authority, when enacted or decided, and how various courts have framed the rule.
✔	Consider sorting out the synthesized rule by making a chart of the relevant authorities.

You will find all of the chapter checklists compiled in Appendix D.

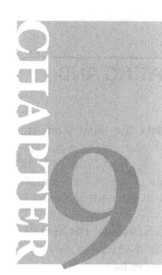

Stating and Explaining the Rule

Do you remember math classes in which you would get the right answer but not all of the available points because you didn't "show all your work"? It never worked to ask the teacher "How did I know the answer was 67.32179 if I didn't follow the steps correctly?" You had to write each of those steps on paper. The fact that you followed them correctly in your head didn't matter. The writing that lawyers do is a lot like those math classes. To succeed you must show how you arrive at your conclusion—in legal writing courses, on exams, or in the practice of law.

In the law, you "show your work" by providing a detailed legal analysis because the reader needs to understand fully the foundations of your analysis to decide whether she agrees with your ultimate conclusion. In this chapter, we'll discuss "showing your work" in terms of stating and explaining the rule. (Chapters 10-12 explain how to "show your work" in terms of applying the rule to your facts.) This "rule explanation" shows how courts in the past have applied the rule, which will, in turn, help the reader understand how the rule is likely to apply in your case.

Terminology notes. Different texts use different terms for the part of your analysis where you elaborate on the rule you have stated. Some of the more common terms are "rule explanation," "rule proof," and "rule illustration." Nearly every text requires you to elaborate on the rule by explaining, proving, or illustrating it through more detailed discussion.

WHAT YOU NEED TO KNOW ABOUT STATING AND EXPLAINING A RULE

"Stating the rule" means to clearly articulate the legal standard that applies in your client's situation. Chapter 8 discusses how to construct a rule. Often you'll have to synthesize the rule from a number of sources. Once you have the rule, the task is to state it in clear and simple terms for the reader. Quote key statutory language and generally quote sparingly from cases.

"Explaining the rule" means citing to, and discussing, the authorities that create the rule. Immediately after stating the rule (or each part of the rule), cite the authority that supports it. If you've had to synthesize a number of sources to create a rule, you'd cite those key sources here. Then, right after the citation(s), discuss precedents that show how courts have previously applied that rule as well as any authority that suggests the rule might differ from your formulation of the rule. When a potential alternative rule formulation exists, explicitly address it so the reader understands there may be alternative arguments about the rule the court will use. As explained more below, you'll also need to explain why the court is more likely to adopt your version of the rule.

Rule explanation helps the reader see that you stated the rule correctly. Citing and discussing the authorities that support your rule statement makes it more likely that you didn't misstate the rule. Provide enough information so the reader can understand why you formulated the rule as you did. Legal readers are skeptical readers!

Even if the reader is inclined to trust your analysis, rule explanation helps her check to be sure you're right. Think of rule explanation as a way to educate the reader. Your analysis might be correct, but without a complete picture of the current state of the law the reader won't have enough information to be sure you correctly analyzed the way the law would apply to your case. With citations and the discussion of the supporting authorities, the reader can judge whether the way you later apply the rule is sound.

Rule explanation allows the reader to understand what the rule means — its contours — and understand how it has been applied in precedent cases. The statement of a rule in the abstract is one thing. Understanding how that rule has affected the outcome in real cases is another, and that understanding often makes the difference in predicting how the rule will affect your client's case. In addition to creating a more complete picture of the rule, discussing the precedent cases here allows you to compare and contrast, or in legal terms, "analogize and distinguish," your client's facts with the facts in the precedent cases.

The appropriate depth for any rule explanation depends on three things: (1) the type of authority; (2) how controversial the rule is; and (3) how central the rule is to your analysis. Sometimes an entire rule explanation can fit into an explanatory parenthetical at the end of a case citation. Usually, though, a longer explanation is more effective. In longer memos, it is not unusual for the rule explanation alone to span several pages of your Discussion section. You might spend a page discussing a key case, a paragraph each discussing other helpful cases, and end with a paragraph that explains several other less significant cases that are still helpful to the reader.

1. *The type of authority:* With constitutional provisions, statutes, and administrative regulations, quoting the relevant language suffices for stating the rule. When it comes to the rule itself, simply quote the statutory language and add the citation. If the rule contains no ambiguous language, you might not need to explain much more.

When the language of the statute is unclear, or when case law is part of the rule, though, the reader needs more than a citation to understand your statement of the rule. The reader needs to understand how case law has interpreted and applied the statute. To this end, it's helpful to explain the facts, issue, and holding of the precedent case or cases. The court's reasoning is also helpful if it isn't explicit in your statement of the issue or holding. This information allows the reader to independently judge your formulation of the rule. And keep in mind that when the rule comes from a case (or series of cases), what the court *did* is key. What happened in the trial court? Was the defendant convicted? Did the plaintiff win on a motion for summary judgment? Next, what was the outcome in the appellate court? Discussing these outcomes helps narrow down the actual issue the court faced and helps ensure your rule formulation is accurate.

On a related note, although you should quote statutory language, quote sparingly from cases. Sometimes the court provides a clear, logical formulation of the rule. Often, as you saw in Chapter 8 though, you need to work through several cases and synthesize the rule. In those instances, it's often difficult to find a concise passage that accurately sums up the rule and you should paraphrase the synthesized rule. Overreliance on quotations makes it more likely you're taking statements out of context.

2. *How controversial the rule (or its parameters) is:* When the rule is settled, you might need to do little more than illustrate how previous courts applied it. When the rule itself could be the subject of debate, though, more is needed. For instance, if you were challenging the admissibility of a defendant's confession, you would likely start your rule with the relevant constitutional provision (the Fifth Amendment), and then with the rule that emerged from the seminal Supreme Court case, *Miranda v. Arizona*. Your rule statement might be very basic: Custodial interrogations are admissible only when the

defendant has been advised of his right to remain silent and has voluntarily waived that right. *Miranda* stands for that proposition, so you would cite the case. You wouldn't expect anyone to disagree with that statement because it comes from a Supreme Court decision that courts have long followed, and so a parenthetical explanation of *Miranda* would be enough here. But if the parties disputed the more specific issue of whether the interrogation occurred while the defendant was "in custody," you would need to explain in more detail any applicable cases that establish what "in custody" means.

3. *How central the rule is to your analysis:* If the rule is not very essential to your analysis, a parenthetical explanation may be sufficient. But if the rule you state is key to your conclusion, then the rule explanation needs to be longer. It may be a paragraph, or a page, or even numerous pages. As with all depth questions, use your best judgment, but consider how important the rule is before you decide how much explanation to include.

HOW TO STATE AND EXPLAIN A RULE

Using the cell phone manslaughter problem in Appendix A, we'll walk you through the process of stating and explaining a rule.

PROBLEMS

Problem

Here is a quick overview of the cell phone manslaughter problem (for details, see Appendix A). Allison King used her wireless phone, without a hands-free device, while driving in dense fog on a winding road on the edge of an ocean cliff. King placed the call to warn her friends about the dangerous conditions, as they would be meeting later. While she was making the call, she hit and killed a bicyclist. The prosecution will attempt to convict King of vehicular manslaughter by showing that she drove while committing an illegal act (driving while using a wireless phone without a hands-free device) and with gross negligence. King will argue that her actions fit within the "emergency purposes" exception to the wireless phone prohibition. She will also argue that she did not act with gross negligence.

Step 1: Clearly articulate your rule. If you need help with this step, review Chapter 8. With the cell phone manslaughter problem, you'd probably identify your main rule like this:

> Vehicular manslaughter is manslaughter—"the unlawful killing of a human being without malice"—that occurs when "driving a vehicle in the commission of an unlawful act, not amounting to felony, and with gross negligence."

Step 2: Add citations to support each component of the rule. For the main rule in the cell phone manslaughter problem, you'd add the citation to the statute:

> Cal. Penal Code § 192 (West 2022).

Put together, the rule would look like this:

> Vehicular manslaughter is manslaughter—"the unlawful killing of a human being without malice"—that occurs when "driving a vehicle in the commission of an unlawful act, not amounting to felony, and with gross negligence." Cal. Penal Code § 192 (West 2022).

If no parts of the statute were ambiguous, you would add no further rule explanation besides adding a citation. Usually you'll also have interpretive case law to address as well, which we discuss in the next step.

If a disputed issue in your case involved the element of gross negligence, you might phrase the "gross negligence" sub-rule like this:

> "'Gross negligence' is the exercise of so slight a degree of care as to raise a presumption of conscious indifference to the consequences." Gross negligence depends on the circumstances of each case. Courts apply the standard objectively. If a "reasonable person in the defendant's position would have been aware of the risk involved," the law presumes that the defendant was aware of the risk and acted with gross negligence, even if he in fact was unaware of the risk. At least one California court held that a defendant "knew or should have known that using his cell phone while driving was endangering the lives of others."

Note that this rule contains several principles. Each of them needs support from authority.

You'd start your rule explanation in the same way you did with the main rule: by adding citations. That rule, with the citations, might look like this:

> "'Gross negligence' is the exercise of so slight a degree of care as to raise a presumption of conscious indifference to the consequences." *People v. Harris*, 89 Cal. Rptr. 3d 904, 906 (Ct. App. 2009). Gross negligence depends on the circumstances of each case. *People v. Newton*, 104 Cal. Rptr. 3d 138, 141 (Ct. App. 2010). Courts apply the standard objectively. *Id.* If a "reasonable person in the defendant's position would have been aware of the risk involved," the law presumes that the defendant was aware of the risk and acted with gross negligence. *Id.*

> This is true even if he in fact was unaware of the risk. *Harris*, 89 Cal. Rptr. 3d at 906. At least one California court held that a defendant "knew or should have known that using his cell phone while driving was endangering the lives of others." *People v. Tompkins*, 104 Cal. Rptr. 3d 131, 134 (Ct. App. 2010).

Notice that for each rule explanation, the citation comes after the rule. Unless the supporting source is especially significant, you do not need to preface your rule statement with a reference to the authority. For instance, you do not need to preface your general rule with language like this: "California's Penal Code, in section 192, defines vehicular manslaughter as follows. . . ." The reader wants to know the rule, and will see where the rule comes from by looking at the citation that follows. Always provide a pinpoint citation to the smallest possible portion of the authority that supports the rule—the statutory section or subsection, and with case law, to the exact page or pages where the relevant material appears.

> *People v. Tompkins*, 104 Cal. Rptr. 3d 131, 134 (Ct. App. 2010).
>
> ↑ pinpoint citation

Step 3: Discuss the authorities that support the rule. Most often, you'll be discussing cases here. But you might also be discussing legislative history or some other source, like the "purposes" section in a statutory scheme that sets out the policy objectives of the statute, to support your formulation of the rule. Either way, your goal is to provide enough detail to explain—to the skeptical reader—how the authority supports your rule.

For instance, imagine that for the statute prohibiting driving while using a cell phone without a "hands-free" device, the purposes section of the statute states the following:

> Drivers on California's roads and highways have caused thousands of deaths and injuries by talking on their cell phones without using a "hands-free" device. This problem is especially severe on some of our State's winding, inherently dangerous roads. The goal of this Act is to protect the lives of our citizens by eliminating the use of cell phones by drivers except when used in a hands-free mode.

The policy behind the statute is helpful. Understanding California's concern about "winding, inherently dangerous roads" can help the reader determine which violations of the statute are committed with gross negligence and which are not. Sometimes policy comes from the legislature, and sometimes courts discuss it. Either way, it's often helpful to include.

When case law helps explain the rule, you'll need to educate the reader about those cases. In your paragraph on "gross negligence" in Step 2, you've stated the rule and you've begun your rule explanation by providing citations to the relevant cases. But you haven't yet fully explained the rule. You do that by describing the facts, issues, holdings, and rationales of the relevant cases. Often, your rule explanation will consist of about one paragraph per case. That paragraph usually begins with the case's rule followed by the case's facts/issue/holding/rationale, as the following example demonstrates:

> A defendant's subjective belief that his actions are safe does not prevent a court from finding gross negligence. *Harris*, 89 Cal. Rptr. 3d at 906. In *Harris*, the defendant struck the back of a car that was waiting for a pedestrian to exit the crosswalk before turning right. *Id.* at 905. The defendant was travelling 45 miles per hour and applied the brakes only three feet before he hit the car, killing its driver. *Id.* The court determined that Harris acted with gross negligence by talking on his cell phone without a hands-free device even though he subjectively thought he was behaving safely. *Id.* at 907. His actions were illegal in California, and even though Harris' home state of Nevada had no such restriction, Harris should have known of the danger posed by using his cell phone while driving. *Id.*

Following this same pattern, the next two paragraphs could explain the other two cases relevant to the statute's gross negligence rule:

> Using a cell phone while driving at high speeds when other vehicles are present demonstrates gross negligence. *Tompkins*, 104 Cal. Rptr. 3d at 134. In *Tompkins*, the court held the defendant acted with gross negligence when, while driving on an interstate, he called home to check on his family's safety after hearing a news broadcast about an earthquake; while placing that call, the defendant hit and killed Mr. Smith. *Id.* at 133. The defendant was driving from San Francisco to Los Angeles, and while dialing the phone, Tompkins did not see that a piece of tire was in the road. By the time the defendant noticed the tire, he had to swerve, and this caused him to hit Smith's motorcycle. The court concluded that the defendant "should have known" that using a cell phone under these circumstances was "endangering the lives of others." *Id.* at 134.
>
> All of the surrounding circumstances are relevant, however, and those circumstances can suggest the absence of gross negligence even when making a cell phone call while driving. *See Newton*, 104 Cal. Rptr. 3d at 141. In *Newton*, the defendant's wife went into labor while he was driving in a predominantly commercial area. *Id.* at 139. His wife was only seven months pregnant and had previous complications. *Id.* The defendant altered his course to drive to the hospital and called his wife's obstetrician from his cell phone without a hands-free device. *Id.* at 140. While on the phone, the defendant hit and killed a jogger. *Id.* The court held the defendant did not act with gross negligence under these circumstances. *Id.* at 141. A reasonable person whose wife was in labor at seven

> months would want the doctor who had been treating his wife and understood her prior complications to be present at the hospital and likely would not be aware of the risks inherent in making the cell phone call. *Id.*

Your rule explanation for cases won't always be one paragraph per case. Recall that sometimes the entire rule explanation for a case can fit into a parenthetical following that case's citation. Parenthetical rule explanations (also called "explanatory parentheticals") directly follow the case citation and usually begin with a present participle—a verb ending with "ing"—and summarize in one short phrase the court's holding:

> Evidence that flows from information obtained during an illegal arrest is inadmissible. *Wong Sun v. United States*, 371 U.S. 471, 487-88 (1963) (holding that narcotics discovered because of a statement given during an illegal search were inadmissible).

Parenthetical explanations can also provide context for a noncontroversial rule as the latter half of this paragraph illustrates:

> Evidence that flows from information obtained during an illegal arrest is inadmissible. *Wong Sun v. United States*, 371 U.S. 471, 487-88 (1963) (holding that narcotics discovered because of a statement given during an illegal search were inadmissible). Based on this exclusionary rule, the Court has reversed criminal convictions in a number of contexts. *See, e.g., id.* (narcotics case); *Brown v. Illinois*, 422 U.S. 590, 604 (1975) (murder case); *Taylor v. Alabama*, 457 U.S. 687, 694 (1982) (robbery case).

At other times, you'll need a page or more to fully discuss one key case. And recall that courts might also indicate the policies that certain rules promote. When you glean those policy rationales from the cases, add them to the rule explanation.

Note also that you haven't included your client's facts as you explain each case. Keep your rule statement and explanation separate from the application of that rule. The goal here is to give your reader a complete understanding of the current state of the law. Later, you'll apply the rule to your facts and analogize (or distinguish) your facts with the facts in the precedent cases. But for now, just explain the cases without reference to your client.

Step 4: Address alternative formulations of the rule. The rule isn't always crystal clear. In fact, if someone has bothered to ask you to write a memo, there's a decent chance the rule is not clear. That means some other rule formulation has some merit, even if you discount it in the end. Rather than ignoring that competing formulation, address it head-on and explain why a court is less likely to adopt that formulation than your formulation.

EXAMPLES

Review the following examples. For each example, there may be more than one correct answer, but try to choose the *best* answer. Explain to yourself why you have chosen that answer. Then read the explanations in the last section of this chapter to check your work.

EXAMPLES

Example 9-1

This question uses the cell phone manslaughter problem, which you can find in Appendix A.

Read the following statutory section for the hypothetical cell phone problem: California Penal Code § 192.

> **Cal. Penal Code § 192. Manslaughter; voluntary, involuntary, and vehicular**
>
> Manslaughter is the unlawful killing of a human being without malice. It is of three kinds:
>
> **(a)** Voluntary—upon a sudden quarrel or heat of passion.
>
> **(b)** Involuntary—in the commission of an unlawful act, not amounting to felony; or in the commission of a lawful act which might produce death, in an unlawful manner, or without due caution and circumspection. This subdivision shall not apply to acts committed in the driving of a vehicle.
>
> **(c)** Vehicular—
>
> **(1)** Except as provided in subdivision (a) of Section 191.5, driving a vehicle in the commission of an unlawful act, not amounting to felony, and with gross negligence; or driving a vehicle in the commission of a lawful act which might produce death, in an unlawful manner, and with gross negligence.

If you were representing Allison King, who is being charged with vehicular manslaughter for causing the death of a person when she was driving and using a wireless telephone, which of the following drafting plans would be helpful in developing the rule explanation section of your memo?

A. Quote all of California Penal Code Section 192—the manslaughter statute—and thoroughly cite to cases that explain how courts determine if a killing is "voluntary."
B. Quote the "unlawful killing of a human being without malice" language of California Penal Code Section 192, and cite to cases that indicate what the phrase "without malice" means.
C. Quote the language of California Penal Code Section 192(c)(1) that mentions the term "gross negligence," and cite to cases that define this legal concept in a vehicular manslaughter scenario.
D. Discuss the language of California Penal Code Section 192(c)(1) but do not quote any of it, as the reader can review the statutory language on her own.

EXAMPLES

Example 9-2

This question uses the copyright and fair use problem, which you can find in Appendix B.

> The second factor in the fair use exception to copyright protection, "the nature of the copyrighted work," is of minimal significance in the context of a parody. *Campbell v. Acuff-Rose Music, Inc.*, 510 U.S. 569, 586 (1994) (reversing a finding of no fair use and stating that the second factor was "not much help" because "parodies almost invariably copy publicly known, expressive works"); *Mattel Inc. v. Walking Mountain Prods.*, 353 F.3d 792, 803 (9th Cir. 2003) (holding an artist's parody of Mattel's Barbie doll was permitted by fair use, noting the second factor is not "terribly useful" and quoting *Campbell*).

A. This is an insufficient rule explanation because each case needs a full paragraph of discussion.
B. This is an insufficient rule explanation because it does not include the issues the cases addressed.
C. This rule explanation is sufficient because when the issue is not likely to be contested, a parenthetical explanation can be enough.
D. This rule explanation is sufficient even if the issue was contested because it includes the facts, issues, and holdings of each case.

EXAMPLES

Example 9-3

This question uses the copyright and fair use problem, which you can find in Appendix B.

> Under the fourth fair use factor, "the effect of the use upon the potential market for or value of the copyrighted work," parodies present a unique situation.

17 U.S.C. § 107(4). "[W]hen a lethal parody, like a scathing theater review, kills demand for the original, it does not produce a harm cognizable under the Copyright Act." *Campbell v. Acuff-Rose Music, Inc.*, 510 U.S. 569, 591-92 (1994).

A. This is an insufficient rule explanation because when a rule that is central to the analysis comes from a case, the reader needs to know the case's facts, issue, and holding to understand why the case stands for that proposition.
B. This is an insufficient rule explanation because the policy behind a statute should be included.
C. This rule explanation is sufficient because it cites both the quoted statutory language and the quoted Supreme Court case.
D. This rule explanation is sufficient because it includes pinpoint citations to the relevant subsection of the fair use statute and the page number within the case where the language can be found.

EXAMPLES

Example 9-4

This question uses the negligent infliction of emotional distress problem, which you can find in Appendix C.

A plaintiff can recover for negligent infliction of emotional distress as a bystander by establishing these four elements:

1) "the death or serious physical injury of another caused by the defendant's negligence";
2) the plaintiff and the victim share a "marital or close blood relationship" or an "intimate, familial relationship";
3) the plaintiff directly observed, or was "sensorially aware," of the "death or injury at the scene of the accident"; and
4) the plaintiff suffered severe emotional distress as a result.

A. This is an insufficient rule statement because language in cases should never be quoted.
B. This is a sufficient rule statement because it includes all four elements and extensions to the original rule that have been added over time.
C. This is an insufficient rule statement because it should state the initial rule only, leaving out later developments, and then explain these extensions later following a chronological development of the law.
D. This is an insufficient rule statement because it numbers the elements, making it harder to follow.

EXAMPLES

Example 9-5

This question uses a hypothetical vehicular manslaughter problem (but *not* the cell phone manslaughter problem in Appendix A).

> An "unlawful killing" for purposes of California's vehicular manslaughter statute, California Penal Code § 192 (West 2022), requires that the defendant's actions contributed to the victim's death, even if another factor also contributed. *People v. Matthews*, 89 Cal. Rptr. 3d 1027 (Ct. App. 2009). In *Matthews*, the victim did not die immediately after being struck by the defendant's car. Instead, she died two days after being released from the hospital. The cause of death was "acute subdural hematoma," which is a collection of blood on the surface of the brain. *Id.* at 1029. The hematoma was caused by the accident, but the hospital failed to diagnose it and released the victim. Had it been properly diagnosed, there was a ninety-eight percent chance that she would have survived. *Id.*

A. This is an insufficient rule explanation because more of the *Matthews* facts need to be included.
B. This is an insufficient rule explanation because although the *Matthews* facts are included, the reader is not told what the issue or holding was in the *Matthews* case.
C. This rule explanation is sufficient because it includes a pinpoint citation to the relevant pages in *Matthews*.
D. This rule explanation is sufficient because it cites both the governing statute and the relevant case.

EXAMPLES

Example 9-6

This question uses a hypothetical Title VII employment discrimination problem.

> Title VII's prohibition on discrimination "because of sex" includes discrimination based on an employee's transgender status. *See, e.g., Barnes v. City of Cincinnati*, 401 F.3d 729, 737 (6th Cir. 2005). In *Barnes*, the Sixth Circuit upheld a jury verdict finding that the city violated Title VII when it demoted a transgender plaintiff for his failure to conform to sex stereotypes. *Id.* at 747. Although some early cases held the opposite, their reasoning is flawed. *See, e.g., Ulane v. Eastern Airlines, Inc.*, 742 F.2d 1081 (7th Cir. 1984), *cert. denied*, 471 U.S. 1017 (1985).

A. Assuming this rule is not very controversial, this paragraph is a sufficient rule explanation for the stated rule because it includes *Barnes'* facts, issue, and holding and cites to them.
B. Assuming this rule is not very controversial, this paragraph is a sufficient rule explanation for the stated rule because in addition to describing *Barnes*, it advises the reader of contrary authority.

C. Even if this rule is not very controversial, this paragraph is an insufficient rule explanation because Title VII's remedies should be included when discussing the *Barnes* case.

D. Even if this rule is not very controversial, this paragraph is an insufficient rule explanation because although the contrary authority is cited, the facts, issue, and holding of that case need to be included as well, at least in a parenthetical explanation, and more information from *Barnes* would be helpful to the reader.

EXPLANATIONS

Explanation 9-1

A is incorrect. Even though there are some parts of Section 192 that will be at issue, there's no need for you to quote the entire section to explain the rule governing your case. In addition, it's highly unlikely that the parties will dispute whether the killing was voluntary or involuntary, so you should avoid going into depth about the definition of a "voluntary" killing. **B** is also incorrect. Although you might want to take the approach of quoting only parts of a statute, you still need to make sure that you are quoting sections that are applicable to your case and that will likely be contested. Here, the issue of whether there was malice probably won't be significant, and therefore you don't need to cite cases that define what the phrase "without malice" means. **C** is the best answer. A significant issue in the case is whether King acted with gross negligence, so it's important to quote the relevant sections of the statute that use this phrase and to cite cases that define this legal term. This type of depth is necessary to fully explain to the reader the meaning of "gross negligence." **D** is not the best answer. Cases can be paraphrased, but the key language used by the legislature should be quoted for the reader.

Explanation 9-2

A is not the best answer. Although many rule explanations for cases are a paragraph or more, if the point is not controversial or central to the analysis, the rule explanation can be condensed into a single sentence or a parenthetical. Here, that is the case because in *Campbell*, the Supreme Court stated that the second statutory factor was largely irrelevant in parody cases. **B** is incorrect. The two parenthetical explanations address the global issue (fair use) as well as the specific question here (the second factor in the fair use test). **C** is the best answer. As stated in A, the length of rule explanations varies. Here, if the issue is not contested, these parenthetical explanations provide enough information for the reader to understand the rule and agree with the writer's formulation. **D** is not the best answer. Although these parentheticals include the cases' basic facts, issues, and holdings, this bare information would likely be insufficient if the issue were contested.

Explanation 9-3

A is the best answer. Because the issue is central to the analysis, simply quoting one line from a case and adding a citation is probably not enough to explain the rule to the skeptical reader. Even though this quote is from the Supreme Court, so it carries more weight, an effective rule explanation would add the case's facts, issue, and holding to show how the case stands for the quoted proposition. **B** is not the best answer. Although it's true that sometimes the policy behind a particular statute is helpful, that isn't always the case. Furthermore, including policy might be helpful, but including the facts, issue, and holding from the controlling Supreme Court case, as discussed in A, is essential. **C** is incorrect. A mere citation with no additional information is sufficient for statutory language, but not for quotations from cases. **D** is also incorrect. Although rule explanations should include pinpoint citations for both statutes and cases, those citations are usually not enough. The writer needs to go further and add the case explanation, as discussed in C.

Explanation 9-4

A is incorrect. It's true that you generally won't quote much from cases in the rule *explanation*. But quoting the rule (or key portions of the rule) in the rule *statement* is fine as long as the court has stated the rule in a helpful or consistent way. **B** is the best answer. The rule you state should be the current, controlling rule. **C** is incorrect for the reasons stated in A. Although common law develops over time, the reader needs to see the current, controlling rule. You can explain, in rule explanation, why particular elements are part of that rule. But you should articulate the complete, current rule in your rule statement. **D** is also incorrect. Numbering elements can generally help the reader, especially when each element is lengthy. Note also that courts often number elements, creating a logical separation for the reader.

Explanation 9-5

A is incorrect. Plenty of the *Matthews* facts are included. What is lacking is the issue and holding. Without those, the reader has no idea what effect these particular facts have on the rule. **B** is the best answer for the reasons A is incorrect. **C** is incorrect. This example does not include the pinpoint citation to the main rule. Although it includes the pinpoint citation at the end of the paragraph, the reader needs the pinpoint citation for the rule. Furthermore, pinpoint citations alone are insufficient to create an effective rule explanation. They are necessary, but not sufficient. **D** is also incorrect. Simply citing a case is not enough for an effective rule explanation. Unless the issue is uncontested and the law is firmly established, adding a parenthetical or a discussion of the facts, issue, and holding of a case is usually needed to explain how the case illustrates the rule or how a court has applied the rule.

EXPLANATIONS

Explanation 9-6

A is incorrect. Although the paragraph does include the basic facts, issue, and holding of *Barnes* (and citations), some explanation for the *Ulane* case should be included, even if the rule is "not very controversial"—because it is clear there is it least some controversy. Furthermore, because there's contrary authority, additional information from *Barnes*, such as the court's reasoning, would be helpful to the reader trying to decide which rule formulation was more likely to be accepted. **B** is not the best answer. It is true that readers should be advised of opposing authority, and the citation to *Ulane* helps here. But adding an explanation of *Ulane* (along with more information about *Barnes*) would be more helpful. **C** is incorrect. The rule this paragraph is explaining is whether Title VII prohibits a particular type of discrimination, not what the available remedies might be. **D** is the best answer for the reasons stated in A and B. The reader needs to know more about *Barnes* and know more about the cases that reach the opposite result. This rule explanation fails to provide that information.

Checklist

Chapter 9: Stating and Explaining the Rule

✔	Clearly state the rule (quote key statutory language and generally quote sparingly from cases).
✔	Add citations to support each component of the rule stated.
✔	Discuss the authorities that support the rule—for example, illustrate the way courts have interpreted and applied the rule by explaining the precedents' facts, outcomes, and rationales.
✔	Consider the types of relevant authorities and put mandatory authority first or give it more space in the rule explanation.
✔	When the precedent is central to the analysis, feature it more prominently or give it more space in rule explanation.
✔	If there are alternative formulations of the rule, explain both.
✔	When the rule is unsettled or controversial, provide detailed explanation of relevant cases.
✔	When the precedent is less central or weighty for the analysis, give it less space and consider simply using a parenthetical.

You will find all of the chapter checklists compiled in Appendix D.

CHAPTER 10

Applying the Law: Fact-Based Analysis

"Just the facts, ma'am," is a favorite admonishment of police officers and prosecutors in many crime stories. And most people think of facts in that way—as fixed and unchanging. Lawyers, on the other hand, know that within certain constraints, facts are what you make of them. And when lawyers apply the law to the facts of a problem, fact-based analysis is one of the most basic skills in the toolbox.

Terminology notes. Some textbooks will call analysis based on the law and just the facts of your assignment "rule-based reasoning" or a "factual argument based on the plain language of the rule." This fact-based analysis is distinct from analysis based on analogies (or distinctions) to facts of precedent or analysis based on policy.

WHAT YOU NEED TO KNOW ABOUT FACT-BASED ANALYSIS

Understand the difference between a fact and an inference. "Kay was driving 120 mph" is a fact. "Kay was driving too fast" or "Kay was breaking the speed limit" are inferences. Sometimes an inference is so commonplace that we forget it's an inference. "When the light turned red, John stopped" is a fact. "John stopped because the light turned red" is an inference.

Depending on the inferences you make, the same fact can often work to help both sides. Once you have some practice with fact-based analysis, you'll be amazed at how many times you can "flip" a fact to work for either side. Here's one example:[1]

> Fact: The car accident happened while a father was driving with children in the car.
>
> First inference: Children in a car can be distracting and thus the accident was the father's fault because he was distracted.
>
> Second inference: Parents drive more carefully when they have children in the car and thus the accident was not the father's fault because he was driving carefully.

Connect the fact to the statute or rule to show why the fact is legally significant. The best legal analysis mixes law and facts. Don't miss that opportunity by simply restating a fact without telling the reader why you think that fact is important. Consider this example from the cell phone manslaughter problem (in Appendix A):

> Bad example: King was driving slowly and attempted to warn her friends of the dangerous conditions in order to prevent an accident.

Specify the connection between the fact or factual inference and the law. One way to do this is by using the word "because" or one of its synonyms. Explain to the reader why you've singled out these particular facts as important. Make your reasoning explicit, as in this example:

> Better example: King likely did not act with "gross negligence" because she was driving slowly and attempted to warn her friends of the dangerous conditions to prevent an accident, demonstrating she was trying to minimize, not ignore, any danger.

To help you plan, you might make a chart that sorts the facts of the problem with the various parts of the rule. If you're a visual thinker, charts can be helpful. (See Chapter 8, Constructing a Rule, for a chart that helps you connect a case to a part of a statute.) Here, with

1. See Albert J. Moore, *Inferential Streams: The Articulation and Illustration of the Advocate's Evidentiary Intuition*, 34 UCLA L. Rev. 611 (1987).

fact-based analysis, you can design a chart that will help you visually connect facts with parts of the rule. The chart can include each relevant fact and the inferences from that fact, divided by which party the fact and inferences favors. And remember that the same fact can have an inference that favors one party as well as an inference that favors the opposite party. We'll work through one of these charts in Step 1 of the next section.

HOW TO WRITE FACT-BASED ANALYSIS

Using the copyright and fair use problem in Appendix B, we'll walk you through the process of writing fact-based analysis.

PROBLEMS

Problem

> Here is a quick overview of the copyright and fair use problem (for details see Appendix B). Page is suing Dash for violating the Copyright Act when Dash wrote a song based on Page's song (which in copyright terms is called the "original"), "Red, White, and Blue." Dash's song uses the structure and many lyrics of the original but changes the original song's political message. The music of the two songs is not at issue, only the lyrics. Page expects that Dash will argue that his song is a parody that falls under the fair use exception to the Copyright Act. The court will consider the relevant factors set out in the fair use statute, 17 U.S.C. § 107: whether the copy was transformative and targeted the original; whether it took more than necessary of the original; and whether it will interfere with the original's market.

Step 1: Sort the facts, deciding which facts support each side (or, in some instances, both sides). You might wish to make notes to yourself in a more casual fashion, but you can also make a chart that states the rule and connects facts to the rule. For instance, pick out a few facts related to the fourth factor of the fair use test: "the effect of the use upon the potential market for or value of the copyrighted work."

Fact Related to Fourth Factor (the effect of the copy on the possible market for original)	Inference That Favors Page	Inference That Favors Dash
Page's song is very famous.	It is more likely that Dash is trying to capture some of the big market for the song.	It is more likely that buyers will know the original and know the copy is not the original.
Both songs make a political statement about America.	This is precisely the same market — rock fans who like political statements.	The political statements are so different that the buyers are unlikely to confuse the songs.
Both songs are rock music.	The copy is a direct assault on the same market as the original.	The specialized rock music audience is more likely to know the original and realize the copy is a parody.
Page's song has been played at patriotic rallies.	Despite the purported difference in message, both songs serve as positive patriotic songs and thus Dash's song will cut into that part of Page's market.	No inferences favor Dash on this fact at first look.
Dash's song uses images of good things in America.	No inferences favor Page on this fact at first look.	The images in the songs are so different that buyers will not be confused.

Step 2: Review the fact-based inferences you've generated and determine which are the strongest. The strongest inferences are those to which the other side will find it difficult to respond. Here, because Page's song has been played at patriotic rallies, a strong inference for Page is that despite the purported difference in message, both songs serve as positive patriotic songs.

Step 3: Write sentences that tie together the fact and the law's text. You want both in the same sentence when possible. Start with the law's text:

> Dash's song is likely to produce an "effect on the market of the original."

And then you'll add the facts to the same sentence and use "because" to explain how the facts and the law combine:

> Dash's song is likely to produce an "effect on the market of the original" because Page's original song has been played at patriotic rallies and despite the

> purported change in message, Dash's song also appeals to the market of those looking for a patriotic song.

You've woven together the facts and law in this fact-based analysis. For the second fact-based rationale, the process is the same. This time start with facts:

> Both songs are in the same genre.

And add law and inference:

> Both songs are in the same genre and thus the copy is likely to affect the original's market because the copy is a direct assault on the market of the original, rock music fans who like songs with a political message.

Step 4: Check to make sure you've told the reader explicitly how the facts and law are connected. Remember that the word "because" is handy here, although it is not the only way to draw that explicit connection. Both of your fact-based analyses above use the word "because" to make the connection explicit.

EXAMPLES

Review the following examples. For each example, there may be more than one correct answer. Explain to yourself why you have chosen that answer or those answers. Then read the explanations in the last section of this chapter to check your work.

EXAMPLES

Example 10-1

This question uses the copyright and fair use problem, which you can find in Appendix B.

The third factor of the fair use test requires the court to weigh the "amount and substantiality of the portion used in relation to the copyrighted work as a whole." The rule allows the author of a parody to take aim at "the heart of the original." Here is a fact-based analysis on this third factor:

> While a parody may take aim at the heart of the copyrighted work, Dash has used over a quarter of Page's lyrics, including an almost identical chorus, which comprises more than just the heart of the original, so the court will likely rule against his fair use claim.

A. This fact-based analysis successfully ties the facts to the law, specifically with regard to the third factor.
B. This fact-based analysis would be better if it used the word "because" to tether the facts to the law.
C. "Dash has used over a quarter of Page's lyrics" is an inference rather than a fact.
D. The amount taken "comprises more than just the heart of the original" is an inference rather than a fact.

EXAMPLES

Example 10-2

This question uses the copyright and fair use problem, which you can find in Appendix B.

Continuing to address the third factor, consider this analysis:

Dash started his phrases in the same way as Page's phrases and then Dash changed the meaning so that the listener would feel the contrast between his message affirming how good America is and Page's message about the problems with America.

A. This fact-based analysis is successful because it implies a connection to the factor that addresses the amount taken and uses the facts in a clever way.
B. This fact-based analysis should be more explicitly tied to the law.
C. This fact-based analysis is strong because it could apply to either factor three about the amount taken or to factor four about interfering with the original's market.
D. This analysis is based on fact not inference.

EXAMPLES

Example 10-3

This question uses the copyright and fair use problem, which you can find in Appendix B.

Continuing to address the third factor, consider this analysis:

The amount and substantiality Dash took was too great for fair use because he copied over twenty percent of the original lyrics and the form of every line. Further, Dash nearly duplicated the chorus.

A. This is a good fact-based based analysis because it connects the facts to the law.
B. This fact-based analysis uses the facts to create an inference that twenty percent is too much to take of the original.

C. This fact-based analysis would be stronger if it connected the law and the facts.
D. This fact-based analysis is weak because it doesn't state the outcome the author wants.

EXAMPLES

Example 10-4

This question uses the negligent infliction of emotional distress problem, which you can find in Appendix C.

The third element requires that the plaintiff "directly observe" or be "sensorially aware" of the injury or death at the scene of the accident. Consider this analysis:

> Although Poe had her back to the accident, because she heard the impact and turned to see Valenzuela's lawnmower flying toward her and Valenzuela bleeding on the ground with the defendant's car nearby, she was "sensorially aware" of his injury at the scene of the accident.

A. This fact-based analysis effectively ties the facts to the law.
B. This fact-based analysis is weak because it includes a fact that negates the author's legal conclusion.
C. This fact-based analysis would be stronger if it included the legal standard.
D. This fact-based analysis is effective even though the word "because" is before the key facts rather than being more closely tied to the key element.

EXAMPLES

Example 10-5

This question uses a hypothetical sexual harassment problem.

The rule requires the harassment to be "severe or pervasive." Consider this analysis:

> The alleged harassment Jennifer Jones experienced was not "severe or pervasive" considering that her coworkers did not call her names every day but only sporadically over almost a year.

A. This fact-based analysis is weak because it's based on inference, not facts.
B. This fact-based analysis would be stronger if it used the word "because."

C. This is not fact-based analysis because it refers to a rule.

D. This is good fact-based analysis because it explicitly tells the reader the legal significance of the facts.

EXAMPLES

Example 10-6

This question uses a hypothetical sexual harassment problem.

The rule requires the harassment to be "based on sex." Consider this analysis:

> Although Jennifer Jones was a transsexual, the alleged harassment she suffered is not actionable because it was not "based on sex" as the statute requires. None of the federal appellate courts have recognized such a claim, nor has the Supreme Court recognized it.

A. This is not fact-based analysis because it focuses on how courts have interpreted the statute and not on analyzing how the rule applies to the facts of the case.

B. This fact-based analysis is strong because it uses the word "because" to connect to the law.

C. This fact-based analysis is strong because it mentions that the best authority, the U.S. Supreme Court, has not yet recognized this claim.

D. This fact-based analysis is weak because it includes only one fact: that Jennifer Jones was a transsexual.

EXPLANATIONS

EXPLANATIONS

Explanation 10-1

A is correct. This analysis is good in that it has a fact and an inference drawn from the fact that it ties to the language of the third factor. It might be even better if it referenced more of the text of the factor, regarding the "amount and substantiality of the portion used in relation to the copyrighted work as a whole." It could also be stronger if the conclusion were specific to the factor. ***B*** is also correct. The answer would be better if it used the word "because" to tie the fact to the text of the factor. It could say "Dash used an amount too great in relation to the whole of the work because he used more than a quarter of the original lyrics, which was more than taking aim at the 'heart of the work.'" Using the word "because" is not strictly required, but it often works well for constructing sentences that clearly link law and fact.

C is incorrect because whether Dash used more than a quarter of the lyrics is a measurable fact and not an inference or conclusion of law. **D** is correct. Whether one has taken "the heart" of something is a judgment call, and thus an inference, not a fact. It's fine to draw inferences for the reader, but you shouldn't confuse them with facts.

Explanation 10-2

A is incorrect. Fact-based analysis is stronger when it is connected explicitly to the law. Although you don't always need to connect the facts and law in one sentence, the connection must be more explicit than the implication here. **B** is correct. Fact-based analysis is stronger when it is connected explicitly to the law. Here, the author might have continued the analysis by saying: "Thus, Dash needed to copy as much as he did to parody the original, and the third factor allows him to copy this amount." **C** is incorrect. The author should analyze one factor at a time. Tying the fact-based analysis to the text of a factor will help you refrain from running your arguments together. **D** is incorrect. The inference here is about what Dash intended and what an audience will draw from the song.

Explanation 10-3

A is correct. The example starts with the law and tells the reader how the facts relate to the law. **B** is also correct. Although the inference is not explicit, the author leads the reader to that conclusion. This inference works well for Page. **C** is incorrect. As explained for answer A, the example starts with the law and tells the reader how the facts relate to the law. **D** is incorrect. Whether you are writing predictively or persuasively, nothing requires you, in the fact-based analysis, to identify a likely outcome or the outcome you seek.

Explanation 10-4

A is correct because this example ties the legal standard—sensorially aware—to the relevant facts in the problem. But this example could be stronger by starting with the law, rather than the facts, so the reader has context for the analysis before the end of the example. Rewritten to be stronger, this analysis would read:

> Poe was "sensorially aware" of Valenzuela's injury at the scene of the accident because she heard the impact and turned to see his lawnmower flying toward her and Valenzuela bleeding on the ground with the defendant's car nearby, even though she had her back to the accident.

B is incorrect. Whether a fact (or factual inference) favors one conclusion or another, including it in your analysis is helpful as long as the reader can follow the connections. In this example, using "although" to preface the fact that contradicts your conclusion signals to the reader that this fact isn't dispositive. Using "because" and adding favorable facts support the writer's conclusion. **C** is incorrect. Fact-based analysis focuses on the facts and references the legal standard. But it doesn't need to fully state and explain the rule; that analysis comes before the fact-based analysis and should *exclude* our problem's facts. (See Chapter 9 for more on stating and explaining the rule.) **D** is not completely correct for the reasons stated in A.

Explanation 10-5

A is incorrect. The example includes facts. Even if it were based on an inference, it might still be good fact-based analysis as long as the inference is strong and tied to the law. **B** is incorrect. Although it's a great idea to use the word "because," the word "considering" is a synonym for "because" here and the sentence connects facts and law. No strict rule requires using the word "because." **C** is incorrect. Fact-based analysis *should* refer to a legal text, such as a rule or a statute. **D** is correct. This is good fact-based analysis, tying the facts to the law.

Explanation 10-6

A is correct. Although you could say that explaining that courts have not recognized a certain claim is a "fact," fact-based analysis usually explains how a rule applies to the facts of the case you're analyzing. **B** is incorrect. Even though we encourage you to use the word "because" to connect facts to law, just adding the word "because" won't automatically make the analysis strong or indicate that it's fact-based analysis. **C** is also incorrect. The analysis is not fact-based and a cite to the Supreme Court doesn't make it fact-based. **D** is only partially correct. If this is fact-based analysis at all, it's true that the fact-based analysis is very weak. Including one fact does not make it fact-based analysis. The analysis still focuses on the state of the law, and not on how the law applies to facts in this case.

Checklist

Chapter 10: Applying the Law: Fact-Based Analysis

✔	Sort the facts, deciding which facts and inferences support each side.
✔	Review the fact-based inferences you have generated and choose the strongest one or two.
✔	Write sentences that tie together the fact and the legal rule.

You will find all of the chapter checklists compiled in Appendix D.

Applying the Law: Analogical Analysis

You've undoubtedly been reasoning by analogy since childhood. Any game that asked you to sort objects into categories asked you to reason by analogy. And just as you tried then to figure out which shared characteristics were important enough to group objects together and label them as alike, now as a lawyer you'll analyze by trying to figure out which shared facts and concepts in similar cases are important enough to group cases together and label them with similar outcomes. (Did you notice that the last sentence was a good example of an analogy?)

Analogical reasoning is important because it's a key way that courts make decisions in a common law system. Courts generally want to treat similar cases alike. Thus, courts will reason by analogy in deciding cases, and lawyers will accordingly argue that their case is like or unlike a precedent. Indeed, when lawyers say that an argument is "well-supported" they usually mean that the argument is based on, or connected to, a text to which the relevant court would defer. When you reason or argue by analogy, that text is a case. And you support your analysis or argument by explaining how your case is the same or different from a precedent case.

Terminology notes. Lawyers talk about "analogizing" to or "distinguishing" from a precedent case. When you "distinguish a case," you tell the reader how your case is different from the precedent and therefore requires a different response or outcome. Distinguishing a case is also sometimes called "counter-analogical reasoning."

WHAT YOU NEED TO KNOW ABOUT ANALOGICAL REASONING

It's not enough to say that your case is like or unlike a precedent case; explain *how* they're alike or different. Sometimes you may feel as though you're stating the obvious, but when making analogies or distinctions, it's best to make your analysis explicit. For instance, if you were making an analogy in the copyright and fair use problem, instead of just saying Dash's work is like the defendant's work in *Mattel*, explain that they're both "transformative" and describe the facts in *Mattel* and in your case that *show* the work is transformative.

Compare or contrast facts that are *relevant* to the precise issue you're addressing. That your case and a precedent are similar or different in some respect isn't what matters; you could find something similar or different about any two cases in the world. Instead, the comparison or distinction needs to be about something that's relevant to the issue—typically, that your case is similar or different with respect to a fact that mattered to the outcome in the precedent.

If you're having a hard time deciding whether a fact is relevant, remove the fact from the narrative and ask yourself whether your analysis would change. If removing a fact would change the analysis, then it's a relevant fact.

You can phrase analogical reasoning effectively in many different ways. The keys are to write clearly, make the connections explicit, and keep the structure parallel so that you compare apples to apples. For instance, if you're analogizing the defendant in your case to the defendant in a precedent, make sure to keep a parallel structure—defendant to defendant.

> Like the defendant in *Poehlen*, the Defendant here also robbed a convenience store at gunpoint.
> *Not:*
> Like *Poehlen*, the Defendant robbed a convenience store at gunpoint.

Here are templates that provide phrasing lawyers might use for analogizing and distinguishing. Where you see brackets, you would insert material from your assignment and the precedent you're discussing.

> **Like the** [defendant/plaintiff/victim/etc.] **in** [*Precedent*], **who** [relevant precedent fact], **here the** [defendant/plaintiff/victim/etc.] **also** [relevant similar fact from your case].

>> Like the defendant in *Jones*, who had a long record of criminal activity, here the Defendant also has a long record of criminal activity.

As the [defendant/plaintiff/victim/etc.] **in** [Precedent] [relevant precedent fact], **here also** [relevant similar fact from your case].

> As the defendant in *Fisher* targeted the same genre of music as the original, here also Dash targeted the same genre of music as Page's original.

In [Precedent], [relevant precedent fact]. **Likewise, here** [relevant similar fact from your case]. **Thus, in both** [Precedent] **and the instant case** [similar relevant facts] **and** [result from the precedent case] **should result here.**

> In *Jones*, the defendant used more than twenty percent of the original's lyrics and the court found that was not fair use. Likewise, here Dash used more than twenty percent of Page's "Red, White and Blue" lyrics. Thus, in both *Jones* and the instant case the defendants used more than twenty percent of the lyrics and no finding of fair use should result here.

Similar to [Precedent], **in which** [relevant precedent fact], **here** [relevant similar fact from your case].

> Similar to *Mattel*, in which the defendant copied part of the original to deliver a social message, here Dash copied part of Page's song to deliver a social message.

Although in [Precedent] [relevant precedent fact], **our case is distinguishable because** [relevant distinguishable fact from your case].

> Although in *Campbell* the copy acceptably used four bars of the original to create the parody, our case is distinguishable because here Dash's copy used every bar of the original by keeping the same form in every line, repeating over twenty percent of the original lyrics, and nearly duplicating the chorus.

Unlike in [Precedent], **where** [relevant precedent fact], **here** [relevant distinguishable fact in your case].

> Unlike in *Jones*, where the defendant was calling a public health official, here King was calling her friends.

In [Precedent], [relevant precedent fact]. **In contrast, here** [relevant distinguishable fact from your case]. **Thus, as** [resulting legal distinction], **it does not follow that** [result from the precedent case] **should result**.

> In *Jones*, the defendant received *Miranda* warnings as soon as she was in custody. In contrast, here the defendant was in custody for several hours before receiving the *Miranda* warnings. Thus, as the defendant in our case

did not know of his right to a lawyer in a timely fashion, it does not follow that his confession should be admissible.

HOW TO ANALOGIZE AND DISTINGUISH

Using the negligent infliction of emotional distress problem in Appendix C, we'll walk you through the process of analogizing and distinguishing.

PROBLEMS

Problem

Here is a quick overview of the negligent infliction of emotional distress problem (for details see Appendix C). Our client, Poe, is suing Defoe for the emotional trauma she suffered after Defoe, while texting, drove his car into Poe's fiancé, Valenzuela. Poe was gardening in her front yard while Valenzuela was mowing the lawn. Poe's back was to the road and she was listening to music on her earbuds when she heard the impact. When she turned, she saw the lawnmower, without Valenzuela operating it, coming toward her. Poe jumped out of the way and ran toward Valenzuela, who was about ten feet away, lying on the ground with Defoe's vehicle just a few feet from him. He was covered in blood and not making a sound. Poe found a weak pulse and tried to get her fiancé to respond. She rode in the ambulance with Valenzuela to the hospital, where he had surgery to repair a punctured lung and internal bleeding. He was hospitalized for three weeks and then continued his recovery at home. After the incident, Poe experienced significant emotional distress.

Let's start with analogizing and distinguishing to precedents concerning the third element of the test for negligent infliction of emotional distress as a bystander—the plaintiff must "directly observe" or be "sensorially aware" of the injury at the scene of the accident.

Step 1: Read the cases and consider the facts of the precedents and the facts of your assignment, looking primarily for facts that are about the precise issue you're addressing. Read the cases, looking for facts and outcomes we can use to make comparisons. There are (at least) four relevant cases on this sub-issue. In *Portee v. Jaffee*, 417 A.2d 521 (N.F. 1980), the plaintiff watched for hours as her seven-year-old son was crushed to death by an elevator. The New Fornia Supreme Court (a court that creates binding precedent for your problem) held the plaintiff could sue for negligent infliction of emotional distress as a bystander, acknowledging she had directly observed her child's death. More recently, the New Fornia Supreme Court created an exception to the "direct observation" requirement when the plaintiff was at the scene and "sensorially aware" of her child's death in a house fire, but was unable to actually see her child burning because of flames and smoke. *Ortiz v. JDP Builders, Inc.*, 689 A.2d 1135, 1138 (N.F. 2015). In two other cases, the New Fornia Appellate Court (also a court that creates binding precedent for your problem) held that plaintiffs did not meet the "direct observation" or "sensorial awareness" element. *Miller v. Davidson*, 794 A.2d 175, 178 (N.F. App. 2017) (upholding summary judgment for the defendant because the plaintiff had been talking on her phone and unaware her boyfriend had been mauled by a leopard until after he had bled to death); *Vargas v. Quinones*, 801 A.2d 1440, 1445 (N.F. App. 2018) (upholding summary judgment for the defendant because the plaintiff was at home when his pregnant wife was involved in a car accident, and he therefore did not observe and was not sensorially aware of the crash and the death of the fetus at the scene of the accident).

These facts seem relevant to the issue of whether Poe directly observed or was sensorially aware of the accident injuring Valenzuela at the scene:

Portee
- The plaintiff watched for hours as rescue workers tried to free her son, who was trapped between an elevator door and the elevator's shaft.
- She heard and saw her son moan, cry out, and flail his arms.
- The son died, still trapped, while his mother watched.

Ortiz
- The plaintiff's house was on fire and she and her mother tried to gather her three children.
- The plaintiff's mother had one child, Jasmine, by the hand, but a window exploded and Jasmine was separated from her grandmother.
- The grandmother handed an infant son to the plaintiff and kept screaming for Jasmine and ran back into the house to look for her.
- The plaintiff saw the grandmother running out of the house, on fire and without Jasmine, hysterically screaming "I can't find her."
- The plaintiff could not see Jasmine because of the flames and smoke but knew the grandmother meant Jasmine was still in the house and yelled to the police that her daughter was still inside.

- The plaintiff learned the next day that Jasmine had died in the fire.

Miller

- The plaintiff and the victim went to the circus and the victim left his seat to use the restroom.
- As the victim was returning, the plaintiff received a phone call, went up the bleachers, and turned her back to the ring so she could hear her call.
- After her call, the plaintiff started to walk back to her seat and realized the victim was not in his seat.
- The plaintiff saw a crowd near the ring and rushed to see that the victim had been mauled by a leopard and had been freed from the leopard's jaw, but had just bled to death.

Vargas

- The plaintiff was at home when he was called because his pregnant wife had been in a car accident.
- He drove to the scene and his wife was already in an ambulance, "bleeding, crying hysterically, and holding her stomach."
- The plaintiff followed the ambulance to the hospital and learned there that the fetus had died.
- The plaintiff was not present when doctors removed the fetus.

Step 2: Choose the facts from your assignment that may be relevant to the particular legal test that applies to your issue. Here, that means choosing facts that address whether Poe directly observed or was "sensorially aware" of Valenzuela's injury at the scene of the accident. Look for facts, both positive and negative, that suggest she does or doesn't meet this element.

We find these facts in the negligent infliction of emotional distress problem.

- Poe was tending to flowers in her yard with her back to the street while Valenzuela was mowing the grass behind her.
- Poe was listening to music through earbuds.
- Poe didn't see Defoe's car hit Valenzuela, but heard the impact.
- Poe didn't know what happened and as she immediately turned, she saw the lawnmower coming toward her without Valenzuela.
- Poe jumped out of the lawnmower's way and saw Valenzuela lying on the ground about ten feet away with Defoe's car near him.
- Poe rushed to Valenzuela, who was bloody and not making a sound.

- Poe tried to get Valenzuela to respond to her and rode to the hospital with him in an ambulance, where he underwent surgery and remained for three weeks.

Step 3: Pick out the key facts from an analogous case, being careful to articulate exactly *how* and why the two cases are similar or different. Here are just a few of the many possible comparisons that you might make.

- Unlike the husband in *Vargas* who was not with his wife during the accident but arrived on the scene later, here Poe was in her yard with Valenzuela, heard the impact when Defoe's car hit him, and saw his injuries ten feet from her, at the scene of the accident, within seconds.
- Like in *Miller*, where the plaintiff had her back to the ring when the circus leopard attacked and killed her boyfriend, Poe had her back to Valenzuela and the road, so she could not directly observe the accident that injured Valenzuela.
- Similar to *Ortiz*, where the plaintiff was aware her daughter was burning inside their house even though she could not actually see the death, Poe heard the impact of Defoe's car hitting Valenzuela and saw his lawnmower coming toward her and forcing her to jump out of the way, making her "sensorially aware" of the accident the injured Valenzuela at the scene.
- Unlike in *Portee*, where the victim's injury was ongoing because of the faulty elevator and the plaintiff directly observed that continuing injury for hours and her son's ultimate death, here the victim's injury occurred when Defoe's car hit him and the plaintiff merely observed the accident's aftermath.

Finally, notice that the extent to which facts are generalized can change their effect. A difference can be framed as a similarity, and vice versa, if you zoom far enough in or out. In objective writing it's a good idea to take a neutral approach, as you would expect a court to do. In persuasive writing, be aware of the importance of these framing choices, while being careful not to stretch too far.

Here is an analogy that stretches the comparison in an acceptable way:

- Similar to the plaintiff in *Ortiz*, who could not see anyone inside the house but was still "sensorially aware" of her daughter, here Poe was sensorially aware, by virtue of hearing the impact and seeing Valenzuela's lawnmower coming at her, of the accident that caused him physical injury.

Here is an analogy that might go too far:

- Like in *Portee*, where the plaintiff arrived after her son had been trapped by the elevator wall but still "directly observed" his death at the scene, here Poe directly observed Valenzuela injured at the scene.

EXAMPLES

Review the following examples. For each example, there may be more than one correct answer. Explain to yourself why you have chosen that answer or those answers. Then read the explanations in the last section of this chapter to check your work.

Example 11-1

This question uses the copyright and fair use problem, which you can find in Appendix B.

> In the copyright and fair use case at hand, just as in *Campbell*, it was fair use because it was transformative.

This is a . . .

- **A.** strong analogy because it says they are both transformative.
- **B.** strong analogy because it refers to *Campbell*, which was decided by the U.S. Supreme Court.
- **C.** weak analogy because it doesn't explain how the facts in the precedent and in the problem are alike.
- **D.** weak analogy because although it uses an important word from the rule, it doesn't explain its conclusion.

Example 11-2

This question uses the copyright and fair use problem, which you can find in Appendix B.

> Like the defendants in *Campbell*, who set up an expectation by using the lyrics and opening bars of the original but shattered it with a different message, Dash uses the music, structure, and lyrics of the original to set up an expectation that he shatters with his different message.

This is a . . .

A. strong analogy because it compares the facts of the precedent to the facts of the copyright and fair use problem.
B. strong analogy because it uses the same words for both cases.
C. weak analogy because it goes on and on about something the reader can figure out without explanation.
D. weak analogy because it's repetitive.

EXAMPLES

Example 11-3

This question uses the copyright and fair use problem, which you can find in Appendix B.

> Unlike *Mattel*, Dash failed to substantially transform his work in order to convey his message. The verse and chorus pattern in Dash's parody is the exact pattern used in Page's song.

A. This successfully distinguishes Dash's case from *Mattel* because it uses facts to support the conclusion.
B. This successfully distinguishes Dash's case from *Mattel* because it compares the facts of the copyright and fair use problem to *Mattel*'s facts.
C. This unsuccessfully distinguishes Dash's case from *Mattel* because it doesn't say why copying a verse and chorus pattern is important.
D. This unsuccessfully distinguishes Dash's case from *Mattel* because it doesn't tell the reader which facts in *Mattel* are different from the facts in Dash's copyright and fair use problem.

EXAMPLES

Example 11-4

This question uses a hypothetical torts problem where a child fell from a ladder.

Consider these three examples:

Example 1: Under *Daniels*, falling is not a danger that fills this rule. Therefore, the plaintiff cannot win.

Example 2: Falling from the height of the boat was a danger a child would understand in *Daniels*. Falling from the height of the ladder and hayloft in our case is also an understandable danger to a child. In both cases the danger of falling from a height is a danger immature minds can comprehend.

Example 3: Jack fell from the ladder in the same manner that the plaintiff in *Daniels* fell from the stationary boat. Jack is also a year or two older than the plaintiff in *Daniels*, strengthening the argument that he should be aware of the danger of falling.

Choose a good observation about these examples:

A. Example 1 is better than Example 2 and Example 3 because it tells what is the same about both cases.
B. Example 2 is better than Example 1 because it uses the facts of the precedent case to show how the facts in the case at hand are similar.
C. Example 1 is not as strong as the others but it's a good analogy using the same case.
D. All of the examples are poor because they use more than one sentence to make the analogies.

EXPLANATIONS

Explanation 11-1

A is incorrect. This is not a strong analogy. **B** is also incorrect. It makes a good point for weight of authority questions, but it doesn't help much for analogical reasoning. **C** is correct and it's probably the best description of why this is a weak analogy, because the example doesn't explain why or how the two cases are similar. The example doesn't compare facts. **D** is also a good answer and it names a common problem first-year students experience: simply using an important word from the test without explaining how it applies. On law school exams, a professor would call this kind of answer "conclusory." It states a conclusion without the reason for it.

Explanation 11-2

A is correct and probably the best description of why this is a strong analogy. The analogy here is very specific, telling the reader how in the precedent case and in our case the writer used enough of the original song to create an expectation about its message and then relayed a significantly different message. **B** is also a good answer. It's fine to repeat phrases to make your point. You may have learned elsewhere to vary your language to keep a reader interested. In law, readers want information they can grasp quickly without doing much work. You're unlikely to be graded down for using the same words to describe similarities. **C** is problematic. Remember to explain the links for the reader as specifically as you can. This is especially true in a first-year class when you are learning to make clear analogies. **D** is incorrect. Although the example repeats certain words and repeats concepts that you explained, this is new information for the reader—how and why the precedent case supports a similar finding.

Explanation 11-3

A is incorrect. Although this example includes facts, there aren't any factual comparisons between Dash's copyright and fair use case and the precedent. Instead, the comparisons are between the two songs in Dash's copyright and fair use problem. **B** is also incorrect. It assumes that mentioning a case name is enough. We know that it's not. **C** is correct. The comparison doesn't really explain much about how the two cases are different. In addition, the structure is not parallel. **D** is also correct and it best characterizes the difficulty here. Reread the example. Is there anything in it about the facts in the precedent case? No. So although the author is thinking about ways the two cases are different, she hasn't provided an explanation. The only facts we see are from Dash's copyright and fair use problem itself. No facts are from the precedent case.

Explanation 11-4

A is not correct. Unlike Examples 2 and 3, Example 1 tells little about what facts are similar in both cases. **B** is correct; Example 2 explains how the facts are alike. **C** is incorrect. Example 1 does not contain an analogy. It merely refers to an appropriate precedent case. **D** is also incorrect. It's fine to use more than one sentence to make an analogy. Sometimes it makes an analogy very strong to fit it all into one sentence. But if putting it all in one sentence is unwieldy, it's fine to use as many sentences as you need.

With this example, it's interesting to see how informative good examples are when you have no background about a case. Examples 2 and 3 are taken directly from first-year student papers and show how much you can learn about an issue merely by reading a couple of sentences of good analysis. Although the students undoubtedly explained more about the precedent earlier in the paper, notice that you quickly learn how the precedent case illustrated the rule that requires a danger to be understandable by an immature mind. And then, almost as quickly, you see how the facts of the problem compare to the precedent.

Checklist

Chapter 11: Applying the Law: Analogical Analysis

✔	Read the precedent cases and consider the facts that are relevant to the applicable legal test.
✔	Choose the facts from the assignment that are relevant to the applicable legal test.
✔	Articulate exactly how and why the facts from a precedent and from the assignment are similar or different.
✔	Compare apples to apples: make sure the facts compared or contrasted are actually parallel to the facts from precedents and the connections are explicit.

You will find all of the chapter checklists compiled in Appendix D.

Applying the Law: Policy Analysis

Law professors are fond of policy rationales. Your Contracts or Property professor probably spends considerable time helping the class see the societal interests served by a rule of law. In practice and when you're learning to write practice documents, fact-based analysis (discussed in Chapter 10) and analogical reasoning (discussed in Chapter 11) are more common and generally more significant. Policy analysis is often most helpful in cases of first impression or when the rule of law and the precedent cases go against your client (if you're in an appellate court that has the authority to change the law). One problem with considering policy is that both sides to a dispute can often make sweeping statements about how the outcome each wants will help society. If these sweeping statements are not substantiated by solid analysis, they will seldom convince the reader. In this chapter, we explain how to make specific, well-supported policy arguments that can be important in practice documents.

Terminology notes. When professors use the term "normative argument," they mean an argument about what *should happen* for the benefit of society. It's a synonym for "policy argument."

WHAT YOU NEED TO KNOW ABOUT POLICY ANALYSIS

"Analyzing policy" means explaining how an outcome will benefit or disadvantage society. Because both sides of an issue can generate reasons why society would be better off if their side won, think of generating policy rationales as looking for the strongest policy reasons that benefit a particular side, rather than looking for the "right answer" or the one "correct" policy.[1]

Make your policy analysis specific to your assignment. Identify exactly how your position will benefit society. Most readers understand that anyone can make broad sweeping policy rationales to benefit either side. Those abstract generalities are rarely important unless the writer also explains specifically and concretely how an outcome will affect society.

Like any other analysis, policy analysis is stronger when supported by citations to mandatory primary authority. Look for authority in a couple of places. Often statutes will begin with a section that states the purpose or goals of the statute—the policy behind the statute. Courts also address the policy behind decisions in opinions. As you might have guessed by the references to citations, you are using policy like a rule, so describe the policy in the section of your document where you explain or prove the rule (for more about stating and explaining a rule, see Chapter 9). Later, in the application section, you'll explain to the reader what that policy means in your particular case.

Policy rationales can show the reader why your analogical analysis or fact-based analysis is important. With analogies or fact-based rationales, you're asking the court to put the facts of your case in a certain category. (For example, you might argue that certain facts fall in the "burglary" category, or that your case is just like the precedent case where the court held that an allegedly infringing use was "fair use.") The policy analysis tells the court *why* it's important to categorize your case your way.

Think about your audience while deciding how much to emphasize policy. The highest court in a jurisdiction will find policy considerations important when deciding a case because the high court's decision will probably affect more subsequent cases and affect a broader section of society. A trial court and intermediate appellate court are less likely to decide a case based primarily on policy reasons. Any court, however, will consider policy when addressing a case of first impression or a case that presents new arguments.

HOW TO GENERATE POLICY RATIONALES

Using the copyright and fair use problem in Appendix B, we'll walk you through the process of generating policy rationales.

1. For more detailed information on making policy arguments, see Ellie Margolis, *Closing the Floodgates: Making Persuasive Policy Arguments in Appellate Briefs*, 62 MONT. L. REV. 59 (2001).

Problem

> Here is a quick overview of the copyright and fair use problem (for details see Appendix B). Page is suing Dash for violating the Copyright Act when Dash wrote a song based on Page's song (which in copyright terms is called the "original"), "Red, White, and Blue." Dash's song uses the structure and many lyrics of the original but changes the original song's political message. The music of the two songs is not at issue, only the lyrics. Page expects that Dash will argue that his song is a parody that falls under the fair use exception to the Copyright Act. The court will consider the relevant factors set out in the fair use statute, 17 U.S.C. § 107: whether the copy was transformative and targeted the original; whether it took more than necessary of the original; and whether it will interfere with the original's market.

Step 1: Generate a list of policy rationales. You need policies that legislatures and courts have already recognized as societal interests. The logical place to start is to check primary, mandatory authority to find policy statements or arguments that might be helpful to your analysis. Because you're working with a statute, first look at the statute's introductory section to see whether it includes a policy statement. Or you might look at the first section of a title or other subdivision of a larger enactment. For example, at the beginning of a state code's section on criminal law, there may be general policy statements about criminal law in that jurisdiction. At the beginning of the Copyright Act, however, you'll find definitions but no statement of policy or of Congress's intention when it adopted the Act.

Next turn to cases, looking first at cases from the courts of last resort as a likely place to find policy. Cases from a high court will also provide the best authority for policy. After evaluating cases from the highest courts, you may consider looking for policy in lower court decisions.

Here, looking at the highexst court for your jurisdiction, you see that *Campbell*, a U.S. Supreme Court case, states that:

> The fair use doctrine thus "permits [and requires] courts to avoid rigid application of the copyright statute when, on occasion, it would stifle the very creativity which that law is designed to foster." *Campbell v. Acuff-Rose Music, Inc.*, 510 U.S. 569, 577 (1994) (*quoting Stewart v. Abend*, 495 U.S. 207, 236 (1990)).

Or looking at a lower court, you find this statement:

> The primary intent of fair use is to weigh the rights of the original owner against the benefit that the secondary use provides to society. *Mattel, Inc. v. Walking Mountain Prods.*, 353 F.3d 792, 806 (9th Cir. 2003).

So, your list of policies looks like this:

- The purpose of the Copyright Act is to encourage creativity.
- The court should not stifle creativity.
- The court will balance the rights of the original owner with the benefit the copy makes to society.

Step 2: If you don't find policy in the primary sources for your assignment, generate a list of ideas and then look for authority to support those ideas. If you find nothing about policy in your statutes or cases, think through the effects of a potential ruling. The analysis will still be stronger with a citation to some kind of authority, so you'll want to look for the authority after you've come up with the idea. If you can't find authority in primary sources, try citing secondary sources or social science outside of legal sources.

To generate the list, think of the consequences, both direct and indirect, of your desired outcome. Some consequences might be moral, economic, or practical. They might implicate our institutions of government such as which branch of government is best situated to make a decision or whether the decision will affect the integrity of the justice system.

Here, the copyright and fair use problem includes an interesting twist in the facts. Dash's song criticizes the politics expressed in Page's original. So when you think of other policies that might help persuade a decision maker to prefer Dash's side, you can say that his copy is a form of political speech. The problem doesn't include a First Amendment claim, which requires an entirely different analysis, but the facts arguably involve political speech, a highly protected form of speech.

Thus, you can look at First Amendment cases for policy statements that help, even though they are not part of copyright law. A useful statement about the importance of political speech appears in a Supreme Court case:

> "Freedom of speech is 'indispensable to the discovery and spread of political truth,' and 'the best test of truth is the power of the thought to get itself accepted in the competition of the market.'" *Consol. Edison Co. of N.Y., Inc. v. Pub. Serv. Comm'n of N.Y.*, 447 U.S. 530, 534 (1980) (internal citations omitted).

We might make this more concrete and take it out of the First Amendment analysis by considering the consequences of a precedent that a court would establish by deciding the controversy between Page and Dash. So you might add to your list that political parody is valuable to society and future artists may hesitate to critique political statements, which would mean the general public would lose the chance to hear both sides of an issue.

Step 3: Craft an argument that is specific to your assignment. A common mistake for beginners is to make a broad, sweeping statement of policy without following through to tell the reader how it applies in your assignment. Remember, the better supported by authority and the more specific the application, the stronger the policy analysis.

Because the court's policy statements are a part of the law, you'll put those in the section of the paper that describes, explains, or proves the law (what we have previously referred to as "rule explanation"). Then in the application or analysis section you'll apply that statement to your assignment (using the CRAC structure described in Chapter 7). So take a look at these policy statements and the arguments you make with them.

Policy statement #1:	The fair use doctrine thus "permits [and requires] courts to avoid rigid application of the copyright statute when, on occasion, it would stifle the very creativity which that law is designed to foster." *Campbell v. Acuff-Rose Music, Inc.*, 510 U.S. 569, 577 (1994) (*quoting Stewart v. Abend*, 495 U.S. 207, 236 (1990)).
Policy application #1:	A finding that Dash's song is not fair use would be counter to the policy of encouraging creativity because artists will refrain from creating a new work of art that comments on the message of an earlier work of art for fear of litigation.
Policy statement #2:	The primary intent of fair use is to weigh the rights of the original owner against the benefit that the secondary use provides to society. *Mattel, Inc. v. Walking Mountain Prods.*, 353 F.3d 792, 806 (9th Cir. 2003). The "freedom of speech is 'indispensable to the discovery and spread of political truth.'" *Consol. Edison Co. of N.Y., Inc. v. Pub. Serv. Comm'n of N.Y.*, 447 U.S. 530, 534 (1980) (internal citations omitted).
Policy application #2:	Here the benefit to society of free and open critique of an earlier political song outweighs the rights of the original artist because a democratic society is more informed and better able to make choices when artists freely exchange opposing ideas. This exchange is "indispensable" in a democratic society. *Consol. Edison Co. of N.Y., Inc. v. Pub. Serv. Comm'n of N.Y.*, 447 U.S. 530, 534 (1980).

EXAMPLES

Review the following examples. For each example, there may be more than one correct answer. Explain to yourself why you have chosen that answer or those answers. Then read the explanations in the last section of this chapter to check your work.

Example 12-1

This question uses the cell phone manslaughter problem, which you can find in Appendix A.

It would be against the public policy interest in safety to convict Allison King of vehicular manslaughter.

Standing on its own, this is a . . .

A. weak public policy analysis because it's not supported by a reference to mandatory authority stating that the state has an interest in safety.

B. strong public policy analysis because it correctly identifies that the state has an interest in the safety of its citizens.

C. weak public policy analysis because it doesn't specify how the outcome the author advocates would further the state's interest in safety.

D. strong public policy analysis because it expressly refers to "public policy."

Example 12-2

This question uses a hypothetical adverse possession problem.

Courts recognize adverse possession as a doctrine that "encourages land be put to its most productive and highest use." *Jones v. Jones*, 116 N.E.2d 1235, 1237 (Mass. 1945). Here, Calvin Kolb was an absentee owner. If the law fails to punish absentee owners, there will be more absentee owners whose land is unused.

This is a . . .

A. good policy analysis because it cites primary authority and is specific about Calvin Kolb being an absentee owner.

B. good policy analysis because it includes how the outcome may influence future cases.

C. poor policy analysis because the analysis relies on an assumption the author hasn't stated.
D. poor policy analysis because it should cite secondary authority rather than a case from the Massachusetts Supreme Court.

EXAMPLES

Example 12-3

This question uses the copyright and fair use problem, which you can find in Appendix B.

> "The purpose of copyright is to create incentives for creative effort." *Sony Corp. of Am. v. Universal City Studios, Inc.*, 464 U.S. 417, 450 (1984). Here, artists, like Page, will lose the incentive to create new works if they are likely to lose profits to copyists, like Dash, who copy so closely that consumers are likely to confuse the two works. Future artists will hesitate to expend creative effort if they cannot reap the reward.

A. This policy analysis is weak because it connects the abstract generality with the specific and concrete effects that the desired ruling will produce, and it talks about the future.
B. This policy analysis is strong because it cites good authority and makes concrete and practical arguments about how a contrary decision would affect society.
C. This policy analysis is weak because it doesn't identify other artists who will be affected by this decision.
D. This analysis will work only if the case is in the U.S. Supreme Court.

EXAMPLES

Example 12-4

This question uses a hypothetical burglary problem.

> Courts recognize that the criminal code protects the safety of the people. *State v. Smith*, 592 N.W.2d 1303, 1306 (Minn. 1999). Our case is similar to *Smith* because both cases are burglary cases. Thus, it is important to convict Harrison of burglary so that the people will be safe.

This is a . . .

A. good policy analysis because it shows the reader why the analogy to *Smith* is important.
B. good policy analysis because it tells the reader why it's important to society to convict the defendant.
C. poor policy analysis because it is so broad that it could be used in any criminal case.
D. poor policy analysis because it cites to primary authority.

EXPLANATIONS

Explanation 12-1

A is correct because public policy analysis is most effective if you've laid the groundwork by citing authority for the proposition that your jurisdiction cares about the policy. **B** is incorrect because this is not strong policy analysis. In fact, the prosecutor could easily make this argument favor the state by saying that the public policy interest in safety *mandates* convicting Allison King of vehicular manslaughter. In addition, it does not specifically explain how the outcome the author advocates or predicts would further the state's interest in safety. **C** is correct. The analysis would be much stronger if the author told the reader that excusing King's cell phone use would promote safety because citizens could warn others of dangerous road conditions without fear of prosecution. **D** is incorrect. Some of the best policy arguments don't use the phrase "public policy," and this analysis is weak for the reasons stated in A, B, and C.

Explanation 12-2

A is partially true because it correctly states that citing primary authority is important in strong policy analysis. But citing to authority isn't sufficient to create good policy analysis. Further, although this example is specific that the landowner does not live on the property, the policy involves the "most productive and highest use" of the land, which doesn't necessarily involve knowing where the landowner lives. **B** is also partially correct because good policy analysis often does connect the current problem to future results. But it's incorrect because this particular example doesn't do a good job of connecting the current problem to future results. It refers to absentee ownership, which may be relevant, but is not the same as failure to put the land to its best use, which is the policy behind adverse possession. **C** correctly identifies that problem. The assumption is that all absentee owners fail to put land to its highest and best use. Even though the example uses specific facts and speculates about how the outcome will influence future cases, it focuses on where the owner lives and not on whether the owner uses the land well. The author could improve it by stating the assumption: "Here Calvin Kolb was an absentee owner and did not put his land to its highest and best use." **D** is incorrect. Primary authority, especially mandatory primary authority, is much stronger support for a policy argument than secondary authority.

EXPLANATIONS

Explanation 12-3

A is incorrect because this policy analysis connects the abstract idea of giving artists incentives to create new works with their fear of losing money when their work is copied. This is exactly the kind of concrete, practical policy analysis that is effective. Further, good policy analysis usually addresses the future. **B** is correct for the reasons stated in A; the analysis is specific and it also cites good authority for the general proposition upon which it's based. **C** is incorrect. This is a well-supported prediction about how a particular outcome will affect artists in general. More specificity in terms of the effects on society aren't needed and could undercut the value of the generalization. **D** is also incorrect. Although the highest courts are more likely to consider policy, all courts might be influenced by it.

EXPLANATIONS

Explanation 12-4

A is incorrect because the analogy to *Smith* has nothing to do with policy. Noting that the criminal charge in both cases was the same does not support the idea that safety is an important policy. Further, the analogy itself is weak. If you'd like to know more about making a strong analogy, see Chapter 11. **B** is only partially correct. It's good to tell the reader why an outcome is important to society, but in this example, the author needs to be more specific about how finding the defendant guilty will further a societal interest. **C** is correct. This rationale is so broad that it would apply in any criminal case and that means it's so broad it fails to convince. **D** is incorrect. Although the answer correctly identifies the example as a poor policy analysis, citing to primary authority is helpful (although not sufficient).

Checklist

Chapter 12: Applying the Law: Policy Analysis

✔	Consider the audience and whether the analysis or arguments will be stronger if you add policy rationales.
✔	If appropriate, specifically articulate or craft an argument about how an outcome in the case will benefit or disadvantage society.
✔	Support policy analysis or arguments with cites to authority, especially mandatory primary authority if available.

You will find all of the chapter checklists compiled in Appendix D.

Writing the Introduction to the Discussion (or Argument)

In the part of this book that covers memo writing, why does the chapter on writing the introduction to the Discussion or Argument come near the end? It's because the introduction will include the points you think are most important and only after you've written the bulk of the analysis contained in the Discussion section or Argument section will you know which important points you will include.

The same principles that apply to the introduction to the Discussion or Argument section will apply whenever you write the introductory paragraph for each issue or sub-issue of the Discussion section. Each section will have an introductory section and you'll put the same types of information into short introductions, or introductory paragraphs, throughout the memo or brief.

Terminology notes. Terminology about this section of your document is varied and rich. Your textbook or teacher may call the introductory section of a document or a section of a document an "introduction," "thesis paragraph," "rule paragraph," "umbrella paragraph," or "umbrella rule paragraph." Although these labels may emphasize different components of an introductory paragraph, the components of a good introductory section or paragraph will be the same. Furthermore, some readers will expect you to use a heading for this section, like "Introduction," and others will expect no heading. Some will use "roadmap" to refer to the entire introduction, while others will use that term to mean only the part of the introduction that tells the reader the sequence in which you'll address the issues and sub-issues.

WHAT YOU NEED TO KNOW ABOUT WRITING INTRODUCTIONS

Write or revise an introduction only after you've identified the points that are most important to your analysis in the Discussion section of a memo or the Argument section of a brief.

An introduction should contain the points you think are most essential for the reader to know before you discuss the details. Although people often imagine writing as organizing your thoughts first and then pouring them perfectly onto the page from start to end, you've probably realized by now that you actually work through your ideas as you write. Writing is thinking. Often you won't know the most important points on each side until you've written the Discussion section. So revise the introductory section of the Discussion or Argument as the last drafting task before you begin the final editing and proofreading to make sure your paper is perfect.

A good introduction to a Discussion section with one main issue that has sub-issues will include:

- *A thesis statement:* A thesis statement is an assertion or series of assertions about how a court will decide the issue or issues you're writing about—the outcome. Some think of a thesis statement as your conclusion put up front. In fact, some teachers will call the entire introduction to the memo a general "thesis paragraph" or the "CR" in the overarching, global CRAC we discussed in Chapter 7.
- *The rule or rules the court will apply to your issue:* Usually the introduction includes only the main rule that applies to the issue, and not the rules that apply to the sub-issues that make up this larger rule. Some teachers will call this the "umbrella rule," or the rule that "covers" the whole issue. Those teachers may call the introduction "the umbrella rule paragraph."
- *A statement about those parts of the rule that will not be at issue, along with a very brief explanation of why not:* When more than one rule, or more than one part of the rule, applies, your Discussion section will address everything the parties are likely to contest. Even if you decide the plaintiff can't prove an essential part of the rule, you'll still need to analyze every part that a plaintiff could make arguments about in case you're wrong about the plaintiff ultimately losing on another point. The only time you can omit an issue from the Discussion section is when you decide a party has no valid arguments to make on the issue. In that situation, your introduction should note the issue that is not likely to be in dispute and explicitly explain why it won't be "at issue."

- *A roadmap of the memo:* A roadmap is a sentence or paragraph that outlines the organization of the discussion that follows for the reader. Legal readers want to know exactly where they are going, without surprises. Usually setting out the rule and explaining which parts of it are at issue acts as the "roadmap" of your paper because the reader will assume that you will proceed in your Discussion section in the same order. But sometimes the organization is more complex, and you will need to spell out the order in which you'll address each issue or sub-issue.

A good introduction to a Discussion section with multiple issues will include:

- *A thesis statement on each main issue:* Here, you'll advise the reader how a court is likely to decide each of the main issues.
- *A statement explaining the connection—or lack of connection—between the main issues:* The reader needs to know whether the issues you address are related; for example, if your client can prevail by winning on either of two issues, make that clear. If she has to win both issues to prevail overall, make that clear. If the first issue is a procedural question and losing on that issue means the second, substantive issue won't matter, explain that. Use phrases and transitions like "independent claims for relief" and "presuming the client prevails on the subject-matter jurisdiction issue" to signal these connections to your reader.
- *A roadmap of the memo:* Because you'll be discussing more than one main issue, it's especially helpful to the reader to understand the order in which you'll be addressing the issues. As noted above, a roadmap is a sentence or paragraph that outlines the organization of the discussion that follows.

Unless your professor or supervisor has specified a sequence she finds most effective, you can put these pieces together in the introduction in any order that makes sense to you. The last piece will often include a sentence that provides a transition from the introductory section to where you begin to analyze the first issue or sub-issue. For more on CRAC and organizational paradigms, see Chapter 7.

You can also include other statements that apply to the issue generally rather than to one particular section. For instance, perhaps the statute or key case identifies policies served by the rule. General policy statements are not usually dispositive, and sometimes have limited persuasive value, but it may make sense to include them in the introduction if they are noteworthy and you can't find a way to weave them into your detailed analysis.

One of the difficulties you'll run into is how much detail to include in the introduction. If you give too little detail, the reader will miss the links that connect the information you've presented and the introduction won't make much sense. If you give too much detail, the reader will be bogged down with information that is not immediately usable. Readers get frustrated if you clutter up their short-term memory with details they can't immediately use. So the key to writing an introduction is really to give readers enough to understand what is going on and what to expect from the memo, but not a bit more.

Finally, writing the introduction may make later sections seem repetitive to you. Remember that the reader may read only parts of your memo rather than reading it like a book from start to finish. Each section has to stand on its own. Don't repeat within a section, but don't worry about repeating something from the introduction in another part of the memo.

HOW TO WRITE INTRODUCTIONS

Using the copyright and fair use problem in Appendix B, we'll walk you through the process of writing introductions and introductory paragraphs.

PROBLEMS

Problem

Here is a quick overview of the copyright and fair use problem (for details see Appendix B). Page is suing Dash for violating the Copyright Act when Dash wrote a song based on Page's song (which in copyright terms is called the "original"), "Red, White, and Blue." Dash's song uses the structure and many lyrics of the original but changes the original song's political message. The music of the two songs is not at issue, only the lyrics. Page expects that Dash will argue that his song is a parody that falls under the fair use exception to the Copyright Act. The court will consider the relevant factors set out in the fair use statute, 17 U.S.C. § 107: whether the copy was transformative and targeted the original; whether it took more than necessary of the original; and whether it will interfere with the original's market.

Step 1: Plan. Develop a thesis, a rule statement, an explanation of why neither side is likely to dispute some part of the rule, if that's true, and a roadmap.

Step 2: Write a thesis statement. Remember that the thesis statement is your conclusion stated up front. When you can identify one primary reason for your conclusion, include that in your thesis statement. Sometimes there won't be just one primary reason for your conclusion. Then you can write a general thesis statement.

Using the copyright case, you could have come to several conclusions, because you have to decide whether Dash violated the Copyright Act and whether the fair use exception will work for him. Let's write several thesis statements that cover most of the possibilities.

For instance, you could decide that Dash violated the Copyright Act and won't be able to prove the fair use exception:

> The court will most likely hold that Dash violated the Copyright Act and Dash cannot prove that his use falls under the fair use exception because he used more of the original than needed for his parody.

Put another way with less detail:

> Page can successfully show that Dash is liable for violating the Copyright Act and that the fair use exception is not available to him.

Or your analysis might show that Dash did the things that would normally constitute a copyright violation, but you might conclude he can avoid liability through the fair use exception:

> Although Page can show Dash infringed upon Page's copyright, Dash can successfully assert the fair use exception as a defense because the court is likely to find the transformative nature of the parody outweighs other factors.

Put another way with less detail:

> The court will find that Dash violated the Copyright Act but that he can escape liability under the fair use exception.

Or you could decide that Dash didn't violate the Copyright Act, and that in any case, he could successfully use the fair use exception:

> Dash will successfully defend the claim of infringement because he did not violate the Copyright Act and even if he did, he can prove the fair use exception because he used only what he needed to make a parody, his work had a different message than the original, and despite being in the same musical genre it was not likely to appeal to the same audience.

Put another way with less detail:

> Page cannot prove Dash infringed his copyright and even if he could, Dash can prove his use falls under the fair use exception.

Some legal writing textbooks suggest putting the relevant thesis statement as the heading that announces that particular section of the paper.

The heading will be an assertion about the outcome of the analysis in that section.

Step 3: State the rule or rules that govern overall. It's important to include enough for the reader to understand which rules apply overall to the problem. This is especially true because the structure of the rule that applies overall will most often form the structure of your analysis and provide an organization for you to follow. That's also why the rule statement so often serves as the roadmap for your paper. But do more than just cut and paste the rule into your paper. Although the reader will expect you to quote statutes or the test that the court sets out, edit the statute or rule to make it easy for the reader to see what the parties need to prove. Too much detail will clutter the introduction and just burden the reader with more than he needs to start.

Sometimes you'll need to make a judgment call on how much context you need to give. The copyright and fair use problem provides a good example. You have choices about which rules to include in your introduction. You can start with the rights given to Page by the Copyright Act, or you can start with the rules for the fair use exception that Dash will assert. Let's look at how they both would work.

If the reader would need some background to understand the Copyright Act section that gives Page the right to sue Dash over using his song, you might write something like this:

> Among the exclusive rights that the Copyright Act, 17 U.S.C. § 106, provides copyright holders are the rights to perform, copy, distribute, and make derivatives of the copyrighted work. These rights are subject to exceptions for fair use, which includes "purposes such as criticism" and "comment." 17 U.S.C. § 107. The statute provides four factors that courts can use to determine whether there is a fair use exception to the infringement:
>
> (1) the purpose and character of the use, including whether such use is of a commercial nature or is for nonprofit educational purposes;
>
> (2) the nature of the copyrighted work;
>
> (3) the amount and substantiality of the portion used in relation to the copyrighted work as a whole; and
>
> (4) the effect of the use upon the potential market for or value of the copyrighted work.
>
> *Id.*

Or, if you decide that the general principles of copyright are so well known to your audience that you don't need to set them out, you could go right to the rules that govern your analysis in this memo:

> Dash is likely to answer a claim of copyright infringement by asserting that he falls under the fair use exception to the Copyright Act. Fair use includes "purposes such as criticism" and "comment." 17 U.S.C. § 107. The statute provides

> four factors that the courts can use to determine whether there is a fair use exception to infringement:
>
> > (1) the purpose and character of the use, including whether such use is of a commercial nature or is for nonprofit educational purposes;
> >
> > (2) the nature of the copyrighted work;
> >
> > (3) the amount and substantiality of the portion used in relation to the copyrighted work as a whole; and
> >
> > (4) the effect of the use upon the potential market for or value of the copyrighted work.
>
> *Id.*

Decide how much information is necessary and useful for the ordinary legal reader. This may be difficult for you as a first-year law student, but it will become second nature to you as you become more experienced as a legal reader and a legal writer. For now, it's not wrong to give a fuller context than necessary for the rules you apply; but it can be a time-waster for the reader and use up valuable words if you're under a strict word count or page limit. In those cases, you may decide to go right to the rules that most apply in your analysis.

Step 4: Tell the reader which parts, if any, the parties are not likely to dispute. If one of the issues in your assignment so clearly falls to one party that the other party has no good arguments to make about it, or if your assignment instructs you to assume particular issues or elements, you should dismiss those issues or sub-issues in the introduction.

In the copyright and fair use problem, the U.S. Supreme Court has held that the second factor is likely irrelevant in cases involving a parody. Thus, you would include a couple of sentences like these:

> In our case, the second factor, the nature of the copyrighted work, is relatively insignificant in a parody case because parodies "almost invariably copy publicly known, expressive works," and this factor has been largely disregarded by the courts in such cases. *Campbell v. Acuff-Rose Music, Inc.*, 510 U.S. 569, 586 (1994). Thus, because the court is not likely to consider this factor here, the parties are not likely to dispute it.

Or

> The second factor, the nature of the copyrighted work, is not likely to be in dispute because the Supreme Court has stated that courts disregard this factor in cases like ours involving parody. *Campbell v. Acuff-Rose Music, Inc.*, 510 U.S. 569, 586 (1994).

Step 5: Make sure you have a roadmap. Most often the rule will act as your roadmap. Usually, your Discussion section will address the issues in the same order that the source of the rule does. For instance, if your rule comes from a statute, you'll address the elements or factors in the same order as the statute does. Or if you're using a rule delineated in a case, address each part of the rule in the same order the court did. In these cases, once you state the large-scale rule in your introduction you don't need to add a separate roadmap.

Sometimes, however, you'll have a good reason for departing from ordering the issues in the same way the rule does. Perhaps one part of the rule is more important to your case. If you're writing a persuasive brief, it might be advantageous to order your arguments by their strength and indicate this order in the introduction to your argument. Or perhaps you're applying more than one rule and no statute or case suggests an order to use for more than one rule. In those cases, you'll add a simple sentence or two, setting out the organization your memo will follow. For instance:

> In our case, the court will probably weigh the third factor, "the amount and substantiality of the portion used in relation to the copyrighted work as a whole," more heavily than the others. Thus, this memo will focus first on that factor before turning to the purpose and character of the use, and the potential effect on markets.

Step 6: Put it all together. Here are a couple of ways you could put together the introduction section. Remember that not all readers will expect this explicit "Introduction" heading:

> **Introduction**
>
> The court will most likely hold that Dash violated the Copyright Act and that his work does not fall under the fair use exception because he used more of the original work than needed for his parody. Dash is likely to answer a claim of copyright infringement by asserting that his use falls under the fair use exception to the Copyright Act. Fair use includes "purposes such as criticism" and "comment." 17 U.S.C. § 107. The statute provides four factors that courts use to determine whether there is a fair use exception to infringement:
>
> (1) the purpose and character of the use, including whether such use is of a commercial nature or is for nonprofit educational purposes;
>
> (2) the nature of the copyrighted work;
>
> (3) the amount and substantiality of the portion used in relation to the copyrighted work as a whole; and
>
> (4) the effect of the use upon the potential market for or value of the copyrighted work.
>
> *Id.* The second factor, the nature of the copyrighted work, is not likely to be in dispute because the Supreme Court has stated that courts disregard this factor in cases like ours involving parody. *Campbell v. Acuff-Rose Music, Inc.*, 510 U.S. 569, 586 (1994).

In our case, the court will probably weigh the third factor, "the amount and substantiality of the portion used in relation to the copyrighted work as a whole," more heavily than the others. Thus, this memo will focus first on that factor before turning to the purpose and character of the use, and the potential effect on markets.

Or you might write this instead:

Introduction

Among the exclusive rights that the Copyright Act, 17 U.S.C. § 106, provides copyright holders are the rights to perform, copy, distribute, and make derivatives of the work. These rights, however, are subject to exceptions for fair use. 17 U.S.C. § 107.

Fair use includes "purposes such as criticism" and "comment." *Id.* The statute provides four factors that courts use to determine whether there is a fair use exception to the infringement:

> (1) the purpose and character of the use, including whether such use is of a commercial nature or is for nonprofit educational purposes;
>
> (2) the nature of the copyrighted work;
>
> (3) the amount and substantiality of the portion used in relation to the copyrighted work as a whole; and
>
> (4) the effect of the use upon the potential market for or value of the copyrighted work.

Id.

In our case, the second factor, the nature of the copyrighted work, is relatively insignificant in a parody case because parodies "almost invariably copy publicly known, expressive works," and this factor has been largely disregarded by the courts in such cases. *Campbell v. Acuff-Rose Music, Inc.*, 510 U.S. 569, 586 (1994). Thus, because the court is not likely to weigh this factor, the parties are not likely to dispute it. Although Page can show Dash infringed upon Page's copyright, the court is likely to find Dash's use falls under the fair use exception because the transformative nature of the parody outweighs other factors.

EXAMPLES

Review the following examples. For each example, there may be more than one correct answer. Explain to yourself why you have chosen that answer or those answers. Then read the explanations in the last section of this chapter to check your work.

EXAMPLES

Example 13-1

This question uses the copyright and fair use problem, which you can find in Appendix B.

Introduction

ISSUE: Copyright law grants specific privileges for copyrighted material under Title 17 U.S.C. § 106. Congress's intention in creating a copyright monopoly of protected uses is grounded in the larger context of societal advancement. Congress recognized elements where society would be better served by allowing "fair use" of copyrighted material and codified this in Title 17 U.S.C. § 107. In that section Congress created four elements that courts should use to weigh when deciding whether a work is "fair use" of copyrighted material. In light of this the case law recognizes there is "fair use" of copyrighted materials that would otherwise violate copyright holder's rights. Specifically, courts have clearly recognized parody as a potential fair use of copyrighted material.

RULE: To determine whether Dash's song "Red, White, and Blue Through and Through" is a "fair use," we must weigh the four factors using the facts of the case. *Campbell v. Acuff-Rose Music, Inc.*, 510 U.S. 578 (1994). The first and arguably the most important factor, the character of use, will show Dash's song is transformative enough to be "fair use." The second factor, the nature of the copyrighted work, is insignificant in parody cases because parodies "almost invariably copy publicly known, expressive works." *Campbell v. Acuff-Rose Music, Inc.*, 510 U.S. 569, 586 (1994). Thus, both sides would agree on that factor. *Id.* The third factor, substantial use, will show that an excessive amount of the copyrighted work was not used. Finally, the fourth factor, market effect, will show that there is potential for market substitution barring "fair use."

THESIS: Considering the balance of the four factors as a whole, it is highly unlikely that Page can have an injunction served against Dash to stop him from using Page's lyrics.

A. This rule statement in this introduction works well because it personalizes the statute and saves the reader the trouble of reading it. This makes the introduction flow well.

B. This introduction works well because it labels the components so that the professor can see the student included everything.

C. This introduction should not include the Copyright Act, because the analysis really focuses on the fair use exception.

D. One of the things this introduction does well is explain what is not in dispute.

EXAMPLES

Example 13-2

This question uses the copyright and fair use problem, which you can find in Appendix B.

Introduction

To prove fair use of copyrighted material, four elements must be considered. 17 U.S.C. § 107. The first element assesses whether the material is for a commercial purpose and what its character is. The second element assesses if the nature of the material is covered under copyright law. The third element assesses the amount of the copyrighted work that was copied and borrowed in relation to the entire copyrighted work. The fourth element determines whether the new song has an economic impact on the copyrighted song.

The first element is partially disputed. That Dash intended his song to be used for commercial purposes is not under dispute. Dash asserts that his song is a parody and is legal under fair use. Here, there is no argument that both the original and the new work are in the same genre and similar lyrical composition, so the work's nature is not in dispute. Page is disputing that Dash's song is a parody. The second factor is not in dispute because invariably the copyrighted work in parody cases involves "publicly known, expressive works." *Campbell v. Acuff-Rose Music, Inc.*, 510 U.S. 569, 586 (1994). In addition, Dash recognizes that Page copyrighted his song. Dash's song was played on the radio. The substantiality of the amount used in reference to the whole will be the last factor addressed. Finally, since these are factors and not elements, the last section will weigh the factors.

A. A weakness of this introduction is that it does not contain a thesis statement and, like the first example, it does not quote the statute.
B. This introduction is strong because it repeats facts to give the reader context for its analysis.
C. A weakness of this introduction is that it uses the words "element" and "factor" as synonyms.
D. A strength of this introduction is that it tells the reader how the court will decide each factor.

EXAMPLES

Example 13-3

This question uses the copyright and fair use problem, which you can find in Appendix B.

Introduction

To decide whether the defendant's parody falls under the fair use exception to the Copyright Act, the court will weigh the four factors of the fair use statute. 17 U.S.C. § 107. The statute provides:

Notwithstanding the provisions of sections 106 and 106A, the fair use of a copyrighted work, including such use by reproduction in copies or photographic records or by any other means specified by that section, for purposes such as criticism, comment, news reporting, teaching (including multiple copies for classroom use), scholarship, or research, is not an infringement of copyright. In determining whether the use made of a work in any particular case is a fair use the factors to be considered shall include:

(1) the purpose and character of the use, including whether such use is of a commercial nature or is for nonprofit educational purposes;

(2) the nature of the copyrighted work;

(3) the amount and substantiality of the portion used in relation to the copyrighted work as a whole; and

(4) the effect of the use upon the potential market for or value of the copyrighted work.

Id.

The fact that a work is unpublished shall not itself bar a finding of fair use if such finding is made upon consideration of all the above factors. *Id.*

In this case, the defendant has the greatest burden of proof because fair use is an affirmative defense. *Campbell v. Acuff-Rose Music, Inc.*, 510 U.S. 569, 590 (1994). The court has established that the plaintiff is the owner of a copyright, and as such, is entitled to protect his work against copyright infringement. 17 U.S.C. § 106. Consequently, the issue of exclusive rights of copyrighted works is beyond the scope of this discussion. *Id.* The court will likely find that Dash's song violates the Copyright Act and that his song does not fall within the fair use defense because three of the four factors weigh against the defendant. The "character and purpose" factor weighs in favor of Dash, but none of the other factors do.

A. This introduction contains a thesis statement.

B. Although this introduction quotes the statute, it quotes so much that the reader will find it hard to see the test the court will apply.

C. This introduction lets the reader know whether the parties are unlikely to dispute any of the factors.
D. This introduction correctly orders the components of a good introduction.

EXAMPLES

Example 13-4

This question uses a hypothetical gift in contemplation of marriage problem.

Introduction

To revoke a gift given in contemplation of marriage, California Civil Code § 1590 requires donors seeking to recover the gift to first show that they indeed gave the gift in contemplation of marriage. A donor gives a gift in contemplation of marriage if the plaintiff can prove the following elements. First, the donor "makes a gift of money or property to the other." Cal. Civ. Code § 1590 (West 2022). Neither party disputes that the facts of this case fulfill this requirement. Second, the donor gives the gift "on the basis or assumption that the marriage will take place." *Id.* The parties are in dispute over this element.

If a gift is given in contemplation of marriage, to recover the gift, the plaintiff must establish that either "the donee refuses to enter into the marriage as contemplated" or the marriage is "given up by mutual consent." *Id.* Then "the donor may recover such gift or such part of its value as may, under all of the circumstances of the case, be found by a court or jury to be just." *Id.*

The court will likely find that defendant Norton can keep the painting because the donor did not give that particular gift in contemplation of marriage, but rather as a token of love. California Civil Code section 1148 governs and provides, "A gift, other than a gift in view of impending death, cannot be revoked by the giver." Cal. Civ. Code § 1148 (West 2022). Norton can also keep the ring her fiancé gave her, even though he gave it in contemplation of marriage, because courts have not construed a fiancée's unforeseen death as "mutual consent" to end the engagement.

A. This introduction is too complicated and has too many rules to be a good introduction.
B. Some of these rules could be described in another order and the introduction would still be successful.
C. The reader needs more facts to understand this introduction.
D. This introduction ends with good thesis statements.

EXAMPLES

Example 13-5

This question uses the negligent infliction of emotional distress problem, which you can find in Appendix C.

Introduction

Poe is unlikely to succeed on her claim of negligent infliction of emotional distress as a bystander. To prevail in New Fornia, four elements must be met:

(1) the defendant's negligence must cause the victim's injury or death;

(2) the plaintiff and victim must be married, close blood relatives, or in an "intimate, familial relationship";

(3) the plaintiff must directly observe or be "sensorially aware" of the injury at the scene of the accident; and

(4) the plaintiff must suffer severe emotional distress.

Ortiz v. JDP Builders, Inc., 689 A.2d 1135, 1138 (N.F. 2015).

The first and fourth elements are not in dispute; the facts suggest the defendant's negligence and the plaintiff's severe emotional distress, and the assigning memo instructs to assume these elements can be proven.

Although this sub-issue is close, Poe is likely to meet the second element and demonstrate she and Valenzuela had an intimate, familial relationship. Poe is unlikely, however, to prevail on the third element. A court is unlikely to find that she directly observed or was sensorially aware of the accident and Valenzuela's resulting injury. Therefore, Poe is unlikely to succeed on her negligent infliction of emotional distress claim.

A. This introduction should address only the main issue, negligent infliction of emotional distress as a bystander, and not raise the sub-issues so it will be easier for the reader to follow.
B. This introduction contains a clear thesis statement.
C. This introduction should not include a final conclusion.
D. This introduction should include more facts.

EXAMPLES

Example 13-6

This question uses the cell phone manslaughter problem, which you can find in Appendix A.

If you represented Allison King, which of the following would be a good thesis statement to include in your introduction?

A. King acted without considering the obvious risk she was creating; therefore, her behavior is nothing short of gross negligence.
B. A court is likely to find King guilty of vehicular manslaughter.
C. King's case has several unfavorable facts, and few favorable ones.
D. The prosecution will likely prove that King is guilty of vehicular manslaughter because she acted with gross negligence and her actions cannot be exempted under the criminal statute's "emergency purposes" exception.

EXPLANATIONS

Explanation 13-1

A is incorrect. It's fine to personalize a rule, and some textbooks teach students to do that. But when a statute is involved, even when personalizing the rule, readers will want to know the exact language of the statute. Generally, quote statutes or the precise tests set forth by cases. (When discussing cases in your analysis, you're often encouraged to paraphrase the intricate language the court uses in its rationale so that it's shorter and easily understood by readers.) Here, the author didn't give the reader the precise language of the statute. And what looks like an effort to make the introduction "flow" is actually a dense writing style. ***B*** is incorrect. Although you might attach these labels internally, the reader will find it amateurish and distracting to find these labels in the text. The same convention applies to exams. Most professors believe all the components should be there (what the issue is, the rule, your analysis, and conclusion), but they also believe the components shouldn't be labeled. **C** is also incorrect. It's fine to include a rule statement about the Copyright Act as context for the fair use exception. It's also fine to include policy statements about the Copyright Act, although this author mistakenly neglected to provide a citation for those statements. Policy analysis is always stronger if supported by mandatory authority. How much context to provide is a judgment call, without a specific answer. Provide as much as the reader needs, without overburdening the reader. ***D*** is correct. The author tells us which factor will not be in dispute, and tells us why not. Further, she gives us a citation to mandatory authority telling us that courts disregard this factor in cases such as this one.

Explanation 13-2

A is correct. This introduction gives the reader no idea how the author predicts the court will rule. Further, like the first example, it doesn't quote the statute. You can probably see even more clearly here that failure to use the statute's exact words can be very confusing for a reader. ***B*** is incorrect. Your professor has probably told you that each section of the Discussion section of a memo should "stand alone," enabling a reader to read just that section and understand what's going on. You can assume, however, that readers either are familiar with the facts or will read the Facts section of the memo before reading the analysis. Don't repeat facts in the introduction. **C** is correct. The words *element* and *factor* are terms of art for legal readers. Each has a specific meaning and they are not interchangeable. An element is a part of the rule that a plaintiff must prove to win on that issue. The plaintiff must prove all of the elements to win. A factor, on the other hand, is a part of a rule that a court weighs against other factors to come to a decision. (See Chapter 8.) Courts may weigh factors equally or with varying levels of importance depending on the applicable law and circumstances of the case. Thus, if a plaintiff fails to prove an element, she will fail to prove her ultimate claim. But if she loses on a factor, it's not dispositive and another factor may be so strong that she can still ultimately prove her claim. ***D*** is incorrect. It's not always wrong to tell the reader how you predict that a court will decide each element or factor. But it's generally not necessary and clutters up the introduction. And to simply announce that a factor will be "at issue" wastes words. Legal readers will assume that both sides have arguments to make about every factor unless you have told them the parties will not dispute it and why.

Explanation 13-3

A is correct. The last two sentences form a thesis statement that gives readers a clear idea of the predicted outcome. ***B*** is also correct. Even though it's a good idea to quote a statute, you probably need to do more than cut and paste the whole statute into your paper. It's important to edit the statute so that all the critical language is there, but it's in a form easy for readers to absorb. Here, the author should include the precise language of the four factors courts apply. But much of the rest of the statute can be discarded. **C** is incorrect. The author neglected to let the reader know that courts in parody cases usually disregard the second factor. ***D*** is incorrect. There is no universally accepted way to order the components of a good introduction. Your professor may suggest an order for you to follow, especially if she views the introduction as the global CRAC, and of course you should follow those individual instructions. But most texts want you to include the components of a good introduction without demanding that you put those components in a certain order.

Explanation 13-4

A is incorrect. Sometimes the law is complicated and you'll need to untangle how several rules will apply. This introduction does a good job of leading the reader through the relevant rules. **B** is correct. The author has made it relatively easy for a reader to follow a complex series of rules. Other ways could be just as successful. For example, you could place the rule about ordinary gifts being irrevocable, California Civil Code § 1148, in the first paragraph, which explains how courts decide whether a gift is given in contemplation of marriage. **C** is incorrect. Chances are good that you understood enough about the law to begin reading this analysis. In any case, legal writing convention requires laying out a Facts section to familiarize readers with the relevant facts of the case. ***D*** is correct. The author has done a good job with the thesis statements.

EXPLANATIONS

Explanation 13-5

A is incorrect. With one issue and multiple sub-issues, the introduction should explain the outcome on each sub-issue as well as the overall issue. This introduction does that well. **B** is correct. The introduction starts and ends with a thesis statement about the overall issue. It also includes thesis statements about the disputed sub-issues. **C** is incorrect. Introductions do not always need a conclusion—which is a thesis statement—at the end, but it is rarely incorrect to include one. ***D*** is incorrect. While facts may be helpful in the introduction when you have adequate space, they are not essential, and the Discussion section will explain in full why each element is (or is not) met.

EXPLANATIONS

Explanation 13-6

A is incorrect. A thesis statement for your introduction should present your overall conclusion, not a minor conclusion. Asserting that King's actions will constitute gross negligence is only a conclusion regarding one of the crucial elements in this case, but not the general conclusion of your memo. **B** is correct. In contrast to A, B presents an overall conclusion. It would be a stronger thesis statement, however, if it included a primary reason for the conclusion. **C** is incorrect. This statement might inform the reader of the weakness of King's case, but it is not a thesis statement. It doesn't tell the reader the overall conclusion of your memo nor of any reasons for reaching that conclusion. ***D*** is correct. This sentence includes the main conclusion of the memo—that King is likely to be found guilty—and two main reasons for reaching this conclusion—that she acted with gross negligence and that the "emergency purposes" exception is likely not met here.

Checklist

Chapter 13: Writing the Introduction to the Discussion (or Argument)

✔	Plan for the components of a good introduction: a thesis, the main rule that applies to the issue, a statement about any parts of the rule that will not be at issue and a very brief explanation of why not, and a roadmap.
✔	Include a thesis statement.
✔	Include the main rule that applies to the issue.
✔	If any parts of the rule will be undisputed by the parties, briefly state and explain that.
✔	Include an explicit roadmap when the rule does not roadmap your paper.
✔	Include any other important statements that apply to the issue generally.
✔	Edit the introduction to include an appropriate amount of detail by giving legal readers enough to understand what the memo or brief addresses without including more detailed information that would be better addressed in the body of the Discussion or Argument.

You will find all of the chapter checklists compiled in Appendix D.

Writing the Question Presented (Objective)

Throughout law school, you're asked to answer difficult questions. This section of the memo lets *you* be the one to ask the question. So even if the issue—the disputed legal question—is provided to you, your task as a writer is to craft a useful "Question Presented." The Question Presented poses the legal question the memo resolves. It identifies the governing authority, tells the reader the precise legal question, and includes the key facts that control the outcome.

Terminology notes. Sometimes the Question Presented is called the "Issue," and sometimes it's referred to by its acronym, "QP."

WHAT YOU NEED TO KNOW ABOUT AN OFFICE MEMO'S QUESTION PRESENTED

A Question Presented includes three parts: (a) the applicable law, (b) the legal question, and (c) the determinative facts. Writers sometimes use a shorthand formula, called "Under/Does/When," to express all three of these parts:

Under: the applicable law

Does: the legal question

When: the determinative facts

Using this structure, the Question Presented is framed like this: "Under (*the applicable law*), does (*the legal question*) when (*the determinative facts*)?" The three parts are not always in this order. Any logical order is fine as long as the Question Presented contains all three components.

A Question Presented should generally be one complete sentence, phrased as a question. Readers need to quickly grasp the issue your memo addresses. Most writers therefore draft the Question Presented as one sentence, although some writers use two or more sentences. Also, the Question Presented is usually a complete sentence (rather than a phrase). The "under/does/when" formula is inherently a question and whether you use that formula or not, the Question Presented is generally just that—a question.

Try to phrase the Question Presented so that the answer would be either "yes" or "no" or a qualified "yes" or "no" (such as "likely yes" or "probably no"). The reader needs to see, as quickly as possible, what your bottom-line answer is. As we explain in Chapter 15 on Brief Answers, you'll add a little more explanation soon after the Question Presented. But the Question itself should be framed so the answer can be a simple yes or no.

Generally include only main issues in the Questions Presented. For instance, when you have two main issues—such as whether the plaintiff can prevail on a breach of contract claim and whether she can prevail on a tort claim alleging intentional interference with a contractual relationship—you would have two Questions Presented.

If you have more than one issue, call this section "Questions Presented" (or "Issues") and number them. As suggested previously, each separate issue addressed should be a separate Question Presented. If you have three main issues (as opposed to one issue with two sub-issues, which would mean you have only one issue), you should have three Questions Presented. Number them 1, 2, and 3, and number the Brief Answers (and call that section "Brief Answers," not "Brief Answer") to correspond to those Questions Presented.

If you write your Question Presented before writing your Discussion section, remember to go back to review and revise it. There's no particular order in which you must write the various sections of your memo. You'll generally want to have a draft Question Presented to get you started and guide your analysis, but after you've fully analyzed the problem you'll better understand which are the key facts and issues. For this reason, it's a good idea to review and revise your Question Presented after you've finished writing the Discussion section.

HOW TO WRITE AN OFFICE MEMO'S QUESTION PRESENTED

This section uses two main scenarios to walk you through the process of writing an objective Question Presented: the cell phone manslaughter problem in Appendix A and a multi-issue problem that includes a social host issue and a negligent entrustment issue.

PROBLEMS

Problems

Here is a quick overview of the cell phone manslaughter problem (for details see Appendix A). Allison King used her wireless phone, without a hands-free device, while driving in dense fog on a winding road on the edge of an ocean cliff. King placed the call to warn her friends about the dangerous conditions, as they would be meeting later. While she was making the call, she hit and killed a bicyclist. The prosecution will attempt to convict King of vehicular manslaughter by showing that she drove while committing an illegal act (driving while using a wireless phone without a hands-free device) and with gross negligence. King will argue that her actions fit within the "emergency purposes" exception to the wireless phone prohibition. She will also argue that she did not act with gross negligence.

Here is a quick overview of a social host liability and negligent entrustment problem that we use in this chapter. Joan Smith hosted a party that many of her co-workers attended, including Suzanne Flynn (and her husband Raymond Flynn) and Holly Hoyt (who drove her boyfriend, Stuart Hampton). Smith did not interact much with Hampton but she provided him and other party guests with beer. Hoyt, Hampton, and Raymond Flynn became intoxicated. Suzanne Flynn knew Hoyt was intoxicated, so at the end of the evening she suggested Hampton drive Hoyt's car. Hampton agreed. Hoyt knew Hampton had been drinking but did not believe he was too intoxicated to drive, so she gave him her car keys. Raymond Flynn rode with Hampton; Hampton caused an accident, seriously injuring Raymond Flynn. The Flynns sued in New Jersey state court alleging Smith is liable as a social host and Hoyt is liable for negligently entrusting her car to a drunk driver, Hampton.

Step 1: State the applicable law—the "under" component. In this part of the Question Presented, identify the relevant jurisdiction and the controlling legal authority in a broad sense. You generally won't identify the specific statutory citation unless it's well known and used as shorthand for the claim (like § 1983, part of the Civil Rights Act). Similarly, you usually won't identify the controlling case unless it's so central to the analysis that the case name serves as a shorthand to the reader for the governing principle (as might be the case with *Miranda* for confessions).

Some readers prefer—and some situations lend themselves to—using a relatively generic description of the applicable law. For instance, if you're asked to research whether there's any theory of liability under federal law under which your client could make a claim, you would probably identify the applicable law very generally:

> Under federal law . . .

On the other hand, often you will have a more discrete problem to address. For instance, imagine you represent Raymond and Suzanne Flynn in the social host liability example above. Assume that social host liability in New Jersey is governed by statute. That section might look something like this:

> Under New Jersey statutory law . . .

Using that same problem, assume that negligent entrustment in New Jersey is governed by common law (rather than a statute). That section might look something like this:

> Under New Jersey common law . . .

Now we'll draft a Question Presented for the cell phone manslaughter problem in Appendix A. That case is governed by a California statute, which makes it illegal to drive "a vehicle in the commission of an unlawful act, not amounting to felony, and with gross negligence." Another California statute makes it illegal (not a felony) to "drive a motor vehicle while using a wireless telephone unless that telephone is specifically designed and configured to allow hands-free listening and talking, and is used in that manner while driving." That section creates an exception when the driver is using the cell phone for "emergency purposes." You need interpretive case law to finally resolve the issue, but in this step identify only the applicable law for the main issue. That law is California's vehicular manslaughter statute, so you could phrase the "under" portion of the Question Presented like this:

> Under California's vehicular manslaughter statute . . .

This wording doesn't refer to the governing statute by its citation. Instead, it's referred to by name, which the reader will understand much more easily. (Few readers memorize statutory citations.)

If the issue were simply whether the cell phone use was for "emergency purposes," the first section might be phrased like this:

> For purposes of California's vehicular manslaughter statute, under the prohibition on using a cell phone while driving . . .

Step 2: State the specific legal question—the "does" component. Here, identify for the reader the underlying legal issue that's in dispute. Use the rule's actual language. If the rule comes from a statute, refer to the legal issue in statutory language, not in the generic wording that you might otherwise use. If your rule comes from court opinions, use the terms of art the courts use. Using these "buzz words" helps the reader understand the key elements you're going to address.

This section of the "under/does/when" formula of the Question Presented might be written like this for the cell phone manslaughter problem:

> . . . does a person commit vehicular manslaughter . . .

Similarly, for the social host issue, you might write:

> . . . is a person liable as a social host . . .

Using the social host problem but considering the second issue, negligent entrustment, you might write:

> . . . is a person liable for negligent entrustment . . .

Generally, you'll refer to the main rule in this section, although some readers will expect more detail here, including the terms of art from the disputed element or elements. (In the latter situation, the main rule's terms of art would be included in the "under" section.) There, the "under" and "does" components might look like this:

> Under New Jersey's social host statute, does a host have knowledge that a guest is intoxicated . . .

Similarly, if you're focusing on the "emergency purposes" exception outlined in the cell phone manslaughter problem, this section might look like this:

> For purposes of California's vehicular manslaughter statute, under the prohibition on using a cell phone while driving does a person use a cell phone for "emergency purposes" . . .

Note how the statute's terms of art are included (both "vehicular manslaughter" and "emergency purposes"). If this were the only contested issue, a Question Presented framed this narrowly immediately lets the reader know the exact issue you're discussing.

Step 3: State the determinative facts — the "when" component. Determinative facts are the key facts that most affect the outcome. You can't include every fact, and you don't need to. But you should remain objective and include the key favorable and unfavorable facts. In addition, the facts should be actual *facts*, not legal conclusions. Similarly, principles of law, like "damages have to be mitigated," aren't facts. Save them for the Discussion section of your memo instead. And what's a fact versus what's a conclusion depends, in part, on your legal issue. For instance, whether a person was "negligent" is generally a legal conclusion, not a fact (the underlying fact creating negligence may be that the defendant ran a red light, for instance). But imagine that it is uncontested that the plaintiff was negligent and the issue is whether the negligent plaintiff is barred from suing the defendant, who also caused the plaintiff's injuries. In that case, the plaintiff's own negligence is a fact. Including the determinative facts in the Question Presented allows the reader who doesn't know your facts to still understand the issue. For this reason, it might help to write the Facts section of your memo before you draft the Question Presented. For more help figuring out which facts are determinative, see Chapter 16.

Let's consider the relevant facts in the cell phone manslaughter problem. If the issue was whether King acted with "gross negligence," the "when" section of the "under/does/when" formula might be written like this:

> . . . when she hit and killed a bicyclist as she dialed her cell phone while driving on a winding two-lane road on the edge of a cliff in dense fog?

If, on the other hand, the issue you're concerned with is whether King was entitled to the "emergency purpose" defense, this section might look like this:

> . . . when she placed the call in order to warn her friends not to drive because road conditions were so dangerous?

Notice how the relevant facts change depending on the issue. The facts necessary to resolve the "gross negligence" element are different from the facts necessary to resolve the "emergency purposes" defense.

For the social host problem, if the issue was whether the social host was liable, the determinative facts component might look like this:

> . . . when she provided alcohol to a guest after the guest displayed signs of intoxication, and the guest later drove and seriously injured his passenger?

Step 4: Put them all together. Simply add the three sections to make one complete sentence phrased as a question. You may need to rearrange the order or edit for conciseness, but generally, you can just plug the steps in using the same order you drafted them. Hence, the Question Presented for the California cell phone manslaughter problem might look something like this:

> Under California's vehicular manslaughter statute, does a person commit vehicular manslaughter when she hit and killed a bicyclist as she dialed her cell phone while driving on a winding two-lane road on the edge of a cliff in dense fog?

Assume you are focusing on the narrow "emergency exception" issue, the final Question Presented might look something like this:

> For purposes of California's vehicular manslaughter statute, under the prohibition on using a cell phone while driving, does a person use a cell phone for "emergency purposes" when she placed the call to warn her friends not to drive because road conditions were so dangerous?

And for the New Jersey social host hypothetical, the complete Questions Presented (notice it is called "Questions Presented" because there are two) might look like this:

1) Under New Jersey statutory law, is a person liable as a social host when she provided alcohol to a guest after the guest displayed signs of intoxication, and the guest later drove and seriously injured his passenger?
2) Under New Jersey common law, is a person liable for negligent entrustment when she handed her car keys to a visibly intoxicated person but she believed the person was capable of driving?

You can also switch the order of the sections. For instance, for the second Question Presented above, you could draft it like this:

> Is a person liable for negligent entrustment under New Jersey common law when she handed her car keys to a visibly intoxicated person but she believed the person was capable of driving?

Each of these Questions Presented works, because the reader understands all of the components (the "under," the "does," and the "when").

EXAMPLES

Review the following examples. For each example, there may be more than one correct answer, but try to choose the *best* answer. Explain to yourself why you have chosen that answer. Then read the explanations in the last section of this chapter to check your work.

EXAMPLES

Example 14-1

This question uses the cell phone manslaughter problem, which you can find in Appendix A.

If you were drafting an objective memo in King's case, which of the following would be determinative facts that should be included in your Question Presented?

A. Gross negligence is the exercise of so slight a degree of care as to raise a presumption of conscious indifference to the consequences.
B. King has been charged with vehicular manslaughter in California.
C. While she was driving, King called her friends to warn them of hazardous road conditions.
D. King failed to appreciate the risk she was causing on the road when she decided to call her friends.

EXAMPLES

Example 14-2

This question uses the cell phone manslaughter problem, which you can find in Appendix A.

Is King likely guilty when she made a cell phone call while driving on a narrow winding road in dense fog, but did so to warn her friends of the dangerous driving conditions?

This is an . . .

A. effective Question Presented because it includes the determinative facts.
B. effective Question Presented because it poses the key legal question—whether King is guilty.

C. ineffective Question Presented because it omits the applicable law.
D. ineffective Question Presented because it provides too much detail in terms of the determinative facts.

EXAMPLES

Example 14-3

This question uses a hypothetical negligent infliction of emotional distress problem (but not the negligent infliction of emotional distress problem in Appendix C).

> The issue is whether Jones is liable for negligent infliction of emotional distress under Indiana common law, considering the fact that the plaintiff was not married to the deceased when he died, and whether Chen is barred from suing because the statute of limitations has expired.

This is an . . .

A. effective Question Presented because it includes the applicable law, the legal questions, and the determinative facts.
B. ineffective Question Presented because it omits determinative facts.
C. ineffective Question Presented because it isn't phrased as a question.
D. ineffective Question Presented for the reasons stated in both B and C.

EXAMPLES

Example 14-4

This question uses the cell phone manslaughter problem, which you can find in Appendix A.

> Under California's vehicular manslaughter statute, does a person commit vehicular manslaughter when she violates a traffic law and drives with gross negligence, killing someone?

This is an . . .

A. ineffective Question Presented because it fails to identify the specific legal question.
B. ineffective Question Presented because it fails to include the determinative facts.
C. effective Question Presented because it includes all three components of a good question presented: under, does, and when.
D. effective Question Presented because it's short and easily readable.

EXAMPLES

Example 14-5

This question uses the cell phone manslaughter problem, which you can find in Appendix A.

> Under California's vehicular manslaughter statute, does a person commit vehicular manslaughter when she makes a cell phone call while driving on a narrow, foggy road, or does she have to do more than drive unsafely even though she thought she was driving safely?

This is an . . .

- **A.** effective Question Presented because it includes the applicable law, the specific legal question, and the determinative facts.
- **B.** effective Question Presented because it identifies both the main legal question and the potential defense.
- **C.** ineffective Question Presented because it isn't capable of being answered with a yes/no answer.
- **D.** ineffective Question Presented because it omits the applicable law and specific legal question.

EXAMPLES

Example 14-6

This question uses the negligent infliction of emotional distress problem, which you can find in Appendix C.

> Under New Fornia common law, is a bystander barred from recovering for negligent infliction of emotional distress when the injured person was the bystander's fiancé and the couple had been dating five years, spent most nights together, and owned a car together?

This is an . . .

- **A.** effective Question Presented because it includes the applicable law, the specific legal question, and the determinative facts.
- **B.** effective Question Presented because it's easy to read, even though it omits some determinative facts.
- **C.** ineffective Question Presented because it omits the determinative facts.
- **D.** ineffective Question Presented because it's too long.

EXPLANATIONS

Explanation 14-1

A is incorrect. This sentence states a legal standard, not a fact. You should leave the presentation and explication of legal standards for the Discussion section of your memo. **B** is also incorrect. The Question Presented needs to include determinative facts—facts that will play a crucial role in resolving a case. Here, the fact that King is being charged with vehicular manslaughter is a fact of the case, but not one that needs to be considered to resolve the main issue or question in this case: whether Ms. King should be found guilty of vehicular manslaughter. **C** is the best answer. The fact that King called her friends while she was driving to warn them of the hazardous conditions will be key in resolving this case, and needs to be included as one of the determinative facts stated in the Question Presented. **D** is incorrect. This statement is not a fact of the case, but a conclusion that could be drawn from the actual facts.

Explanation 14-2

A is not the best answer because this Question Presented is not effective. This Question Presented describes the determinative facts, and it does so objectively by including facts that suggest King might have acted with gross negligence as well as facts that suggest she may be eligible for the "emergency purposes" exception. But it doesn't identify the applicable law, so it isn't effective. **B** is also not the best answer. This Question Presented is ineffective at least in part because the ultimate legal question can be phrased more clearly than "is King guilty." The reader doesn't know what King might be guilty of. In the broadest sense, the legal question is more clearly phrased as "does a person commit vehicular manslaughter." In a more narrow sense, the underlying legal question may be whether King acted with gross negligence or whether King made the call for an emergency purpose. Any of these three options would provide the reader with more guidance than the generic "is she guilty" phrase. **C** is the best answer. This Question Presented doesn't identify the applicable law, which is the California vehicular manslaughter statute. The Question Presented could also be improved by phrasing the ultimate legal question more clearly, as explained in B. **D** is incorrect. As noted in the explanation for answer A, the determinative facts are well described.

EXPLANATIONS

Explanation 14-3

A is incorrect. Although the Question Presented includes the applicable law for the first issue, it doesn't for the second. It's also phrased as a statement rather than a question, and it doesn't include sufficient determinative facts to understand the issues. It's therefore ineffective. In addition, most professors would expect this Question Presented to be divided into two separately numbered questions (one for each issue). ***B*** is true, but it isn't the best answer because **C** is also true; hence, **D** is the best answer. This Question Presented includes two separate legal questions—negligent infliction of emotional distress and the statute of limitations. But as noted in B, the example omits determinative facts. How long after the incident occurred was the suit filed? And what was the relationship between the plaintiff and the deceased? The Question Presented tells us they weren't married, but it doesn't tell us what their relationship was. In addition, as noted in C, a Question Presented isn't usually phrased as a statement. Readers will generally expect a question that is answered by the Brief Answer (see Chapter 15).

EXPLANATIONS

Explanation 14-4

A is incorrect. This Question Presented does identify the specific legal question—vehicular manslaughter. ***B*** is the best answer. The phrases "violates a traffic law" and "drives with gross negligence" are legal conclusions, not facts. The reader needs to know the underlying determinative facts, such as "when she uses a cell phone while driving" (the act that violates the traffic law) or "when she places a call while driving on a narrow two-lane road over a cliff in a dense fog" (the acts that constitute gross negligence). In addition, this Question Presented merely states the elements of the statute, making the answer an indisputable "yes": if a person violates a traffic law and drives with gross negligence and kills someone, she has committed vehicular manslaughter. But the reader needs to know whether, *in this case*, the defendant has in fact violated the traffic law and driven with gross negligence. More facts are necessary to answer that question. **C** is incorrect. Although the Question Presented uses "under," "does," and "when," for the reasons stated in B the determinative facts are absent. ***D*** is also incorrect. This Question Presented is short, which is good, but it omits determinative facts, which outweighs the benefit of having a shorter and easily read Question Presented.

EXPLANATIONS

Explanation 14-5

A is incorrect. Although this Question Presented includes all the necessary components, it's ineffective for the reason C is correct. **B** is also incorrect. Having to "do more than drive unsafely" isn't a defense. To the extent it infers a lack of gross negligence it's simply the absence of an element. **C** is the best answer. This Question Presented isn't capable of being answered with a simple yes/no answer. It's also phrased a bit casually for a Question Presented. ***D*** is not the best answer. The Question Presented is ineffective, but not for the reasons stated in D. The applicable law and specific legal question are included. But they are clouded by the complex question.

EXPLANATIONS

Explanation 14-6

A is the best answer. This Question Presented includes all the necessary components—the under/does/when sections—and they are properly developed. ***B*** is not the best answer. Even though this Question Presented is effective and relatively easy to read, it doesn't omit any determinative facts. **C** is incorrect for the reasons stated in B. ***D*** is also incorrect. Questions Presented should be as short as possible, but they need to contain all three parts of the "under/does/when" formula, and this example does that in one (although slightly long) sentence.

Checklist

Chapter 14: Writing the Question Presented (Objective)

✔	Use a format your professor recommends, "under, does, when" or "whether, when."
✔	State the applicable law (the "under" component).
✔	State the specific legal question (the "does" component).
✔	State the determinative facts (the "when" component).
✔	Put the components together.
✔	Usually make the Question Presented one complete sentence.
✔	Phrase the Question Presented as a question so the answer would be either "yes" or "no" or a qualified "yes" or "no" (such as "likely yes" or "probably no").
✔	Include only the main issue in the QP.
✔	If you have more than one QP, use numbers to separate them and use that same scheme for later parts of the memo.

You will find all of the chapter checklists compiled in Appendix D.

CHAPTER 15

Writing the Brief Answer

Unlike television detective shows, legal memos are best when they tell the reader the answer in the beginning. That's because lawyers tend to be most comfortable when they know exactly where they're going. When busy readers know the answer at the outset they can read the rest of the memo to discover the reasons for this and ask themselves whether it seems correct.

WHAT YOU NEED TO KNOW ABOUT A BRIEF ANSWER

The Brief Answer should answer the Question Presented and briefly summarize the key reasons for that answer. Assert your answer and then give your main reasons for it, which will typically include key "buzz words" from the legal rule that applies, combined with the determinative facts. Don't go into unnecessary detail. Most lawyers think it's sufficient to write the Brief Answer in a way that assumes the reader is familiar with the legal and factual analysis you provide in your Discussion. Brief Answers are typically two to three sentences. Some professors and attorneys may prefer a slightly longer version that includes a concise statement of the applicable rule and more summary of the reasons for the conclusions. Generally, even counting these "slightly longer" versions, Brief Answers come in two sizes: small and extra small!

The first sentence should be a one- or two-word answer to the Question Presented, such as "Yes.", "No.", "Probably Yes.", or "Probably No." Aim to indicate an accurate degree of certainty about your answer. Avoid sending mixed signals about your level of certainty within your Brief Answer or between your Brief Answer and the rest of your memo. Also, don't waffle when you have confidence in an answer. But if you really can't accurately answer the Question Presented because of legal or factual uncertainty, use a term that suggests your uncertainty such as "Maybe yes . . ." and explain briefly why your conclusion is tentative or what additional facts you'd need to know.

Be conclusory: don't discuss or evaluate the strength of arguments. Writing is conclusory if it states a legal conclusion without supporting it with analysis. In your Brief Answer, that's the approach to take: state your answer and the key reasons for that conclusion, without explaining your underlying analysis. (Conclusory writing is usually a mistake in the Discussion, but in the Brief Answer, it's the right thing to do. The answer is supposed to be brief.)

For instance:

> Yes. The defendant committed burglary because he entered his neighbor's apartment without permission and with intent to steal her jewelry.

And if you wanted to include a concise statement of the rule in your Brief Answer, it might instead look like this:

> Yes. Under relevant state law, a person commits burglary when he enters a building without authority and with intent to commit a felony or theft inside. The defendant committed burglary here because he entered his neighbor's apartment without permission and with intent to steal her jewelry.

These examples provide the key conclusions that led to the answer ("because . . ."), melding law and fact without going into a detailed explanation of the analysis that supports the conclusions. Don't explain that the answer depends on whether the facts show the legal conclusion at issue, such as "Whether the defendant committed burglary depends on whether he had authority to enter. Several facts show that he had authority, such as his past history of helping his neighbor bring in the mail while she was on vacation and that they recently started dating. But some facts do not, such as that she was not on vacation when he entered and that she had not asked him for help for over a year or given him a key." The reader can turn to your Discussion section for your analysis and discussion of alternative arguments. Keep your Brief Answer concise and conclusory.

Generally, don't include citations or discussions of authority. Your conclusions will come from your analysis of authority, but your Brief Answer shouldn't cite or discuss any particular authorities. There are a couple of exceptions. First, when the Question Presented poses a statutory issue, you may refer to the statute and include any essential statutory requirements in your Brief Answer. Second, when you have a seminal case that controls all or nearly all of your analysis, it's okay to note and cite the case.

You should have a Brief Answer for each Question Presented. As explained in Chapter 14, when you have multiple Questions Presented, number them 1, 2, and 3, and number the Brief Answers to correspond to them. In those instances, remember to use the header "Brief Answers," not "Brief Answer."

HOW TO WRITE A BRIEF ANSWER

Using the copyright and fair use problem in Appendix B, we'll walk you through the process of writing a Brief Answer.

PROBLEMS

Problem

Here is a quick overview of the copyright and fair use problem (for details see Appendix B). Page is suing Dash for violating the Copyright Act when Dash wrote a song based on Page's song (which in copyright terms is called the "original"), "Red, White, and Blue." Dash's song uses the structure and many lyrics of the original but changes the original song's political message. The music of the two songs is not at issue, only the lyrics. Page expects that Dash will argue that his song is a parody that falls under the fair use exception to the Copyright Act. The court will consider the relevant factors set out in the fair use statute, 17 U.S.C. § 107: whether the copy was transformative and targeted the original; whether it took more than necessary of the original; and whether it will interfere with the original's market.

Step 1: Carefully read your Question Presented and decide on the answer. You'll want to do this after you've written the Discussion section of your memo because often writing that section will crystallize the answer in your mind. Look at the phrasing of the Question Presented. Does the factual and legal analysis warrant a certain "Yes." or "No." answer? Would a "Probably yes." or "Probably no." better capture your degree of certainty?

An office memo on the copyright and fair use problem might include the following Question Presented:

> Does Billy Dash's rock song fall under the Copyright Act's fair use exception when it purposely used lyrics from Jenna Page's anti-establishment rock anthem to imitate its pattern but critiqued its message by celebrating patriotism?

Step 2: Write the first sentence of your Brief Answer, starting with a one- or two-word answer to the Question Presented. Imagine that after a thorough legal and factual analysis in the Discussion section you decide that Dash's song is probably fair use. Responding to the Question Presented, the first sentence of your Brief Answer might be:

> Probably yes.

Step 3: Write another sentence or two summarizing the reasons for the answer; be conclusory. If your professor or supervising attorney expects a slightly longer version that includes more detail, then your Brief Answer might be a bit longer and include more specificity.

Here, you might add the following:

> Probably yes. Dash used Page's song as a means to criticize the original and create an identifiable parody. The copy thus transforms the original work's anti-establishment message to an opposing political viewpoint and creates a different market for the critique.

This Brief Answer works. It starts with a one- or two-word answer to the Question Presented. It briefly summarizes the key reasons for that answer in a conclusory manner, melding law and fact, without evaluating the strength of various arguments. It doesn't cite or discuss specific authority. It's brief.

EXAMPLES

Review the following examples. For each example, there may be more than one correct answer, but try to choose the *best* answer. Explain to yourself why you have chosen that answer. Then read the explanations in the last section of this chapter to check your work.

EXAMPLES

Example 15-1

This question uses the copyright and fair use problem, which you can find in Appendix B.

Question Presented

Does Billy Dash's rock song fall under the Copyright Act's fair use exception when it purposely used lyrics from Jenna Page's anti-establishment rock anthem to imitate its pattern but critique its message by celebrating patriotism?

Brief Answer

Likely yes. The fair use statute provides various factors to weigh when determining whether an allegedly infringing work is fair use. Whether the parody is transformative enough or borrows too heavily from the original are questions that a jury will end up deciding, as there is no bright line rule to determine these factors. It is undisputed that Dash's song is for commercial purposes and, while not a pivotal issue, this nonetheless weighs in Page's favor. Also, Dash's song uses the same musical genre and might compete in the same market. On the other hand, Dash could argue that his work criticizes the political message of Page's song and as such is parody that falls within the fair use exception.

A. This is typical of a good Brief Answer because it tells the reader about the various important arguments.
B. This Brief Answer should be more concise and conclusory instead of weighing alternative arguments.
C. This Brief Answer should include specific references to cases and provide citations.
D. This is a strong Brief Answer because it begins with "Likely yes", immediately signaling the conclusion to the reader.

EXAMPLES

Example 15-2

This question uses the copyright and fair use problem, which you can find in Appendix B.

Question Presented

Does Billy Dash's rock song fall under the Copyright Act's fair use exception when it purposely used lyrics from Jenna Page's anti-establishment rock anthem to imitate its pattern but critique its message by celebrating patriotism?

Brief Answer

Dash's song is parody, which constitutes a fair use of copyrighted material for commercial use. Although the large amount of original lyrics he used may weigh against fair use, his critical transformation of the lyrics changed the song in such a way that it would no longer appeal to the same market as the original.

The writer could improve this Brief Answer by . . .

A. starting with a "yes" or "no" type of answer.
B. cutting out the factual detail.
C. softening the first sentence's tone.
D. this Brief Answer cannot be improved.

EXAMPLES

Example 15-3

This question uses the copyright and fair use problem, which you can find in Appendix B.

Question Presented

Does Billy Dash's rock song fall under the Copyright Act's fair use exception when it purposely used lyrics from Jenna Page's anti-establishment rock anthem to imitate its pattern but critique its message by celebrating patriotism?

Brief Answer

Probably not. Dash's lyrics are not entitled to fair use protection because his song would likely serve as a substitute for Page's original. Unlike the allegedly infringing work in *Mattel v. Walking Mountain Productions*, 353 F.3d 792 (9th Cir. 2003), which served a different market than the original, Dash's work is similar to Page's in that both provide political commentary set to rock music, potentially confusing listeners and causing market harm to the copyright holder.

A. This Brief Answer should state what action the client wants the court to take.
B. This Brief Answer should state and explain the rule of law first.
C. This Brief Answer should include more facts.
D. This Brief Answer should not include the case reference and citation.

Example 15-4

This question uses the copyright and fair use problem, which you can find in Appendix B.

Question Presented

Does Billy Dash's rock song fall under the Copyright Act's fair use exception when it purposely used lyrics from Jenna Page's anti-establishment rock anthem to imitate its pattern but critique its message by celebrating patriotism?

Brief Answer

Probably yes. The owner of a copyrighted work usually has exclusive rights over the work. There is, however, a fair use exception. To qualify as fair use, a work must transform the original work without copying more than necessary or harming its market value. These are statutory factors. Dash borrowed significantly from twenty-three of the original thirty-six lines of Page's song. Some words and phrases are exactly the same, such as "Red, white, and blue." By changing some of the lyrics, however, Dash significantly changed the meaning of Page's song. Specifically, the political message of Dash's song is different than that of Page's song. A court will therefore probably rule in favor of Dash because he borrowed the amount of lyrics necessary to invoke the tension of a parody between his work and Page's. A court will probably also rule that Dash's parody will do minimal damage to Page's market value because Page has an established fan base of listeners who are concerned about economic inequality and are critical of the government's response; those fans will not support Dash's lyrics. Thus, Dash's song probably falls within the fair use exception to the Copyright Act.

The writer could improve this Brief Answer by . . .

A. editing it to make it more conclusory.
B. adding analogical reasoning.
C. concluding more broadly at the end.
D. this Brief Answer cannot be improved.

EXAMPLES

Example 15-5

This question uses a hypothetical negligence problem.

Question Presented

Under Illinois common law, is Jones liable for negligence when she saw a fire and yelled that she would call 911, but then took an incoming call and did not call for emergency services for another seven minutes?

Brief Answer

Probably yes. Although there is no general duty to rescue those in danger, once a person begins a rescue attempt she creates a duty. Others who might have attempted a rescue may be dissuaded once they know of another rescue attempt. Jones acted negligently because she announced she would call 911, creating a duty to follow through on that rescue attempt. Waiting for seven minutes before she actually made the call increased the likelihood of danger.

Which of the following sentences in this Brief Answer is a strong legal conclusion?

A. Although there is no general duty to rescue those in danger, once a person begins a rescue attempt a duty is created.
B. Others who might have attempted a rescue may be dissuaded once they know of another rescue attempt.
C. Jones acted negligently because she announced she would call 911, creating a duty to follow through on that rescue attempt.
D. Waiting for seven minutes after yelling she would call 911 before she actually made the call increased the likelihood of danger.

EXAMPLES

Example 15-6

This question uses the negligent infliction of emotional distress problem, which you can find in Appendix C.

Question Presented

Under New Fornia common law, is a bystander barred from recovering for negligent infliction of emotional distress when the injured victim is the bystander's fiancé and the couple had been dating five years, spent most nights together, and owned a car together?

Brief Answer

No.

A. This Brief Answer should be more concise and conclusory.
B. This Brief Answer is ineffective because Brief Answers should never simply state the conclusion but instead should always include factual details to support the legal conclusion.
C. This Brief Answer would be more effective if it included—briefly—the reasons that support the writer's conclusions.
D. This Brief Answer is ineffective because Brief Answers should always be qualified with a "probably" or "likely" to avoid being wrong.

EXPLANATIONS

Explanation 15-1

A is incorrect. Save your evaluation of reasons and alternative arguments for your Discussion. The Brief Answer should simply state your conclusions and very briefly summarize the essential reasons in a way that assumes the reader is familiar with your legal and factual analysis. You can tell that this example weighs alternative arguments because it uses language like "on the other hand." Likewise, you can tell that this example doesn't assume the reader is familiar with the law because it starts out by explaining that the statute provides factors and that there's no bright line rule. Further, you may have spotted the language "while not a pivotal issue" and noted that this example fails to focus on only essential reasons. **B** is the best answer. This Brief Answer should be more conclusory instead of weighing alternative arguments. **C** is incorrect. Brief Answers typically do not provide specific references to cases or citations. **D** is not the best answer. Although it's true that starting with "likely yes." (or "likely no.") is helpful to the reader, this Brief Answer is not strong for the reasons stated in B.

Explanation 15-2

A is the best answer. A Brief Answer should start with a one- or two-word answer to the Question Presented. **B** is incorrect. Unless the Question Presented is a pure legal question, good Brief Answers meld legal conclusions with the facts. **C** is also incorrect. The conclusory tone is characteristic of a good Brief Answer. **D** is incorrect for the reasons stated in A.

EXPLANATIONS

Explanation 15-3

A is incorrect. Brief Answers don't state what action the client wants the court to take. They provide answers to Questions Presented, giving legal conclusions based on the essential facts. **B** is not the best answer, though perhaps partly correct. Some readers indeed prefer a concise statement of the applicable rule in the Brief Answer. But Brief Answers typically don't include an explanation of the rule. The Discussion section is where the memo provides more detailed rule development, as addressed in Chapter 9. **C** is incorrect. This example includes the determinative facts, and that is all a Brief Answer should include. **D** is the best answer. Brief Answers usually don't refer to specific cases or provide case citations. In this example, the reference to *Mattel* is unnecessary because, although useful, it's not a blockbuster case that controls all of the analysis. The Brief Answer would be improved by editing out this case reference and citation.

EXPLANATIONS

Explanation 15-4

A is the best answer. Readers' tastes will vary, but most would probably agree that you could improve this Brief Answer by distilling down its critical conclusions and reasoning and stating those in a concise, conclusory manner. Here's one way you could revise it:

> Probably yes. Dash borrowed the amount of lyrics necessary to invoke Page's original and changed some of the lyrics to transform it into a critical parody of Page's anti-establishment stance. The parody will do minimal damage to Page's market value because Page has an established fan base of listeners who are concerned about economic inequality and critical of the government's response and who will not support Dash's lyrics.

B is incorrect. Brief Answers should not include analogical reasoning. Save that for the analysis in your Discussion. **C** is also incorrect. A Brief Answer should summarize conclusions precisely and doesn't need to broaden its conclusions at the end as essays in the liberal arts sometimes do. **D** is also incorrect for the reasons stated in A.

Explanation 15-5

A is incorrect. This sentence is a statement of the rule, not the legal conclusion. **B** is also incorrect; it provides the justification for the rule, but does not include a legal conclusion. Most readers wouldn't find this sentence necessary in the Brief Answer (although it would be helpful to explain the rule in the memo's Discussion section). **C** is the best answer. This sentence explains that Jones acted negligently and it explains, briefly, the reasons for that legal conclusion. The word "because" helps signal the reader that these are the key conclusions that lead to the answer on the issue of negligence. **D** is not the best answer. This sentence states the rationale that supports the legal conclusion, but it isn't a strong statement of the legal conclusion itself.

EXPLANATIONS

Explanation 15-6

A is incorrect. It is impossible to have a more concise and conclusory Brief Answer than the word "no." **B** is also incorrect; although Brief Answers will usually include factual details to support the legal conclusion, that isn't always required. For example, if the Question Presented asked a legal issue with a clear-cut answer, a single word may be an appropriate Brief Answer. **C** is the best answer. Most readers expect some preview, before reading the entire Discussion section, about why the answer is no. Furthermore, in cases without an obviously correct answer—such as this case—you may want to qualify your answer with "probably" or "likely." **D** is not the best answer for the reasons stated in B.

Checklist

Chapter 15: Writing the Brief Answer

✔	Aim to indicate an accurate degree of certainty about your answer to the Question Presented.
✔	Start with "Yes" or "No" and if it is really a close call, add "Probably" or "Likely" before the "yes" or "no."
✔	Briefly summarize the key reasons for the answer, melding law and fact.
✔	Be conclusory without discussing or evaluating authorities and arguments.
✔	Usually do not include citations.
✔	Keep it short—typically about two or three sentences.
✔	Have a Brief Answer for each Question Presented and if there is more than one, make the numbers match.

You will find all of the chapter checklists compiled in Appendix D.

CHAPTER 16

Writing the Facts

In the Facts section of the memo, you tell the story. It's probably the easiest section to write—because the facts are often (but not always) the easiest part of the problem to understand. But don't let this lull you into believing you can write the Facts section without much thought or effort. And don't just copy and paste into your memo the facts provided by your professor in the assignment (which may be considered plagiarism). This is a genuine writing task requiring effort and skill.

WHAT YOU NEED TO KNOW ABOUT AN OFFICE MEMO'S FACTS SECTION

Include every fact you mention in the Discussion section as well as any other fact that is necessary for the story to make sense. Describe the client and what she wants first, and then develop the facts more fully. Some writers like to think of this as the "who, what, where" part of the memo. Include as much detail as necessary either for the analysis or to understand the story. Because including lots of specific dates can clog up your writing and make it harder for the reader to follow, leave out specific dates unless they're relevant to the legal issue (for instance, when the legal issue depends on the timing of particular events, such as in statute of limitation issues, claims regarding default for failure to file an answer, etc.).

Include procedural facts. The Facts section should note what has happened in terms of legal action to date. And as with substantive facts, specific dates aren't necessary unless they're legally significant.

State the facts and just the facts. This section is called the "Facts" for a reason. Don't include the law. That will go in the Discussion section. Similarly, the Facts section is not the place for analysis, characterizations of the facts, or inferences. You'll have plenty of space to do that in the Discussion section. Keep the Facts section clearly factual. You can, though, include a description of what each party is claiming, as their claims are facts. Just don't state whether those claims have merit in the Facts section. Save that for the Discussion.

Frame the facts objectively. The facts should not be told just from your client's perspective (assuming you have been put in the role of an attorney drafting a memo on behalf of your client). The reader needs to understand all sides of the issue. Include facts that hurt your client's case, not just those that help.

Because objective memos are usually used for predictive purposes and strategy, you're not doing the client any favors by making the facts sound more compelling than they actually are. Be accurate, objective, and neutral. This contrasts with a persuasive brief, where you still have to avoid making overt arguments and leaving out relevant facts, but your goal there is for the facts to have a subtly persuasive effect.

Generally write the facts in chronological order. Stories usually make the most sense when they start at the beginning, then explain what happened in the middle, and then tell what happened at the end. Sometimes, though, another organization makes more logical sense. For instance, if two parallel situations were brewing, explaining the facts in true chronological order would jumble the two scenarios together and likely confuse the reader. As with all writing tasks, use your best judgment, but absent a reason to do otherwise, ordering the facts in chronological order is wise. And because the facts already happened, you'll generally use past tense in the Facts section.

Facts sections are usually written in regular paragraph format. Unlike complaints and some Statements of Material Facts for motions, which are often drafted using numbered sentences or very short numbered paragraphs, Facts sections in office memos are most often written in regular narrative format. If you have a long Facts section, consider using subheadings to break the facts into logical chunks. This will make the Facts section easier to read and understand.

Be sure to revise the Facts section after you've completed the Discussion section. Some writers like to begin with the Facts because it's the part of the memo they understand the best. If you do that, first be sure that you don't spend too much time on the facts and run out of time (or space) for the harder analysis. Second, be sure to go back and review the

Facts section after you've completed the Discussion section, because only then can you appreciate which facts are truly relevant and which aren't.

Every fact that's necessary for the analysis needs to be in the Facts section, so double-check to make sure you've included them all (and correspondingly omitted facts irrelevant to the legal analysis unless they're necessary to understand the story). Even though it may seem repetitive to include everything in the Facts section (because all the necessary facts are also in the Discussion section), readers won't always read the memo in order. They may jump around. And Facts sections have a separate purpose. Clients are often told to review the Facts section carefully and make sure that all the facts are correct and none are omitted. In that sense, the Facts section ensures the factual basis for your analysis is accurate and it protects you in the event your analysis is based on a fact that turns out to be inaccurate.

HOW TO WRITE AN OFFICE MEMO'S FACTS SECTION

This section uses two scenarios to walk you through the process of writing the Facts section of an office memo. We'll write a Facts section for a hypothetical employment law problem for this chapter and use some examples from the copyright and fair use problem.

PROBLEMS

Problems

Here is a quick overview of the employment discrimination problem for this chapter. Mark Yokus, who owns R & J Construction Company, was recently served with a complaint by the Equal Employment Opportunity Commission (EEOC). One of his employees filed a complaint with the EEOC alleging R & J Construction engaged in unlawful employment discrimination in violation of Title VII. The claimant, Sarah Clark, worked for R & J for five years as a supervising electrician. In that capacity, she regularly earned overtime (averaging 57 hours of work per week).

On Friday, May 28, 2010, Yokus learned that Clark was four months pregnant. Yokus became concerned about health and safety risks for Clark and her fetus if she were to continue working as a supervising electrician. The same day, Yokus shared his concerns with Clark and offered to transfer her to an office job for seven months while continuing to pay her at her current hourly rate. That position is a 40-hour-a-week job that rarely involves overtime, and thus Clark would suffer a reduction in total pay. Clark declined this offer on the spot, but Yokus refused to allow her to continue performing electrician duties.

Clark's next day at work was Tuesday, June 1. (Monday, May 31, was a holiday.) Yokus again refused to allow Clark to perform electrician duties. At noon that day, Clark went home. On the following day, June 2, Yokus told Clark her employment was formally terminated. Clark filed a complaint with the EEOC on November 29, 2010.

And here is a quick overview of the copyright and fair use problem (for details see Appendix B). Page is suing Dash for violating the Copyright Act when Dash wrote a song based on Page's song (which in copyright terms is called the "original"), "Red, White, and Blue." Dash's song uses the structure and many lyrics of the original but changes the original song's political message. The music of the two songs is not at issue, only the lyrics. Page expects that Dash will argue that his song is a parody that falls under the fair use exception to the Copyright Act. The court will consider the relevant factors set out in the fair use statute, 17 U.S.C. § 107: whether the copy was transformative and targeted the original; whether it took more than necessary of the original; and whether it will interfere with the original's market.

Step 1: Gather and read all the facts, whether in a case file, a memo from the assigning attorney, or some other source your professor has provided. In the employment discrimination problem, the facts are provided in a short summary form. Often, the relevant facts have to be gleaned from other documents. For instance, for a breach of contract claim, you might review the contract and possibly a complaint and answer. Discovery may also be relevant; you may need to review deposition testimony, affidavits, responses to interrogatories, and other evidence. In whatever form you find the facts, your task is to locate and closely review every source that may contain factual information.

Step 2: Determine which facts are relevant. To determine whether a particular fact is relevant, you need to have some knowledge of the legal issue and the applicable rules. Whether a particular fact is relevant also depends on the surrounding circumstances. For instance, in a negligence suit, the fact that a car involved in an auto accident was white is generally irrelevant. If, however, the accident occurred during a blizzard and the defendant claims he couldn't see the plaintiff's vehicle, the fact that the car was white may very well be relevant.

A good way to tell if a fact is relevant is to remove it from your scenario. If the outcome would change, the fact is relevant. If the outcome would be the same, the fact is irrelevant. In determining which facts are relevant, you might look at any charts you created to form a rule or to make fact-based arguments. See Chapters 8 and 10. For the copyright and fair use problem, you might review the factors the court will use to decide the copyright fair use exception and make lists of the facts that you will use when discussing those factors.

First determine which facts are relevant in the employment discrimination problem. If you represent Yokus and the only issue you're asked to address is a question of law such as whether Title VII's definition of "sex" includes pregnancy, the Facts section might be very short, like in this example:

> Our client, Mark Yokus, owns R & J Construction Company. One of R & J's employees, Sarah Clark, became pregnant, and Yokus attempted to transfer her position. Clark refused, and Yokus terminated her employment. Clark then filed a complaint with the EEOC alleging sex discrimination in violation of Title VII.

It's often the case when a memo addresses only a question of law that the Facts section is relatively short. However, with a factual issue, such as whether R & J Construction unlawfully engaged in sex discrimination in violation of Title VII, the Facts section would be longer and might look like this:

> Our client, Mark Yokus, owns R & J Construction Company. R & J employed Sarah Clark for five years as a supervising electrician. Yokus learned that Clark was four months pregnant. Concerned for her health and safety as well as the fetus's, Yokus offered to transfer Clark, at her usual hourly rate, to an office position until after the baby was born. Clark refused that offer because the office position did not include regular overtime and as a supervising electrician Clark had averaged seventeen hours of overtime per week.
>
> Clark then filed a complaint alleging sex discrimination in violation of Title VII with the EEOC. The EEOC recently filed a complaint against Yokus on behalf of R & J Construction.

This Facts section doesn't include specific dates. Imagine, though, that Clark has now sued, and the issue is whether Clark filed suit within the 180 days required by Title VII. Several events happened and the question is which one of them triggered the start of the 180-day time limit. In that case, additional facts—including dates—would be relevant. That Facts section might look like this:

> Our client, Mark Yokus, owns R & J Construction Company. On May 28, 2010, Yokus learned that one of R & J's employees, Sarah Clark, was pregnant. On that day, Yokus told Clark that she could not continue to work as a supervising electrician and could be transferred to an office position at the same rate, although she would lose her customary overtime pay. Clark refused that offer on the spot, and Yokus refused to allow her to perform electrician duties. Her next workday was June 1, 2010, and Yokus again refused to allow her to perform

> electrician duties. Clark went home at noon. The next day, June 2, Yokus formally terminated Clark's employment.
>
> Clark filed her complaint with the EEOC on November 29, 2010, 185 days after May 28, when Clark was told that she could not continue to work as a supervising electrician and when she refused Yokus' offer to transfer to an office position. November 29, 2010 was 181 days after June 1, when Clark was again prohibited from performing supervising electrician duties and went home at noon. It was 180 days after June 2, when Yokus told Clark that her employment was terminated.

Note how which facts are relevant changes depending on the specific legal issue being addressed. The facts themselves don't change, but because the issue changes, their relevancy changes. Some facts are relevant to one issue, and some are relevant to another issue. Some are relevant to all issues. Your Facts section would include the facts relevant to the issue or issues you're addressing. For this reason, don't just copy and paste the facts you were given into your memo.

Step 3: Be especially careful to include the relevant facts that allow you to analogize or distinguish the facts in the precedent cases from the client's facts. In the employment law problem, the fact that the company offered to transfer Clark is relevant because it allows you to compare the way Yokus treated her after learning of her pregnancy with precedent cases where companies offered other alternatives to pregnant employees. Using that precedent effectively will depend on you including those facts when you write the Facts section. If you need a refresher on analogical reasoning, see Chapter 11.

In the copyright and fair use problem, the following facts might be helpful in the Facts section—first because they are relevant, and second because they allow you to compare and contrast those facts with the facts in the controlling cases:

> Page's song is critical of America, and Dash's song reflects pride in America.

These facts are relevant and helpful under the Copyright Act's first statutory factor, the "purpose and character of the use." But these facts also create a point of comparison with the *Mattel* case: In *Mattel*, the defendant's works criticized women's traditional role in society, emphasizing that role can put women in ridiculous and even dangerous positions. On the other hand, Mattel's works represented women's traditional role positively, associated with beauty, wealth, and glamour. You'll be able to create stronger analogies and distinctions in the Discussion section if you've included enough facts in the Facts section to draw those explicit comparisons later.

Step 4: Draft a preliminary Facts section. Start at the beginning and work your way through the facts chronologically (unless some other structure works better in your particular case). At this stage, err on the side of including too much. You can always delete facts later, but if you've left them out here, you might forget about them when drafting the Discussion section, and that can cause greater problems. Don't worry too much yet about whether each fact will ultimately be relevant. You'll be better able to answer that question after you've completed the legal research and considered how all of the pieces fit together.

Step 5: After you've completed the Discussion section, revise the Facts section. Now you're ready to decide whether each fact in your Facts section is relevant or needed for context. You can tell how much detail the reader needs to understand the analysis in the Discussion section. And now you're ready to revise—not just edit—your Facts section. Recall the first thing you need to know about Facts sections: "Describe the client and what she wants first, and then develop the facts more fully." So start there, explaining, briefly, the client's legal predicament. Then tell the story, making sure that every fact in the Discussion section is indeed in the Facts section. Also make sure the Facts section leaves out irrelevant facts, unless they are necessary for the story to make sense. And make sure it flows, so the reader can follow the story with one quick read.

EXAMPLES

Review the following examples. For each example, there may be more than one correct answer, but try to choose the *best* answer. Explain to yourself why you have chosen that answer. Then read the explanations in the last section of this chapter to check your work.

EXAMPLES

Example 16-1

This question uses the cell phone manslaughter problem, which you can find in Appendix A.

It would be helpful here to review the facts on the first page of Appendix A.

Facts

Allison King has been charged with vehicular manslaughter.

On October 22, 2010, Ms. King was driving from Jenner to Gualala on State Highway 1. This road is well known for being a winding two-lane highway on the edge of a cliff with the sea below. The highway offers very few places to pull over. Ms. King planned to meet several friends from San Francisco for a weekend vacation on the coast near Gualala.

The night Ms. King was driving, the fog was rolling in from the ocean and driving conditions were even more hazardous than usual. She was terrified and kept her bearings in near-whiteout conditions by hugging the road on the side of the cliff.

She also became concerned that the fog presented such dangerous driving conditions that she should warn her friends and suggest that they refrain from driving until road conditions improved.

Ms. King pulled out her cell phone and, while driving slowly along the cliff, she dialed one of her friends, June Coughlin, to give the warning. Suddenly a bicyclist appeared from out of the fog. Ms. King's car struck the cyclist, and he slipped across the road and over the cliff. The fall killed him. Ms. King has been charged with vehicular manslaughter.

This is an . . .

A. effective Facts section because it includes all the facts provided by the supervising lawyer verbatim.
B. effective Facts section because it includes names and dates, and without those details, the reader would be confused by the story.
C. ineffective (but thorough) Facts section primarily because it repeats the exact fact summary provided to the writer without considering the relevance of each particular fact.
D. ineffective Facts section because it's too long and fact statements should never exceed two paragraphs.

EXAMPLES

Example 16-2

This question uses the cell phone manslaughter problem, which you can find in Appendix A.

Consider the following opening paragraph to the Facts section:

Allison King, who turned forty-six years old on May 11, 2010, drove a silver 2006 Mercedes-Benz four-door sedan. On Friday, October 22, 2010, she was driving approximately 23 miles per hour heading northbound on California State Highway 1 near milepost 56. The time was 7:47 p.m.

This is an . . .

A. ineffective opening paragraph in the Facts section because it doesn't include the deceased bike rider's name, which is a relevant fact.

B. ineffective opening paragraph in the Facts section because it doesn't state the client's problem.
C. effective opening paragraph in the Facts section because it includes enough relevant facts to allow the reader to picture the story.
D. effective opening paragraph in the Facts section because Facts sections should read like novels: they should be interesting and include lots of detail.

EXAMPLES

Example 16-3

This question uses the cell phone manslaughter problem, which you can find in Appendix A.

Facts

Our client, Allison King, was charged in California with vehicular manslaughter. Ms. King was driving in dense fog when her car struck a cyclist, who died. Ms. King had been trying to call a friend on her cell phone when the accident happened.

This is an . . .

A. effective Facts section because it includes all the relevant facts.
B. effective Facts section because it's brief and avoids unnecessary detail.
C. ineffective Facts section because the reader isn't told the date of the accident, the name of the cyclist, or which friend King was calling when the accident happened.
D. ineffective Facts section because it omits relevant facts.

EXAMPLES

Example 16-4

This question uses a hypothetical breach of contract problem.

Facts

Our client, Steve Morris, has been sued for breach of contract. He entered into a written contract last fall to supply B & G Foods with 3,000 pounds of pineapples. Because of an early winter frost, all of his crops were destroyed. Morris was therefore unable to deliver the pineapples to B & G.

The contract includes no provision for inability to perform or Acts of God. B & G claims Morris is liable for the difference in price between their contracted price and the price B & G had to pay for pineapples on the open market. Morris claims B & G should bear the risk of natural disaster, as Morris was unable to perform through no negligence or acts of his own and any potential breach was not voluntary.

This is an . . .

A. effective Facts section because it begins with the legal claim and includes the relevant facts.
B. ineffective Facts section because it includes argument.
C. ineffective Facts section because the reader isn't told the exact date of the contract, the date of the frost, and the date the crops were destroyed.
D. ineffective Facts section because it includes the parties' claims about the contract.

EXAMPLES

Example 16-5

This question uses the cell phone manslaughter problem, which you can find in Appendix A.

Facts

Our client, Allison King, has been wrongfully charged with vehicular manslaughter. King acted reasonably and responsibly and should not be found guilty.

The accident occurred on October 22, 2010, when Ms. King was driving on California State Highway 1. Highway 1 is a winding two-lane road that sits atop a high cliff with the sea below. It was exceptionally foggy on Oct. 22, with "near white-out" conditions. Despite these hazardous conditions, a bicyclist decided to ride on the narrow cliff-top road.

Ms. King was terrified of the road conditions and feared that her friends, whom she would be meeting, would be in danger by driving on Highway 1 in those conditions. There was no place to pull over, so Ms. King called her friends to warn them not to drive. This single act of using her cell phone is the sole reason she is charged with vehicular manslaughter.

This is an . . .

A. effective Facts section because it includes all the relevant facts.
B. effective Facts section because it's told from the client's perspective.
C. effective Facts section because it begins by introducing the client and the legal claim.
D. ineffective Facts section because it omits negative facts, does not frame the facts objectively, and includes legal argument.

EXAMPLES

Example 16-6

This question uses a hypothetical employment contract problem.

Facts

Bob Fulton and José Garcia got into a heated argument in March. They had previous negative encounters, at least in part because Fulton believed Garcia was paid too much. In August the year before, Fulton, Garcia's immediate supervisor, told his department manager that Garcia was "underperforming" and began making a record in an effort to fire him. After the March argument, Garcia demanded to speak with the department manager, claiming Fulton had made working conditions unbearable. Fulton was paid only $3,000 per year more than Garcia, and Fulton believed he should be paid substantially more.

Finally, in July, Fulton fired Garcia. Garcia's previous performance reviews, for two years before August, were all "satisfactory" or "excellent." Garcia wishes to sue Premier Banking for wrongfully terminating his employment contract.

This is an . . .

A. ineffective Facts section because the facts are not organized logically.
B. effective Facts section because the facts are framed objectively.
C. effective Facts section because it includes all the relevant facts.
D. ineffective Facts section because it omits the legal claim.

EXPLANATIONS

EXPLANATIONS

Explanation 16-1

A is incorrect. Although this Facts section is thorough, it's not particularly effective because the writer has simply copied, verbatim, the facts provided. Part of your job as a writer is to discover which facts are (and which are not) relevant, and to leave the irrelevant facts out. **B** is also incorrect. It's unlikely the reader would be confused if she weren't told the name of the friend Allison King was calling, for instance. **C** is the best answer for the same reasons that A is wrong. It's your job to distinguish between relevant and irrelevant facts, and to relate only the relevant facts to the reader. ***D*** is not the best answer. Although a Facts section should omit irrelevant facts or details, it should be as long as needed to convey all the relevant facts. A strict rule on length—such as that all Facts sections should be two paragraphs or less—won't work when you have a complex case that requires greater space to recount all the relevant facts.

Explanation 16-2

A is not the best answer. This opening paragraph is ineffective, but not because *more* facts are needed. The bike rider's name isn't a relevant fact. (Is King guilty only if the bike rider's name is Smith and not if it is Jones?) What's relevant—and what the reader needs to know—is that he was riding a bike when King drove her car into him and killed him. **B** is the best answer. Telling the reader at the beginning that King has been charged with vehicular manslaughter helps frame the rest of the facts in context. Without knowing that, the reader wonders why it's worth caring about King, what she was driving, or where she was. **C** is incorrect. Facts sections generally don't need to personalize the client to this degree. This level of detail is irrelevant both to the legal issue and to understanding much about the client. In persuasive briefs, personalizing the client may be more appropriate, but still this much detail is likely unnecessary. **D** is also incorrect for the reasons stated in C. Furthermore, the reader needs to know the legal issue at the beginning.

Explanation 16-3

A is incorrect. This Facts section fails to include many relevant facts, including where she was driving, the characteristics of Highway 1, and why King made the call. **B**, too, is incorrect. Although the Facts section should be as brief as possible, it needs to include all the relevant facts, and this one doesn't for the reasons stated in A. Furthermore, this Facts section doesn't avoid unnecessary detail. Instead, it leaves out *necessary* detail. **C** is not the best answer. The reader needs more facts, but not, for instance, the cyclist's name. Instead, the reader needs to know more about the driving conditions, the accident, and the reason for the call because these facts are relevant to the issues of whether the elements of vehicular manslaughter are met and whether the emergency exception would apply. **D** is the best answer for the reasons stated in A, B, and C.

Explanation 16-4

A is the best answer. A good Facts section identifies the client and his legal problem, and then includes the relevant facts in chronological order. This Facts section does that. The reader is told that the client is being sued for breach of contract and why he didn't perform under the contract. The reader is also told that the contract's language does not address this situation together with what each party claims at this stage. **B** is incorrect. An objective description of the claims being made isn't the same thing as argument. The Facts section doesn't suggest one version is correct, so that is not a problem. **C** is incorrect. The exact date of the contract, the date of the frost, and the date the crops were destroyed do not appear, from the claims made, to be relevant to the issue. If the issue had been one of timing—such as a statute of limitations issue—some of those dates might be relevant. But as the problem is posed, the dates do not appear to be relevant, and the Facts section wisely omits them. **D** is also incorrect. As noted in the explanation for answers A and B, the parties' claims are facts. Including them here helps the reader understand the significance of the legal arguments.

Explanation 16-5

A is incorrect. This Facts section omits a number of key facts, including that King's car hit a bicyclist, who then slid across the highway and off the cliff, resulting in death. **B** is also incorrect. A memo's Facts section should identify the client and include facts relevant to the client, but it needs to be told from an objective point of view, not the client's point of view. The reader can't decide whether to agree or disagree with your analysis if the facts aren't stated here objectively. (In persuasive writing, on the other hand, facts are most often told from the client's point of view—although negative facts still need to be included and addressed. See Chapter 25.) **C** is incorrect. Although this Facts section introduces the client and legal claim, it's not effective, for the reasons stated in A, B, and D. **D** is the best answer. This Facts section omits negative facts. Here, King's hitting and killing a bicyclist is essential to the analysis. Furthermore, these facts aren't framed objectively. Criticizing the bicyclist's decision to ride on Highway 1 and at the same time portraying King's decision to drive on that road—and place a cell phone call—as "reasonable and responsible" highlights the lack of objectivity in the writer's description of the facts. In addition, the last sentence in the Facts section misstates the facts. King's "single act of using her cell phone" is not the "sole reason she is charged with vehicular manslaughter." Rather, she has been charged because she hit and killed a bicyclist when she placed that call during dangerous driving conditions. Finally, this Facts section includes legal argument. The Facts section isn't the place to state that King has been "wrongfully charged with vehicular manslaughter." That's argument. If it's true, it belongs in the Discussion section. And whether she acted "reasonably and responsibly" and therefore "should not be found guilty" are not facts, but instead are legal conclusions that belong in the Discussion section.

Explanation 16-6

A is the best answer. The organization of this Facts section detracts from its effectiveness. The facts are not relayed chronologically, making it hard for the reader to follow the sequence of events. **B** is not the best answer. Even if the facts are framed objectively, that is not enough—alone—to make a Facts section effective. And here, the facts might be a bit slanted in Garcia's favor. **C** is incorrect. Some key facts are missing, including how the working conditions were unbearable and what information was used to "make a record" against Garcia. In addition, as with B, even if all of the facts are included, that does not guarantee an effective Facts section. The information must be organized logically, as noted in A. **D** is incorrect. This Facts section does include the legal claim—wrongful termination of an employment contract.

Checklist

Chapter 16: Writing the Facts

✔	Gather and read all the facts, whether in a case file, a memo from the assigning attorney, or some other source your professor has provided.
✔	Decide which facts are relevant by asking if removing the fact would change the analysis.
✔	Include all relevant facts.
✔	Include background and procedural facts necessary for context.
✔	Write in a regular paragraph format, usually without numbered lines.
✔	Frame facts objectively and do not include opinion or argument.
✔	Usually organize facts in chronological order and use past tense.
✔	For lengthy Facts sections, consider using subheadings to break it into logical chunks so it's easier to read and understand.
✔	After completing the Discussion section, go back to check that all the facts you use in the analysis are stated in the Facts section.

You will find all of the chapter checklists compiled in Appendix D.

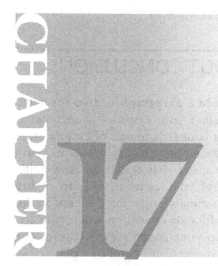

Writing the Conclusion Section (Objective)

Conclusions are important enough that Shakespeare named an entire play after them: *All's Well That Ends Well.* We like stories to have an ending that makes narrative sense with the path the author has drawn for us as readers. Similarly, legal readers want memos to have a conclusion that makes sense of where they've been.

Just as the terms "brief" and "roadmap" can mean several things in legal writing, your professor may use the word "Conclusion" in several ways. A Conclusion may be the final section of a memo that summarizes all of the issues addressed. Although we think of conclusions as always occurring at the end of a document, the "first conclusion" in a CRAC (for a refresher on the organization of your analysis, see Chapter 7) may be the thesis statement at the beginning of a section or chunk of analysis. Or it may be the last sentence of a section addressing a sub-issue. But in this chapter, we are talking about the section at the end of a memo that sums up and answers the primary questions you've addressed.

Terminology notes. Some professors use the term "mini-conclusion" to describe the conclusion to a sub-issue. Others might use a term like "landing" for sub-issues, saving the term "Conclusion" for an entire issue or an entire memo.

WHAT YOU NEED TO KNOW ABOUT CONCLUSIONS

Conclusion sections usually include a paragraph or two for each main section of the memo. And whether your Conclusion includes a summary of the sub-issues or only main issues is a matter of judgment; if your memo has three main issues, for example, you may decide to summarize only those main issues. If your memo has one main issue with two or three contested sub-issues, though, the reader is likely to expect the analysis of those sub-issues to be summarized in the Conclusion. As always, follow the conventions of the office or classroom where you are working, and tailor your Conclusion to your reader's expectations. (In contrast with the Conclusion in a memo, the Conclusion in a persuasive brief filed with a court is usually short—rarely more than a sentence or two. To see the difference, see Chapter 27 on Writing the Conclusion Section (Persuasive).)

The Conclusion is generally longer than a Brief Answer and shorter than a Discussion section. It's usually organized around the structure of the rule (just like your memo!). The Conclusion section of a memo is often similar to the "Summary of the Argument" in a brief. (See Chapter 24 for a preview.) In memos, it's helpful to readers if the Conclusion section "stands alone"; readers may refer to it when they are rushed and don't have time to read the entire Discussion section. Making sure your Conclusion is complete on its own means including everything the reader needs to know without reference to other sections. One useful guideline is for the Conclusion to start with an introductory paragraph setting out the main rule and then include one paragraph for each subsequent section of the memo. In these subsequent paragraphs, all you need to do is state the rule for that particular issue or sub-issue and then write a sentence or two about how it applies. Most often you won't need headings in a Conclusion, but use your judgment about whether your Conclusion needs them depending on the length of the memo and how many issues are involved.

HOW TO WRITE THE CONCLUSION SECTION

Using the copyright and fair use problem in Appendix B, we'll walk you through the process of writing a Conclusion.

PROBLEMS

Problem

Here is a quick overview of the copyright and fair use problem (for details see Appendix B). Page is suing Dash for violating the Copyright Act when Dash wrote a song based on Page's song (which in copyright terms is called the "original"), "Red, White, and Blue." Dash's song uses the structure and many lyrics of the original but changes the original song's political message. The music of the two songs is not at issue, only the lyrics. Page expects that Dash will argue that his song is a parody that falls under the fair use exception to the Copyright Act. The court will consider the relevant factors set out in the fair use statute, 17 U.S.C. § 107: whether the copy was transformative and targeted the original; whether it took more than necessary of the original; and whether it will interfere with the original's market.

Step 1: Restate your prediction for the outcome of the case and the rule that applies to the entire memo. Here, because the Conclusion is really a summary, you can go directly to the rule that will govern the outcome in its simplest form. With the copyright problem, you won't need to include the constitutional provision or the provision that sets out the exclusive rights of the copyright holder. You'll go right to what's at issue in this memo, the fair use exception. So the first paragraph of your Conclusion—your prediction and rule statement—might look like this (note that the relevant statutory language is quoted directly):

> Dash is likely to prevail on a claim of copyright infringement by asserting that his parody falls under the Copyright Act's "fair use" exception. Fair use includes purposes "such as criticism" and "comment." 17 U.S.C. § 107. The statute provides four factors used to determine whether there is a fair use exception to copyright infringement:
>
> > (1) the purpose and character of the use, including whether such use is of a commercial nature or is for nonprofit educational purposes;
> > (2) the nature of the copyrighted work;
> > (3) the amount and substantiality of the portion used in relation to the copyrighted work as a whole; and
> > (4) the effect of the use upon the potential market for or value of the copyrighted work.
>
> *Id.* The second factor, the nature of the copyrighted work, is not likely to be in dispute because the Supreme Court has stated that courts disregard this factor in cases like ours involving parody. *Campbell v. Acuff-Rose Music, Inc.*, 510 U.S. 569, 586 (1994).

Step 2: Review the sections or subsections in your memo's Discussion section and write one or two paragraphs for each section. As noted above, usually the structure of the rule will determine the structure of your Conclusion. For the copyright problem, three factors are at issue, so plan on three to six paragraphs summarizing the Discussion section. If your memo included a section on how the court will weigh the various factors to come to a conclusion, also include a paragraph that summarizes that analysis. Your Conclusion should follow the same order as the body of the memo unless there is a good reason to organize the Conclusion differently.

Step 3: In the paragraph or two that summarizes the sections (or sub-sections) of the Discussion, start with the rule for that issue (or sub-issue), then add a sentence or more of application, and then state a mini-conclusion for that issue (or sub-issue). After you set out the rule for a particular issue, provide a citation to each rule, using your best authority, just as you did in the Discussion section. In the sentence or two about how that rule applies in your case, there's generally no need to describe how previous courts have applied the rule or to support arguments with analogies (even though this is necessary in the memo's Discussion section). But do use the facts of your case as you describe the best argument for how the rule applies.

So the next paragraph of the Conclusion section in the copyright problem would start with your prediction on the first factor, the "purpose and character of the use, including whether such use is of a commercial nature or is for nonprofit educational purposes." Then provide a rule or the most important rules about that factor. Here, there is no need for "rule explanation" or "rule proof." Go straight to a few sentences of application that use our facts. Thus:

> When the court analyzes factor one, whether the "purpose and character of the use, including whether such use is of a commercial nature or is for nonprofit, educational purposes," the facts likely weigh slightly in favor of Dash. For this factor, the court focuses on whether the work is "transformative" by adding new meaning which furthers its purpose or changes its character. *Campbell v. Acuff-Rose Music, Inc.*, 510 U.S. 569, 579. The more transformative the work, the less significance other factors will have in finding fair use. *Id.*
>
> Here, although both works are political in nature, the parody alters the context of the original by providing a positive view of patriotism, rather than the negative view in the original. Thus, even though Dash's work is commercial in nature, it is probably transformative.

Step 4: Repeat this process by summarizing each section (or subsection) of the Discussion and end with a strong statement of how you believe the court will decide the overall issue. You can make this last statement a sentence or a paragraph. If the memo and the Conclusion section are fairly short, a sentence tacked onto the last paragraph of the Conclusion will probably suffice. If the Conclusion section is longer, you may want to write a short paragraph that predicts the outcome for the entire memo. Here, for example, you might come up with this:

> Weighing the fair use factors, the court will most likely find that Dash cannot show fair use and thus Page can demonstrate copyright infringement. Although Dash's work is probably transformative, considering the amount and substantiality he took when 70% of the lyrics are similar, the probable harm to Page's market, and the likelihood that customers will confuse the two works, overall the factors weigh in favor of Page. Thus, the court will likely find for Page.

EXAMPLES

Review the following examples. For each example, there may be more than one correct answer, but try to choose the *best* answer. Explain to yourself why you have chosen that answer. Then read the explanations in the last section of this chapter to check your work.

EXAMPLES

Example 17-1 and Example 17-2 are based on the Conclusion section below. These examples use the cell phone manslaughter problem, which you can find in Appendix A.

Conclusion

It is unlawful in California to "drive a motor vehicle while using a wireless telephone unless that telephone is specifically designed and configured to allow hands-free listening and talking, and is used in that manner while driving," except in cases where "using a wireless telephone for emergency purposes, including, but not limited to, an emergency call to a law enforcement agency, health care provider, fire department, or other emergency services agency or entity." Cal. Vehicle Code § 23123 (West 2022). Further, California's vehicular manslaughter statute, Penal Code § 192(c)(1), applies to those drivers who drive "a vehicle in the commission of an unlawful act, not amounting to felony, and with gross negligence." Thus, King is guilty unless (1) she placed the call "for emergency purposes" or (2) she acted without gross negligence.

First, King likely did not place the call for "emergency purposes." To prove an emergency, King must show a threat of imminent danger. *People v. Thompkins*, 104 Cal. Rptr. 3d 131, 133 (Ct. App. 2010). Here, the court will likely find King's friends were not threatened with imminent danger because King was not even sure her friends were on the same road and had not already safely driven through the fog. King could have waited for an opportunity to pull over and make the call when it was safe, and legal, to do so.

Second, the court will probably find King acted with gross negligence. Courts use an objective test to determine gross negligence: whether a reasonable person in the defendant's position would be aware of the risk involved. *People v. Harris*, 89 Cal. Rptr. 3d 904, 906 (Ct. App. 2009). King must have realized the driving risk because she was actually calling her friends to warn them of that same risk. Despite that, King chose to place a call on her cell phone. King therefore acted with gross negligence.

Hence, King drove while committing an unlawful act, not committed for an emergency purpose, and she was grossly negligent. King is therefore likely to be convicted of vehicular manslaughter.

EXAMPLES

Example 17-1

This Conclusion is:

A. probably too long.
B. probably too short.
C. about the right length, but should all be one paragraph and should not include citations.
D. about the right length, and the paragraph breaks and citations are proper.

EXAMPLES

Example 17-2

This Conclusion:

A. needs to cite more cases and explain how they apply.
B. stands on its own and needs no improvement.
C. needs a thesis statement in the first paragraph.
D. would be much better with headings.

EXAMPLES

Example 17-3

This question is based on the negligent infliction of emotional distress problem, which you can find in Appendix C.

Conclusion

Poe will likely succeed on her claim under New Fornia common law.

First, the assigning memo instructs to assume that elements one and four are met, and the facts suggest they can be proved. So I won't analyze those elements.

Next, the second element is close, but Poe will likely prevail on this element. The factors weigh in her favor, even though she and Valenzuela weren't married. *Dunphy v. Gregor*, 642 A.2d 372, 376 (N.F. 2013). Hence, she meets elements one, two, and four.

Finally, Poe will very likely prevail on the third element. She was present at the scene and was therefore at least "sensorially aware." *Ortiz v. JDP Builders, Inc.*, 689 A.2d 1135, 1139 (N.F. 2015). Because she meets all four required elements, Poe is likely to prevail.

This Conclusion:

A. is ineffective because it simply states that Poe can prevail but never states the claim, the underlying rule's actual elements, or the factors used for the third element.
B. is ineffective because the reader will not understand the relevance of the facts that are included.
C. is ineffective because the language is too casual for an office memo.
D. all of the above.

EXAMPLES

Example 17-4

This question is based on the negligent infliction of emotional distress problem, which you can find in Appendix C.

Conclusion

Poe is likely to succeed on her claim of negligent infliction of emotional distress as a bystander for the accident that seriously injured her fiancé, Valenzuela. In New Fornia, a bystander can prevail by showing: (1) "the death or serious physical injury of another caused by defendant's negligence"; (2) a "marital or close blood relationship," or an "intimate, familial relationship," between "the plaintiff and the injured person"; (3) the plaintiff's "direct observation" or "sensorial awareness" of "the death or injury at the scene of the accident; and (4) resulting severe emotional distress in the plaintiff." *Ortiz v. JDP Builders, Inc.*, 689 A.2d 1135, 1139 (N.F. 2015) (internal citations omitted). The assigning memo instructs to assume that elements one and four are met, and the facts suggest they can be proved. They are therefore not analyzed here.

Poe can likely demonstrate that she and the victim had an "intimate, familial relationship." Courts consider four factors to determine whether unmarried, non-blood relatives meet this standard: "the duration of the relationship; the type of relationship (dating, engaged, cohabitating, etc.); the degree of financial intermingling; and the extent and quality of shared experiences." *Dunphy v. Gregor*, 642 A.2d 372, 376 (N.F. 2013).

Here, Poe and Valenzuela had been dating for five years. They were engaged and planned to move in together within the next few months to save money for their wedding. Their finances were generally separate, but they had jointly purchased a car. In addition, they stayed over at each others' houses almost every night, spending significant time together. On balance, a court is likely to find Poe and Valenzuela had an intimate, familial relationship.

Furthermore, although close, Poe will likely be able to demonstrate that she "directly observed" or was "sensorially aware" of Valenzuela's injury at the scene. The bystander must be at the scene for her emotional injury to be foreseeable; simply arriving at the scene after the accident is over and the victim is already in an ambulance will not suffice. *Vargas v. Quinones*, 801 A.2d 1440, 1443 (N.F. App. 2018). When the plaintiff is at the scene but her view of the injury is obstructed, as with fire and smoke, she can still recover if she is aware of the injury. *Ortiz v. JDP Builders, Inc.*, 689 A.2d 1135, 1139 (N.F. 2015).

Here, Poe had earbuds in and her back to the street when the defendant's car struck Valenzuela, who had been mowing the lawn. Although she did not see the impact, Poe heard the impact and turned immediately to see Valenzuela's lawnmower coming toward her. She had to jump out of the way and saw her fiancé on the ground, ten feet from her and just a few feet from the defendant's car. Valenzuela was covered in blood; Poe tried to get him to respond and, when the ambulance arrived, rode with him to the hospital. Although this element is close, a court is likely to find this element is met because Poe was at the scene when the accident occurred, heard the accident's impact, and immediately witnessed the injuries. Because she meets all four required elements, Poe is likely to prevail on her claim of negligent infliction of emotional distress.

This Conclusion:

A. should quote less from the cases.
B. is effective.
C. should be shorter.
D. needs to draw direct analogies and distinctions with the precedent cases.

EXPLANATIONS

Explanation 17-1

A is incorrect. Although you could develop this conclusion a bit more, the length is typical for an office memo Conclusion. **B** is incorrect because this Conclusion is a length typical for memos. But remember, the form and length of Conclusions can vary. Your professor or office may prefer one paragraph or even one sentence. **C** is incorrect. Although this Conclusion is about the right length, it is far too long to all be one paragraph. Each main point (or sub-point, if you include them in your Conclusion) should be a paragraph or two long. Furthermore, even though you do not need to include analogies and distinctions to the cases in your Conclusion, you should provide citations for the rules. ***D*** is correct for the reasons A, B, and C are incorrect.

Explanation 17-2

A is incorrect. Typically, a memo's Conclusion doesn't have to include "rule explanation" or "rule proof." Although Conclusions may cite a case for a rule, it is rare that the Conclusion reviews the case law and precedent facts applied in the Discussion section. **B** is incorrect; although this Conclusion does a good job of standing on its own, it's missing a thesis statement at the beginning of the first paragraph. Readers who turn to this Conclusion would have the law and the facts they need to understand the most important points in the memo, so this Conclusion "stands alone." But it would be more effective if the section began with a thesis statement. **C** is correct. A thesis statement to start off the first paragraph would improve this Conclusion. ***D*** is not the best answer. Headings are often a matter of personal preference. In general, the longer the Conclusion, the more likely headings would be helpful. Here, although you could add headings, they are probably not necessary because this entire Conclusion is only four paragraphs.

Explanation 17-3

The statement in answer ***A*** is correct, but because this isn't the only reason this Conclusion is ineffective, it is not the best answer. Recall that Conclusion sections need to stand on their own; you should assume the reader is not familiar with your entire memo. This Conclusion only tells the reader that the author thinks Poe will win—but the reader doesn't even know that she sued for negligent infliction of emotional distress as a bystander. Even if she knew the alleged tort, the reader is not likely to know the four elements of that claim off the top of her head or the factors courts use to determine whether the plaintiff and victim have an "intimate, familial relationship." As with A, the statement in **B** is correct, but this is an incomplete answer. The reader won't understand the relevance of the facts in this Conclusion, because the reader hasn't been told what test the courts will apply. Similarly, the statement in **C** is correct but incomplete. Memos should avoid contractions and using the first-person point of view (so avoid words like "I"). **D** is the best answer for the reasons in A, B, and C.

EXPLANATIONS

Explanation 17-4

A is wrong. Although it's true that legal writers should generally quote from statutes and paraphrase from cases, it's fine to quote rules (as opposed to facts) from cases. **B** is correct. This Conclusion section works. It provides the reader with a stand-alone summary of the memo and the reasons for the author's objective conclusions. **C** is incorrect. The length of a good conclusion will vary, but generally one to two paragraphs per issue is fine. Especially when the rule for a particular element is long (as it is here), it's fine to have the thesis and rule (with a citation) in one paragraph and the application (and final conclusion) in another paragraph. **D** is wrong. It's important in a memo to draw direct analogies and distinctions with the precedent cases, but that should happen in the Discussion section, not the Conclusion section.

Checklist

Chapter 17: Writing the Conclusion Section (Objective)

✔	Conclusion sections usually include a paragraph or two for each main section of the memo.
✔	A memo's Conclusion is generally longer than the Brief Answer and shorter than the Discussion, but be sure to consider your audience's preferences.
✔	Conclusions are usually organized around the structure of the rule, just like your memo.

You will find all of the chapter checklists compiled in Appendix D.

PART III

Persuasive Writing

Overview: Motions and Briefs

Picture a lawyer at work. You're probably picturing someone arguing a case in court. After all, that's what lawyers get paid to do, right? We picture the brilliant lawyer bantering with the Supreme Court or eliciting that confession as the witness breaks down on the stand. There's some truth in that picture, but it's not the whole picture.

When lawyers advocate, a good chunk of it occurs in writing. In a very small percentage of appellate cases, the outcome may turn on the oral argument (assuming the court allows argument in that case). Usually, however, the written briefs are most influential.

The good news is that in persuasive writing, you'll use many of the same analytical and organizational tools that you'll use in objective writing—so the principles discussed in Parts I and II of this book apply here as well. But persuasive writing has some unique features. To excel at persuasive writing, you need to know certain techniques of persuasion and understand some unique document sections that appear primarily in appellate briefs. You also need to think about a theory of your case and themes that can tell a persuasive story.

This chapter provides an overview of the audience, purpose, and format of motions and briefs. It also discusses some helpful tips and some common pitfalls to avoid.

Terminology notes. A "brief" generally refers to a document lawyers file with an appellate court, and some textbooks also use that term to refer to the document of legal analysis that lawyers file with a *trial* court when seeking a specific ruling. Some call it a "trial brief." Some call it a "motion brief." Others call it a "motion memo." Those terms are also used for the document the opposing lawyer submits asking the trial judge to deny the motion. For conciseness, this book uses the more simplified term "motion" to describe the persuasive document that accompanies a request to the trial court as well as the document the opposing lawyer submits. When discussing these documents in class or with your professor, we suggest you use whatever term your textbook or your professor uses.

AUDIENCE AND PURPOSE OF MOTIONS AND BRIEFS

Even though the analytical process is the same, the audience and purpose for objective and persuasive writing are very different. In terms of audience, you're now writing for a judge (and perhaps for the judge's clerks as well as secondary audiences like your opponent, who might be persuaded to settle the case). Judges are busy and usually won't spend extra time trying to understand poorly made arguments.

In terms of purpose, in contrast to office memos, your goal when drafting a motion or a brief isn't to "inform" the reader or provide an objective analysis of the case. As a writer, your goal with persuasive writing is to make the reader agree with you. Whether that reader is a judge reading your motion, an appellate judge reading a brief, or someone else, you're trying to get the reader to act in a way that favors your client. Even if you objectively think your client should lose, you must argue as though you believe in your client's position.

MOTION AND APPELLATE BRIEF FORMAT

There's no universal format for motions and briefs. That's because documents filed with courts are subject to various court rules. Be sure to check the rules in your jurisdiction. But here are a few general guidelines.

Motions usually have fewer restrictions in terms of required sections, but they typically have formatting requirements (margins, page limits, etc.). Motions usually have two parts: (1) the motion page itself, stating very briefly what you want, and (2) the memorandum or brief in support of the motion, arguing that the trial court should grant your motion. The lawyer on the other side of the case can also submit a memo or brief arguing that the court should deny the motion. As we said at the beginning of this chapter, textbooks use different terms to describe these memos or briefs, and for conciseness we simply use the term "motion" to refer to them. In many jurisdictions, certain motions, most notably motions for summary judgment, also include a separate statement of facts.

The supporting memorandum or brief often has three parts: (1) an Introduction or Factual Statement to give the reader an overview or factual background (see Chapter 25 on writing a persuasive Fact Statement, sometimes also called a Statement of the Case); (2) an Argument, which is organized like an objective memo's Discussion section (see Chapter 7 and Chapter 13) but framed persuasively (see Chapters 20, 21, 22, and 23); and (3) a short Conclusion, which typically states the action you want the court to take (see Chapter 27).

Appellate briefs also follow court rules, so their format also varies by jurisdiction. But the typical sections that are required in appellate briefs and not in trial-level motions or memos include:

- the Question Presented, where you state the question the court must answer (see Chapter 26);
- a Table of Contents, where you identify each section in the brief and reproduce the text of your point headings and subheadings, with page references;
- a Table of Authorities, where you list all the statutes and cases and other authorities cited, with page references;
- a Statement of Jurisdiction, where you state the basis for the court's jurisdiction over the case;
- a Summary of the Argument, where you provide a concise overview of your arguments (see Chapter 24);
- a Standard of Review section or statement, where you explain how much deference the reviewing court should give to the lower court's decision (see Chapter 19); and
- a Conclusion, where you state the specific relief you are requesting (see Chapter 27).

You'll often include the verbatim language of any relevant statutory provision or provisions, sometimes near the beginning of the brief and sometimes as an appendix at the end.

SOME TIPS FOR PLANNING YOUR TIME

Just like when you're writing memos, writing motions and briefs takes a lot more time than you probably expect.

Start researching and writing as early as possible. In addition to the research and writing taking a long time, revising and polishing will also take more time than you expect, so plan for that on the front end. Judges are not likely to trust your arguments if you don't cite cases correctly or follow other basic rules. Furthermore, because you're trying to do more than convey objective legal analysis, you'll want to spend extra time working on persuasion after you have the analysis and arguments down. So build in time for that as well.

Just as with office memos, you'll rarely write a motion or brief from the first section to the last. You'll usually write some form of introduction or summary last, even though those sections appear near the beginning of the final document.

One key difference between memo writing and motion or brief writing is that court rules apply to motions and briefs. These court rules may cover items such as font size, page limits, citation style, and required document sections. Some of these sections take significant time to format, so add that to your time estimate. Court rules vary by jurisdiction, so be sure to find and read the court rules that apply to the document you're drafting.

SOME COMMON PITFALLS

Pitfall: Leaving out unfavorable facts or authorities. This sometimes happens in office memos as well, but it happens more often in persuasive writing. Just remember that you can't refute that negative information, whether it's factual or legal, unless you address it. Don't leave the only discussion on the point to the other side. See Chapters 22, 23, and 25.

Pitfall: Framing your argument as a response to your opponent's argument. This problem is the reverse of the first problem; here, the writer uses statements like this: "Although the State argues that the Defendant is guilty of aggravated assault for shooting Mr. Smith, he should be acquitted because he acted in self-defense." Rather than wishing away the other side and their arguments, you start with their arguments and react. A defensive position isn't persuasive, though. Instead, try to make an affirmative argument showing why you should win, like: "Mr. Collins justifiably defended himself against Smith's display of deadly force, and hence is not guilty of aggravated assault for shooting Smith." Again, see Chapters 22, 23, and 25. Chapters 20, 21, 24, and 26 might also help. Generating and using a persuasive theory of the case and themes that help advance your position will help ensure you aren't just reacting defensively to your opponent's arguments. Chapters 20 and 26 will be helpful with these skills.

Pitfall: Not supporting your factual assertions. Courts expect proof for each assertion you make, including factual claims. Citations to the underlying facts are less common in office memos. But when drafting persuasive documents, you need to cite documents that you put in the factual record as sources of support for your factual assertions. Follow whatever citation format your reader expects, but be sure to cite to the underlying documents that support your factual assertions.

Pitfall: Not including all the required sections for your document (or not including them in the required order). This problem is usually the result of not budgeting enough time for the project. Legal analysis and drafting take time, and when you're reading authorities for the first time at 4:30 in the morning and the brief is due at 9:00, chances are you're going to miss something. So look at the authorities early and create a template with all the document sections. Figure out from the court rules which sections count toward the page limit and which don't. Format your template so that once you add the content, you're ready to submit.

Pitfall: Going overboard with exaggerated attempts at persuasion. This problem is the reverse of using waffling language in memos, and it usually happens because students haven't had enough exposure to good persuasive writing this early in their careers. For example, words like "clearly" and "obviously" usually send the opposite message; the reader will generally assume that your point isn't clear or obvious so you are reaching for labels to make up for substance that is lacking. So avoid those words. Chapters 22 and 23 will help with striking the right balance in persuasion, as will time and experience. To get some of that experience more quickly, take the time and review some good persuasive writing. Read briefs submitted to the U.S. Supreme Court, for example, especially those by the Solicitor General, which are often excellent. But no matter where you find them, reading good briefs will help. Chapter 33 also has some suggestions for finding models of good persuasive writing.

Checklist

Chapter 18: Overview: Motions and Briefs

✔	Plan time for multiple drafts and polishing.
✔	Include relevant, unfavorable facts and binding authorities.
✔	Make your own affirmative argument and do not just respond to your opponent's arguments.
✔	Support factual assertions with citations to the record.
✔	Read local rules and/or the assignment and include what the rules require.
✔	Do not go overboard with exaggerated attempts at persuasion.

You will find all of the chapter checklists compiled in Appendix D.

CHAPTER 19

Handling Standards of Review

Standards of review are part of appellate practice. You don't need this chapter if you're writing for a trial court. Come back to it later if you're assigned an appellate brief.

"Counsel, what's the standard?" If you're appearing before an appellate court, the court is likely asking you about the standard of review, meaning the level of deference it should apply to the finding or ruling of the lower court. This can be quite important, and in many appeals, outcome determinative. Because courts and lawyers use the term *standard of review* in various ways, however, it's natural to feel confused. In fact, standard of review is a complex topic and the subject of several legal treatises. This chapter describes, on a basic level, the various usages and meanings of the term *standard of review* and explains how to write the standard of review section for an appellate brief.

WHAT YOU NEED TO KNOW ABOUT STANDARDS OF REVIEW

When an appellate court hears an appeal it reviews the decision below; it does not retry the case. Instead of holding a new trial with witnesses, cross-examinations, and the like, the appeals court reviews the written record of the claims made on appeal and considers the evidence already in the record for those claims. This system promotes judicial economy and respects factual findings made at trial where the fact-finder observed the witnesses firsthand, rather than having the appellate court rely on a "cold" record.

The appellate court's power to decide is limited by the standard of review applicable to the lower court's decision. The standard of review determines the level of *deference* the appellate court must give to the decisions of the court below. This level can range from no deference to a lot of it.

In this sense, to defer is to accept, at least to some extent, someone else's decision, largely because of who, or what institution, made it. If you give someone no deference at all, you judge her decisions on their own merits, without assuming that she's probably right because of her knowledge or skill. If you give a lot of deference, you start off assuming that she's probably right and disagree only if you have some special reason for doubting her in this instance. How much doubt do you need before you'll disagree? That depends on how much deference you're giving.

For some types of issues, appellate courts give trial courts no deference and will reverse if they simply disagree with the trial court. For others, appellate courts defer to some extent, but not a lot. They'll reverse only if they disagree strongly. For still other types of decisions, appellate courts defer a great deal to trial courts, and they'll reverse only if they disagree emphatically with what the trial court did.

The standard of review is itself a matter of law that you must research to determine and cite authority to support. Appellate courts apply standards of review on an issue-by-issue basis, so there may be more than one that applies in any given case. Research the applicable standard of review in your jurisdiction for each issue. In many instances, you'll be able to find a recent case from the appellate court your case is before, or the highest one in the jurisdiction, that provides the applicable standard of review for your issue.

Usually the applicable standard of review is not a controversial issue and the research required is not terribly time-consuming. Sometimes, however, it's not clear what standard applies and the standard will determine the outcome. In those instances, the standard of review may be at the core of the parties' dispute. For instance, one party might argue that the appropriate standard of review is deferential to the favorable ruling below while the other party might argue that the appropriate standard of review is no deference to the lower court's ruling. At higher appellate levels, one party might argue that an intermediate appellate court applied the wrong standard of review below and if it had applied the correct one, that party would have prevailed. As you might have guessed, when the standard of review is controversial, you'd need more than a simple statement and a citation to a case or two. The standard of review argument in those cases might be a significant portion of your brief.

The standard of review the court applies depends on what it is reviewing: a factual finding, a legal ruling, an evidentiary ruling, or some other type of decision. The standard for factual findings is usually very deferential, while the standard for legal conclusions is usually low or no deference. This reflects the relationship among different levels of courts and the view that the fact-finder—either trial judge or jury—is in the best position to evaluate the evidence, particularly witness testimony, while the appellate court is in the best position to rule on the law and promote a uniform body of law.

The three most common appellate standards of review in civil proceedings are de novo, clearly erroneous, and abuse of discretion. These phrases don't have definitions agreed upon by all courts, and courts haven't uniformly applied them, but the basic concepts can be generally summarized as follows:

- **De novo review** applies to questions of law (about what the law means) and often to mixed questions of law and fact (usually a question about how the law applies to certain agreed-upon facts, such as whether the facts meet a legal standard). De novo review means reviewing the issue anew, without any deference to the lower court.
- **Clearly erroneous review** applies to factual findings. It requires a high level of deference to the lower court. The appellate court will not reverse unless the lower court made a decision based on a clearly erroneous understanding of the facts.
- **Abuse of discretion review** applies to procedural rulings and other discretionary decisions such as admissibility of evidence, objections, and nondispositive motions. Like the clearly erroneous standard, abuse of discretion requires the appellate court to give a high level of deference to the lower court's decision. Depending on the circumstances, this may amount to a determination that the decision was one no reasonable person would have made or that it was arbitrary and capricious.

Follow court rules, if any, about where to address the standard of review in your brief. If court rules don't specify where to put it, use good writing judgment. You could put it in a separate section with its own heading or in the beginning of your Argument section. If you have multiple issues with different standards of review, you could put the applicable portion in the introduction to each issue. If the standard is controversial, then treat it like any other major issue and develop the section further with argument, as noted above.

If a deferential standard of review applies, that standard will frame the brief's argument. When the applicable standard of review is deferential, do more than just state it: incorporate it into your argument as well and use the terms of art that apply to that standard of review. It's like a filter or lens through which the court will be viewing your arguments, so when the standard of review favors your side, emphasize it, and when it's not favorable, show how you should win even with the bar set that high.

For instance, if you're appealing an evidentiary admissibility ruling, you must assert that the trial court "abused its discretion" by admitting certain evidence, identify that evidence and the ruling with a citation to the record, and argue why the decision changed the outcome of the case. It wouldn't be enough for the appellate court to be persuaded that it would've ruled differently. It must be persuaded that the trial court abused its discretion in admitting certain evidence and that this changed the outcome of the case.

The phrase "standard of review" can be confusing because courts also use the phrase to describe the legal tests or constitutional standards for trial-court motions and government actions. Specifically, courts use the term to refer to the legal test the trial court applies to decide whether to grant a motion and the standard that courts use to review the constitutionality of a statute or government action (i.e., strict scrutiny, intermediate scrutiny, and rational basis). Sometimes the necessary certainty and evidence for trials, known as the burden of persuasion and burden of proof, is also confused with standard of review. Don't let this confuse you into thinking that appellate courts are applying trial burdens. If you're writing an appellate brief that doesn't concern the constitutionality of a statute or government action, then "standard of review" simply refers to the appellate standard of review as discussed in this chapter.

HOW TO WRITE THE STANDARD OF REVIEW SECTION OF AN APPELLATE BRIEF

Using the copyright and fair use problem in Appendix B, we'll walk you through the process of writing a standard of review section.

Problem

> Here is a quick overview of the copyright and fair use problem (for details, see Appendix B). Page is suing Dash for violating the Copyright Act when Dash wrote a song based on Page's song (which in copyright terms is called the "original"), "Red, White, and Blue." Dash's song uses the structure and many lyrics of the original but changes the original song's political message. The music of the two songs is not at issue, only the lyrics. Page expects that Dash will argue that his song is a parody that falls under the fair use exception to the Copyright Act. The court will consider the relevant factors set out in the fair use statute, 17 U.S.C. § 107: whether the copy was transformative and targeted the original; whether it took more than necessary of the original; and whether it will interfere with the original's market.

Step 1: Identify the issue or issues on appeal and figure out the standard or standards of review that apply in your case. To do this, you'll need to do legal research. Look for binding case law that states the standard of review that a court applied to the same kind of decision that is at issue in your appeal.

Here are some considerations that can help you think about what you're looking for. Who made the ruling on the record below? Was it a judge, jury, or administrative body? Also consider the kind of decision. Was it an evidentiary ruling (e.g., that certain evidence was admissible)? A procedural ruling (e.g., that a motion should be granted)? A factual finding (e.g., whether the defendant pulled the gun's trigger)? A decision of law (e.g., whether a collateral debt obligation is a "security" within the meaning of the statute)? A mixed question of law and fact (e.g., a district court's finding of fair use under the Copyright Act)?

Imagine that the copyright and fair use problem resulted in litigation between the parties in a district court within the Ninth Circuit. Page claimed that Dash infringed her copyright. Dash argued that his song was a parody and within the fair use exception to the Copyright Act. Imagine further the district court granted summary judgment to Dash, holding that Dash's parody was indeed fair use. If you were working on Page's appeal of the district court's grant of summary judgment, you'd need to find the standard of review that the Ninth Circuit would apply when reviewing such a ruling. Preferably, you'd find this information in a recent case on a similar posture and area of law.

Here, your research discovers the *Mattel* case in Appendix B, which provides that an appellate court reviews de novo a district court's grant of summary judgment. Likewise, an appellate court reviews de novo a "district court's finding of fair use under the Copyright Act," which is a "mixed question of law and fact." It's always a good idea to check that your research results are still "good law" and up to date, and assuming that *Mattel* is, you'd be able to say this so far:

> A court reviews de novo a district court's grant of summary judgment. A "district court's finding of fair use under the Copyright Act," a "mixed question of law and fact," is also reviewed de novo.

Step 2: Once you've found the standard or standards of review that apply, make a note of the authority that stands for that proposition. Cite authority for the standard of review: it's a legal proposition. Here, make a note of the proper citation for *Mattel* and include a pinpoint citation to the part of the opinion that discusses the applicable standard of review. You'd now have the following:

> A court reviews de novo a district court's grant of summary judgment. *Mattel Inc. v. Walking Mountain Prods.*, 353 F.3d 792, 799 (9th Cir. 2003). A "district court's finding of fair use under the Copyright Act," a "mixed question of law and fact," is also reviewed de novo. *Id.*

Step 3: Check whether the court where you are submitting your brief has rules regarding where the standard of review should be included and whether it should be in a separate section with its own header. If the court rules don't require a separate statement, then, as noted previously, use your good writing judgment about where to fit it into your organization.

Here, you'd check what the Ninth Circuit requires. Ninth Circuit Rule 28-1 provides that appellate briefs should conform with the Federal Rules of Appellate Procedure (FRAP) Rule 28, which in turn provides that the appellate brief must contain "for each issue, a concise statement of the applicable standard of review (which may appear in the discussion of the issue or under a separate heading placed before the discussion of the issues)." Ninth Circuit Rule 28-2.5 similarly provides: "As to each issue, appellant shall state where in the record on appeal the issue was raised and ruled on and identify the applicable standard of review." Thus, when filing a brief in the Ninth Circuit you could either state the applicable standard of review in one main section labeled "Standard of Review" just before the Argument section, or you could include the standard of review within the Argument for each issue. Decide which makes more sense in your particular case; if the standard is controversial for one issue but not another, for example, you might want to address the standard of review within the argument on each issue. Think about how much emphasis you want the reader to place on the standard of review (which will vary depending on the applicable standard and whether it favors your position) and what best fits your particular case.

Step 4: State the applicable standard of review for each issue on appeal and cite authority. Either paraphrase or use a direct quote. Use simple language, and frame the standard of review in terms of its effect on the reviewing court.

Here, you might write, in a separate section just before the brief's Argument section:

> **Standard of Review**
>
> This Court reviews de novo a district court's grant of summary judgment. *Mattel, Inc. v. Walking Mountain Prods.*, 353 F.3d 792, 799 (9th Cir. 2003). A "district court's finding of fair use under the Copyright Act," a "mixed question of law and fact," is also reviewed de novo. *Id.*

This statement of the standard of review works. You researched the applicable standard or standards, you checked local court rules for formatting, and you stated simply the standard of review and cited binding authority.

Step 5: If a deferential standard of review applies and favors your client, you should incorporate that standard into your argument. Using the copyright and fair use problem, the standard of review is de novo, so the appellate court would give no deference to the lower court's decision. However, if the problem involved an issue on appeal that required applying the clearly erroneous, abuse of discretion, or some other deferential standard, then you'd want to frame your argument in terms of that standard of review.

For example, imagine you represent the plaintiff in a civil case and the trial court granted your motion to continue the trial. The defendant lost at trial and is appealing, claiming the continuance unfairly prejudiced his case. You'd want to frame your argument to reflect that your opponent has to demonstrate that the court "abused its discretion" in granting the continuance. This is a hard standard to overcome, so within the Argument section, frame headings (and your entire argument) to emphasize this burden:

> The Defendant Cannot Demonstrate that the Trial Court Abused its Discretion in Granting the Continuance.

You might then begin your argument by stating that the trial judge's decision wasn't "arbitrary and capricious" if the law in your jurisdiction required that showing to reverse the decision. You'd make similar arguments in any situation where the standard of review favors your position.

EXAMPLES

Review the following examples. For each example, there may be more than one correct answer, but try to choose the *best* answer. Explain to yourself why you have chosen that answer. Then read the explanations in the last section of this chapter to check your work.

Example 19-1

EXAMPLES

This question uses a hypothetical problem where one party appeals the district court's award of costs to the prevailing party under a federal statute.

Standard of Review

This Court reviews de novo a district court's interpretation of a federal statute. In addition, this Court reviews de novo whether the district court has the authority to award costs to a prevailing party.

This standard of review statement . . .

- **A.** works well and both issues are properly included in one section.
- **B.** needs citations to authority.
- **C.** needs to tell the appellate court how much deference to give the lower court's decision.
- **D.** is too repetitive.

Example 19-2

EXAMPLES

This question uses a hypothetical problem where one party appeals the district court's order compelling arbitration and dismissing the action for failure to prosecute pursuant to Federal Rule of Civil Procedure 41(b).

Standard of Review

The Plaintiffs-appellants brought a proposed class action in federal court against the Defendant company, alleging that it had sold defective products to them in violation of California state law. Based on the terms and conditions of the product purchase agreement, the Defendant moved to stay proceedings and compel arbitration. The district court granted the motion, and the Plaintiffs refused to comply with it. Subsequently, the Defendant moved under Federal Rule of Civil Procedure 41(b) for the district court to dismiss the action for failure to prosecute or comply with a court order. The district court granted the Defendant's motion to dismiss. The Plaintiffs-appellants now appeal the district court's dismissal, which this Court should review for abuse of discretion. *Omstead v. Dell, Inc.*, 594 F.3d 1081, 1084 (9th Cir. 2010). Further, this Court should review the district court's order compelling arbitration de novo. *Davis v. O'Melveny & Myers*, 485 F.3d 1066, 1072 (9th Cir. 2007).

This standard of review statement . . .

A. works well.
B. needs more citations to authority.
C. includes unnecessary information for the section.
D. confuses the standard the trial court applied to the motions it granted with the appellate standard of review.

EXAMPLES

Example 19-3

This question uses a hypothetical problem where one party appeals the district court's award of attorneys' fees to the defendant under the Copyright Act and the Lanham Act.

Argument

The district court's award of attorneys' fees should be reversed. First, the district court abused its discretion in awarding attorneys' fees under the Copyright Act. Based on the factors to be considered in copyright infringement cases in this Circuit, the Defendant was not entitled to attorneys' fees here. The Defendant had not advanced the purpose of the Copyright Act and the award was not an appropriate deterrent to further the purposes of the Copyright Act. Second, the district court abused its discretion in awarding attorneys' fees under the Lanham Act because it failed to apportion the attorneys' fees for work only related to the Lanham Act claim, as required.

This Court reviews decisions by the district court awarding attorneys' fees under the Copyright Act and under the Lanham Act for abuse of discretion. *Stephen W. Boney, Inc. v. Boney Servs., Inc.*, 127 F.3d 821, 825 (9th Cir. 1997).

The writer . . .

A. should revise this because the standard of review needs to be in its own separate section of the brief.
B. has made an acceptable choice to include the standard of review in the beginning of the Argument.
C. should add more citations to authority supporting the standard of review.
D. should specify how much deference to give the lower court's decision.

EXAMPLES

Example 19-4

This question uses a hypothetical problem where the plaintiff appeals a jury's factual finding that the plaintiff didn't mitigate her damages.

If you were writing the reply brief, the best way to frame your argument would be:

A. The Plaintiff did not mitigate her damages.
B. The jury correctly decided that the Plaintiff did not mitigate her damages.
C. The jury's finding that the Plaintiff did not mitigate her damages was not clearly erroneous.
D. The Plaintiff cannot demonstrate that the jury's factual finding that she failed to mitigate her damages was clearly erroneous.

EXAMPLES

Example 19-5

This question uses the negligent infliction of emotional distress problem, which you can find in Appendix C. Assume the defendant, Defoe, prevailed on summary judgment in the trial court. The plaintiff, Poe, appeals.

Standard of Review

This Court reviews a trial court's summary judgment dismissal de novo. *Klinger v. Brighton*, 564 A.2d 476, 478 (N.F. 2018).

This standard of review statement . . .

A. works well.
B. should be longer and include why the trial court granted summary judgment, as well as why that ruling was erroneous.
C. does not require a citation.
D. should not be a separate section because it is so short; instead, it should be incorporated into the Argument section of the brief.

EXPLANATIONS

Explanation 19-1

A is not the best answer. This is a good start and if the court's rules permit it, it seems to make sense to include the standard of review on both issues in one section because they are both de novo, requiring no deference to the trial court's ruling. But the statement lacks the necessary citations to authority. **B** is the best answer. The applicable standard of review is a legal proposition that should be supported by authority. Each sentence in this example should have a citation to authority after it. **C** is not the best answer. It's true that the standard of review should tell the court how much deference to give, but this statement does just that because it states the review is "de novo." This means that the appellate court will review the matter anew with no deference to the lower court's decision. **D** is not the best answer. Although it repeats the phrase "de novo," this statement is not too repetitive because there's a question of statutory construction and a question of authority to award costs, and the standard of review for each issue should be explicit.

Explanation 19-2

A is not the best answer. In this example, the author chose to put the standard of review in a separate section of the brief with its own header. After so choosing, the author should have put only the standard of review in this section and shouldn't have included the procedural history as well. **B** is incorrect. The portions of this example that relate to standard of review have appropriate cites to authority. The author should, however, edit the section by moving the beginning portion devoted to procedural history to a different section of the brief. **C** is the best answer. As discussed in A, this separate standard of review statement shouldn't include tangential information such as the procedural history. Note, though, that the problem with this example isn't length. Sometimes the applicable standards of review can be complicated and require a detailed explanation or argument. The problem here is simply a lack of focus on the standard of review in a section devoted to it. A better standard of review statement would be as follows:

> **Standard of Review**
>
> This Court reviews for abuse of discretion a district court's dismissal pursuant to Federal Rule of Civil Procedure 41(b) for failure to prosecute or comply with a court order. *Omstead v. Dell, Inc.*, 594 F.3d 1081, 1084 (9th Cir. 2010). This Court reviews de novo a district court's order compelling arbitration. *Davis v. O'Melveny & Myers*, 485 F.3d 1066, 1072 (9th Cir. 2007).

D is incorrect. Although the section unnecessarily includes procedural history, it doesn't discuss the legal test that the trial court applied in granting the motions. If you're feeling confused about the term *standard of review*, you might review the beginning of this chapter again.

EXPLANATIONS

Explanation 19-3

A is not the best answer. Depending on court rules, the standard of review can be included in its own separate section of the brief, but it doesn't have to be. If court rules don't specify where to put it, use good writing judgment. You could put it in a separate section with its own header or in the beginning of your Argument section, as the writer did in this example. **B** is the best answer for the reasons explained in A. **C** is incorrect. The writer has appropriately included a citation to authority for the standard of review—the *Stephen W. Boney, Inc.* case, which states that the standard of review is abuse of discretion for awards of attorneys' fees under the Copyright Act and under the Lanham Act. **D** is incorrect. This statement does tell the court how much deference to give because it states the review is "abuse of discretion," which means that the appellate court must give a high level of deference to the lower court's decision.

EXPLANATIONS

Explanation 19-4

A is not the best answer. It adequately states the underlying issue the appellate court is addressing—whether the Plaintiff mitigated her damages—but it completely ignores a favorable standard of review. **B** is also not the best answer. Although it refers to the jury, it simply states that their decision was correct. This might be proper if the standard of review was de novo, but for factual findings, the standard of review is clearly erroneous. As with A, this framing fails to take advantage of that favorable standard. **C** is a good answer, but arguably not the *best* answer. It incorporates the proper standard of review—clearly erroneous—but it could emphasize the Plaintiff's burden here. It also uses a double negative, which might be confusing to the reader. ***D*** is the best answer. It emphasizes that it's the Plaintiff who has to prove this, and it emphasizes that the Plaintiff has to prove not only that the jury was wrong in determining she didn't mitigate her damages, but that the jury's finding was "clearly erroneous."

Explanation 19-5

A is the best answer. This standard of review is clearly stated and includes a citation to mandatory authority. ***B*** is not the best answer. In a section labeled "Standard of Review," the writer should avoid summarizing the substantive arguments. The task is to clearly and concisely set out the applicable standard of review, which this statement does. Other sections of the brief will contain a summary of the argument. If the writer chose instead to not have a separately labeled section (assuming court rules permitted that), this statement of the standard of review might be appropriate in the Argument section of the brief or at the end of a summary of the argument. **C** is wrong. Standards of review are legal principles; they always require a citation to controlling authority. ***D*** is not the best answer. Although incorporating the standard of review into the Argument might make sense, sometimes court rules require an explicit section of the brief labeled "Standard of Review." In addition, when the standard of review favors your client (or at least is not detrimental), you may want to break it out separately for persuasive effect.

Checklist

Chapter 19: Handling Standards of Review

✔	Understand what a standard of review is and how it can affect the case.
✔	Identify the issue or issues on appeal.
✔	Conduct research to figure out the standard or standards of review that apply in the case.
✔	Consider whether the standard of review itself might be at issue.
✔	Check and follow the court rules about where to address standard of review in the brief.
✔	State the applicable standard of review for each issue on appeal and cite authority.
✔	If the standard of review favors your client's case, emphasize it where you can to strengthen the arguments.

You will find all of the chapter checklists compiled in Appendix D.

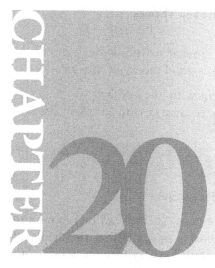

Developing a Theory of the Case and Themes

A good brief isn't just a patchwork of required sections. A good brief tells a coherent story. It makes the reader understand the issue from your client's point of view and why your client should prevail. An excellent brief can in fact make the reader believe that your client prevailing is not only the legally correct result, but also the just result.

"Theory of the case" is a term that lawyers use to describe the overarching narrative or idea about a case that a lawyer uses as a guide when making decisions about the trial plan and brief writing process. A good theory of the case is the glue that holds your brief together, forming a cohesive storyline between facts and argument that illuminates what the case is about and the key reasons your client should win.

WHAT YOU NEED TO KNOW ABOUT A THEORY OF THE CASE AND THEMES

A theory of the case is an overarching narrative or idea that concisely explains the key issues and why your client should prevail. It's a view of the law and facts that puts your client in a favorable light and makes the result you advocate seem both legally correct and just. You might not state your theory of the case expressly in your brief, but after reading your brief, the reader should have a clear idea of what you think the case is about and why your client should prevail. Thus, a good theory of the case:

- accounts for, or is at least consistent with, the key facts;
- plausibly explains the controversy, consistent with common sense;
- has a solid legal basis;
- is concise;
- is easily understandable;
- is persuasive; and
- leads to a conclusion that your client should win.

Themes support the theory of the case. Themes can be captured in words, phrases, or even a sentence that evokes or symbolizes the theory of the case or related key points. Themes should be easy to understand, concrete, and emotionally compelling. For instance, in a breach of contract case where your client is seeking to enforce the contract, a word that evokes the theory of the case might be "promise."

Don't worry about trying to vary your word choice so as to avoid repetition. Using the same word or words—like "promise"—that evoke your core themes throughout your brief will enhance its cohesion and clarity. But carefully choose the labels you use to describe the parties as well as those facts that can subtly reinforce your themes. For instance, if you're writing a brief in support of prosecuting a minor as an adult, you might call the minor a "juvenile" instead of a "minor" or "child" because the word "juvenile" may evoke a juvenile delinquent who seems more like an adult than the word "child" would suggest. In a case about an automobile collision, the defendant might describe it as an "accident," whereas the plaintiff might call it a "car crash."

A theory of the case can be formed at various stages of litigation and it might change over time as the key facts develop and litigation continues. For instance, in civil litigation a lawyer might form a theory of the case based on a client interview or informal investigation even before formal discovery starts. In a criminal case a lawyer might develop a theory of the case after reading the initial facts such as in a police report. The theory of the case could start as a broad idea and get refined as more evidence is gathered, as you better understand the strengths and weaknesses of your case, or as the litigation continues and the court rules on motions and issues. Remember, though, that the theory of the case must be driven by the facts; don't try to force or manipulate facts to fit into a theory that doesn't account for the key facts and the particular situation at hand.

A good brief will weave the theory of the case and core themes throughout, while not overpowering the reader. Every part of your brief is a potential persuasive moment that should advance or at least comport with (and not conflict with) your theory of the case.

The introduction is an entryway for the reader to understand your overarching narrative and what you're asking the court to do. If your brief includes a Question Presented or a Summary of the Argument, craft these so that they're consistent with your theory of the case. For example, if you decided that the word "promise" was a theme you wanted to use in a brief about a breach of contract issue, then "promise" should appear in the introduction and Question Presented or Summary of the Argument.

Carry the theory of the case through your Facts section, which should tell a compelling story, with persuasive techniques that are not obvious. Avoid an argumentative tone because it may appear so slanted that you will lose credibility. Similarly, avoid factual overstatements and using words like "clearly" and "obviously."

Include, though, contextual facts that help to subtly build your narrative. In the breach of contract case, for example, you could include the details about forming the contract—details that show there was an intentional decision to make the "promise." Of course, you must present the key facts accurately, even unfavorable ones. But ask yourself whether you can also present them in a light favorable to your client while maintaining accuracy and integrity. Use vivid, specific detail to describe facts you want the reader to remember. Use less detail and less space for facts you want to deemphasize. In addition, tell the facts from your client's perspective, making the reader start from and follow the story through your client's eyes or a favorable vantage point. In terms of organization, a chronological order is usually easiest for the reader to understand. You might consider starting at a point in the chronology that is favorable to your side, or using a non-chronological order if you carefully ensure it is still easy for the reader to digest. Chapter 25 explains more about writing a persuasive Fact Statement.

Finally, your arguments should also fit your theory of the case. Use words and phrases that evoke the core themes of your narrative. Emphasize the strong aspects of your theory of the case, whether that is the law itself, the facts, or policy. And choose arguments that are coherent with each other, or easily understandable alternatives that still fit with your theory of the case.

HOW TO DEVELOP AND USE A THEORY OF THE CASE AND THEMES

Using the copyright and fair use problem in Appendix B, we'll walk you through the process of developing a theory of the case and themes.

PROBLEMS

Problem

> Here is a quick overview of the copyright and fair use problem (for details, see Appendix B). Page is suing Dash for violating the Copyright Act when Dash wrote a song based on Page's song (which in copyright

terms is called the "original"), "Red, White, and Blue." Dash's song uses the structure and many lyrics of the original but changes the original song's political message. The music of the two songs is not at issue, only the lyrics. Page expects that Dash will argue that his song is a parody that falls under the fair use exception to the Copyright Act. The court will consider the relevant factors set out in the fair use statute, 17 U.S.C. § 107: whether the copy was transformative and targeted the original; whether it took more than necessary of the original; and whether it will interfere with the original's market.

Step 1: Gather and review foundational information to determine what will likely matter to the outcome of the case. Research and review the legal requirements, such as elements for the claims or defenses, and the relevant facts, whether favorable, unfavorable, or neutral. A good theory of the case has to have a solid basis in the applicable law and it must take into account the facts that will matter to the outcome.

Using the copyright and fair use problem, this would mean reviewing the materials in Appendix B, which includes the background facts, the lyrics of the two songs, and the applicable law.

Step 2: Identify each side's strengths and weaknesses, considering the evidence for each side and the weight of authority supporting each side's arguments. Most first-year writing courses begin with "objective," rather than persuasive, analysis and writing so that students can really evaluate a case with a clear sense of where it is strong and where it is weak. At this point you're evaluating the foundational information with an analytical purpose.

With the copyright and fair use problem, you might jot down a list of strengths and weaknesses for Page's side. For instance, you might note that a strong point for Page's case is that Dash used a lot of Page's song lyrics. The third statutory factor for determining fair use considers whether "'the amount and substantiality of the portion used in relation to the copyrighted work as a whole' . . . [is] reasonable in relation to the purpose of the copying." *Campbell v. Acuff-Rose Music, Inc.*, 510 U.S. 569, 586 (1994) (internal citations omitted). The fact that Dash used a lot of Page's song is a strength, but a weakness for Page might be that Dash's song is a parody of hers, and while it uses some of the lyrics and evokes Page's song, Dash's song critically changes the message. This creates the argument that the amount of Page's song that Dash used was reasonable in light of his purpose in copying—parody. Furthermore, the first statutory factor for determining fair use considers this "purpose and character of the use." Under that factor, "transformative" work, like Dash's parody, weighs in favor of finding fair use. You'd continue in this way making a list of strengths and weaknesses in light of the applicable law and facts.

Step 3: Brainstorm ways of looking at the case that would make your client a winner. Reviewing and analyzing the applicable law and facts probably got your brain buzzing with ideas. Now it's time to think of a logical and persuasive narrative about what happened. It should emphasize your side's strengths, while neutralizing or at least being consistent with your side's weaknesses. This stage can be quite creative and it's often best to focus on simply generating ideas. You might try jotting down ideas without stopping to evaluate them—phrases or sentences for a theory of the case and words to use for your themes. If you get stuck, imagine you're telling a colleague about the case by completing the sentence "My client should win because . . ." or "This case is about . . . ." Don't worry too much about the phrasing at this stage because you won't necessarily use the same language in your brief.

With the copyright and fair use problem, you might start by jotting down words for Page's side:

- unreasonable
- unfairly
- inequitable

Phrases and full sentences would be good too, so you might jot down:

- Dash takes too much
- Dash's song does not creatively transform
- Dash attempts to capitalize on Page's work
- Dash's song supplants the original

And then you might start thinking about completing a sentence, with results like these:

- My client Page should win because Dash unfairly took too much from Page's song in an attempt to financially capitalize on the market for Page's song.
- My client Page should win because instead of creating a new or transformative work, Dash stole an unreasonable amount from Page to try to take advantage of the market for Page's song. It's not fair because Dash took too much.
- This case is about a guy who lacked creativity and tried to take advantage of a successful musician by copying her song and targeting the original song's market.

It's okay if you start to feel your mind wander and you start jotting down ideas that go a little beyond the construct of "My client should win because . . ."

or "This case is about . . . ." At this stage, you're just brainstorming. For instance, you might start to feel your emotions rise and write down:

- People like Dash shouldn't be able to hide behind the fair use defense when they unfairly steal from someone else's successful work.
- It's okay to make a parody, but it's not okay to copy huge amounts from someone else and try to get people to buy your song instead of theirs.

Step 4: Evaluate possible strategies and choose what you think will be the most effective theory of the case and themes. This may be a matter of simply choosing the best idea from your brainstorming session if you have something good or it may require you to synthesize and distill multiple ideas into one concise theory.

Remember the theory of the case needs to be a credible and specific explanation of what happened, consistent with the evidence and not in legalese. Choose a theory of the case that fits with the case you have—the applicable law and actual facts. It should persuade your audience that your client should win. For instance, "the defendant infringed the copyright" or "the fair use exception does not apply" is too generic and conclusory, and won't likely persuade a juror or judge.

With the copyright and fair use problem, the court will weigh the statutory fair use factors. Which would be strong factors for you to emphasize in your theory?

Reviewing the case law, you'd find that the second factor, "the nature of the copyrighted work," is usually not significant in cases involving parodies. So you could ignore that factor for purposes of your theory. The first factor, though, is significant; it considers whether the new work is "transformative." Although you've brainstormed the idea that Dash didn't creatively transform Page's work, the facts suggest that Dash's song is arguably a parody and that many of the lyrics actually were different and critical of Page's message. Therefore, the first factor probably doesn't weigh very strongly in Page's favor. You might avoid emphasizing it in your theory of the case for that reason. The theory of the case must fit well with the facts you have, not the facts you wish you had. It would therefore be better for Page to emphasize the third and fourth factors regarding "the amount and substantiality of the portion used" and "the effect of the use upon the potential market for or value of the copyrighted work." The ideas from your brainstorming highlight these with the core themes of Dash taking too much of Page's song and Dash trying to take advantage of the market for Page's song. Synthesizing these, you might come up with something like:

- Dash took an unreasonable amount from Page and unfairly tried to take advantage of the market for Page's song.

Step 5: Use the theory of the case and themes throughout your brief. Unify your key points and assertions with your theory of the case and themes.

For instance, when writing an introduction to your brief consider the purpose of the section and what you need to include, such as some contextual facts and stating what action you'd like the court to take. Also consider how you might get in your theory of the case or core themes. Start with a line that will spark the reader's interest and that suggests a narrative explanation for the case. For the copyright and fair use problem, you might start with this:

- Although the fair use exception protects certain parodies from violating the Copyright Act, in this case Billy Dash has taken too much of Jenna Page's original popular song lyrics to qualify for such protection.

This orients the reader to your situation, where Dash claims his song is a parody that falls under the fair use exception but Page claims that Dash took too much of the original and infringed her copyright. This sentence subtly gets in the core theme of "taking too much" and you can build on this in the rest of the introduction.

Remember that you'll want to use the theory of the case and themes at multiple places throughout your brief. You won't necessarily use the exact words that you jotted down. This is just to get the idea clear in your mind as you're writing your brief. Keep your notes close by, however, so that they can guide your choices and provide a memorable focal point for the reader to grasp.

EXAMPLES

Review the following examples. For each example, there may be more than one correct answer, but try to choose the *best* answer. Explain to yourself why you have chosen that answer. Then read the explanations in the last section of this chapter to check your work.

Example 20-1

EXAMPLES

This question uses the cell phone manslaughter problem, which you can find in Appendix A.

Which of the following is the most comprehensive and persuasive theory of the case on behalf of Allison King? (Answering this example gives you a chance to test your ability to strategically evaluate whether, given the relevant law and facts, a theory of the case would persuasively explain why your client should prevail.)

A. The near-whiteout conditions were dangerous and Allison King's decision to use her cell phone to prevent others from entering is what most anyone would have done in that situation.

B. Allison King's decision to give June Coughlin a call was the right thing to do because she was a friend and they were planning to get together. King was terrified and was doing her best. She had to dial the friend to be able to warn her. The law allows for this kind of cell phone use when there's an emergency.

C. Allison King did not drive with gross negligence, so she is not guilty of vehicular manslaughter.

D. The bicyclist appeared from out of the fog, so it wasn't Allison King's fault that she couldn't see him.

EXAMPLES

Example 20-2

This question uses the cell phone manslaughter problem, which you can find in Appendix A.

If you were prosecuting King for vehicular manslaughter, which of the following facts would best help develop a theme or theory of your case?

A. King used her cell phone to call a friend, and not to contact a law enforcement agency, fire department, or health care provider.

B. The highway on which King was driving offered no places to stop.

C. King was concerned for the safety of her friends because of the unusually hazardous driving conditions.

D. While she was driving down the highway, King was grossly negligent by using her cell phone.

EXAMPLES

Example 20-3

This question uses the copyright and fair use problem, which you can find in Appendix B.

Can you identify a theory of the case in this introduction? What words and phrases express the theory of the case and themes that the author is trying to convey? Circle or underline the portions you identify and then read the explanation.

Although the fair use exception protects certain parodies from violating the Copyright Act, in this case Billy Dash has taken too much of Jenna Page's original popular song lyrics to qualify for such protection. Dash produced and marketed a song entitled "Red, White, and Blue Through and Through," targeting Page's copyrighted original "Red, White, and Blue." Dash patterned song lyrics after Page's in an attempt to capitalize on Page's significant financial and musical success. The Copyright Act protects rightful copyright holders like Page from this kind of unfair use. Under the statutory four-factor test, Dash's use, which closely copies a famous original work, taking more than necessary from the original and targeting its market, does not constitute a fair use and therefore infringes Page's copyright. Accordingly, the Court should deny Dash's motion for summary judgment.

EXAMPLES

Example 20-4

This question uses the copyright and fair use problem, which you can find in Appendix B.

Assume your theory of the case is that instead of creating a sufficiently transformative work, Dash copied an unreasonable amount from Page to take financial advantage of the successful musician's original work. Which of the following thesis statements would best weave in this theory of the case?

A. Dash's song is not fair use because it conjures up the original song by targeting a recognizable refrain and unfairly transforms its political message.
B. The fair use exception does not protect parodies that copy too much of the original copyrighted work.
C. This Court should deny the motion to dismiss because under the relevant statutory factors, Dash's song infringes Page's work.
D. Dash's song is not fair use because it unreasonably copies too much from Page's copyrighted song without sufficiently transforming it and while aiming to usurp the original market.

EXPLANATIONS

Explanation 20-1

A is the best answer. This theory of the case would plausibly work. It melds relevant facts and law: that the near-whiteout conditions Allison King was in were dangerous, which goes toward showing that the call was for an "emergency purpose" under California Vehicle Code § 23123 and therefore that King was not driving "in the commission of an unlawful act" or "in an unlawful manner" for purposes of California Penal Code § 192, vehicular manslaughter. It also concisely melds relevant facts and law as to section 192's gross negligence requirement, suggesting that it was not vehicular manslaughter because King acted how others would have acted in that situation, not with gross negligence. **B** is not the best answer. Although it has the makings of a plausible theory of the case, this version is not concise and lacks the coherence necessary for an overarching narrative or idea that concisely explains why King should prevail. **C** is not the best answer. When choosing a theory of the case, avoid lawyerly language and simply stating the legal conclusion that you hope your audience will reach. Gross negligence is a legal term and simply asserting that King did not act grossly negligent does not provide reasoning or a concise narrative to understand her actions. **D** is not the best answer. Although D melds law (the concept of fault) and fact (that the bicyclist appeared from out of the fog), it doesn't provide a precise explanation or narrative explaining why King isn't guilty of vehicular manslaughter. In addition, it doesn't involve the idea of King making a cell phone call and this omission might leave the reader wondering a number of things, such as: (1) whether the cell phone call is relevant to the writer's theory of the case; (2) whether the writer's theory is that fault is related to visibility or that fog creates an emergency; (3) whether the legal question presented is whether King could see the bicyclist; or (4) whether she was grossly negligent for not seeing him. In short, while D might be a decent start in a brainstorming session, it isn't yet a clearly crafted, precise theory of the case for the cell phone manslaughter problem.

Explanation 20-2

A is the best answer. This is a potential strength in your argument, because the "emergency purposes" exception in the statute implies that an "emergency" involves calling the local authorities or a medical provider. **B** isn't the best answer. According to the facts, the highway offered few places to pull over, not none. Although this fact is not as strong as the one in A, it may nonetheless still help establish gross negligence. The prosecution could use this fact to portray the conditions in which King was driving as obviously hazardous and establish the theory that a reasonable person would have acknowledged the risk of using a cell phone under the same circumstances. **C** is incorrect. King's concern for the safety of her friends is not a good fact to develop a theory of a case for her conviction. This fact might actually be a weakness in your case, and although it is important to address it, you don't want to create your theme based on it. **D** is incorrect. This is not a fact; it is a legal conclusion. Develop your theory of the case and themes using persuasive facts.

EXPLANATIONS

Explanation 20-3

This introduction uses the theory of the case discussed in "How to Develop and Use a Theory of the Case and Themes" above, that instead of creating a sufficiently transformative work, Dash copied an unreasonable amount from Page to take financial advantage of the successful musician's original work. It uses the related themes of Dash's use as unfair and unreasonable. The bolded portions weave in this theory of the case and themes:

> Although the fair use exception protects certain parodies from violating the Copyright Act, in this case Billy Dash has **taken too much** of Jenna Page's original popular song lyrics to qualify for such protection. Dash produced and marketed a song entitled "Red, White, and Blue Through and Through," targeting Page's copyrighted original "Red, White, and Blue." **Dash patterned song lyrics after Page's in an attempt to capitalize on Page's significant financial and musical success.** The Copyright Act protects rightful copyright holders like Page from this kind of **unfair** use. Under the statutory four-factor test, Dash's use, which closely copies a **famous** original work, **taking more than necessary** from the original and **targeting its market**, does not constitute a fair use and therefore infringes Page's copyright. Accordingly, the Court should deny Dash's motion for summary judgment.

EXPLANATIONS

Explanation 20-4

A is incorrect. It uses reasoning that doesn't reflect the theory of the case and in fact would likely weigh against the conclusion you're advocating. A parody may copy to a limited extent so that it "conjure[s] up" the original work, particularly memorable parts of an original, and a work's transformative nature weighs in favor of finding fair use. *See* Appendix B; *Campbell v. Acuff-Rose Music, Inc.*, 510 U.S. 569, 588, 579 (1994). **B** is not the best answer. Although this thesis statement weaves in the part of the theory regarding Dash using "too much," D is a better choice because it also weaves in the part of the theory regarding Dash trying to capitalize on Page's financial success by targeting the original work's market. Also note while B uses generic language about the fair use exception, D uses facts that are more specific to the copyright and fair use problem at hand and so is overall a stronger thesis statement. **C** is incorrect. This thesis statement is conclusory and doesn't weave in a theory of the case. A reader might wonder what key facts specifically show that Dash's song infringes Page's work. Key facts are important to a strong theory of the case because they help to create an understandable narrative with persuasive effect. **D** is the best answer. This thesis statement gets in the theory of the case that Dash unfairly took "too much" from Page's original and is trying to capitalize on the original's financial success by taking over its market.

Checklist

Chapter 20: Developing a Theory of the Case and Themes

✔	Consider each side's strengths and weaknesses, thinking about the evidence and weight of authority supporting each side's arguments.
✔	Create an overarching narrative or idea that explains the key issues and why your client should win—the theory of the case and core themes.
✔	Weave the theory of the case and core themes through the brief, while not overpowering the reader.

You will find all of the chapter checklists compiled in Appendix D.

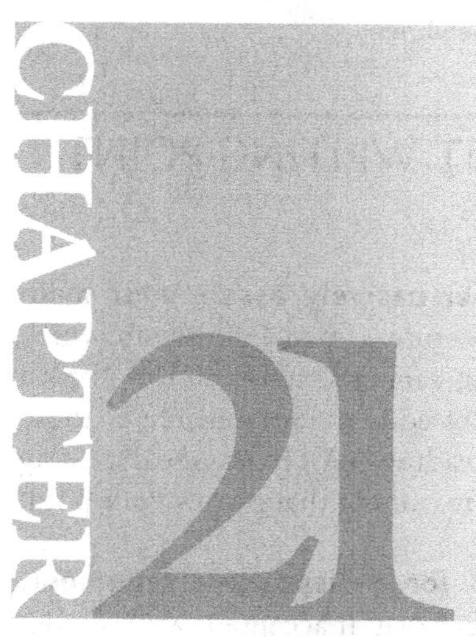

Writing Point Headings and Subheadings

Point headings and subheadings are sometimes an afterthought for student writers, but they are often the first thing judges read. The point headings and subheadings do a lot of structural and persuasive heavy lifting because they briefly summarize your entire argument. The reader will either page through the body of the Argument itself to find them or will find them neatly presented in outline form in a Table of Contents.

Two important aspects contribute to effective point headings and subheadings: organization and persuasive writing. Making good choices about how many point headings and subheadings to use and where to put them requires you to make smart choices about the organization of your Argument section. You'll want to think about how many separate legal issues you have, what you have to show to win, how your applicable legal rule is divided, and where logical spots for point headings and subheadings would be. A natural place to get more help on this is Chapter 7 on Organizing the Discussion. Once you've got a logical organization in place, use this chapter to help you write persuasive point headings and subheadings.

Terminology notes. This chapter addresses the argumentative headings in the Argument section of your motion or brief. Your professor may call all of them "point headings," or may identify the headings at the highest level as "point headings" or simply "headings" and the various divisions as "subheadings." In this book, the ones at the highest level are called your "point headings" and any that come at a level nested below those are called "subheadings."

WHAT YOU NEED TO KNOW ABOUT WRITING POINT HEADINGS AND SUBHEADINGS

Point headings and subheadings persuasively assert your main arguments, arranged in a logical order. Picture a formal outline in which your big points—the point headings—are each a sentence at the Roman numeral level of the outline (I., II., . . .). Nested at the level inside of those bigger point headings you have your subheadings (A., B., . . .), each being a sentence that provides a logical chunk of reasoning that proves your point headings.

A point heading is generally used for a dispositive argument. A "dispositive argument" means an argument that, if accepted, would independently win what you're seeking in the motion or brief. Some professors expect that you'll use a point heading only for making such a dispositive argument. Other professors recognize that while this is the general custom, it's not a strict rule and there may be reasons to use a point heading for a nondispositive argument. For instance, you may have a threshold issue that, although not dispositive, should be addressed before your first main point heading. Some writers would use a point heading for that threshold issue.

Use subheadings to set forth the steps of logic or conclusions that prove your point heading. Subheadings can neatly separate a long and complex argument into logical chunks that go toward demonstrating the assertion in your point heading.

Each point heading and subheading should generally (a) include one or more key facts; (b) relate to the legal issue; and (c) identify what you want the court to do or what conclusion you want it to reach. If your issue is a purely legal one, such as an argument before an appeals court about what the law is, then you won't include facts because they won't be necessary to your argument. But in most cases, your issue will not be purely legal, and you'll want to include facts because point headings that meld legal issues and key facts are more persuasive. Be specific, not generic. And phrase the point heading in terms of what you want the court to do ("This Court Should Dismiss . . .") or as the conclusion you want it to reach ("The Defendant Breached the Contract by . . .").

There's no official rule on numbering and typesetting, but there are typical conventions that most lawyers and professors follow. Use Roman numerals (I., II., III.), letters (A., B., C.), and numbers (1., 2., 3.) as in a formal outline. Professors and practicing lawyers tend to have varying views about whether you should give a point heading a Roman numeral if you have only one point. Some consider it permissible, while others believe that if you have only one point heading, there's no point in giving it a number. What about subheadings? Most lawyers and professors agree that you should not use subheadings unless you have at least two subheadings for that level. For instance, you would not use a subheading "A." unless you also had a subheading "B."

Your best bet is to ask which typesetting convention your professor considers most effective and to follow your professor's or supervisor's recommendation. Traditionally, lawyers have used all capital letters for point headings at the Roman numeral level (I.). All caps can be difficult to read, however. Furthermore, spellcheck doesn't always catch errors in all caps, so be sure to proofread carefully. Some use bold print instead of all caps, in part for the reasons stated above. Subheadings may be in italics, in bold, or underlined, but be sure to follow court rules for formatting the Table of Contents. The first letter of each significant word is capitalized. All headings should be single-spaced.

Here are three versions of typeface choices you might make in your point headings:

I. DASH'S PARODY IS FAIR USE BECAUSE IT TARGETS A RECOGNIZABLE REFRAIN OF THE ORIGINAL SONG AND CRITICALLY TRANSFORMS ITS POLITICAL MESSAGE FOR A DIFFERENT ECONOMIC MARKET.

A. Dash Fairly Created a Parody of Page's Song That Transformed Its Political Anti-Establishment Message to Support for Traditional Values.

B. Dash Fairly Used a Reasonable Amount of Page's Copyrighted Work as Necessary to Invoke the Original for Dash's Parody.

C. Evidence Shows That Dash's Critical Parody Has a Different Market and Will Not Affect the Market for Page's Original Song.

I. Dash's Parody Is Fair Use Because It Targets a Recognizable Refrain of the Original Song and Critically Transforms Its Political Message for a Different Economic Market.

A. Dash Fairly Created a Parody of Page's Song That Transformed Its Political Anti-Establishment Message to Support for Traditional Values.

B. Dash Fairly Used a Reasonable Amount of Page's Copyrighted Work as Necessary to Invoke the Original for Dash's Parody.

C. Evidence Shows That Dash's Critical Parody Has a Different Market and Will Not Affect the Market for Page's Original Song.

I. Dash's Parody Is Fair Use Because It Targets a Recognizable Refrain of the Original Song and Critically Transforms Its Political Message for a Different Economic Market.

A. *Dash Fairly Created a Parody of Page's Song That Transformed Its Political Anti-Establishment Message to Support for Traditional Values.*
B. *Dash Fairly Used a Reasonable Amount of Page's Copyrighted Work as Necessary to Invoke the Original for Dash's Parody.*
C. *Evidence Shows That Dash's Critical Parody Has a Different Market and Will Not Affect the Market for Page's Original Song.*

You can use your point headings and subheadings to ensure that you have an effective structure to your Argument. Read your point headings in order and perhaps copy and paste them out onto another page as you would when creating a Table of Contents for an appellate brief. Considered together, your point headings and subheadings should set out a complete and persuasive outline of your Argument. Ask yourself: Do they assert my Argument's main points? Are there gaps or inconsistencies? If you're not using enough point headings and subheadings, you'll see that you don't have an accurate and complete outline of your Argument. If you notice that two point headings or subheadings are similar, you might be making only one point and you should consider consolidating those sections of your Argument and adjusting your headings accordingly.

HOW TO WRITE POINT HEADINGS AND SUBHEADINGS

Using the copyright and fair use problem in Appendix B, we'll walk you through the process of writing point headings.

PROBLEMS

Problem

Here is a quick overview of the copyright and fair use problem (for details, see Appendix B). Page is suing Dash for violating the Copyright Act when Dash wrote a song based on Page's song (which in copyright terms is called the "original"), "Red, White, and Blue." Dash's song uses the structure and many lyrics of the original but changes the original song's political message. The music of the two songs is not at issue, only the lyrics. Page expects that Dash will argue that his song is a parody that falls under the fair use exception to the Copyright Act. The court will consider the relevant factors set out in the fair use statute, 17 U.S.C. § 107: whether the copy was transformative and targeted the original; whether it took more than necessary of the original; and whether it will interfere with the original's market.

Step 1: Start with your draft outline. Assuming you represented Dash, the Defendant in the copyright and fair use problem, you might start with this draft outline:

I. Fair Use
   A. The purpose and the character of the use
   B. The amount and substantiality of the portion used in relation to the copyrighted work as a whole
   C. The effect of the use upon the potential market for or value of the copyrighted work[1]

This draft outline organizes the defendant's Argument section by three of the four statutory factors that courts consider in evaluating whether an appropriation of copyrighted material is fair use. The second factor, "the nature of the copyrighted work," is omitted because the case law shows that courts have consistently concluded it is of negligible significance in cases where, as in this copyright and fair use problem, the defendant claims the allegedly infringing work is "parody." This omission could be briefly explained in the introduction (also known as the umbrella section) of the Argument. That leaves the other three factors for the Argument section.

Step 2: Consider whether your headings are point headings or subheadings and whether you've appropriately numbered them. The draft outline envisions "Fair Use" as the big point of the brief. This makes sense because you're imagining writing a brief for the defendant who wants to assert fair use as a defense to copyright infringement. If the defendant prevails with the fair use defense, he wins the case and so it's a dispositive argument that warrants using a point heading.

What about the three statutory factors? None of them are dispositive. Each one, however, is a logical step toward showing that the use falls within the fair use exception to the Copyright Act. So these make sense as subheadings as in the draft outline.

Step 3: Craft a sentence for each point heading and subheading that melds the legal issue with key facts and is phrased as the conclusion you want the court to reach or the action you want it to take. Think about writing a point heading about fair use.

What's the legal issue here? The plaintiff sued the defendant for copyright infringement of her original song's lyrics, "Red, White, and Blue." The defendant wants to argue that the fair use defense applies to his song's lyrics, "Red, White, and Blue Through and Through." You could say the issue is whether the defendant's use of the original work in his parody song falls

1. 17 U.S.C. § 107.

within the fair use exception. And you know the defendant will argue that the three relevant statutory factors weigh in favor of the court finding that his song's appropriation of the original falls within the fair use exception. You would then capture that idea in the point heading.

What are the key facts that you could use to show this? Look at your arguments under each of the relevant statutory factors and consider what the most persuasive facts are for each factor. Is there a fact that goes to more than one factor and that you think will be especially important?

Finally, you want to phrase this as a conclusory sentence, either identifying what you want the court to do or the conclusion you want it to reach. Here, you want the court to conclude that the song is not an unlawful infringement because it falls within the fair use exception. Stated more briefly, Dash's song is fair use.

Capturing all three of these components, you might have:

> I. DASH'S PARODY IS FAIR USE BECAUSE IT TARGETS A RECOGNIZABLE REFRAIN OF THE ORIGINAL SONG AND CRITICALLY TRANSFORMS ITS POLITICAL MESSAGE FOR A DIFFERENT ECONOMIC MARKET.

This one's a bit on the long side, but it's readable and gets in the important components. Next, you'd craft the subheadings using the same method.

Step 4: Check that your point headings and subheadings set out a complete and persuasive outline of your Argument. Some people write point headings before they've written the Argument section and others keep a marker in the spot and write the point headings after they've finished writing the Argument section. Whichever way you do it, after you've finished writing the Argument section, go back and check your point headings and subheadings. Make any necessary adjustments to the number or phrasing of the headings.

EXAMPLES

Review the following examples. For each example, there may be more than one correct answer, but try to choose the *best* answer. Explain to yourself why you have chosen that answer. Then read the explanations in the last section of this chapter to check your work.

Note. We've all-capped these point headings only because that's commonly done in practice. In your own writing, as noted earlier in this chapter, you should use the typesetting your professor or supervisor considers most effective.

EXAMPLES

Example 21-1

This question uses the copyright and fair use problem, which you can find in Appendix B.

DASH'S SONG COPIES SOME OF PAGE'S SONG, TARGETING THE MOST MEMORABLE PARTS, AND CRITICIZES PAGE'S NEGATIVE POLITICAL MESSAGE TO APPEAL TO A DIFFERENT AUDIENCE.

This point heading . . .

A. should state a legal conclusion or what the court should do.
B. is strong for a pure question of law and needs no improvement.
C. should include more key facts.
D. would be strong in a motion or brief for Dash but not Page.

EXAMPLES

Example 21-2

This question uses the copyright and fair use problem, which you can find in Appendix B.

DASH'S SONG IS FAIR USE BECAUSE, ALTHOUGH IT COPIES SOME OF PAGE'S SONG, IT TARGETS THE MOST RECOGNIZABLE REFRAINS AND TRANSFORMS THE SONG INTO A PARODY CRITICIZING PAGE'S NEGATIVE MESSAGE ABOUT AMERICA AND ECONOMIC INEQUALITY, WHILE NOT SUPERSEDING THE MARKET FOR PAGE'S ORIGINAL, WHICH CONSISTED OF MANY LOYAL AND LIBERAL FANS.

A. The Relevant Statutory Factors Weigh in Favor of Dash's Song Being Fair Use.

A. The subheading is better than the point heading—it should be substituted for the point heading.
B. The point heading should explicitly state the action the writer wants the court to take.
C. The point heading and subheading are strong and need no improvements.
D. The point heading is too long and the subheading should be cut.

EXAMPLES

Example 21-3

This question uses the copyright and fair use problem, which you can find in Appendix B.

> IN LIGHT OF THE APPLICABLE STATUTORY FACTORS AND LONGSTANDING DOCTRINE, THE COURT SHOULD FIND THAT DASH'S SONG IS FAIR USE.

This point heading . . .

- **A.** would be more persuasive if it included facts supporting the legal conclusions.
- **B.** is strong and needs no improvement.
- **C.** should cite authority.
- **D.** is too short.

EXAMPLES

Example 21-4

This question uses the cell phone manslaughter problem, which you can find in Appendix A.

Assume you are responding to a motion by Allison King to dismiss the vehicular manslaughter charge against her. She argues that the court should dismiss the case, as a matter of law, because she placed the cell phone call for an "emergency purpose" under the statute. Which of the following point headings would best articulate the state's argument?

- **A.** KING IS NOT ENTITLED TO THE STATUTE'S "EMERGENCY PURPOSES" EXCEPTION BECAUSE SHE WAS CALLING HER FRIEND, NOT AN EMERGENCY SERVICE PROVIDER AS THE STATUTE REQUIRES.
- **B.** KING'S MOTION SHOULD BE DENIED BECAUSE THE "EMERGENCY PURPOSES" EXCEPTION APPLIES ONLY WHEN CALLING A LAW ENFORCEMENT AGENCY, A HEALTH CARE PROVIDER, A FIRE DEPARTMENT, OR ANOTHER EMERGENCY SERVICES AGENCY OR ENTITY.
- **C.** KING DID NOT ACT FOR AN "EMERGENCY PURPOSE" AND HENCE, HER MOTION TO DISMISS SHOULD BE DENIED.
- **D.** KING CALLED JUNE COUGHLIN, NOT THE POLICE OR ANOTHER AGENCY DESIGNED TO DEAL WITH EMERGENCIES.

EXAMPLES

Example 21-5

This question uses the negligent infliction of emotional distress problem, which you can find in Appendix C.

Assume the plaintiff, Poe, prevailed at trial and the defendant, Defoe, appealed. He claims Poe failed, as a matter of law, to demonstrate two of the required elements because she and Valenzuela were not cohabitants and because she did not witness the accident that injured her fiancé, Valenzuela. The outline that follows is the point heading and subheadings in Poe's responsive brief.

THE JURY VERDICT SHOULD BE UPHELD BECAUSE DEFOE NEGLIGENTLY RAN OVER POE'S FIANCÉ, VALENZUELA, WHILE POE WAS ONLY FEET AWAY FROM THE CRASH AND POE SUFFERED SEVERE EMOTIONAL DISTRESS.

A. Poe and Valenzuela had an "intimate, familial relationship" because they were engaged, had been dating for five years, jointly owned a car, and stayed at each others' houses almost every night.

B. Poe was "sensorially aware" of the crash because she heard the impact, had to jump to avoid being hit by the lawnmower Valenzuela had been operating, and immediately saw Valenzuela on the ground near Defoe's car, covered in blood and nonresponsive.

This point heading and subheadings...

A. should have a Roman numeral "I" for the main heading.

B. effectively outline the argument for Poe on appeal.

C. contain too many facts to be effective.

D. should not include, in the main heading, points that are not included in the subheadings.

EXPLANATIONS

EXPLANATIONS

Explanation 21-1

A is the best answer. A point heading should include key facts, relate to the legal issue, and identify what the court should do or what conclusion it should reach. This example is heavy on the facts and fails to identify what the court should do or conclude. You could start to revise it by adding to the beginning "DASH'S SONG IS FAIR USE BECAUSE . . ." It would then be phrased as the conclusion that Dash wants the court to reach. With a few more small changes, you might then have: "DASH'S SONG IS FAIR USE

BECAUSE IT IS A PARODY THAT TARGETS THE MOST MEMORABLE PARTS OF PAGE'S SONG TO CRITICIZE THE NEGATIVE POLITICAL MESSAGE AND THUS APPEAL TO A DIFFERENT AUDIENCE." **B** is incorrect. Our copyright and fair use problem is not a pure question of law. The issue requires the court to determine how the law applies to the facts. **C** is also incorrect. This point heading already includes lots of facts. What's missing is the conclusion or action the writer seeks from the court. **D** is not the best answer. Although this point heading would be *stronger* in a motion or brief for Dash than for Page, it isn't a *strong* point heading for the reasons stated in A.

EXPLANATIONS

Explanation 21-2

A is incorrect. The subheading does a good job clearly and concisely stating its point, but it does not incorporate key facts. So it wouldn't be a good idea to simply substitute the subheading for the point heading. In fact, because most professors agree that you shouldn't use a subheading if you have only one point to make under the point heading, it would make sense here to cut the subheading. Alternatively, if you liked the text of the subheading better than the text of the point heading in this example, you could revise the subheading to incorporate the key facts and use it instead of the point heading. For instance, you might revise the subheading to this point heading:

> DASH'S SONG IS FAIR USE UNDER THE RELEVANT STATUTORY FACTORS BECAUSE IT IS A PARODY THAT TARGETS THE ORIGINAL'S MOST RECOGNIZABLE REFRAINS, CRITICALLY TRANSFORMING ITS POLITICAL MESSAGE, WHILE NOT SUPERSEDING ITS MARKET.

B is not the best answer. Point headings should either state what you want the court to do or state the conclusion you want the court to reach; this point heading states the conclusion—Dash's song is fair use—so it isn't necessary to say what you want the court to do in this point heading. **C** is incorrect. Although the point heading has some strong aspects, it's hard to read and could be improved by editing its length. Also, most professors agree that you shouldn't use a subheading if you have only one point to make under the point heading. Because there's only one subheading here, it should be cut. **D** is the best answer. This point heading is pretty good, but it's too long and needs some editing. Also, as noted in C, the subheading should be cut because you don't use a subheading if you have only one point to make under the point heading. The point heading should make that point.

EXPLANATIONS

Explanation 21-3

A is the best answer. Supplying reasons, particularly with key facts, is more persuasive than generic conclusions of law. **B** is incorrect. This point heading could be improved by explaining its conclusion, particularly with key facts. **C** is also incorrect. Although point headings occasionally cite authority if there's a key statute or seminal case, they usually don't and there's no requirement that they should. **D** is not the best answer. It's true that this point heading needs more information (it needs key facts, as noted in A)—so it needs to be longer to add that information—but in general you want your point headings to be short enough to be easily readable. Hence, there is no such thing as a point heading that is "too short" as long as it has all the required components.

EXPLANATIONS

Explanation 21-4

A is the best answer. This point heading includes a key fact (she called her friend, not an emergency services provider), relates to the legal issue (the "emergency purposes" exception under the statute), and identifies the conclusion the writer wants the court to reach (King isn't entitled to the "emergency purposes" exception). **B** is not the best answer. This point heading sounds good—it starts with what we want the court to do (deny King's motion), includes "because" (so it sounds like it has facts), but it includes only law. This point heading never explicitly states that King didn't call one of these agencies or entities; it needs to say she called her friend instead. The judge won't know your facts, so you need to be explicit in the point heading. Furthermore, this point heading misstates the law. The statute itself lists these emergency service providers but expressly states that the exception applies to a "person using a wireless telephone for emergency purposes, *including, but not limited to,*" the list of agencies and entities in the point heading. Hence, the exception doesn't apply *only* when calling one of those agencies or entities listed. **C** is not the best answer. This point heading includes the key legal test and states what the writer wants the court to do, but it includes no facts. This is problematic for the reasons stated in B. **D** is also not the best answer. This point heading has the opposite problem of B—it states only a fact (and the friend's name probably isn't helpful) and doesn't clearly tie this fact to the statute's "emergency purposes" exception or state what the court should do or conclude.

Explanation 21-5

A is not the best answer. Although some lawyers include a Roman numeral when there is only one main heading, some lawyers (and professors) expect no number if the writer has only one main heading. **B** is correct. The main point heading provides a quick overview of the reasons the claim succeeds, and the subheadings highlight the contested elements and use facts to persuasively argue these elements are met. **C** is incorrect. Facts are key to strong headings (unless the issue is a purely legal issue), and these headings include the key facts and are still relatively easy to read. **D** is not the best answer. Although on appeal the defendant did not challenge his negligence and the plaintiff's emotional distress, it can help for persuasive purposes to make those elements clear. You wouldn't need sections in your brief devoted to those points, so you wouldn't have subheadings on those issues. But it might help the judge understand the incident and be more inclined to rule in favor of your client.

Checklist

Chapter 21: Writing Point Headings and Subheadings

✔	Point headings meld the legal issue with key facts and are phrased as the conclusion you want the court to reach or the action you want it to take.
✔	Use a point heading for each dispositive argument.
✔	Use subheadings to set out the steps of logic or conclusions that prove your point heading or headings.
✔	Follow conventions of using different formatting and numbering for different levels of headings.
✔	Point headings and subheadings set out a complete and persuasive outline of the argument.

You will find all of the chapter checklists compiled in Appendix D.

CHAPTER 22

Making Persuasive Arguments

If you came to law school because you love to argue, this part of writing ought to make you happy. Although the art of persuasion is just that—an art—certain principles will make your arguments more likely to succeed. After all, who likes to *lose* an argument?

WHAT YOU NEED TO KNOW ABOUT MAKING PERSUASIVE ARGUMENTS

Your goal with persuasive writing is to get the reader to agree with you. As noted in Chapter 18, persuasive writing differs from objective writing. With objective writing, your purpose is to answer the Question Presented with objective/predictive analysis. With persuasive writing, on the other hand, you're trying to convince the judge that your client's position is the correct position. Sometimes this is your task even though you believe the opposing side has a stronger legal argument. But even in those situations, you need to write as though you are confident that your position is the winner. Analyze each sentence to ensure that it helps your client or at a minimum it is neutral. Even though you will sometimes cite adverse law, sentences that are adverse to your client need to be reframed.

The substance of your argument is the most important factor in overall persuasiveness. A losing argument, even when made artfully, is still almost always a losing argument. The good news is that (at least in law school) you'll rarely need to make arguments that are clear "losers." Usually, each side's position has merit—which is why your professor assigned the problem in the first place.

Your argument should include both (1) the reasons you are *legally entitled* to win (the "justifying" arguments), and (2) the reasons you *should* win (the "motivating" arguments).[1] The justifying arguments convince the judge she won't be overruled for deciding in your favor. But the motivating arguments are those that make the judge want to rule in your favor in the first place. Although rarely dispositive, in a close case making the judge think your side is right can matter. Your arguments need to incorporate all the relevant law and the record or the other factual basis for your argument.

Furthermore, limit your arguments to those with a reasonable chance of success. If you want a refresher on legal analysis and different types of arguments, you can review Chapters 10 through 12. And unless a weak argument is essential to your client's success (or unless you're trying to preserve the record in a criminal case by raising all possible arguments), generally you'll be more persuasive if you focus your attention, in detail, on the strongest reasons you should prevail. This allows greater focus on those winning arguments.

The second most important factor in a document's persuasiveness is the structure of your argument, and two organizational tools can help: (a) starting each section, argument, and paragraph with a thesis statement; and (b) putting important information at the beginning and end. The first tool, starting with thesis statements, helps with the second: putting important information at the beginning. But each technique involves different considerations.

Thesis statements: Your thesis is, at a very basic level, your main point. Some people think of the thesis statement as the conclusion that you state at the beginning of your argument. The same structure you use to organize an office memo's Discussion section—CRAC—is the foundation for persuasive organization. For a refresher on CRAC, see Chapter 7. For some tips on writing effective thesis statements, see Chapter 30.

The beginning and end: Readers have certain expectations: mainly, that the most important information will be at the beginning and end, and these expectations should influence the organization of your argument. Knowing that the beginning and end are positions of strength—the beginning is the "topic" position[2] and the end is the "stress" position[3]—will help you write more persuasively. Furthermore, the concepts of primacy and recency

1. *See* Richard K. Neumann, Jr., Legal Reasoning and Legal Writing: Structure, Strategy, and Style 309-13 (6th ed. 2009).

2. Joseph M. Williams & Gregory G. Colomb, Style: Lessons in Clarity and Grace 76 (10th ed. 2010).

3. *Id.* at 85.

suggest that readers remember most what is at the beginning and the end, and you want the reader to remember favorable information.

Although the end—the stress position—is the position of greatest emphasis and readers remember that information most clearly, this principle is trumped by a special expectation in the law: Judges expect your strongest argument first. If you wait until the end, the judge may have stopped reading by then (or may only be skimming the document by that point). So if you have three main arguments, a good strategy is to start your Argument section with the strongest argument. Some readers expect the next strongest argument to follow, and so on; others expect a strong argument at the end, so they would suggest you save the second strongest argument for last and put the weakest argument in the middle. If you have more than three arguments, many writers put the weakest next to last.

Make your organization obvious with headings and transitions. This is true even for objective writing. Headings and transitions simply make your writing easier to read. But in motions and briefs, headings should be persuasive phrases or sentences that assert the conclusion you argue for, not just a word or phrase to introduce the issue. Chapter 21 explains point headings; point headings are all thesis statements as well. Your thesis statement for a section ought to become that section's heading. And the thesis statement for a subsection ought to be that section's subheading if you have subheadings.

Transitions are also key to your document making sense. Whether it's a simple "first, . . ." "second, . . ." "third, . . ."; "therefore"; or transition phrase or sentence, the reader will better understand your argument if you include explicit signals and transitions. See Chapter 32 for more help with transitions.

Your writing style can also add to the persuasiveness of your argument. Just as the way you write your facts can affect how the judge perceives your case, as noted in Chapter 25, the same holds true for your arguments. As with all legal documents, and especially all documents filed in a court, your writing style should be formal. Avoid contractions, using parentheses other than for citations, and writing in the first person. Similarly, as with other legal writing, avoid unnecessary legalese. The bottom line is this: If the judge has to stop and think about why you chose a particular word, you've lost the persuasion battle. Your word choice should help persuade the judge without him even thinking about it.

Techniques of persuasion work best when they are subtle, not obvious. Judges like to think of themselves as objective, neutral decision makers. If you make it obvious that you're attempting to sway a judge, she might put less trust in your brief or resist adopting your position. So follow all of the tips provided here, but don't go overboard in your attempts at persuasion. Similarly, you should avoid words like "clearly" and "obviously."

HOW TO MAKE PERSUASIVE ARGUMENTS

Using the cell phone manslaughter problem in Appendix A, we'll walk you through the process of writing persuasive arguments.

PROBLEMS

Problem

> Here is a quick overview of the cell phone manslaughter problem (for details, see Appendix A). Allison King used her wireless phone, without a hands-free device, while driving in dense fog on a winding road on the edge of an ocean cliff. King placed the call to warn her friends about the dangerous conditions, as they would be meeting later. While she was making the call, she hit and killed a bicyclist. The prosecution will attempt to convict King of vehicular manslaughter by showing that she drove while committing an illegal act (driving while using a wireless phone without a hands-free device) and with gross negligence. King will argue that her actions fit within the "emergency purposes" exception to the wireless phone prohibition. She will also argue that she did not act with gross negligence.

Step 1: Draft a thesis statement for each argument. Because the most important piece of persuasion is the substance of your argument, thoroughly research your problem to ensure that you aren't missing helpful authorities or contentions. The same processes you used in objective writing apply to persuasive writing, even though the ultimate goal is different.

In persuasive writing, headings and subheadings that just name an issue, like "robbery," aren't very effective (although some readers prefer them in objective office memos). Hence, you should craft thesis statements—the main point of each argument. Those thesis statements will become your descriptive (and persuasive) section and subsection headings. You can write these thesis statements whether you're at the outlining stage or already have a draft.

For instance, the beginning of your objective outline (in IRAC format) of the cell phone manslaughter problem might look like this:

Vehicular Manslaughter

1. Unlawful Act
2. Gross Negligence

Using this outline, make the short phrases into complete sentences by adding the determinative facts and key terms of art (like "emergency purposes"). Transforming the objective headings below into thesis statements in a motion or brief for King, you might come up with this:

King did not commit vehicular manslaughter.

1. King's use of her cell phone did not constitute an "unlawful act" because she called for "emergency purposes."
2. King did not act with "gross negligence."

Most readers will treat the point headings and subheadings as the "conclusion" (using the CRAC structure described in Chapter 7). Those readers expect you to jump right into the rule as you begin the text below the heading. Some readers, though, expect each conclusion to be restated at the beginning of the textual paragraph that follows the heading. As with all writing choices, knowing your audience's preferences should help you decide which choice to make.

Step 2: Organize your arguments by ranking their strength. Usually put the strongest argument first and order the rest by strength as well, but be sure to end on a strong note. Even if your last argument is the weakest you choose to include, don't end a section by trailing off with a weak argument. You should include a final sentence or two that reminds the reader of your strongest points. Using the previous outline, you might rank the sub-issues as follows:

Rank 2:	King's use of her cell phone did not constitute an "unlawful act" because she called for "emergency purposes."
Rank 1:	King did not act with "gross negligence."

Even though the "gross negligence" element is last in the statute, if you determine that it's the strongest argument in your client's favor, you would probably lead with it. This general rule of leading with your strongest argument can be trumped, though. For example, readers generally expect threshold issues—those that would dispose of the case, like procedural questions—to be addressed first, even if not the strongest argument. Similarly, some readers expect the argument to parallel the test's elements (or factors) unless there's a good reason to vary from that structure. Here, if you assume the point ranked 1 is stronger than the point ranked 2 and the reader won't be confused by this order, putting it first makes sense. The same holds true of claims or contentions supporting each main argument. Rank them, and lead with the strongest unless that order is likely to confuse the reader.

When you have three or more arguments, you should find a way to end on a strong note. Typically, legal writers put the strongest argument first. The convention to start strong is so widespread that readers will think whatever you put first is your strongest point. Many writers would then follow with the next strongest argument, afraid that if the first two arguments failed to convince the judge, she might stop reading. When dealing with the weakest argument, some might put it last while others might decide to minimize its impact by burying it in the middle or eliminating it entirely. But because readers tend to remember more about what they read last, you'll need to end the section with a reminder of the strong arguments that best support your position.

And just as you'll use the points of emphasis in your favor, use the points of de-emphasis—the middle—in your favor. As noted, weaker arguments might be put in the middle or cut altogether (unless they are essential for your success). Similarly, you might address unfavorable precedent or unfavorable facts in the middle of paragraphs or sections.

You might wonder why you should include negative information at all in a persuasive document. The answer is that your opponent will include it, and you don't want the judge left with only the other side's explanation of those arguments, authorities, or facts. You want to do the best you can to minimize their negative effect. Anticipate the other side's arguments. Don't make their arguments for them, but you can't just leave them out. For suggestions on this topic, review Chapter 23 on Making Persuasive Counterarguments. In addition, lawyers are ethically bound to disclose binding, adverse authority when the opposing party fails to disclose it to the court.

Step 3: Follow these first two principles when drafting subsections and even paragraphs. Just as these principles—starting with a thesis statement and putting your strongest argument first—provide an effective, persuasive organization for your main arguments, they are effective for subsections within each argument. Begin each section with the point of that section by using strong thesis statements. Similarly, start each paragraph with the point of that paragraph. If you need suggestions on doing this, review Chapter 30 on Starting Paragraphs Powerfully.

Organizationally, put your strongest contention or subsection within each argument first because the judge will expect it there. As noted above, the next strongest argument can go next or at the end. Similarly, at the paragraph level, start strong and make sure the last sentence is important and favorable. And with sections and paragraphs, bury potentially harmful information in the middle, where it's less likely to be remembered.

Look at the first main argument in our cell phone manslaughter problem: King did not act with "gross negligence." Imagine you had these three main points to demonstrate that King's actions did not rise to the level of gross negligence:

1. King exercised due care, so the presumption of "conscious indifference to the consequences" is not present.
2. A reasonable person in King's position would not have been aware that placing the call posed a serious risk.

3. King was attempting to minimize—not disregard—the risk to others, and these unique circumstances negate gross negligence.

You'd frame each as a thesis statement, as these samples do. Then, you'd rank them in terms of strength. If you concluded that the strongest contention was #3 and the weakest was #1 (hence, leaving #2 as a reasonably strong point, but not as strong as #3), you might reorder them as follows:

1. King was attempting to minimize—not disregard—the risk to others, and these unique circumstances negate gross negligence.
2. King exercised due care, so the presumption of "conscious indifference to the consequences" is not present.
3. A reasonable person in King's position would not have been aware that placing the call posed a serious risk.

The paragraphs within each of these contentions would all begin with thesis statements and be ordered in the same persuasive way: They'd have a strong beginning (the thesis statement), include less favorable information, including counterarguments, in the middle, and then end on a strong note.

Imagine you're drafting a paragraph within the strongest contention—that King was attempting to minimize risk, so she couldn't have disregarded risk. As with all persuasive writing, you'd need to address counterarguments. Here, you might expect the prosecutor to argue that the risk created by King's friends driving is different and a lesser risk than the risk King created when she made a phone call while driving on a dangerous, narrow, cliff-side road in fog. The paragraph where you address that might be structured like this:

> King was attempting to minimize—not disregard—the risk to others, and these unique circumstances negate gross negligence. The purpose of King's call was to warn others that the road conditions were dangerous. Although placing the call may have created a different risk, the overall purpose of the call demonstrates King's actions were not grossly negligent. Rather, the circumstances of this case suggest just the opposite; King acted reasonably.

This same persuasive structure that works for addressing counterarguments with entire issues works for paragraphs as well. For additional suggestions on dealing with counterarguments, review Chapter 23 on Making Persuasive Counterarguments.

Step 4: At the sentence level, be sure to end strong and think about your stylistic options. Readers tend to read a clause or sentence as the story of whoever shows up first—that is, in the "topic" position. So use the sentence's beginning to frame that story. And remember that the final portion of the sentence will garner the most attention, so place the most important information there.

Think about this sentence:

> King acted as carefully as any conscientious driver would in an emergency situation and not with "gross negligence."

This sentence is a story about King. Note how the sentence ends on a strong note: King did not act with "gross negligence." Furthermore, consider these two sentences:

> Mary is a good student, even though she sometimes fails to conduct the deeper analysis.
>
> Although Mary sometimes fails to conduct the deeper analysis, she is a good student.

Audiences are more likely to think the first sentence's Mary isn't as good of a student as the second sentence's Mary.[4] You can use the end of the sentence to make your point. Which Mary do you want the reader to know?

Stylistically, six particular considerations are worth mentioning.

- sentence/paragraph length
- active vs. passive voice
- repetition
- level of detail
- word choice
- transitions

Sentence/Paragraph Length: First, short sentences and paragraphs are more persuasive than longer ones. They draw more attention. And attention often equals persuasion.

Chances are the previous paragraph, and especially the final sentence, captured your attention. As tempted as you may be to say everything you can in one sentence, avoid that temptation if you want to emphasize your point. Simply state the point:

> King called to warn others.

4. *See generally* JOSEPH M. WILLIAMS & Gregory G. Colomb, Style: LESSONS IN CLARITY AND GRACE 82-98 (10th ed. 2010).

Active vs. Passive Voice: Style manuals generally encourage writers to use active voice, and in persuasive writing, active voice is usually stronger. Sentences written in the active voice are usually shorter than sentences written in passive voice and as we noted, short sentences are often strong sentences. The active voice is also easier to follow because the actor in the sentence does the acting. The reader creates a mental picture of who is doing what to whom, as in the following examples:

> John kicked the ball.
> Jim screamed.
> Bob fell.

Each of these sentences creates a strong visual image of the action—kicking, screaming, and falling. It's easy to spot sentences written in active voice because they begin with the actor, then state the action, and usually end with the object.

Despite the general preference for active voice, there's a time and place for passive voice. When your client has done something wrong, you may not want to emphasize that to the reader. For instance, if Mr. Smith is your client, the following statement isn't very persuasive:

> Mr. Smith punched Mr. Cole.

Instead, you can omit the actor and minimize the damage to your client:

> Cole was punched.

Passive voice also makes sense when you want the reader to focus on the object of the sentence rather than the actor. For instance, if your point is that the defendant was arrested, you probably don't want to say "the police arrested the defendant."

You can also use nonaction verbs to deflect attention away from your client. If King was your client in the cell phone manslaughter problem, it would be more persuasive to state that King "placed the call" rather than "called." "Call," an action verb, presents a particular mental image that "place" doesn't, even though the sentences mean the same thing.

Repetition: Third, repeat or otherwise connect topics that appear at the beginning of your sentences to create cohesion. You can fill the topic position with information that links it to previous sentences and topics to transition the reader from the old to the new. Or you can fill the topic position with contextual information that looks forward. Either way, the reader will more easily move through your writing and understand how your various ideas are connected. Using the paragraph from Step 3 about King and the cell phone manslaughter problem, we might connect topics as follows:

> King was attempting to minimize—not disregard—the risk to others. King attempted to minimize the risk to others by calling to warn them that road conditions were dangerous.

Level of Detail: Fourth, use more detail to emphasize favorable information. As you might have guessed, readers remember material better when it is told with more detail. Conversely, they are more apt to forget less detailed information. Therefore, spend more time on favorable arguments, on favorable points within those arguments, and on favorable facts. This doesn't mean you should be redundant. It just means you should be more detailed in your discussion of positive, rather than negative, information.

If you were prosecuting King for vehicular manslaughter, you'd likely want to include a lot of details (without going obviously overboard) showing the dangerous road conditions when King decided to make a call on her cell phone. Although these facts may help King to some extent in showing an emergency, they also show that placing a call was risky. And you'd start by identifying the features of the road to show that although usually dangerous, the conditions were even more dangerous that night. You'd begin with a thesis statement, and then proceed with the facts:

> King was driving on California's State Highway 1, a road well known for its dangerous conditions. Highway 1 is a winding, narrow, two-lane highway. It sits on the edge of a cliff. The Pacific Ocean lies below the cliff, and Highway 1 offers very few places to pull over.
>
> Conditions were even more precarious than usual when King pulled out her non-hands-free cell phone and called her friend. King was driving at night, and visibility was inherently lessened. Most significantly, a dense fog was rolling in from the ocean, creating near-whiteout conditions.

Word Choice: Fifth, think about each word you use and whether it helps or hurts your case. Words create particular connotations. Although you can't stretch the truth or appear to be "playing" the judge, some words are more likely to help than others. For instance, imagine you represent a plaintiff suing her former employer for wrongful termination. Think about the persuasiveness of these sentences:

> Crawford diligently completed every task her employer assigned to her.

> Crawford diligently completed every project her employer assigned to her.

The words "task" and "project" might be used interchangeably, but one suggests minimal effort and the other implies substantially more work.

Similarly, whether you call a company a "corporation" or "conglomeration" or "family business" may impact the reader's perception of that entity.

Transitions: Finally, help the reader. Connect concepts (when appropriate) by using helpful transitions. "Therefore," "however," "furthermore," "similarly," and other common transitions make your writing easier to follow. After all, your goal is to make it as easy as possible for the reader to agree with you, and adding transitions is a relatively simple step toward that goal. If you need suggestions on transitions and making your document flow more smoothly, you can review Chapter 32.

EXAMPLES

Review the following examples. For each example, there may be more than one correct answer, but try to choose the *best* answer. Explain to yourself why you have chosen that answer. Then read the explanations in the last section of this chapter to check your work.

EXAMPLES

Example 22-1

This question uses a hypothetical civil tort assault problem that includes questions about self-defense and jurisdiction.

Assume that the following draft outline shows the arguments that the Defendant intends to make in order.

1. The trial court lacked jurisdiction over the Defendant and hence the ruling for the Plaintiff should be reversed.
2. Reversal is proper because the Defendant acted in self-defense.
3. The case should be reversed because the Defendant did not injure the Plaintiff.
4. Reversal is proper because the Plaintiff consented to any contact between the Plaintiff and the Defendant and hence the Defendant is not liable for assault.

This is . . .

A. a persuasive structure only if point #4 is the Defendant's strongest argument.

B. a persuasive structure only if point #1 is the Defendant's strongest argument.
C. a persuasive structure even if point #2 is the Defendant's strongest argument.
D. an unpersuasive structure because you should never make more than three main arguments.

EXAMPLES

Example 22-2

This question uses the copyright and fair use problem, which you can find in Appendix B.

> It is claimed that the "fair use" exception permits the use of a portion of Page's lyrics. Dash sought to parody Page's lyrics and criticized Page's message of anti-patriotism. This statutory "fair use" defense, however, is unavailable to Dash. Using Page's lyrics constitutes copyright infringement because the songs appeal to the same market. This is true even though the messages are different and the point of Dash's song is to reflect positively on pride in America without taking a critical look at our nation's failures.

This paragraph is . . .

A. unpersuasive in a brief for Page because it fails to state her underlying legal claim.
B. unpersuasive in a brief for Page because it puts the negative information at the beginning and end rather than in the middle and the writing style emphasizes the wrong facts.
C. persuasive in a brief for Page because it asserts her copyright infringement claim.
D. persuasive in a brief for Page because it responds to Dash's fair use claim.

EXAMPLES

Example 22-3

This question uses the copyright and fair use problem, which you can find in Appendix B.

> Jenna Page does not want Dash to use her lyrics. Page holds the copyright to "Red, White, and Blue," and the song has been quite successful. Dash, though, is marketing his song "Red, White, and Blue Through and Through," obviously a copyright violation of Page's original song under the Copyright Act, which prohibits reproducing copyrighted works, like Page's song.

In a motion or brief for Page, this paragraph is . . .

A. persuasive because it clearly states the legal argument—copyright infringement.
B. unpersuasive because it does not begin with a thesis statement.
C. persuasive because it includes details about Page's song, which will reinforce those facts to the reader.
D. unpersuasive because it should include more words like "obviously" and "clearly."

EXAMPLES

Example 22-4

This question uses the copyright and fair use problem, which you can find in Appendix B.

> Dash is not entitled to the "fair use" exception to the general ban on reproducing copyrighted material. 17 U.S.C. § 107. Dash used over twenty percent of Page's lyrics, including almost all of the chorus. Although parody may constitute a fair use of copyrighted material, Dash's extensive use here goes beyond what is permitted to create a parody. Hence, Dash cannot rely on the exception for fair use.

This paragraph is . . .

A. unpersuasive in a motion or brief for Page because it addresses the counterargument that parody can constitute fair use.
B. unpersuasive in a motion or brief for Page because it does not begin with a thesis statement.
C. persuasive in a motion or brief for Page because it includes a percentage, and numbers are always persuasive.
D. persuasive in a motion or brief for Page because it focuses on Dash's wrongdoing and frames fair use as an exception to the general rule that prohibits reproducing copyrighted material, although it would be stronger if it used case law to support the argument.

EXAMPLES

Example 22-5

This question uses a hypothetical wrongful death problem.

> Williams did not see the victim until just before Williams smashed into him with his large SUV.

This sentence is . . .

A. unpersuasive in a brief for Williams because it uses active voice and poor word choice.
B. unpersuasive in a brief for Williams because it does not indicate the model of his SUV.
C. persuasive in a brief for Williams because it includes details of the incident.
D. persuasive in a brief for Williams because it's short and to the point.

EXAMPLES

Example 22-6

This question uses the negligent infliction of emotional distress problem, which you can find in Appendix C.

> Poe, the bystander suing Defoe for negligent infliction of emotional distress, and Valenzuela, the person who was hit by the car, did not live together, did not have a wedding date set, and other than one joint purchase of an automobile, had entirely separate finances. Therefore, they were not in an "intimate, familial relationship." Furthermore, Poe and Valenzuela were not married and not blood relatives.

This paragraph is . . .

A. unpersuasive in a motion or brief for Poe because it should state why she is suing Defoe.
B. unpersuasive in a motion or brief for Defoe because it should begin with a thesis statement rather than a long sentence purely about facts.
C. persuasive in a motion or brief for Defoe because it identifies the parties and points out why the plaintiff cannot meet the "intimate, familial relationship" test.
D. persuasive in a motion or brief for Poe it explains her claim and tells the reader she and Valenzuela jointly own a car.

EXPLANATIONS

Explanation 22-1

A is incorrect. Although the end is the place of highest emphasis, legal readers expect your strongest argument first, not last. Hence, saving your best argument for last is generally not an effective persuasive technique. **B** is not the best answer. It's true you should generally start with your strongest argument. But in this case, there's a threshold issue—jurisdiction—and courts often expect you to lead with that argument even if it isn't your strongest claim. **C** is the best answer. For the reasons stated in B, beginning with a procedural or other threshold issue is still a persuasive structure. You'd then follow that argument with your strongest substantive claim. ***D*** is incorrect. The number of arguments will depend on the number of colorable claims. You shouldn't create a full argument for every minor point, but you shouldn't artificially limit the number of claims, either.

Explanation 22-2

A is not the best answer. The paragraph is unpersuasive in a brief for Page, but not because it doesn't state Page's claim—it does state her underlying copyright infringement claim, but it downplays that claim by burying it in the middle of the paragraph. **B** is the best answer. As noted in A, the favorable information to Page—her copyright claim—is buried in the middle. The paragraph starts and ends with information favorable to Dash, and those positions of emphasis should not be used for negative information. The paragraph also uses passive voice where active voice would highlight what Dash has done: "use" Page's lyrics (note the first sentence contains no actor; "It is claimed that the "fair use" exception permits the use of a portion of Page's lyrics."). Similarly, it uses active voice ("Dash sought to parody Page's lyrics") where passive voice might be more effective. **C** is incorrect. Although it states the legal claim, burying it mid-paragraph is not very effective. ***D*** is incorrect for the reasons stated in B. Although you should respond to anticipated arguments, this paragraph emphasizes them rather than refuting them. See Chapter 23 for more help with Making Persuasive Counterarguments.

EXPLANATIONS

Explanation 22-3

A is incorrect. The paragraph does state that Dash's song is "obviously a copyright violation," but that statement doesn't make the paragraph persuasive. First, the reference to the copyright violation is buried in the middle of the paragraph. In addition, subtlety persuades more than bluntness. Terms like "obviously" and "clearly" actually detract from, rather than increase, persuasiveness. **B** is the best answer. The first sentence of the paragraph introduces the two parties, but it doesn't assert a thesis. It simply states what our client "wants," and that is rarely persuasive to a court (or to anyone else, for that matter). **C** is incorrect. This paragraph includes almost none of the actual facts. It includes broad characterizations, which are far less memorable. ***D*** is not the best answer. Although the paragraph is unpersuasive, using more words like "obviously" and "clearly" will hurt, not help, as stated in A.

EXPLANATIONS

Explanation 22-4

A is incorrect. To be persuasive, you need to address counterarguments. You should address them persuasively, but ignoring them won't strengthen your case. **B** is also incorrect. This paragraph begins with a thesis statement, and the paragraph develops that thesis. **C** is not the best answer. This paragraph is at least arguably persuasive, but not because numbers are always persuasive. Numbers can be helpful, but they aren't always necessary or even relevant. In addition, if the numbers aren't helpful, leave them out unless you need to refute them in some way. ***D*** is the best answer. This paragraph is generally persuasive, although as noted, comparisons to the case law would make it stronger.

EXPLANATIONS

Explanation 22-5

A is the best answer. Active voice is generally preferred, but when your client has behaved badly or you want to minimize her actions, use passive voice. In addition, the word choice is poor. Identifying the person Williams hit as the "victim" suggests Williams was an intentional perpetrator, and that is not an image Williams wants the court to have. Saying Williams "smashed" into the victim is also not helpful, and calling his vehicle a "large SUV" is probably also not the image of this incident that it makes sense for Williams to create. **B** is not the best answer. This sentence is unpersuasive, but adding more information about the SUV would only exacerbate the problems identified in A. **C** is incorrect. Although related to the point in B, fewer details deemphasize the material. ***D*** is not the best answer. Short sentences can have more impact, but for the reasons in A, this sentence is unpersuasive in a brief for Williams.

EXPLANATIONS

Explanation 22-6

A is incorrect. This paragraph *does* state why Poe is suing Defoe. But it's unpersuasive for her because the facts are framed in a way that hurts her position. In addition, even though it's buried in the middle of the paragraph (which is the least persuasive placement), the paragraph explicitly says Poe and Valenzuela didn't have an intimate, familial relationship. **B** is the best answer. This paragraph begins with facts, not connected to the legal standard in any way. The second sentence in this paragraph is much stronger, and should be the thesis statement—and therefore, the first sentence in the paragraph. Recall that the middle is the place of least emphasis. **C** is not the best answer for the reasons stated in B. In addition, the first sentence is long and somewhat hard to follow because it contains so many clauses. **D** is incorrect. Even though this paragraph includes one fact that favors Poe, nothing else about the paragraph favors her position.

Checklist

Chapter 22: Making Persuasive Arguments

✔	The substance of the argument is most important so concentrate on that first.
✔	Be subtle when using persuasive techniques so the reader does not notice the technique but is persuaded.
✔	Usually put strongest arguments first and also end on a strong note.
✔	Structure the argument to persuade by using thesis statements at the start of every section, argument, and paragraph.
✔	Structure the argument to persuade by putting the most important information at the beginning or the end of units of information.
✔	Use headings and transitions to persuade.
✔	Use a forceful writing style with thoughtful stylistic choices (e.g., active vs. passive voice, word choice, etc.) to persuade.

You will find all of the chapter checklists compiled in Appendix D.

CHAPTER 23

Making Persuasive Counterarguments

Puzzled about how to make your paper stronger? One way is to think of arguments and counterarguments as two jigsaw puzzle pieces that fit together. That's because one side's strongest argument is often the other side's weakest argument. And if you ignore your weaknesses, you'll give the other side a clear shot at influencing how a decision maker will view that part of the argument. So although it may seem paradoxical, you can strengthen your argument by addressing its weak points.

Counterarguments are important for two reasons. First, you want the court to know why weaknesses shouldn't prevent a ruling in your favor. Some might call this a "defensive counterargument"—a response to what you expect your opponent will point out is a weakness in your case. Second, you can often strengthen your position by pointing out specific flaws in your opponent's arguments. Some might call this an "affirmative counterargument"—an argument where you point out the weaknesses in your opponent's case. Regardless of these labels, these two counterarguments are, as noted above, flip sides of the same coin, because your strong arguments are your opponent's weak arguments and vice versa. In short, make counterarguments in two situations: (1) when you can anticipate and weaken strong arguments against your case or address the court's likely concerns; and (2) when you're writing a brief responding to the other side and you have the opportunity to directly point out specific, significant flaws in the other side's arguments.

WHAT YOU NEED TO KNOW ABOUT MAKING PERSUASIVE COUNTERARGUMENTS

A counterargument is usually more persuasive when it's framed as part of the brief's affirmative argument, rather than as a digression that labels itself as a counterargument. This is called "anticipating" the counterargument. For instance, instead of saying "The defendant may argue that it gave the employee written warnings, but these were insufficient because . . .," rephrase your point to sound like part of your own affirmative argument: "Although the employee received written warnings, they concerned only her attire and not the type of conduct which her employer ultimately cited as the cause for firing her." This phrasing emphasizes why a potential weakness is not convincing and the phrasing avoids emphasizing the opposing argument itself.

When brainstorming possible counterarguments, consider these commonly used techniques. Common ways to counter an argument include showing that it's based on:

- an incorrect or incomplete view of the facts;
- an incorrect or incomplete view of the law;
- case law that is distinguishable from the case at hand;
- a misapplication of the law to the facts; and
- flawed reasoning or policy arguments.

In addition, as you think about your own arguments, if you're having trouble coming up with arguments your opponent might make against your points, pretend for a moment you represent the other side. What would you argue? If a judge might be persuaded by that argument, you need to address it.

Put your best arguments first, and then make your counterarguments. Most brief writers put their strongest arguments first because most readers expect them first. See Chapter 22 for more on Making Persuasive Arguments and the organization that is expected. Your counterarguments, by their nature, usually aren't your strongest arguments even when you phrase them as an affirmative argument, so most writers wouldn't lead with them.

Be careful about using more space to address counterarguments than the arguments you planned for your side. You'll likely weaken the overall impression that the reader gets from your brief if you spend too much "air time" in your brief addressing defensive points.

Don't make arguments for the other side. Anticipating counterarguments in your brief should generally be limited to points that you think the other side will very likely raise, that the court will be concerned with, and that you can neutralize relatively well. For instance, whenever you see obvious weaknesses in your own arguments, you should preemptively address them. But be careful to only raise those points that will likely concern the court or arguments that the other side is likely to actually raise. Don't score points for the other side! If you're writing a reply brief in response to the other side's brief, then this is less of a concern because you have seen what the other side has actually argued.

Don't nitpick or create weak arguments just to shoot them down. You usually don't have enough space in the brief to devote time to anticipating weak or silly arguments the other side probably won't make. This applies to potential legal or factual arguments. For instance, in the cell phone manslaughter case, imagine that you represent King. You shouldn't waste time arguing against the proposition that the only calls that qualify as being made for "emergency purposes" are calls made to those agencies included in the statutory list. That's because the statute makes clear, in express terms, that the list is not inclusive. The state shouldn't make that argument (it's a loser) and you shouldn't worry about refuting it.

From a factual standpoint, in a suit over a car accident you could probably come up with a million reasons the defendant *might* have run the red light. But don't bother anticipating far-reaching claims, like "maybe there had just been a robbery and he was worried the robber was going to come shoot him." Similarly, in an assault case, don't worry about addressing whether the victim might have been a karate expert, making the defendant/assaulter feel like he had to strike first. Of course, if there are facts that suggest any of this was plausible, then you ought to address it. But don't make up wild facts and theories just so you can respond to potential counterarguments.

HOW TO MAKE PERSUASIVE COUNTERARGUMENTS

Using the cell phone manslaughter problem in Appendix A, we'll walk through the process of making persuasive counterarguments.

> **Note.** The first two steps explore identifying arguments your opponent is likely to make. The final four steps address anticipating those arguments persuasively in your writing.

PROBLEMS

Problem

Here is a quick overview of the cell phone manslaughter problem (for details, see Appendix A). Allison King used her wireless phone, without a hands-free device, while driving in dense fog on a winding road on the edge of an ocean cliff. King placed the call to warn her friends about the dangerous conditions, as they would be meeting later. While she was making the call, she hit and killed a bicyclist. The prosecution will attempt to convict King of vehicular manslaughter by showing that she drove while committing an illegal act, driving while using a wireless phone without a hands-free device, and with gross negligence. King will argue that her actions fit within the "emergency purposes" exception to the wireless phone prohibition. She will also argue that she did not act with gross negligence.

Step 1: Put yourself in the other side's shoes. Some students become so engaged with the arguments for their side that they find it a struggle to see the other side at all. It's natural to identify with your client and to want her to win. But that tendency can blind you to your side's weaknesses.

If you're having difficulty putting yourself in the other side's shoes, make a list of your weaknesses because your weaknesses will usually be their strengths. Do you have any "bad" or undesirable facts? Is the lack of a fact making it hard for you to make an argument? Are there precedents you wish weren't out there? Answering these questions will uncover your weaknesses.

To apply some of these questions to the cell phone manslaughter problem, if you represented King you might start with whether you wish any of the facts had been different:

> It would be better for King if it had been impossible for her to pull her car over before calling her friends.

Next, ask if any facts that are lacking make your argument tougher. Once again, you find a situation you wish were different:

> The facts are silent about exactly when King's friends would be on the road. It might even be possible that they were ahead of King, because the facts just say that the group of friends planned to meet at a town on this road. Then her call would have been pointless for the purpose of warning them of the dangerous conditions.
>
> The facts are also silent about whether her friends could have learned of the dangerous road conditions without the use of a cell phone. It would be better

for King if it was clear that her phone call was the only way her friends might learn of the potential problem.

Viewing these weaknesses as a strength for the State might look like this:

> King's phone call was not made for "emergency purposes" because it is possible that her friends had already driven on the foggy highway.
>
> King's phone call was not made for "emergency purposes" because a reasonable person would expect her friends to check road conditions before starting out.

Step 2: Identify the other side's arguments. Once you've put yourself in the other side's shoes and can see the weaknesses in your side, figure out what the corresponding arguments will be for the other side. One way to do that is to reread the facts and cases through your opponent's eyes. What are your opponent's strongest arguments? What will your opponent emphasize, whether facts or law? How will your opponent likely respond to your arguments?

To identify counterarguments in the cell phone manslaughter problem, review the facts and law. First the facts: Allison King used her wireless phone, without a hands-free device, while driving on a winding road on the edge of a cliff over the ocean in dense fog. Her purpose was to warn her friends, who she planned to meet, about the dangerous conditions. And now the law: One way to convict King of vehicular manslaughter is to prove that she drove while committing an illegal act. Because it's illegal to use a wireless phone without a hands-free device unless the call is made for emergency purposes, the State will try to prove that King's call was not for an emergency purpose and King will try to prove that it was.

Suppose you're King's lawyer. You've made a strong argument that King's call was made for emergency purposes because her concern about the physical safety of her friends was justifiable, as she knew her friends were likely to be driving over the same dangerous road. You've compared your case to the *Newton* precedent in which the court found a call was made for emergency purposes when a husband was driving when his wife went into labor, so he headed toward the hospital and called his wife's obstetrician who had been caring for her throughout her high-risk pregnancy. And you've distinguished King's situation from the *Tompkins* case, where the court found that a driver's call to check on the safety of his family after danger had passed—an earthquake had already occurred—was not made for emergency purposes. So, how can you lose?

Start by looking more closely at the cases. As you read *Newton* you see that although the appellate court found the call was made for emergency purposes, the trial court had stated that the husband could have pulled over to make the call. The appellate court rejected that argument because a reasonable person would not want to pull over while his wife was in labor and they were on the way to a hospital. If you read *Newton* through the eyes of the prosecutor, you see that the prosecutor could argue that in *Newton* the time it would take to pull over might further endanger the pregnant woman. But King would not further endanger her friends by taking a minute or two to pull over. And that's one of the State's likely arguments:

> King's call was not made for "emergency purposes" because she could have waited to use one of the pull-offs provided.

Step 3: Evaluate whether your adversary is likely to raise the arguments you've identified, whether a court would be concerned with them, and whether your response lessens their sting. Decide what's worth including in your brief. This depends in part on whether you're writing an opening brief or reply brief and whether you'll have a chance to respond later.

Here, representing King, you might decide that the strongest argument the State would probably make is that King could have pulled over, instead of continuing to drive, while calling. The State is likely to raise this argument. Your next question is whether a court will likely be concerned about this claim. Here, rather than putting yourself in your opponent's position, put yourself in the judge's position. Does this seem like a reasonable concern? If so, even if you have a good response, assume that the judge will also be concerned. The only remaining question is whether you will have a chance to respond later.

Step 4: Generate a response to the likely opposing argument. What are your best responses to arguments about your weaknesses? Why are they not fatal to your success? If you get stuck while brainstorming, consider the list of common ways to counter an opposing argument. Here, you can say that it's an incomplete view of the facts: The facts say that there were few places to pull off the road and that it was difficult to see, and they give no indication that King had an option to pull off.

Step 5: When writing a persuasive document, respond to the counterargument by anticipating it and not by making it for the other side. Phrase the counterarguments as part of your affirmative argument. Here, instead of saying "the State may argue" or "the State's argument X must fail because," just turn your response into an affirmative argument.

Here is a bad example. Instead of writing this:

> The State may contend that King could have pulled off the road to make a wireless call. King answers, however, that the road she was driving on had few places to pull off and furthermore it was foggy and she probably could not see them. She was not able to pull off.

You could avoid making the other side's argument and state your argument in the affirmative:

> Further, unlike cases in which a driver can pull off the road to make a wireless phone call, the road upon which King was driving had few places at which to pull over and the dense fog likely prevented her from seeing them. Pulling over to make the call was not an option for King.

Step 6: Check that you have not overemphasized or given too much "air time" to the opposing arguments. Note how the previous paragraph anticipates the other side's argument in just a short paragraph. Remember as well to lead with your own strongest arguments. That's the way to win.

EXAMPLES

Review the following examples. For each example, there may be more than one correct answer. Explain to yourself why you have chosen that answer or those answers. Then read the explanations in the last section of this chapter to check your work.

EXAMPLES

Example 23-1

This question uses a hypothetical torts problem.

Assume these facts. At approximately 5:15 p.m. on December 12, your client, Jessica Faulkner, was driving west in a Mini Cooper on Stetson Avenue when she hit another car at the intersection of Stetson Avenue and First Street. The other car, a Cutlass sedan, was driven by Elbert Rutledge. The speed limit on Stetson Avenue was 35 mph and the speed limit on First Street was 25 mph. The police estimated that Faulkner was travelling at 43 mph and Rutledge at 22 mph. There were a few shrubs and tall signs near the intersection, but the view was mostly unobstructed. Both Faulkner and Rutledge claim they had the green light and there were no other witnesses present. Rutledge has filed suit and the relevant jurisdiction has a "last clear chance" rule, whereby drivers have an obligation to avoid an accident if they can, even if the collision would otherwise be the other driver's fault.

Circle or underline each of the facts in the preceding paragraph that might present a weakness to your case and then check the explanation.

EXAMPLES

Example 23-2

This question uses the copyright and fair use problem, which you can find in Appendix B.

Regarding the first factor, "the purpose and character of the use," Page expects that Dash will argue that his song is a parody that transforms the original song and that therefore that factor favors Dash. Page wants to anticipate this argument. Which of the following presents the most persuasive counterargument?

A. Dash argues that the factor weighs in his favor because his song is a parody that transforms the original's meaning from criticizing America to praising America. But although the original song is critical of America, its refrain has become a popular chant at patriotic rallies.

B. Both songs are patriotic because Dash's song expressly praises America and its values and Page's song is popular at patriotic rallies.

C. Dash will likely assert that his song transforms the meaning of the original because it has a different viewpoint. However, both songs are political rock songs.

D. Page's song is a political statement with several levels of meaning. This makes it nearly impossible to "transform" the song by choosing one meaning to parody.

EXAMPLES

Example 23-3

This question uses the copyright and fair use problem, which you can find in Appendix B.

Regarding the second factor, "the nature of the copyrighted work," courts have often ignored it in cases involving parody, because parodies "almost invariably copy publicly known, expressive works." Consider the following statements about how Dash might make a counterargument about this factor.

A. Dash's counterargument should read: "Although courts usually do not apply this factor in parody cases, Page will argue that the court should apply it in this case. This argument will fail because precedent supports that the courts usually do not weigh this factor."

B. Dash should not waste space addressing this argument. He should deal with the factor in the introduction to the Argument section of the brief.

C. Dash should address this argument because there are four factors and there should be an argument and counterargument for each.

D. Dash's counterargument should read: "Page contends that this factor weighs in her favor. This factor, however, is not important in parody cases."

EXAMPLES

Example 23-4

This question uses the copyright and fair use problem, which you can find in Appendix B.

Regarding the third factor, "the amount and substantiality of the portion used," Dash adopted the structure of the song and some of the lyrics. He will maintain, however, that the facts show it was a small amount of copying that was necessary for listeners to identify the song he was parodying. What is Page's best counterargument?

A. Page should not respond because she should not bring the court's attention to her opponent's strong arguments.

B. "Any argument that Dash had to copy as much of 'Red, White, and Blue' as he did must fail. Page's song is so well known that even the smallest reference to it would be recognized."

C. "Dash's argument that he needed to copy so much of the song is weak. Page's argument is much stronger and this Court should reject Dash's contention."

D. "Dash took the entire structure of Page's song without changing enough lyrics. Hence, the facts do not support the conclusion that Dash took only what was necessary to identify the target of the parody."

EXAMPLES

Example 23-5

This question uses the copyright and fair use problem, which you can find in Appendix B.

Regarding the fourth factor, "the effect of the use of the copy on potential markets," Dash is likely to rely on *Campbell* where the Court concluded that the parody would not affect the market for the original. At least part of the rationale was that rappers and country western singers appeal to different markets. Which of these counterarguments for Page are most effective?

A. "In response to Dash's argument analogizing our case to the facts in *Campbell*, our case is different. In our case, Dash's song is likely to interfere with Page's market because Dash's song is the same type as Page's."

B. "Dash's reliance on *Campbell* is misplaced. This case is unlike *Campbell* because there the songs were performed in different genres and here both songs are rock songs with political messages."

C. "In contrast to *Campbell* where the two songs were different genres, here both songs are in the rock music genre and the change in lyrics is so slight that music buyers may confuse the two songs."

D. "Under *Campbell*, Dash's copy will interfere with Page's market."

EXPLANATIONS

EXPLANATIONS

Explanation 23-1

This example requires you to think about facts in a nuanced way and anticipate arguments your opponent might reasonably make.

> At approximately **5:15 p.m. on December 12**, your client, Jessica Faulkner, was driving west in a **Mini Cooper** on Stetson when she hit another car at the intersection of Stetson and First Street. The other car, a Cutlass sedan, was driven by Elbert Rutledge. **The speed limit on Stetson was 35 mph** and the **speed limit on First Street was 25 mph**. The **police estimated that Faulkner was travelling at 43 mph and Rutledge at 22 mph.** There were a **few shrubs** and tall signs **near the intersection**, but **the view was mostly unobstructed**. Both Faulkner and **Rutledge claim they had the green light** and there were no other witnesses present. Rutledge has filed suit and the relevant jurisdiction has a "last clear chance" rule, whereby drivers have an obligation to avoid an accident if they can, even if the collision would otherwise be the other driver's fault.

First, the time and date: Those facts might be harmful because at that time of the year, heading west, she might have had the sun in her eyes. If so, she might have had the red light but not have realized it. This isn't certain, but it's something to consider. Next, why is the type of car she was driving relevant? Mini Coopers are small, and she might not have seen Rutledge's car. This might help her under the last clear chance rule if she actually had the green light. It might hurt her, however, because Rutledge might not have seen her, considering how small her car is and there were shrubs near the intersection that might have obstructed the view, even though the view was "mostly unobstructed." Finally, the obvious fact—Faulkner was speeding—hurts. Rutledge was driving below the speed limit, which might mean he had a yellow or red light, but also suggests he was being careful, and Faulkner's speed suggests she was not. This might hurt even if she had the green light, as she possibly could have avoided the collision if she had been driving the speed limit.

Explanation 23-2

A is incorrect. Its phrasing makes Dash's argument first, which is not the most persuasive structure. It also presents Page's argument defensively instead of affirmatively as part of Page's own argument. **B** is a pretty good start, but it's not yet a strong counterargument because it isn't clear how it's tied to the issue of whether Dash's song transformed Page's original. **C** is incorrect; it has the same problem as A because it makes the other side's argument before answering it. **D** is correct. It does the best job of anticipating the counterargument without making the other side's argument.

Explanation 23-3

A is incorrect. This counterargument isn't persuasive. It's a good example of wasting space to address a weak opposing argument. Most good writers would handle this factor by explaining that it's "not in dispute" in the introduction to the Argument section of the brief. **B** is therefore correct. If the other side has only a very weak argument on a factor, neither side will want to spend space or time addressing it. Both will most likely dispose of it in the introduction. **C** is incorrect because often some part of a rule is not at issue. In those instances, you can usually use the introduction to tell the reader why it's not addressed. **D** is incorrect because it wastes space setting out a contention Page will probably not make.

Explanation 23-4

A is incorrect. When the other side has a strong argument, it's important to address it or else you will let the other side be the only voice the court hears on the issue. **B** is better, but still not correct because it has the common problem of making the argument before answering it. **C** is incorrect. It's a weak counterargument because it doesn't tell why one argument is stronger than another. **D** is correct. It illustrates how you might make an affirmative counterargument by showing how the facts don't support the other side's position.

EXPLANATIONS

Explanation 23-5

A is incorrect because it announces itself as a counterargument by stating "in response to Dash's argument." That wastes words and weakens the argument. **B** is a good counterargument that illustrates making a counterargument by showing how the other side has misread the law. This might work well in a reply brief. **C** is also a strong counterargument because it anticipates Dash's position and refutes it. ***D*** is weak as either an argument or counterargument because it doesn't say why the copy will interfere with the original's market.

Checklist

Chapter 23: Making Persuasive Counterarguments

✔	Put yourself in the other side's shoes and identify the other side's arguments.
✔	Evaluate whether your adversary is likely to raise the arguments identified, whether a court would be concerned with them, and whether your response lessens their sting.
✔	Do not nitpick or create weak arguments just to shoot them down; only address opposing counsel's argument if the court is likely to be concerned with it.
✔	Phrase counterarguments as an affirmative argument rather than a response to your opponent's arguments.
✔	Put your best arguments first, and then address counterarguments.
✔	Give more space to your arguments than to your counterarguments.
✔	Anticipate your opponent's argument but do not score points for the other side.

You will find all of the chapter checklists compiled in Appendix D.

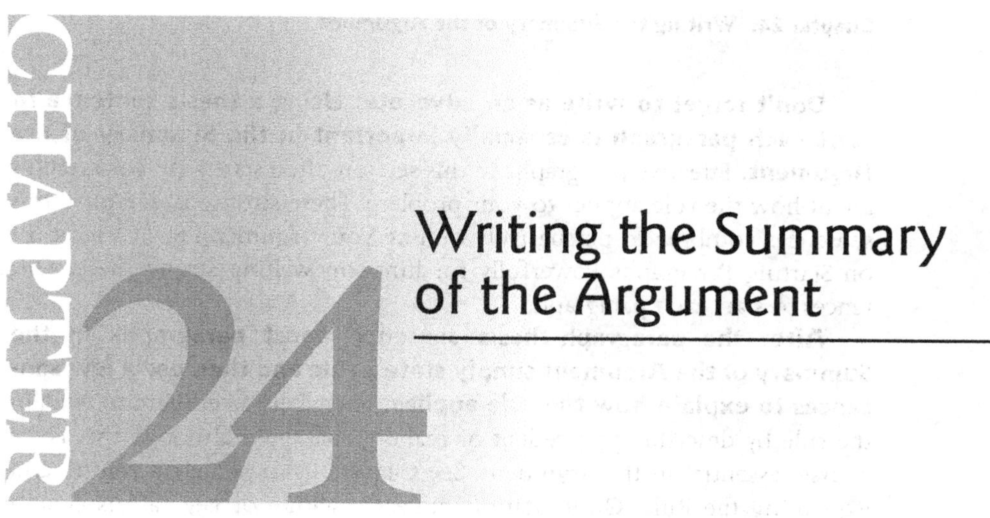

Writing the Summary of the Argument

"You never get a second chance to make a first impression." This old saying illustrates what we all know: First impressions count, whether formed when meeting a new person or reading a new brief. Many readers form first impressions of a brief while reading the Summary of the Argument. Often court rules require a Summary of the Argument in appellate briefs, and some courts may require them in other contexts. The summary quickly orients your reader to the dispute and your client's position, without overwhelming the judge with details that the fuller Argument explores in depth. You can make a good first impression if you rely on a few simple rules about writing this important section.

WHAT YOU NEED TO KNOW ABOUT WRITING THE SUMMARY OF THE ARGUMENT

Begin with an introductory paragraph that sets out a thesis statement and the rules that apply to the whole brief. If parts of the rule will not be in dispute, let the reader know. Keep it as short as you can.

Write only one or two paragraphs for each main issue in the brief. The Summary of the Argument should be concise and not include the details of your Argument. Often one paragraph per main point is adequate.

Don't forget to write as an advocate: Using a thesis sentence to start each paragraph is especially important in the Summary of the Argument. Effective paragraphs in this section often start with an assertion about how the rule applies to your problem. These strong paragraph-thesis sentences combine to persuasively outline your argument. See Chapter 30 on Starting Paragraphs Powerfully for hints on writing strong thesis sentences to start each paragraph.

After the paragraph-thesis sentence, most paragraphs in the Summary of the Argument simply state a rule and then use a few sentences to explain how the rule applies. There's no need here to explain the rule by describing precedent or making analogies, although that is, of course, essential in the Argument. See Chapter 9 for more on Stating and Explaining the Rule. Omit citations unless a statute or key case is central to your position. Similarly, omit weaker arguments. Anticipate counterarguments rarely and only when they are unusually strong. Just state a rule, choose your strongest argument about this issue or sub-issue, and make the argument succinctly in a sentence or two. Within the Summary of the Argument, writers generally do not include headings.

Although the Summary of the Argument is one of the first sections of the brief, most writers draft it after they have finished the Argument section. You won't really know which arguments are your best until you've made them. If you instead draft your Summary of the Argument before you finish writing the Argument section, go back later and revise to be sure it is, in fact, a "summary" of the Argument you actually wrote.

HOW TO WRITE THE SUMMARY OF THE ARGUMENT

Using the cell phone manslaughter problem in Appendix A, we'll walk you through the process of writing a Summary of the Argument for the State.

PROBLEMS

Problem

Here is a quick overview of the cell phone manslaughter problem (for details, see Appendix A). Allison King used her wireless phone, without a hands-free device, while driving in dense fog on a winding road on the edge of an ocean cliff. King placed the call to warn her friends about the dangerous conditions, as they would be meeting later. While she was making the call, she hit and killed a bicyclist. The prosecution will attempt to convict King of vehicular manslaughter by showing that she drove while committing an illegal act (driving while using a wireless phone without a hands-free device) and with gross negligence. King will argue that her actions fit within the "emergency purposes" exception to the wireless phone prohibition. She will also argue that she did not act with gross negligence.

Step 1: Start by writing an introductory paragraph that sets out a thesis and the rules that apply to the whole brief. Assume you are the prosecutor. Begin by drafting a thesis statement:

> King is guilty of vehicular manslaughter because she hit and killed a cyclist while using her cell phone without a hands-free device on a dangerous road during hazardous driving conditions.

Then set out the rules. The State is seeking to convict Allison King based on two statutes, so you'd set those out:

> California's vehicular manslaughter statute, Penal Code § 192(c)(1), holds accountable those drivers who drive "a vehicle in the commission of an unlawful act, not amounting to felony, and with gross negligence." Additionally, California Vehicle Code § 23123 declares it an unlawful act to "drive a motor vehicle while using a wireless telephone unless that telephone is specifically designed and configured to allow hands-free listening and talking, and is used in that manner while driving" unless an exception applies.

Setting out the two statutes is not complete, but the paragraph is growing lengthy. You might start a new paragraph to explain the exception. And then end the introductory section by stating the outcome you advocate.

> Further, King cannot escape culpability under the exception to the prohibition on using a cell phone while driving without a hands-free device because she was not "a person using a wireless telephone for emergency purposes, including, but not limited to, an emergency call to a law enforcement agency, health care provider, fire department, or other emergency services agency or entity." § 23123. King is therefore guilty because (1) she did not make her call for "emergency purposes" and (2) she was driving with gross negligence in treacherous conditions. Her conviction for vehicular manslaughter should therefore be upheld.

Step 2: Once the general introduction is complete, summarize your argument on the first main issue in one or two short paragraphs. Usually, you'll follow the same organization of issues that you used in the Argument. Assume here that means you should address driving "a vehicle in the commission of an unlawful act" before gross negligence. You'll start the paragraph with a thesis statement on that issue—why King doesn't meet the exception—and then state the rule. So the beginning of the one or two paragraphs of the Summary of the Argument devoted to that section of your brief might look like this:

> First, King violated California law prohibiting the use of a wireless phone while driving, unless that phone is used with a hands-free device, and she does not meet the "emergency purposes" exception. California Vehicle Code § 23123 makes driving a car while using a wireless phone without a hands-free listening device an unlawful act, unless the person is using the wireless phone for "emergency purposes." An emergency purpose exists only if there is a threat of imminent danger.

Then, you'll summarize your facts, bringing together the argument. Again you'll want to start the paragraph with a strong thesis statement:

> No emergency purpose existed here because King's friends were not threatened with imminent danger. King placed the call to advise her friends, whom she was to meet that day, that driving conditions were dangerous. King could have waited for an opportunity to pull over and make the call when it was safe, and legal, to do so. There is no indication that her call would have prevented any danger or that the friends were driving on or near the same stretch of road at the time King placed the call.

Step 3: Repeat the same process for each main argument, summarizing your points in one or two short paragraphs. After addressing the wireless phone statute and its exception, you'll turn to the second argument: that King acted with gross negligence. Remember to begin with a thesis statement, then the rule, and then apply that rule, very briefly, to your facts.

> Second, King acted with gross negligence. Courts use an objective test to determine gross negligence: whether a reasonable person in the defendant's position would be aware of the risk involved. King called her friend to advise her of the dangerous driving conditions. This demonstrates her appreciation of the risks involved in making the call. She knew driving in the dense fog on a winding road on the side of a cliff was dangerous. Despite that, King chose to place a call on her cell phone without a hands-free device. King therefore acted with gross negligence.

Step 4: Finally, end on a strong note by stating your conclusion or your desired result. Should the court affirm the lower court? Reverse?

> Hence, King drove while committing an unlawful act, not committed for an emergency purpose, and she was grossly negligent. King's conviction for vehicular manslaughter should be affirmed.

Putting it together, the Summary of the Argument might look like this:

> King is guilty of vehicular manslaughter because she hit and killed a cyclist while using her cell phone without a hands-free device on a dangerous road during hazardous driving conditions. California's vehicular manslaughter statute, Penal Code § 192(c)(1), holds accountable those drivers who drive "a vehicle in the commission of an unlawful act, not amounting to felony, and with gross negligence." Additionally, California Vehicle Code § 23123 declares it an unlawful act to "drive a motor vehicle while using a wireless telephone unless that telephone is specifically designed and configured to allow hands-free listening and talking, and is used in that manner while driving," unless an exception applies.
>
> Further, King cannot escape culpability under the exception to the prohibition on using a cell phone without a hands-free device because she was not "a person using a wireless telephone for emergency purposes, including, but not limited to, an emergency call to a law enforcement agency, health care provider, fire department, or other emergency services agency or entity." Cal. Vehicle Code § 23123 (West 2022). King is therefore guilty because (1) she did not make her call for "emergency purposes" and (2) she was driving with gross negligence in treacherous conditions. Her conviction for vehicular manslaughter should therefore be upheld.
>
> First, King violated California law prohibiting the use of a wireless phone while driving, unless that phone is used with a hands-free device, and she does not meet the "emergency purposes" exception. California Vehicle Code § 23123 makes driving a car while using a wireless phone without a hands-free listening device an unlawful act, unless the person is using the wireless phone for "emergency purposes." An emergency purpose exists only if there is a threat of imminent danger.
>
> No emergency purpose existed here because King's friends were not threatened with imminent danger. King placed the call to advise her friends, whom she was to meet that day, that driving conditions were dangerous. King could have waited for an opportunity to pull over and make the call when it was safe, and legal, to do so. There is no indication that her call would have prevented any danger or that the friends were driving on or near the same stretch of road at the time King placed the call.
>
> Second, King acted with gross negligence. Courts use an objective test to determine gross negligence: whether a reasonable person in the defendant's position would be aware of the risk involved. King called her friend to advise her of the dangerous driving conditions. This demonstrates her appreciation of the risks involved in making the call. She knew driving in the dense fog on a winding road on the side of a cliff was dangerous. Despite that, King chose to place a call on her cell phone. King therefore acted with gross negligence.
>
> Hence, King drove while committing an unlawful act, not committed for an emergency purpose, and she was grossly negligent. King's conviction for vehicular manslaughter should be affirmed.

EXAMPLES

Review the following examples. For each example, there may be more than one correct answer. Explain to yourself why you have chosen that answer or those answers. Then read the explanations in the last section of this chapter to check your work.

> **Note.** Each of the examples in this chapter focuses on a different paragraph of the following Summary of the Argument in a motion for the alleged copyright infringer, Dash, in the copyright and fair use problem in Appendix B.

Summary of the Argument

Dash's use of Page's original work was fair use. The fair use statute sets out a four-factor test to determine whether the use of copyrighted material is allowed. It requires the court to weigh: "(1) the purpose and character of the use, including whether such use is of a commercial nature or is for non-profit educational purposes; (2) the nature of the copyrighted work; (3) the amount and substantiality of the portion used in relation to the copyrighted work as whole; and (4) the effect of the use upon the potential market for or value of the copyrighted work." 17 U.S.C. § 107. The second factor is not relevant in cases of parody, such as this case.

Under the first factor, Dash's work criticized and transformed Page's song from an anti-establishment anthem that criticized American politics and economic inequality into a pro-America song that directly counters Page's original message. The Court has found that such transformation satisfies the elements of a parody, a use allowed under the first factor.

Dash copied only the amount and substance he needed to successfully parody the original. The third factor of the copyright statute requires the court to consider the "amount and substantiality" the copyist took. Dash did take a substantial portion of the structure of Page's song to create his parody. However, he took less than a quarter of the words and only the material he needed to provide a direct point-by-point attack on the original. This factor favors Dash because the strong element of parody in Dash's work justifies the amount of material he took under the third factor of the statute.

Finally, it is unlikely that a Jenna Page fan will find Dash's song a satisfactory substitute for the original. Just as the rappers' market was different from the country western market in *Campbell*, the market for Dash's pro-America song is also different from the anti-establishment market for the original. Dash's song may decrease the demand for the original, but only because of its different message, an effect the fourth factor allows. Because the new work satisfies the criteria included in the four-factor test, the Court should find it was fair use and Dash is not liable for copyright infringement.

EXAMPLES

Example 24-1

This question uses the copyright and fair use problem, which you can find in Appendix B.

This example involves the first paragraph of the Summary of the Argument above, the introductory paragraph:

> Dash's use of Page's original work was fair use. The fair use statute sets out a four-factor test to determine whether the use of copyrighted material is allowed. It requires the court to weigh: "(1) the purpose and character of the use, including whether such use is of a commercial nature or is for non-profit educational purposes; (2) the nature of the copyrighted work; (3) the amount and substantiality of the portion used in relation to the copyrighted work as whole; and (4) the effect of the use upon the potential market for or value of the copyrighted work." 17 U.S.C. § 107. The second factor is not relevant in cases of parody, such as this case.

This Summary's introductory paragraph is . . .

A. strong because it begins with a thesis statement.
B. weak because it analyzes factor two before factor one.
C. strong because it sets out the rule.
D. not very persuasive even though it starts with a thesis statement.

EXAMPLES

Example 24-2

This question uses the copyright and fair use problem, which you can find in Appendix B.

This example involves the second paragraph of the Summary of the Argument above, the paragraph about the first factor, whether the copy transforms and targets the original:

> Under the first factor, Dash's work criticized and transformed Page's song from an anti-establishment anthem that criticized American politics and economic inequality into a pro-America song that directly counters Page's original message. The Court has found that such transformation satisfies the elements of a parody, a use allowed under the first factor.

This paragraph . . .

A. is concise and complete.
B. starts with a thesis statement.
C. is not as strong as it could be because it doesn't state the rule that governs this factor.
D. applies the law to the facts of the problem (although the paragraph might have faults).

EXAMPLES

Example 24-3

This question uses the copyright and fair use problem, which you can find in Appendix B.

This example involves the third paragraph of the Summary of the Argument above, the paragraph about the third factor—the amount and substantiality the copyist takes from the original:

> Dash copied only the amount and substance he needed to successfully parody the original. The third factor of the copyright statute requires the court to consider the "amount and substantiality" the copyist took. Dash did take a substantial portion of the structure of Page's song to create his parody. However, he took less than a quarter of the words and only the material he needed to provide a direct point-by-point attack on the original. This factor favors Dash because the strong element of parody in Dash's work justifies the amount of material he took under the third factor of the statute.

This paragraph . . .

A. starts with a strong thesis statement.
B. states the rule that governs the factor.
C. applies the law to the facts of the problem.
D. ends strongly by telling the court how to weigh the factor.

EXAMPLES

Example 24-4

This question uses the copyright and fair use problem, which you can find in Appendix B.

This example involves the fourth paragraph of the Summary of the Argument above, the paragraph about the fourth factor, whether the copy will interfere with the original's market:

Finally, it is unlikely that a Jenna Page fan will find Dash's song a satisfactory substitute for the original. Just as the rappers' market was different from the country western market in *Campbell*, the market for Dash's pro-America song is also different from the anti-establishment market for the original. Dash's song may decrease the demand for the original, but only because of its different message, an effect the fourth factor allows. Because the new work satisfies the criteria included in the four-factor test, the Court should find it was fair use and Dash is not liable for copyright infringement.

A. This paragraph begins with a strong thesis statement.
B. Although this paragraph doesn't state the rule from the statute, it appropriately states the rule by comparing the case at hand to an important precedent case.
C. This paragraph applies the law to the facts of the problem.
D. As the last paragraph in the Summary of the Argument, this paragraph appropriately identifies the decision it wants the court to reach.

EXPLANATIONS

Explanation 24-1

A is correct in that it's good to start with a thesis statement. This thesis statement might be stronger if it included facts or more of the main reason supporting Dash's claim of fair use. **B** is incorrect. It's fine to explain why one of the factors will not be in play. Although you ordinarily don't cite to cases in the Summary of the Argument, you might provide a citation for this assertion. **C** is correct. When a rule governs the entire issue, it's helpful to include it in the introductory paragraph of the Summary of the Argument. This example does so with the four-factor fair use test. **D** is correct. This example could be more persuasive by briefly stating that the relevant factors all favor Dash.

Explanation 24-2

A is incorrect. Although the paragraph is concise and has good points, it's not complete. It needs a thesis statement and a rule. **B** is incorrect. The first sentence tells how the rule applies to the facts, but it's not a thesis statement for this factor. A good thesis statement for this factor would be: "The first factor weighs in Dash's favor because he targeted Page's work and transformed it." **C** is correct. The paragraph should contain the rule governing the first factor. **D** is correct. The first sentence uses the problem's facts persuasively.

EXPLANATIONS

Explanation 24-3

A is correct. ***B*** is correct. **C** is correct. ***D*** is correct. This is an example of a good paragraph addressing one of the issues in a Summary of the Argument. It uses a strong thesis statement, states the relevant rule, applies the law to the facts of the problem, and ends strongly by stating what the court should conclude.

EXPLANATIONS

Explanation 24-4

A is incorrect. The paragraph starts by applying the law to the facts, without telling the reader about the law. ***B*** is incorrect. The sentence making an analogy to *Campbell* is not appropriate in a Summary of the Argument because the reader may know nothing about the precedent case. Further, you would not want to take the space in the Summary of the Argument to set out what the reader would need to know about that precedent to understand the comparison. **C** is correct. The author does apply the law to the facts of our problem. ***D*** is correct. As the last sentence of the entire section, this final sentence appropriately tells the court the precise outcome the author desires.

Checklist

Chapter 24: Writing the Summary of the Argument

✔	Begin the Summary of the Argument with an introductory paragraph that sets out a thesis statement and the rules that apply to the whole argument.
✔	Write only one or two paragraphs for each main issue in the brief.
✔	Use a topic thesis sentence to start each paragraph in the Summary of the Argument.
✔	State a rule, choose the strongest argument about this issue or sub-issue, and make the argument succinctly in a sentence or two.
✔	End the Summary of the Argument on a strong note for your side.
✔	Check the Summary of the Argument when you've finished writing the Argument section to make sure it's complete.

You will find all of the chapter checklists compiled in Appendix D.

CHAPTER 25

Writing a Persuasive Fact Statement

Stories persuade. In fact, some experts in legal writing focus primarily on how storytelling or narrative techniques win cases. Your task in the Fact Statement of a trial memo or appellate brief is to tell a persuasive story that shows the judge the facts from your client's perspective. Sound legal arguments are key to successful persuasion, but it's also important to persuade the judge, on a human level, that it's right to decide in your client's favor. You need both convincing arguments *and* a compelling story. The Fact Statement is where you begin to tell that compelling story.

Terminology notes. In some jurisdictions, this section is called the "Statement of Facts." In others, it's the "Statement of the Case." Some professors and some jurisdictions will call the client's story the Statement of Facts, and the procedural history of the case the Statement of the Case. You should use the term in your textbook or in the applicable court rules. In this chapter, however, we'll refer to it simply as the Fact Statement.

WHAT YOU NEED TO KNOW ABOUT PERSUASIVE FACT STATEMENTS

Tell the facts from your client's point of view. Contrary to the Facts section in an office memo, where you frame the facts objectively, in a persuasive Fact Statement your goal is subtly to influence the reader to see your client's position more favorably. The reader ought to be able to tell who you represent just by reading the Fact Statement. That's not to suggest that the facts should be obviously biased—note the word "subtly" in the sentence above—but the reader shouldn't wonder who was in the right after reading your Fact Statement.

Tell the whole story. Be sure the story is complete and makes sense to a reader who does not know your case. Even facts that aren't legally relevant can help your reader understand the story. The Fact Statement also needs to include unfavorable facts, so don't leave them out. If you do, you lose credibility with the judge and have no ability to discount them.

Don't analyze or argue in the Fact Statement. Keep it purely factual. Avoid using an argumentative tone—save that for the Argument section. In the Argument, you'll persuade the reader by telling her what you want her to believe and then explaining logically why she should believe it. In the Fact Statement, only *state* the facts. That also means you shouldn't overtly demonize your opponent.

Tell the story in a compelling way using persuasive organization, detail for emphasis, and influential words. The Fact Statement should not be argumentative, but it can be persuasive if you follow a few basic techniques.

First, the Fact Statement must be logically organized, and telling the story chronologically is often the easiest way for the reader to follow along. That said, if some other organization makes sense, is easy to follow, and is more persuasive, use that structure. From a persuasive standpoint, you can emphasize favorable information by putting it at the beginning and end of the Fact Statement, of paragraphs, and even of sentences. See Chapter 22 on Making Persuasive Arguments for more on organizing for persuasion. The beginning and end are points of emphasis, so use those positions wisely. On the flip side, you can't leave them out, but you can bury negative facts in the middle.

Second, use vivid detail for facts you want the reader to remember and more broad generalizations for facts you don't want to emphasize. If your client punched a security guard, going on for a paragraph about the assault will paint a picture you might not want the reader to remember. As with all persuasive techniques, though, be subtle.

Third, sentence length makes a difference. Short sentences create emphasis, and longer sentences can be used to downplay negative facts. You can't omit or characterize facts, but you can decide how to make them work in your favor.

Finally, word choice matters. Use strong action verbs when describing your opponent's bad conduct, for example, but not your client's bad conduct. Similarly, as noted in Chapter 22, "task" and "project" can mean the same thing, but "project" suggests a much more comprehensive assignment than "task." The bottom line is this: think about each word in the Fact

Statement and its connotation, and choose words that help tell your story both truthfully and persuasively.

In the Fact Statement, don't say anything that your adversary could justifiably claim to be inaccurate. If you do, you're probably arguing and you might be losing credibility with your reader. Your story works only if your opponent has to admit that everything you say in the Fact Statement is true.

Unless the rules or your professor ask you not to, include the procedural posture. "Facts" include the underlying events that gave rise to the litigation as well as what has happened in the court case so far. If you are writing a motion or brief, it's because you're trying to get a judge to do something. Give the judge some context for that decision by describing the court action. Explain who sued whom and for what. If you're in trial court, state what kind of motion is before the court and who filed it. If you're in an appellate court, explain who won at trial, who appealed, and on what basis. Most writers put this information either at the beginning or end of the Fact Statement; use your judgment about where it makes the most sense in your story.

Include every fact you mention in the Argument. Your Fact Statement will likely include facts that don't reappear in your Argument, because some facts help tell the story but don't necessarily help with your legal arguments. But any fact that you use in the Argument must also appear in the Fact Statement. A judge needs to able to see all the relevant facts in one place, and that's in the Fact Statement.

Every fact in the Fact Statement must be supported by a citation to the record. The record includes whatever information could be the basis for a court's decision: pleadings, testimony, and affidavits, for instance. For every fact, cite to the place in the record where the reader can find that fact. Citations to the record are also needed in the Argument wherever you refer to a fact.

You can use the same techniques that great writers in other genres use to make your legal writing more persuasive. Some experts believe that storytelling is "hardwired" into our thinking; give human beings a few facts and they will hear a story. Topics like *plot, setting, point of view, narrative hooks, pacing, motivating characters,* and *"showing not telling"* are just a few of the many fiction-writing techniques that might apply to writing a Facts Statement. For example, plot is nothing more than a problem and a resolution. Your job in the Fact Statement is to explain how a problem came about and to use the facts to imply a resolution that is best for your client. Point of view is a powerful technique. Telling the story from your client's point of view—making your client the hero of the story—is a skill many professors will ask you to develop. Think about how fiction writing craftsmanship can help you write your Fact Statement.

HOW TO WRITE A PERSUASIVE FACT STATEMENT

Using the cell phone manslaughter problem in Appendix A, we'll walk you through the process of writing a persuasive Fact Statement.

PROBLEMS

Problem

Here is a quick overview of the cell phone manslaughter problem (for details, see Appendix A). Allison King used her wireless phone, without a hands-free device, while driving in dense fog on a winding road on the edge of an ocean cliff. King placed the call to warn her friends about the dangerous conditions, as they would be meeting later. While she was making the call, she hit and killed a bicyclist. The prosecution will attempt to convict King of vehicular manslaughter by showing that she drove while committing an illegal act (driving while using a wireless phone without a hands-free device) and with gross negligence. King will argue that her actions fit within the "emergency purposes" exception to the wireless phone prohibition. She will also argue that she did not act with gross negligence.

Step 1: Think about your client's story. What did he do? What happened to him? How was he wronged? Or how were his actions justified? Start making a list of all the relevant facts, telling the story from your client's perspective. For instance, if you represented King, this might be a story about a conscientious friend trying to protect others by calling those she knew would be traveling on a dangerous road to warn them about the conditions. If you were prosecuting King, this might be a story about a woman more concerned with the gathering with her friends than with others on the road, including the cyclist she killed when she made a cell phone call. Pay attention to who you place as the subject of the sentence. The subject of the sentence will create the point of view.

Be sure to include all of the facts that are relevant to the applicable legal rules, so in the cell phone manslaughter problem, include the fact that she was driving in California, that she used her cell phone without a hands-free device, that her car hit and killed the cyclist, the driving conditions, and the reason for her call. All of these facts are relevant under the controlling law. You might also include other facts, even if not legally relevant, if they help persuade. If you were prosecuting King, for instance, that might include information about the victim, such as that he was a father of three and a teacher; it isn't relevant in a technical sense, but it might help your position if the judge can identify with him as a person rather than an anonymous cyclist.

Also be sure that you've included harmful facts. Like them or not, facts are facts. You can argue about their relevance in the Argument section, and in the Fact Statement, you can try to minimize negative facts. But you can't leave them out. For instance, if you represented King, you shouldn't omit the fact that the cyclist died after being hit by King. That fact is legally relevant, and you can bet the prosecution is going to tell the judge that he died because your client hit him.

Step 2: Organize the facts so the reader can easily understand them and so they tell a persuasive story. Generally, this means you'll tell the story chronologically, from beginning to end. Sometimes, however, a topical organization works better. For instance, if your complaint alleges two separate causes of action based on mostly separate facts, you could first address the facts relevant to claim one and then address the facts relevant to claim two. If the facts overlap significantly, of course, this might not be the best structure.

Use the positions of emphasis—the beginning and end—for persuasive effect and save the middle (the position that will receive the least attention) for negative or less helpful facts. For instance, if you represented King, you likely would not begin your Fact Statement telling about the accident that killed the cyclist. The prosecutor, however, might do exactly that.

Follow this pattern of using the beginning and end to emphasize favorable facts within paragraphs and even sentences. For instance, you can emphasize King's good intentions with the following sentence:

> King was concerned for the safety of others on the road, so using her cell phone to call June Coughlin, she warned her about the dangerous conditions.

This sentence includes the negative fact—that she made a cell phone call on this dangerous road—but it is placed in the middle of the sentence and surrounded by facts that help King appear responsible and thoughtful.

Step 3: Vary the level of detail depending on how much you want to emphasize a particular fact. Explaining helpful facts in detail helps the reader picture them and remember them. Suppose, for instance, you are prosecuting King. You decide that your best fact is that the road King was driving on (while using her cell phone) is on the edge of a cliff with a limited opportunity for survival in the event of an accident. To be persuasive, paint a vivid picture of the cliff. Give enough detail so the reader can visualize the sheer drop to the ocean below. (Don't make up details, however. They all must be in the record.)

Other favorable facts include the dense fog and the narrow, winding two-lane road. After describing the cliff in detail, when you start discussing the fog, mention the cliff again so the reader can understand the cumulative effect of the dangers:

> The defendant drove along this cliff in dense fog with limited visibility when she decided to take her eyes off the road to dial her friend's number on her cell phone.

In contrast, when you want to downplay a fact (because you can't just pretend it doesn't exist!), use less detail. King might describe the few places to pull over, but she likely would not describe hitting the cyclist in detail; devoting more than a few words to the actual accident will give the reader a mental image of the cyclist's death that will be difficult to forget.

Step 4: Think about each and every word and its persuasive effect. Your goal in the Fact Statement is to subtly persuade, and you can do that best when you use words with precision. Each word in the Fact Statement should serve a purpose—to tell your client's story, to neutralize a negative fact, or to help the judge understand the procedural posture.

Words carry certain connotations, so take advantage of the mental imagery words create and avoid creating negative images. Using the earlier example in King's prosecution, it isn't just detail that helps persuade but word choice; note the mental image that is created here:

> The defendant drove along this cliff in dense fog with limited visibility when she decided to take her eyes off the road to dial her friend's number on her cell phone.

In contrast, avoid using action verbs to describe your client's bad conduct, like in this example from earlier:

> King was concerned for the safety of others on the road, so using her cell phone to call June Coughlin, she warned her about the dangerous conditions.

The verb in this sentence is "using"—not a word that creates a strong mental image—rather than "called" or "dialed," which lets the reader picture King's actions much more clearly.

Similarly, use words and phrases like "although" and "even though" to connect favorable and unfavorable facts, helping to neutralize the unfavorable one. Even without a truly favorable fact, you can use gaps in the record to neutralize unfavorable facts. If you were prosecuting King, for instance, your most unfavorable fact is the reason for her phone call. You might write something like this:

> Although the defendant telephoned her friends to warn them, no evidence in the record suggests that she was unable to stop her car for the few moments needed to make that call. Instead, she continued to drive while taking her eyes off the road to dial.

Just as you should choose your words with care, think about what *not* to include in the Fact Statement. Keep the procedural explanation as short as possible (just enough so the judge knows what is before him). Similarly, eliminate factual clutter. Too much information distracts from the most persuasive aspects of your story, so mention the date, time, place, and any other fact only if it's essential to the story.

Step 5: Go back and forth between the Argument and the Fact Statement, making sure every fact in the Argument also appears in the Fact Statement and revising, rewriting, and proofing in a coordinated way so these two parts of your document support each other. As elsewhere in legal writing, you can't produce an effective document without rewriting it frequently. As you rewrite the Fact Statement, make sure you've included all the necessary facts, including those you use in the Argument. Review the Fact Statement to ensure that it tells a compelling story and that it doesn't contain argument. Make sure the Fact Statement includes the procedural posture and that you've supplied a citation to the record for every fact.

EXAMPLES

Review the following examples. For each example, there may be more than one correct answer. Explain to yourself why you have chosen that answer or those answers. Then read the explanations in the last section of this chapter to check your work.

Example 25-1

This question uses the copyright and fair use problem, which you can find in Appendix B. It would be helpful here to review the facts on the first page of that problem.

> Jenna Page is a successful rock musician who wrote and recorded the hit song, "Red, White, and Blue." She filed this copyright infringement action against a relatively unknown rock singer, Billy Dash, for his rendition of "Red, White, and Blue Through and Through." Dash's chorus is almost identical to Page's original and Dash's lyrics parallel the lyrics in Page's original.

This portion of a Fact Statement is . . .

A. effective in a motion for Page because the story is told from Page's perspective.

B. effective in a motion for Page because it uses the emphasis point at the end of the paragraph well and the words it uses are persuasive.
C. ineffective in a motion for Page because the facts should be told more objectively and much of this paragraph is argument.
D. ineffective in a motion for Dash because although it is true, these facts are not told from Dash's perspective.

EXAMPLES

Example 25-2

This question uses the copyright and fair use problem, which you can find in Appendix B.

Jenna Page is a successful rock musician who wrote and recorded the hit song, "Red, White, and Blue." She filed this copyright infringement action against a relatively unknown rock singer, Billy Dash, for his rendition of "Red, White, and Blue Through and Through." Dash's chorus is almost identical to Page's original and Dash's lyrics parallel the lyrics in Page's original.

This paragraph would be ineffective as the entire Fact Statement in a motion for Page because . . .

A. it doesn't tell the whole story.
B. it doesn't include negative facts (those favoring Dash).
C. it doesn't state what motion has been filed or by whom.
D. it doesn't include the elements of the copyright statute.

EXAMPLES

Example 25-3

This question uses a hypothetical breach of contract problem

David McKeon contracted with Susan Holland on January 20, 2013. Holland Aff. Attach. A. The written contract provided that beginning March 1, 2013, McKeon would provide landscaping services to thirty-seven commercial properties in Santa Fe, New Mexico that were managed by Holland. Holland Aff. ¶ 3. The terms required McKeon to mow all grass, trim all trees and bushes, and clear away all landscaping debris from each property once each week. Holland Aff. Attach. A, ¶ 17. McKeon was also responsible for maintaining the irrigation systems at all properties. Holland Aff. Attach. A, ¶ 18. In return, Holland would pay McKeon $12,800 on the 25th of each month. Holland Aff. Attach. A, ¶ 26.

Holland paid McKeon as required under the contract on March 25th, April 25th, and May 25th, 2013. Holland Aff. Attach. B-D. In total, Holland paid $38,400 to McKeon. Holland Aff. ¶ 6.

In early June, 2013, Holland discovered that McKeon had not been maintaining the irrigation systems, trimming all of the trees and bushes, and clearing away the landscaping debris at a minimum of nineteen of the thirty-seven properties. Holland Aff. ¶ 8. Holland began receiving a number of complaints about the state of the landscaping at each of those nineteen properties. Holland Aff. ¶ 8; Holland Aff. Attach. E-P. Holland called McKeon to discuss the problem and McKeon did not return those calls. Holland Aff. ¶ 10.

Problems with the unmaintained irrigation systems caused excessive drying of trees, bushes, and grass. Williams Aff. ¶ 3. Properties where the irrigation systems continued to run properly experienced very little drying of trees, bushes, and grass, despite unusually high temperatures. Williams Aff. ¶ 6. On properties where the irrigation systems were not running properly, debris from the drying trees, bushes, and grass damaged swimming pools by clogging their filters and causing excessive algae to grow. Valenzuela Aff. ¶¶ 4; 5. In total, landscaping debris clogged the filters of swimming pools at seven properties: Aspire, Collonade, Desert Run, Haymore, Hudson, Millennium, and Mission. Valenzuela Aff. ¶ 4. In total, landscaping debris caused excessive algae in swimming pools at nine other properties: Apollo, Bridgeton, Crescent, Grayhawk, Juniper, Norwalk, Park West, Sunbridge, and Wellington. Valenzuela Aff. ¶ 5.

As a direct result of this landscaping debris, Holland paid $19,278.36 in pool repairs for the sixteen properties. Holland Aff. ¶ 16; Holland Aff. Attach. Q.

Holland now moves for summary judgment in this breach of contract action.

A. This Fact Statement is ineffective because it includes a lot of unnecessary and unhelpful information that dilutes the persuasive effect, such as dates, the names of the various properties, and the fact that Holland called McKeon and he didn't call back.

B. The writer should not have admitted, in the third paragraph, that temperatures were unusually high because that might suggest McKeon was not at fault.

C. This Fact Statement is effective for Holland because it tells the story of this contract breach from her perspective.

D. This is an ineffective Fact Statement because it should begin with the cause of action and explain the particular motion before the court, not end on it.

EXAMPLES

Example 25-4

This question uses the cell phone manslaughter problem, which you can find in Appendix A.

King testified that she was surrounded by fog, could barely see over the hood of her car, and could not see whether there was any place to pull off the road. She knew that if she stopped on the road, another car could crash into hers. She also knew that parts of the road ran along the top of a cliff. She testified that she kept driving because she was afraid to do anything else.

A. This testimony should be cited to the record.
B. The reader can't tell whether the writer represents King or the prosecution.
C. The word "crash" does a better job here than "collide" or "hit" would have done.
D. This passage does nothing to neutralize any of the unfavorable facts.

EXPLANATIONS

Explanation 25-1

A is correct. It should be obvious to a reader that this paragraph is in a motion for Page; it tells her story. She is the main character, and we can immediately tell what her claim is against Dash. **B** is also correct. The paragraph ends strongly, making the point about how similar Dash's song is to Page's original song. Rather than just stating the songs are very similar, it breaks up the chorus and rest of the lyrics. It also repeats the phrase "Page's original" two times, subtly driving home the point that this is Page's song and suggesting without saying so that Dash stole the song. **C** is incorrect. In an office memo's Facts section, objectivity is expected. In a motion's Fact Statement, however, the facts should be told from your client's perspective. The judge expects it, and if you simply state the facts objectively, you've lost an opportunity to persuade him. Furthermore, everything in this Fact Statement is factual, not argument. **D** is correct for the reasons stated in A and C.

Explanation 25-2

A is correct. This paragraph gives a nice overview, but it doesn't include a number of details that would be essential for a persuasive Fact Statement in this copyright infringement case. For example, we know that the copyright statute considers the purpose of the copying, and that Dash will claim his song is a parody entitled to fair use. None of the facts relevant to those arguments are present here. Any fact that appears in the Argument section has to be included in the Fact Statement, and it's hard to imagine writing an effective Argument without a number of additional facts. **B** is also correct. There are a number of facts that favor Dash, but none of them are present in this paragraph. Dash's song has a different message—one of pride in America rather than being critical of U.S. politics and economic inequality—and that is relevant to Dash's claim that his song is a legitimate parody and therefore doesn't violate the Copyright Act. **C** is correct. This paragraph includes the nature of the suit, copyright infringement, but it doesn't tell the judge what she is being asked to decide here: the particular motion that has been filed and who filed it. **D** is incorrect. The Fact Statement shouldn't include the law. Save that for the Argument.

Explanation 25-3

A is incorrect. It's true that you shouldn't include unnecessary and unhelpful facts as they will detract from your persuasive facts, but here, the information is helpful to Holland's story, even if some of it isn't absolutely necessary to her legal claim. For example, the dates are helpful because they show Holland met all of her obligations under the contract. The property names are not necessary, but they help emphasize the breadth of the problem and might make the judge think about actual places rather than abstract "properties." Finally, McKeon not calling Holland back isn't relevant, but it makes McKeon look unappealing, and that helps Holland. **B** is also incorrect. Facts that hurt your client's case have to be included; ignoring them doesn't make your Fact Statement more persuasive. Instead, do just what the writer did here—admit this harmful fact, but dilute its impact by explaining why the unusually high temperatures are not fatal to your case. Note also how that admission is in a position of little emphasis, the middle of the paragraph, and it follows yet another statement that favors Holland: "Properties where the irrigation systems continued to run properly experienced very little drying of trees, bushes, and grass," and then ends with the harmful fact, but qualifies it with "despite" as follows: "despite unusually high temperatures." The next sentence directly connects McKeon's inaction to the damages, when it states: "On properties where the irrigation systems were not running properly, debris from the drying trees, bushes, and grass . . ." **C** is correct. This Fact Statement tells Holland's story. **D** is incorrect. The Fact Statement should describe the procedural posture, including the claim that's been filed and the particular motion or appeal before the court, and the beginning of the Fact Statement is a common place to find the procedural posture. But the procedural posture is also commonly included at the end of the Fact Statement, and including it anywhere within the Fact Statement is fine as long as it makes logical sense.

EXPLANATIONS

Explanation 25-4

A is correct. Citations to the record are mandatory in a Fact Statement. **B** is incorrect. This testimony supports King by explaining the desperate situation in which she found herself and in which she had no good alternatives. **C** is correct. "Crash" helps you imagine the violent effect of one car running into another. "Collide" and "hit" don't provide the same vividness. **D** is incorrect. A fact that hurts King is that she continued to drive in a blinding fog. The passage helps to neutralize that by showing that each of the alternatives was dangerous, too.

Checklist

Chapter 25: Writing a Persuasive Fact Statement

✔	Use your client's point of view.
✔	Tell the whole story to be credible and so the reader can understand what happened.
✔	Don't analyze or argue in the Fact Statement and avoid an argumentative tone.
✔	Pay attention to organization, positions of emphasis, sentence construction, detail, and word choice for nonobvious persuasion in the Fact Statement.
✔	Don't make statements your opponent could justifiably claim are inaccurate.
✔	Follow local rules or professor's rules on whether to include procedure in the Fact Statement.
✔	Include every fact you use in the Argument section.
✔	Include a cite to the record for every fact.
✔	Use storytelling techniques to tell a persuasive story.

You will find all of the chapter checklists compiled in Appendix D.

CHAPTER 26

Writing the Question Presented (Persuasive)

The Question Presented is where you frame the question (or questions) the court is being asked to address. It's rare for a motion or other trial court document to have a Question Presented, but appellate briefs almost universally require a separate Question Presented section. As you might have guessed from learning about persuasive writing in general, you'll use the Question Presented not just as a means to provide the technical issue to the court, but also to subtly sway the court in favor of your client's position. And unlike in memos, where the Question Presented is followed by a Brief Answer, in appellate briefs, the Summary of the Argument (see Chapter 24) fulfills a similar role.

Terminology notes. Sometimes professors will call the Question Presented the "QP." In some courts the Question Presented is called the "Issue" or "Issue Presented." If you have more than one Question or Issue, that part of the brief would be called Questions Presented (or Issues or Issues Presented).

WHAT YOU NEED TO KNOW ABOUT WRITING A PERSUASIVE QUESTION PRESENTED

The way a question is asked often influences the way it's answered. Suppose, for instance, that a cable news network has hired a pollster to find out whether the public feels Congress is doing a good job. A newspaper has hired a different pollster to do a poll on the same subject. One of the pollsters asks question A, and the other asks question B.

A. Do you think Congress is doing a good job of passing legislation that generally benefits the country?
B. Do you think Congress is failing in its responsibility to pass legislation that would resolve some of the basic problems facing the country?

Tomorrow the cable news network and the newspaper will separately announce their poll results. Based on the questions they asked, would you predict that these polls will agree or differ on the extent to which the public has confidence in Congress? What answer does each question encourage?

Keep this in mind as you craft your Question Presented. Use the Question Presented as an opportunity to persuade by framing the issue with the most essential facts of your theory of the case and themes (see Chapter 20).

Don't confuse a persuasive Question Presented with an office memo's objective Question Presented, explained in Chapter 14. They look similar. Both are called the Question Presented. Both define an issue as precisely as possible. And they follow many of the same general rules, such as keeping them to one sentence capable of being answered with a "yes" or "no" and including a Question Presented only for main (not sub-) issues.

But a persuasive Question Presented has the added function of influencing the court to see the case from your point of view. A persuasive Question Presented includes the most essential facts of your theory of the case. You can persuade by choosing your strongest facts and by expressing them in words that will motivate a judge to rule in your client's favor.

A persuasive Question Presented combines three ingredients: (1) a reference to the applicable law; (2) the legal question the court must answer; and (3) the facts you consider most significant to your theory.

A reference to the applicable law: Although the next two examples are phrased differently, they are essentially the same Question Presented. One uses *Under* to introduce the law. The other uses a verb (*Does*).

> Under the Antiquities Act, does the President have the authority to create a National Monument when . . .

> Does the Antiquities Act confer authority on the President to create a National Monument when . . .

The legal question: These three examples use different interrogatory verbs: *Did, Do,* and *Is.*

> Did the police violate the defendant's Fifth Amendment rights when . . .

> Do school boards have the power to . . .

> Is a Congressional delegation of authority unconstitutional under the Separation of Powers Clause when . . .

The facts: An easy way to start the list is with the word "when," as you did in the objective Question Presented in an office memo (see Chapter 14). Or you might incorporate them into the core of the sentence:

> Does Wyoming violate the Due Process Clause by exercising personal jurisdiction over a Nigerian citizen who has never been in the state, never caused harm there, and never derived any benefit from interests there?

Because of the nature of this particular issue, the facts flow without the introductory word "when." In many situations, however, you will need to use "when" to introduce the facts.

Assemble these ingredients in the most persuasive order as long as the reader can quickly grasp the question. General principles of persuasion should help you decide what order works best for your particular case. The beginning and end are positions of emphasis. Think about whether you want to emphasize the controlling law (which you may want to if, for example, it's unsettled and the court is being asked to clarify it), the legal question (which is often a good starting point), or the significant facts (which help if you have a particularly compelling factual scenario). Recall that the middle will be the position of least emphasis, so use that spot for any negative or less important part of the Question Presented.

But make sure the judge can easily understand the Question Presented; for this reason, it's often wise to put the wordiest ingredient at the end of the sentence, whether law, legal question, or facts. A sentence is most easily understood if the most complicated part comes at the end.

It takes a lot of writing and rewriting to make a Question Presented both concise and understandable. In many briefs, the Question Presented is the single hardest sentence to write.

Some readers prefer, and some courts require, that the Question Presented be framed as a declarative sentence beginning with "Whether," rather than a question. Most persuasive Questions Presented are framed in one complete sentence that ends with a question mark. Framing the Question Presented this way makes it easy to read and grammatically correct. In the U.S. Supreme Court, however, Questions Presented begin with "Whether" and end with a period. Some readers prefer this format even for briefs outside the Supreme Court, so as with all writing projects, consider your reader's preferences.

If you are following the "Whether" format, your Question Presented might look like this:

> Whether Wyoming violates the Due Process Clause by exercising personal jurisdiction over a Nigerian citizen who has never been in the state, never caused harm there, and never derived any benefit from interests there.

And if you had a purely legal issue, using the "Whether" format you might draft this Question Presented:

> Whether this state should recognize the tort doctrine of social host liability in light of the increasing number of deaths and injuries caused by drunken driving.

Phrase the Question Presented to invite a "yes" answer. Most lawyers draft persuasive Questions Presented to invite "yes" answers, and judges are used to reading them phrased that way. If you write one to invite a "no" answer, you'll confuse the judge, who will have to try to figure out whether you really want "no." And if you do, your Question Presented will suggest that your theory of the case is based on a negative reaction to the other side's argument rather than the positive merits of your own arguments.

HOW TO WRITE A PERSUASIVE QUESTION PRESENTED

Using the copyright and fair use problem in Appendix B, we'll walk you through the process of writing a persuasive Question Presented.

PROBLEMS

Problem

Here is a quick overview of the copyright and fair use problem (for details, see Appendix B). Page is suing Dash for violating the Copyright Act when Dash wrote a song based on Page's song (which in copyright terms is called the "original"), "Red, White, and Blue." Dash's song uses the structure and many lyrics of the original but changes the original song's political message. The music of the two songs is not at issue, only the lyrics. Page expects that Dash will argue that his song is a parody that falls under the fair use exception to the Copyright Act. The court will consider the relevant factors set out in the fair use statute, 17 U.S.C. § 107: whether the copy was transformative and targeted the original; whether it took more than necessary of the original; and whether it will interfere with the original's market.

Step 1: Articulate the applicable law. As with objective Questions Presented, you'll generally refer to the law descriptively rather than with a case name or citation. Depending on the issue, you might do this broadly:

> Under the Copyright Act . . .

Or more specifically:

> For purposes of the Copyright Act's fair use exception, . . .

Step 2: State the specific legal question as briefly as possible. Express the legal concepts precisely.

> . . . is a work "transformative" when . . .

Where a statute is involved, the statutory wording is usually the most precise way to express the concepts. In the copyright statute, for instance, the word "transformative" has a precise meaning.

Step 3: State the key facts briefly in words that best encapsulate your theory. State only facts and state each fact in carefully chosen words so that your adversary cannot reasonably claim that you've stated the fact inaccurately. Don't include factual inferences or conclusions of law. "The defendant did not stop at the stop sign" is a fact. "The defendant carelessly ignored the stop sign" contains two factual inferences: that the defendant acted carelessly and that he ignored the stop sign (rather than didn't see it, for example). "The defendant negligently entered the intersection" is a conclusion of law. Unless your adversary concedes a factual inference or a conclusion of law, you cannot assume it in a Question Presented. In addition, list only the most essential facts and eliminate unnecessary details.

Furthermore, if a court doubts that you've accurately stated the facts, the Question Presented will not persuade. A good Question Presented persuades with facts that imply this message: "Judge, these undeniable facts are so strong that you should decide for my client." A judge who doubts that you've stated the facts accurately will ignore that message.

For instance, if you represent Dash in the copyright and fair use case, you might use these facts to show that Dash's song transformed Page's original song:

> . . . the work celebrates pride in America and its values rather than portraying the original's critical view of America and its traditions?

Step 4: Combine the components in a persuasive, easily read sentence. Assemble the applicable law, the legal question, and the key facts into one sentence phrased as a question. Place the longest part at the end of the sentence unless that part is particularly compelling and the sentence can still be understood quickly with that part at the beginning. Suppose it takes the following numbers of words to express each part:

applicable law	5 words
legal question	7 words
facts	16 words

Here, if you put the facts first, the reader might struggle to understand the sentence. The facts are more than half of the sentence, and the reader could get lost before realizing how the sentence is structured. Often—but not always—lawyers put the facts at the end of the Question Presented because the facts make sense only after the reader knows what the legal question is.

On the other hand, if the facts are unusually persuasive—even if the key facts can't be expressed very concisely—you might experiment to see if you can find a way to emphasize them by putting them first in the sentence without making the Question Presented hard to read.

Using our copyright and fair use example, we might come up with this:

> For purposes of the Copyright Act's fair use exception, is a work "transformative" when the work celebrates pride in America and its values rather than portraying the original's critical view of America and its traditions?

If you represent Page, you might write this instead:

> Does a copy fail to be "transformative" under the Copyright Act when both the copy and the original are in the same genre and both are chanted at patriotic rallies?

EXAMPLES

Review the following examples. For each example, there may be more than one correct answer. Explain to yourself why you have chosen that answer or those answers. Then read the explanations in the last section of this chapter to check your work.

EXAMPLES

Example 26-1

This question uses a hypothetical murder problem.

Did Nguyen commit first-degree murder when he shot the security guard?

A. This is an effective Question Presented because it's concise and can be read and understood quickly.
B. This is an ineffective Question Presented because it omits the applicable law.
C. This is an ineffective Question Presented because it doesn't completely state the key facts.
D. This is an ineffective Question Presented because the writer has not used the facts to persuade the reader.

EXAMPLES

Example 26-2

This question uses the cell phone manslaughter problem, which you can find in Appendix A.

Did King commit vehicular manslaughter under Cal. Penal Code § 192 (c)(1) when she violated Cal. Vehicle Code § 23123 by using a cell phone that was not configured for hands-free use, while operating a motor vehicle and, while using this cell phone, struck a bicyclist and forced him to fall to his death from a cliff?

A. This Question Presented is not concise.
B. This Question Presented contains unnecessary detail.
C. The statutory section citations in this Question Presented are distracting.
D. The statement that King violated § 23123 is a conclusion of law.

EXAMPLES

Example 26-3

This question uses the cell phone manslaughter problem, which you can find in Appendix A.

> Under California law, does a motorist commit vehicular manslaughter when she makes a cell phone call, creating an unreasonable risk to others, and strikes and kills a bicyclist?

A. This Question Presented adequately identifies the applicable law.
B. This Question Presented is concise.
C. The facts listed in this Question Presented could be disputed by the opposing lawyer.
D. This Question Presented doesn't state all the essential facts.

EXAMPLES

Example 26-4

This question uses the cell phone manslaughter problem, which you can find in Appendix A.

> When King drove on a winding, two-lane road in dense fog near the side of a cliff while recklessly dialing her cell phone and hit a bicyclist, causing him to fall over the cliff to his death, did she commit vehicular manslaughter under California law?

A. The word "dense" expresses a factual inference that does not belong in a Question Presented.
B. The word "recklessly" does not express a factual inference that King could challenge because her conduct was undeniably reckless.
C. This Question Presented is hard to read because of the way it's structured.
D. Because the facts are compelling, placing them at the beginning of the sentence is effective.

Example 26-5

This question uses the negligent infliction of emotional distress problem, which you can find in Appendix C.

> Is a bystander "sensorially aware" of the accident, under New Fornia's negligent infliction of emotional distress common law, when she hears the defendant's car hit her fiancé, has to jump to avoid being hit by her fiancé's lawnmower, and sees her fiancé lying on the ground feet from the defendant's car, covered in blood and unresponsive?

A. This Question Presented should start with the applicable law.
B. This Question Presented contains too many facts.
C. The facts in this Question Presented are framed persuasively.
D. This Question Presented adequately identifies the applicable law.

EXPLANATIONS

Explanation 26-1

A is incorrect. Although this Question Presented is concise and can be easily read and understood, it's nevertheless ineffective for the reasons stated in B, C, and D. **B** is correct. This Question Presented fails to articulate the applicable law. It could be improved by specifying the controlling state law, and specifically, the statutory provision at issue, though you could do this in descriptive terms rather than with a citation. **C** is also correct. This Question Presented doesn't state that the guard died, which is an essential fact for the prosecution in this murder case. ***D*** is also correct. The writer could do more to make this Question Presented persuasive. For example, it could refer to the death, as noted in C, and use details so the reader can visualize how the death occurred. It should also include facts that show, or negate, the "first-degree" nature of the murder charge, such as facts showing premeditation or the commission of a specified felony.

EXPLANATIONS

Explanation 26-2

A is correct. The same thoughts could be expressed in fewer words. For example, instead of "operating a motor vehicle," it would be enough to write "driving." The reader knows from the context that there's a car. **B** is incorrect. The details used here—such as "forced him to fall to his death from a cliff"—help the reader visualize the actual incident and can help persuade the reader to favor the prosecution. The problem here is too many words (see A), not too many facts. **C** is correct. A description of the statutes, such as "the California vehicular manslaughter statute," would be sufficient without citations. If a statutory section is ambiguous and the court must settle its meaning, it can be helpful to identify that section by its number. But typically, the description of the statute—such as California's vehicular manslaughter statute—is enough for the Question Presented. Of course, you'll refer to the specific statutory section, and cite it properly, within the Argument. But it doesn't help the reader much in this Question Presented. **D** is also correct. This Question Presented treats King's violation of § 23123 as a fact—which it isn't. In fact, it's part of the underlying question that helps resolve whether King is guilty of vehicular manslaughter, and the State must prove it in the Argument. One clue that the writer treats this as a fact and not a question is its location in the under/does/when structure: It's in the list of facts that follows the word *when*.

EXPLANATIONS

Explanation 26-3

A is incorrect. Most readers would think that the applicable statute should be specified. Some readers would prefer a descriptive approach to identifying the relevant statute—like "California's vehicular manslaughter statute"—and others would rather see a reference to the statute by section number, especially if the court is being asked to settle the meaning of that section. **B** is incorrect. This Question Presented is short, but that's not the same as being concise. Conciseness is expressing ideas in few words. This Question Presented is short because it expresses too few ideas. The statute is not specified, and most of the key facts are missing. **C** is correct. The assertion that King "creat[ed] an unreasonable risk to others" is a conclusion of law. Because "gross negligence" is defined as creating an unreasonable risk, reasonableness is part of the governing legal rule. Thus, it's a conclusion of law to say that she acted unreasonably. **D** is correct. Many of the persuasive facts in this case, such as the dangerous driving conditions, are missing.

Explanation 26-4

A is incorrect. "Dense" is an inference, but King will not challenge it. She will argue that in a dense fog, on a narrow road near a cliff, she had no choice but to keep driving, and she needed to call her friends and warn them of the fog, which would establish an emergency purpose under § 23123(c). If the fog isn't dense, her defense will fall apart. The prosecution needs a dense fog, too, to support its argument that she was ignoring risks. Both parties want this fog to have been dense. **B** is incorrect for two reasons. First, one could reasonably argue that she was reckless, but one could just as reasonably argue that she was not. Whichever it was would be decided by argument, and it can't be inserted into a Question Presented as an undeniable fact. Second, whether or not she was reckless is irrelevant. None of the statutory tests in Appendix A measure recklessness. They do measure gross negligence, which is a different concept. **C** is correct. This Question Presented is made up of facts (the first 37 words of the sentence), a legal question (5 words, "did she commit vehicular manslaughter"), and a reference to applicable law (3 words, "under California law"). The reader gets lost in the first 37 words without being able to identify the sentence's structure. Generally, a reader will understand a sentence most easily if the wordiest or most complicated part comes at the end. This Question Presented should begin with the legal question and applicable law because they're expressed in few words and can be instantly understood. The facts should follow because they're wordier and more complicated, even if they are persuasive. It's not always true that the facts should come last in a Question Presented. But it is true here. **D** is incorrect. The facts are compelling, but placing them at the beginning of this Question Presented makes it hard for the reader to understand them.

Explanation 26-5

A is incorrect. Questions Presented often start with the applicable law, but that isn't required. Here, the legal question is shorter than the applicable law—8 words versus 10 words—so it makes some sense to start with the legal question. This structure also takes advantage of the positions of emphasis by using the beginning of the sentence for the legal question and the end for the facts. **B** is also incorrect. You should be as concise as possible, but it's more important to be persuasive (as long as the sentence isn't too long to read) than brief. The "facts" portion of this Question Presented contains 38 words—which is a lot, but it's not difficult to digest because they come at the end of the sentence. **C** is correct. These facts are persuasive because they include vivid detail to help the reader understand how the plaintiff was aware of the accident as it happened. **D** is also correct. This Question Presented tells the reader that New Fornia common law governs, the legal claim is negligent infliction of emotional distress as a bystander, and the specific legal issue is whether the plaintiff was "sensorially aware" of the accident.

Checklist

Chapter 26: Writing the Question Presented (Persuasive)

✔	Phrase the Question Presented to invite a "yes" answer that would result in your client prevailing.
✔	Include the applicable law, the precise legal question, and the facts most significant to your theory of the case.
✔	Make the Question Presented persuasive by using the techniques used elsewhere in the brief to persuade: emphasis, word choice, level of detail, and storytelling.
✔	Rewrite several times to make sure the Question Presented is as strong as possible.

You will find all of the chapter checklists compiled in Appendix D.

CHAPTER 27

Writing the Conclusion Section (Persuasive)

In persuasive writing, Conclusions are generally much shorter than they are in memos (objective writing). But just because they are short, you shouldn't discount them. The point of motions, briefs, and other persuasive documents is to persuade. Don't throw away that opportunity. Decision makers like to be reminded of exactly what you expect from them based on the outcomes you've predicted or advocated.

The word "Conclusion" can have several meanings. In a brief, it could be the final sentence or paragraph that reminds the court what action the author hopes it will take. It can also mean the initial conclusion—the "C" in CRAC (see Chapter 7 for more on organizing your analysis). In this chapter, "Conclusion" refers to the section at the end of a motion or brief that explicitly tells the court the relief you seek.

WHAT YOU NEED TO KNOW ABOUT CONCLUSIONS

Conclusions in motions and briefs tend to be very short. Persuasive documents traditionally end with just a short sentence or two (or at most a paragraph) that specifically reminds the court what outcome and form of relief the party seeks. As with all writing, you should be cognizant of your reader's expectations, including applicable court rules.

Traditional Conclusions in documents addressed to a court simply begin with the words, "For the foregoing reasons." The Conclusion then clearly states the specific action the party wants, such as asking the court to "grant this motion" or "affirm the judgment of the lower court" or "reverse and remand."

There is a modern trend to making Conclusions in persuasive documents "count" (meaning including more than traditional boilerplate language) by including just a phrase or two that identifies what you believe are the strongest elements of your argument. Even when following this trend, though, the Conclusion in a motion or brief is rarely more than four or five lines of text and it should still specify the action or actions you want the court to take.

HOW TO WRITE THE CONCLUSION SECTION

Using the copyright and fair use problem in Appendix B, we'll walk you through the process of writing a Conclusion.

PROBLEMS

Problem

Here is a quick overview of the copyright and fair use problem (for details see Appendix B). Page is suing Dash for violating the Copyright Act when Dash wrote a song based on Page's song (which in copyright terms is called the "original"), "Red, White, and Blue." Dash's song uses the structure and many lyrics of the original but changes the original song's political message. The music of the two songs is not at issue, only the lyrics. Page expects that Dash will argue that his song is a parody that falls under the fair use exception to the Copyright Act. The court will consider the relevant factors set out in the fair use statute, 17 U.S.C. § 107: whether the copy was transformative and targeted the original; whether it took more than necessary of the original; and whether it will interfere with the original's market.

Step 1: Generate a list of the most important reasons the prevailing party should win. When you're writing as an advocate, you need to know the best argument for your client. Some Conclusions include no specific reasons at all:

> For the foregoing reasons, Appellant Page asks this Court to reverse the decision of the lower court and remand the case for trial.

If your professor or your office prefers the slightly longer version, you need to add a reason or two why the court should find for your client. Assume you are representing Dash (rather than Page) and you think the best arguments in favor of Dash's fair use claim are that he transformed the original by changing the political viewpoint of the song and customers are unlikely to confuse the two songs. You could add these reasons to your Conclusion, as demonstrated below.

Step 2: Check the procedural posture of the case to identify the relief you seek. Whether you are writing a motion or brief, you need to know precisely what you want the court to do. Are you seeking dismissal for failure to state a claim? Maybe you expect the court to reverse and remand to the lower court. Know the procedural posture and exactly what you want the court to order. In our copyright problem, assume the trial court found in favor of Dash and dismissed Page's copyright infringement complaint.

Step 3: Combine the best argument(s) and the specific relief you are requesting into one or two well-crafted sentences. The best Conclusions combine both facts and law. Continuing with our choices above, we know we will ask the court to affirm the lower court's decision because the new work was "transformative" and unlikely to substantially affect the original's market:

> For the foregoing reasons and because Dash transformed the original by changing the political viewpoint so that listeners are unlikely to confuse the parody with the original, this court should affirm the lower court's decision dismissing the case.

EXAMPLES

Review the following examples. For each example, there may be more than one correct answer, but try to choose the *best* answer. Explain to yourself why you have chosen that answer. Then read the explanations in the last section of this chapter to check your work.

Example 27-1

EXAMPLES

The Conclusion below is based on the cell phone manslaughter problem, which you can find in Appendix A.

> Defendant King's motion to dismiss should not be granted. It is unlawful in California to "drive a motor vehicle while using a wireless telephone unless that telephone is specifically designed and configured to allow hands-free listening and talking, and is used in that manner while driving," except in cases where "using a wireless telephone for emergency purposes, including, but not limited to, an emergency call to a law enforcement agency, health care provider, fire department, or other emergency services agency or

entity." Cal. Vehicle Code § 23123 (West 2022). Further, California's vehicular manslaughter statute, Penal Code § 192(c)(1), applies to those drivers who drive "a vehicle in the commission of an unlawful act, not amounting to felony, and with gross negligence."

King did not place the call for "emergency purposes." To prove an emergency, King must show a threat of imminent danger. King could have waited for an opportunity to pull over and make the call when it was safe, and legal, to do so.

Furthermore, King acted with gross negligence. Courts use an objective test to determine gross negligence: whether a reasonable person in the defendant's position would be aware of the risk involved. King must have realized the driving risk because she was actually calling her friends to warn them of that same risk. Despite that, King chose to place a call on her cell phone. King therefore acted with gross negligence.

Hence, King drove while committing an unlawful act, not committed for an emergency purpose, and she was grossly negligent. For these reasons, this Court should deny the Defendant's motion to dismiss her vehicular manslaughter charge.

This Conclusion in a responsive motion is . . .

A. effective because it highlights the important sub-issues and it quotes and cites the key statutory provisions.
B. ineffective because it should include citations to the key cases supporting the sub-rules.
C. ineffective because it's too long.
D. effective because it uses one paragraph per main section of the brief and explicitly begins and ends by stating the action the writer wants the Court to take in this case.

EXAMPLES

Example 27-2

This question is based on the following Conclusion in an appellate brief:

For the foregoing reasons, this Court should reverse.

This Conclusion . . .

A. is incomplete because it should ask for the complete relief the party seeks.
B. is short and effective.
C. is wrong because it should list the reasons supporting the conclusion.
D. is too short.

EXAMPLES

Example 27-3

The Conclusion below is based on the negligent infliction of emotional distress problem, which you can find in Appendix C.

Defoe is entitled to summary judgment on Poe's claim for negligent infliction of emotional distress because Poe and Valenzuela did not have an "intimate, familial relationship," and because Poe did not "directly observe" and was not "sensorially aware" of the accident that caused Valenzuela's injury.

This Conclusion . . .

A. is too long to be effective in a trial motion.
B. should only reference the main claim, not the sub-issues.
C. should not begin with "Defoe is entitled to summary judgment" but should save that for the last sentence.
D. is a bit long, but probably effective.

EXAMPLES

Example 27-4

The Conclusion below is based on the negligent infliction of emotional distress problem, which you can find in Appendix C.

For the foregoing reasons, Poe should prevail.

This Conclusion . . .

A. should state the specific relief Poe is requesting.
B. should at least reference Poe's main claim.
C. is short and effective.
D. should highlight the underlying reasons Poe should prevail.

EXPLANATIONS

Explanation 27-1

A is incorrect. It's true that some Conclusions in motions and briefs state the reason the requested relief is proper. But even in those instances, the Conclusion shouldn't be more than a few lines. This example is much too long. Furthermore, authorities do not need to be quoted (or even cited) in the Conclusion. **B** is incorrect because persuasive Conclusions generally do not cite any authority, especially case law. **C** is correct. Although there is no hard and fast rule on length, in most writing classes or jurisdictions, this Conclusion would be too long in a persuasive document. The Conclusion for a motion (or brief) is often just one sentence and is rarely longer than a few sentences. **D** is incorrect. Using one paragraph per main section is proper in an objective Conclusion section in a memo (see Chapter 17), but not in a persuasive Conclusion section. Furthermore, although the Conclusion should explicitly state the action the writer wants the Court to take, it does not need to be repeated.

Explanation 27-2

A is correct. The Conclusion in a document addressed to a court should take into account the procedural posture of the case and tell the court precisely the actions the party hopes the court will take. Asking the court to "reverse" is helpful, but should the court remand for trial? Grant summary judgment for the moving party instead? What *exactly* do you want the court to do? That should be explicitly stated. Note the suggestions in "What You Need to Know About Conclusions," above. Asking to affirm the judgment below works, but if you're asking for reversal, more is usually needed ("reverse and remand," etc.). **B** is incorrect for the reasons stated in A. **C** is incorrect because it uses the word "wrong." Various audiences—whether your professor or the conventions of the jurisdiction where you work—may have a variety of expectations. Conclusions in persuasive documents *may* briefly list the most important reason or reasons you believe your client should prevail, but it's not necessary that they do. **D** is incorrect. Conclusions in persuasive documents are often one short sentence beginning with "For the foregoing reasons." The real problem with this Conclusion is that it does not explicitly state what action the writer wants the court to take other than to reverse.

Explanation 27-3

A is incorrect. This Conclusion pushes the boundaries on length, but it's still less than five full lines of text and relatively easy to read. It includes the main claim as well as the reasons summary judgment is appropriate and makes explicit that summary judgment is the requested outcome. If, however, you knew the particular judge on this case (or your professor) preferred a shorter Conclusion, then a shorter Conclusion would be more effective. **B** is incorrect. The Conclusion needs to be short, but if you can summarize, briefly, why the underlying elements are not met, you can include that in your Conclusion. **C** is also incorrect. The Conclusion can begin or end with the requested relief, as both of those positions are positions of emphasis. **D** is correct. Although somewhat long, a persuasive Conclusion can be one short paragraph. As noted in A, though, if you knew your reader preferred a more traditional Conclusion, then follow that reader's preference.

Explanation 27-4

A is correct. "Poe should prevail" doesn't tell the judge what action he should take. Be explicit: "For the foregoing reasons, this Court should deny the defendant's motion for summary judgment." **B** is incorrect. Traditional Conclusions are very short and do not restate the underlying claim. **C** is incorrect. This Conclusion is short, but it's not effective for the reasons stated in A. **D** is also incorrect. Unless your reader prefers a traditional Conclusion, the writer can briefly highlight the underlying reasons supporting the requested outcome. Including those reasons isn't mandatory, however.

Checklist

Chapter 27: Writing the Conclusion Section (Persuasive)

✔	Conclusions in motions and briefs tend to be very short—one to two sentences (a short paragraph at most).
✔	Persuasive conclusions often begin with the words "For the foregoing reasons" and then state, in one short phrase, the relief the party requests.
✔	In stating the relief requested, be aware of the procedural posture of the case.
✔	As with all writing to a court, follow court rules or court expectations regarding Conclusions.

You will find all of the chapter checklists compiled in Appendix D.

PART IV

Revising and Rewriting

CHAPTER 28

Overview: Revising and Rewriting

Revising and rewriting are essential to good legal writing. Everyone has to do it. Analysis, organization, and writing style in early drafts nearly always need polishing. Revise over and over again, polishing documents until they shine.

Knowing how to revise your written work is a valuable skill that you can learn. The next chapters aim to help you learn this skill and improve your writing.

- Chapter 29 helps you tighten and add clarity to your sentences. This may be particularly useful when you receive comments like "awkward" next to sentences.
- Chapter 30 provides the essentials of crafting strong thesis sentences to start paragraphs and keep the reader moving effortlessly through your document.
- Chapter 31 focuses on using a concise writing style. It will help you write clearly and crisply, while staying within the word count or page limit of your assignment or court filing.
- Chapter 32 tackles the big-picture topic of coherence and gives you practice with transitions.
- Chapter 33 provides suggestions for transitioning from a good legal writer to a great legal writer.

In Part IV, we've prioritized topics law students may find most useful as they revise. Even if you don't have a page limit problem or find yourself confused about sentence structure, this part of the book offers some of the key writing style principles that most lawyers value. In addition, if you find yourself struggling with writing mechanics or style, a number of good books can help you in more detail with writing basics. Don't be afraid to turn to other sources to get more practice. The payoff for being a good writer is immense.

SOME TIPS FOR PLANNING YOUR TIME

Keep in mind that you should leave plenty of time for your revision process. Have a smart plan of attack. These tips should help.

Plan to revise your document in multiple sessions. This way you'll have a fresh mind and fresh eyes to tackle revising unclear analysis or to spot errors.

Revise in layers from big to small. Don't try to revise for everything all at once. It's nearly impossible to do a great job this way.

In your first session, you might check that your document has all the right components or sections, work on large-scale organization issues, and work on any sections where you need to do a lot of rewriting. Don't be afraid to scrap portions that aren't working well and start over! Be brutal with your written work. Don't keep something just because it's already written.

In your next session, work on the small-scale organization within your sections. Then, perhaps in another session or two, move on to the more detailed revising work of going line by line, editing out passive voice, revising for conciseness and sentence structure, fixing citation errors, and so on.

The substance of your document is critical, but appearances count a lot, too. The polish of your document reflects on you not only as a writer but also on the care you take with your research and analysis. If you're sloppy with your writing, the reader might assume that you were also sloppy with your research and analysis. If your writing shines, the reader is more apt to assume that you were also careful and smart with your research and analysis. In short, your hard work revising your document is simply part of the process of excellent legal writing.

SOME COMMON PITFALLS

Pitfall: Not budgeting enough time for revising. This is the easiest to avoid pitfall and it occurs when writers have to turn in unpolished documents because they didn't leave enough time to revise the document. Plan on spending about a quarter of the total time revising and rewriting.

Pitfall: Revising only once. Few writers can write amazing first drafts. Amazing writing comes from lots of thoughtful revisions made over a period of time when the writer devoted focus and energy to the project.

Pitfall: Trying to revise and proofread for all issues, big and small, at the same time. Your revision process will be more effective if you focus on one part at a time. Few writers can see every potential improvement at once.

Pitfall: Being too hesitant to make changes. It can feel difficult to cut or revise a sentence or paragraph you worked hard to write, especially if you've gotten some good comments on the draft. But in the revision process it's important to be tough with yourself. Ask yourself if that sentence or paragraph expresses something important and relevant to your analysis or argument. Think about the famous quote to "kill your darlings," often attributed to William Faulkner: even though you love a phrase or a sentence you've created, if it doesn't advance the project, then get rid of it. Also ask yourself whether you've stated the point as accurately and concisely as you can. Don't be afraid to rewrite something from scratch or delete a portion entirely if it will make the document better. It might be easier to edit if you keep a second document open; when you want to change or cut something, copy and paste that section into your blank document. You can make changes there without feeling like you're changing the whole document, and simply replace it when you're done. And you can keep the parts you cut so you won't worry about the possibility of needing them later.

Pitfall: Not giving the revision process enough focus and energy. True revision (which by now should be clear means more than proofreading) takes time and thought. When we read something, we think it says what we expect it to say. Errors aren't always obvious. So leave a few hours—or even days, if possible—between your draft and the due date. Pick the document up a day later, and you'll be amazed at how much more you notice and how many improvements you can make.

Checklist

Chapter 28: Overview: Revising and Rewriting

✔	Plan your revision and rewriting strategy.
✔	Revise in several sessions and focus each session on just one or two types of edits.
✔	Revise in layers from big to small.
✔	Don't hesitate to make changes—even big changes.
✔	Appearance and visual presentation matter.
✔	Proofreading is critical because even small errors chip away at your credibility.

You will find all of the chapter checklists compiled in Appendix D.

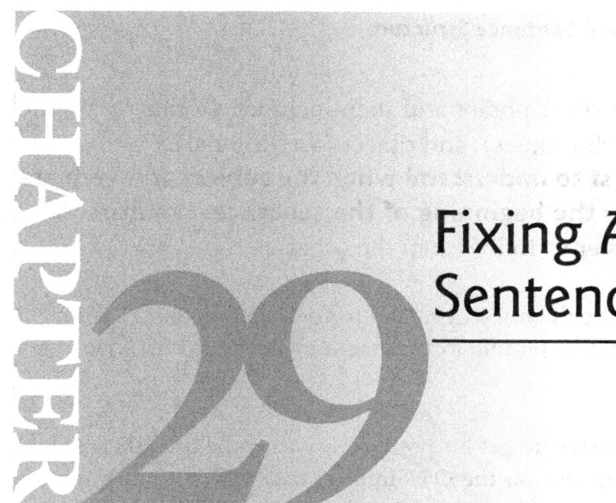

Fixing Awkward Sentence Structure

Just what you need! A margin comment tells you that the reader finds your sentence "awkward," but gives you no clue how to fix it. Chances are that your problem involves sentence structure. The best way to solve this problem is to structure your sentences in the way that conveys information to the reader as quickly and painlessly as possible.

WHAT YOU NEED TO KNOW ABOUT FIXING AWKWARD SENTENCE STRUCTURE

Sentences are easiest to understand when they use a "subject–verb–object" structure. Compare these two sentences. One is easier to follow than the other:

> Due to the recognizable nature of the refrain in the original, which repeats the title four times, Dash's use, which repeats his similar title three times alone, will be recognized by anyone familiar with the song.

> Anyone familiar with the song will recognize the way Dash's song copies the original by repeating the title three times in the refrain.

In the first sentence, it's difficult to even determine the subject on a quick read. Is it the song? The nature of the refrain? This makes the writer's point difficult to ascertain. The second sentence is much easier for readers to follow; it starts with a short phrase and then includes, in this order, the subject (Dash's song), verb (copies), and object (the original).

Sentences are easiest to understand when the subject and verb are close together and near the beginning of the sentence. Compare these two sentences. One is easier to follow than the other:

> Using the original children's book as a vehicle to comment on the O.J. Simpson trial, the defendant, without putting forth something new, copied a style to get his point across.

> The defendant copied a style to get his point across when he used the original children's book to comment on the O.J. Simpson trial without putting forth something new.

The first sentence begins with a long clause and forces the reader to sift through a lot of information before getting to the point: the defendant copied a style. Three commas in this sentence tell you the reader has to do a lot of work to understand the sentence's message. Commas don't always mean the style is awkward, but they are one clue because they often mean the subject and verb are separated by a clause. The second sentence states the point clearly and right at the beginning of the sentence, which is a point of emphasis: the defendant copied a style.

Keep the length of sentences to four lines of type or less. This is one of those "rules" that isn't really a rule, but a handy guideline. In fact, the guideline may vary from professor to professor, with some suggesting three lines of type and others finding a sentence long if it is 25 words or more. See Chapter 32 on coherence. It's possible to structure long sentences in ways that are easy to follow, but it's difficult. Save yourself the trouble by keeping sentences from growing beyond four lines of type. If it's four lines of text or more, break it up.

As you gain experience, you'll get better at drafting easy-to-follow sentences, but as a beginner, plan on time to review each sentence for structure and length. Reading each sentence out loud should help you identify those awkward sentences. The most successful students plan time for a line-by-line edit before turning in their papers.

HOW TO STRUCTURE SENTENCES

Using the copyright and fair use problem in Appendix B, we'll walk you through the process of fixing awkward sentence structure.

PROBLEMS

Problem

> Here is a quick overview of the copyright and fair use problem (for details, see Appendix B). Page is suing Dash for violating the Copyright Act when Dash wrote a song based on Page's song (which in copyright terms is called the "original"), "Red, White, and Blue." Dash's song uses the structure and many lyrics of the original but changes the original song's political message. The music of the two songs is not at issue, only the lyrics. Page expects that Dash will argue that his song is a parody that falls under the fair use exception to the Copyright Act. The court will consider the relevant factors set out in the fair use statute, 17 U.S.C. § 107: whether the copy was transformative and targeted the original; whether it took more than necessary of the original; and whether it will interfere with the original's market.

Step 1: Read your draft sentence by sentence. Choose a sentence that is long or seems hard to follow, and use that to work on editing. Let's say you find this one:

> In examining how the infringing work further cuts against the fair use defense, the use of the title and the copying of the first stanza did not amount to an effort, decided the appellate court, to create a transformative work with new expression.

Step 2: Pull the sentence apart. Start with that long introductory clause. Do you need it? What does it add? Not much. It's not clear you need a signal or transition here, but if you do, it doesn't need to be this long introductory clause. Try deleting it:

> The use of the title and the copying of the first stanza did not amount to an effort, decided the appellate court, to create a transformative work with new expression.

Step 3: Reorganize the sentence if necessary. In this step, decide what the actions in the sentence are and who is doing them. Here you have a court deciding, and the defendant copying and perhaps creating, and the defendant using the title. Recasting the sentence to order it into a subject–verb–object structure means you must choose one of these as the subject of the sentence. Try it both ways:

> The appellate court decided that copying the title and the first stanza did not create a transformative work with new expression.

> The defendant copied the title and the first stanza but did not create a transformative work with new expression.

Both of these sentences significantly improve the original. They are structured as subject–verb–object; the sentences are shorter; and the subject and verb are close together at the beginning of each sentence. Your choice may depend on what you want to emphasize—the court's decision or the defendant's actions. And, of course, you'll want to be careful to accurately characterize the law.

EXAMPLES

Review the following examples. For each example, there may be more than one correct answer. Explain to yourself why you have chosen that answer or those answers. Then read the explanations in the last section of this chapter to check your work.

EXAMPLES

Example 29-1

This question uses the copyright and fair use problem, which you can find in Appendix B.

> When a court decides, depending on the situation and the ease in conjuring up the original in its medium, that the parody uses a greater amount of the original than necessary to assure identification, it finds against fair use.

A. Even though the subject and a verb are close together here, the real action of the courts here is "finding," and because it's separated from the subject "courts," the sentence is difficult to understand.

B. One way to fix this sentence is to break it into more than one sentence.

C. This is a good solution for the sentence: "Depending on the situation and the ease in conjuring up the original in its medium, when a court decides that the parody uses a greater amount of the original than necessary to assure identification, it finds against fair use."

D. This is a good solution for the sentence: "Courts find against fair use when the parody uses a greater amount of the original than necessary to assure identification."

EXAMPLES

Example 29-2

This question uses the copyright and fair use problem, which you can find in Appendix B.

> Mattel, noting that the defendant used the entire image of the Barbie doll, argued that it was copyright infringement by the defendant using more than needed to evoke the original, but the court stated that the purpose of the defendant's work was to critique the stereotyped female roles in American society, and as such it was acceptable for the defendant to use the entire image of the doll.

A. This sentence is too long and one way to fix it is to break it into more than one sentence.
B. The subject and the verb are close together because the subject is "Mattel" and the verb is "noting."
C. This is a good solution for the sentence: "Mattel argued the defendant used more than needed to evoke the original. The court decided that fair use protected the defendant's use of the entire image of the doll to critique stereotyped female roles in American society."
D. This is a good solution for the sentence: "The *Mattel* court found it acceptable to use the entire image of the Barbie doll in a critique of the stereotyped female roles in American society."

EXAMPLES

Example 29-3

This question uses the copyright and fair use problem, which you can find in Appendix B.

> The court has stated that no negative effect, regardless of the number of similar points in the product, is seen on the value or market for the original when the copy has been significantly transformed from the original, and confusion with the original is therefore not likely.

A. Although the subject "the court" and the verb "has stated" are close together at the start of the sentence, this sentence is too long and the intervening clause is confusing.
B. This is a good solution for the sentence: "When the copy has significantly transformed the original, and confusion with the original is not likely, there is no negative effect of the market."

C. This sentence is too long and one way to fix it is to break it into more than one sentence.

D. This is a good solution for the sentence: "The copy will not affect the original's market negatively if the copy is sufficiently transformative. If the copy is sufficiently transformative confusion with the original is not likely."

Example 29-4

EXAMPLES

This question uses the copyright and fair use problem, which you can find in Appendix B.

> Dash's song identifiably adapts Page's "Red, White, and Blue" through its use of similar lyrics, just as 2 Live Crew identifiably adapted Orbison's "Oh, Pretty Woman" song through its use of the distinctive opening lyrics and thus, just as the U.S. Supreme Court found 2 Live Crew's use to be fair, a court is likely to find Dash's song is fair use.

A. This sentence is too long to understand easily and the author should break it into two sentences.

B. This sentence is long but it is fairly easy to follow because the subject and verb are close together and at the beginning of the sentence. You don't need to break up this sentence.

C. This sentence is long and you could best separate it into two sentences by breaking off the end of it, deleting the word "and" that comes before "thus," and starting the new sentences with "thus."

D. This sentence is long and you could best separate it into two sentences by making the break between the first part that describes Dash's song and the second part that describes 2 Live Crew's parody.

EXPLANATIONS

Explanation 29-1

A is correct. **B** may be correct. The phrase "Depending on the situation" doesn't add substance and you could delete it. If the part about the "ease of conjuring up the original" is important, you could make two sentences: "Courts consider the ease of conjuring up the original. If the parody uses more of the original than necessary to assure identification it is not fair use." **C** is incorrect. You still have a long introductory clause that makes the sentence hard to follow, or "awkward." **D** is correct. The revised sentence is easy to understand. It's okay that the phrase "Depending on the situation" was cut because it does not add substance to the sentence. If the part about the "ease of conjuring up the original" was important, however, you could put that concept in a separate sentence as noted in B.

Explanation 29-2

A is correct. The sentence runs "four lines or more" and would be easier to follow if it were shorter. **B** is incorrect. The subject here is "Mattel," but the verb is "argued." **C** is one possible solution that works well. Breaking this into two sentences, each which begins with the subject and verb, is easier for the reader to follow. **D** is another possible solution that works pretty well. This sentence is short and to the point. Although it omits the defendant's arguments (focusing instead on the court's findings), the court's findings and rulings are generally enough. If the point of your sentence was the particular arguments made, however, this sentence doesn't express that point.

Explanation 29-3

A is correct. Although a subject–verb combination starts the sentence, the sentence does not follow the expected subject–verb–object structure that would make it easy to follow. **B** is incorrect. Although the proposed solution is slightly better, it lacks the subject–verb–object structure with the subject and verb close together at the start of the sentence. **C** is correct. The sentence has two ideas. It would work better as two sentences. **D** is correct. This solution, where the author has reorganized and broken the sentence into two sentences, is much easier to read.

EXPLANATIONS

Explanation 29-4

A is at least partially correct. It follows the guidance that if a sentence is more than four lines, you should break it up. But this sentence, although long, is fairly easy to follow. And thus, **B** is also partially correct. This is a pretty good example of a long sentence that works because the subject and verb of each of the major clauses come at the front of the clause and are close together. The parallel structure the author used to write an analogy between the current case and the precedent also makes this long sentence easier to follow. Despite good structure, however, it is a very long sentence. **C** is correct. This answer preserves the parallel construction and the analogy in the sentence, but makes it easier on the reader by breaking it up. **D** is incorrect. The purpose of the sentence is to make the analogy between the two cases, so breaking up the sentence in the middle of the analogy is a poor choice. You can make analogies in more than one sentence, but you don't have to here. The other options are better choices. (For more on making analogies, see Chapter 11.)

Checklist

Chapter 29: Fixing Awkward Sentence Structure

✔	Use a subject–verb–object sentence structure.
✔	Keep the subject and the verb close together.
✔	Keep sentence length to no more than three to four lines of type.

You will find all of the chapter checklists compiled in Appendix D.

CHAPTER 30

Starting Paragraphs Powerfully

Students often ask, "How do I change my B+ into an A?" Here is one practice that may not explicitly be listed on the grading matrix, but nevertheless contributes subtly and powerfully to making your paper one of the top papers in the class. *Use a well-crafted topic sentence that states a thesis for the paragraph.*

In grade school you learned to write paragraphs with a topic sentence—a sentence that tells the reader the topic discussed in the paragraph. In law school, that topic sentence should become a *thesis sentence*—a sentence that announces the topic of the paragraph *by making an assertion that the paragraph supports or proves.* The assertion should advance the argument made in the memo or brief. In this book we call them "paragraph-thesis sentences."

Terminology notes. Talking about a "thesis" in legal documents can get confusing. It can mean the point or claim you want to make for the entire document; it can mean the point you want to make in a particular section of the document; or, as it's used here, it can mean the point of a paragraph. Some textbooks call these "persuasive topic sentences." Others will just say to put a thesis sentence at the beginning of your paragraph. To distinguish these thesis sentences at the beginning of a paragraph from other ways the term might be used, we call them "paragraph-thesis sentences."

WHAT YOU NEED TO KNOW ABOUT PARAGRAPH-THESIS SENTENCES

A thesis sentence at the beginning of a paragraph makes an assertion that tells the reader how the paragraph will advance your argument. The rest of the paragraph will either explain the legal sources that support the assertion or it will make the arguments about your case that support the assertion (or both). Thus, you'll use paragraph-thesis sentences in the "rule" sections of your document, both where you state the rule and where you explain it (see Chapter 9). You'll also use them in the "application/analysis" sections of your document (see Chapters 10 through 12). Note also that within the CRAC structure, the portions other than the rule and application are already conclusions—which are thesis statements by definition. For a refresher on CRAC, see Chapter 7. Some people would say that the paragraph "proves" the assertion you made in the topic or thesis sentence.

When you include a paragraph-thesis sentence that tells readers the point of a paragraph, you ensure that the paragraph actually has a point. You also ensure that it's not making so many points that it should be broken into separate paragraphs.

A paragraph-thesis sentence comes at the beginning of the paragraph. You may have learned that a "topic sentence" can appear anywhere in the paragraph. In contrast, a paragraph-thesis sentence works best at the start of each paragraph for a couple of reasons. First, it allows readers to see if the paragraph actually proves or supports the assertion you start with. Legal readers are critical thinkers and they expect this organization so that they can evaluate your argument. Second, putting it first makes it easy for readers to skim your argument and get the main points. If you write a list of your document's paragraph-thesis sentences in the order in which they appear in your paper, the list should form an outline of your argument.

To determine whether the paragraph-thesis sentence makes an assertion (a thesis) rather than an announcement (of a topic), ask yourself whether a reader would naturally ask "Why?" or a similar question.[1] A reader might want to see support for the sentence, but she should not be left asking, "and what did the court say about that?"

With practice you'll get better at writing strong paragraph-thesis sentences. But as a beginner, plan on going back over a draft to check paragraphs and add paragraph-thesis sentences as needed.

---

1. Thanks to Professor Michael Higdon for this tip. Michael Higdon, *The Legal Reader, the Legal Writer and the All-Important Thesis Sentence*, NEVADA LAWYER, September 2007. Professor Kirsten Davis also has useful suggestions for using strong thesis sentences to start paragraphs. *Persuasion Through Organization: Another in a Series*, ARIZONA ATTORNEY, September 2005.

HOW TO WRITE PARAGRAPH-THESIS SENTENCES

Using the copyright and fair use problem in Appendix B, we'll walk you through the process of writing a paragraph-thesis sentence.

PROBLEMS

Problem

> Here is a quick overview of the copyright and fair use problem (for details, see Appendix B). Page is suing Dash for violating the Copyright Act when Dash wrote a song based on Page's song (which in copyright terms is called the "original"), "Red, White, and Blue." Dash's song uses the structure and many lyrics of the original but changes the original song's political message. The music of the two songs is not at issue, only the lyrics. Page expects that Dash will argue that his song is a parody that falls under the fair use exception to the Copyright Act. The court will consider the relevant factors set out in the fair use statute, 17 U.S.C. § 107: whether the copy was transformative and targeted the original; whether it took more than necessary of the original; and whether it will interfere with the original's market.

Step 1: Read the paragraph you've written and decide what point you're trying to make. Look at this paragraph from the section of the memo addressing the first factor of the fair use test, "the purpose and character of the work," where courts look at whether the copy "transforms" the original work.

> In *Mattel v. Walking Mountain Productions*, the court concluded that the first factor weighed in favor of fair use because the defendant's use of Mattel's Barbie doll in his artwork was transformative in nature. 353 F.3d 792, 802-03 (9th Cir. 2003). The court reasoned that Mattel established Barbie as "'the ideal American woman.'" *Id.* at 802. Mattel's advertisements showed the dolls "dressed in various outfits, leading glamorous lifestyles, and engaged in exciting activities." *Id.* To sell its product, Mattel used "associations of beauty, wealth, and glamour." *Id.* For purposes of social commentary, the defendant transformed these associations by using Barbie dolls in his photography. In some of his photos, kitchen appliances are about to destroy or harm Barbie dolls. Other photos portray a nude Barbie in sexual poses and contexts. The transformative nature of the work made clear that the defendant's commentary intended to show the harm that he perceived in Barbie's influence on gender roles in society. *Id.*

Here, the author is explaining what the court means by "transformative" by illustrating with facts from a previous case where the copy was transformative of the original.

Step 2: Put the main point in one declarative sentence. So far, the first sentence of the paragraph just tells you what the topic is—it's a topic sentence, but not a paragraph-thesis sentence. So, what is the point this paragraph makes? You want to illustrate what it means to be transformative, so start with that:

> A parody is "transformative" when . . .

Now go back to the paragraph. Which are the key facts used to point out what it means to be transformative? The second, third, and fourth sentences describe how Mattel has characterized the original. The fifth sentence tells the reader what the parody does to transform the original work's message. It is the last sentence, though, that makes the key point about the facts from *Mattel* when it says the parody "intends to show the harm that he perceived in Barbie's influence on gender roles and the position of women in society." Put that point in the paragraph-thesis sentence:

> A parody is "transformative" when it criticizes the original and what it signifies by showing its harmful social influence.

Notice that instead of naming Mattel or Walking Mountain Productions, this paragraph-thesis sentence uses the labels that make it easiest for readers to understand how a precedent will compare to the case—labels like "original," "copy," and "defendant."

What else does it need? A citation to authority:

> A parody is "transformative" when it criticizes the original and what it signifies by showing its harmful social influence. *Mattel, Inc. v. Walking Mountain Prods.*, 353 F.3d 792, 802-03 (9th Cir. 2003).

Notice that the citation tells the reader that your statement comes from the case even though the sentence doesn't start with: "In *Mattel*," or "In *Mattel, Inc. v. Walking Mountain Productions*, 353 F.3d 792, 802-03 (9th Cir. 2003), ..." Adding the citation after the sentence not only made a stronger statement that advances your argument, but also saved words and eliminated the clutter at the beginning of the sentence. Effective paragraph-thesis sentences rarely start with a citation in text.

So putting the paragraph-thesis sentence in place, your paragraph might look something like this:

> A parody is "transformative" when it criticizes the original and what it signifies by showing its harmful social influence. *Mattel v. Walking Mountain Prods.*, 353

> F.3d 792, 802-03 (9th Cir. 2003). For example, the court in *Mattel* concluded that the first factor weighed in favor of fair use because the defendant's use of Mattel's Barbie doll in his artwork was transformative in nature. *Id.* The court reasoned that the plaintiff established Barbie as "the ideal American woman." *Id.* at 802. Mattel's advertisements showed the dolls dressed in various outfits, leading glamorous lifestyles, and engaged in exciting activities. *Id.* To sell its product, Mattel used associations of beauty, wealth, and glamour. *Id.* For purposes of social commentary, the defendant transformed these associations by using Barbie dolls in his photography. In some of his photos, kitchen appliances are about to destroy or harm Barbie dolls. Other photos portray a nude Barbie in sexual poses and contexts. The transformative nature of the work made clear that the defendant's commentary intended to show the harm that he perceived in Barbie's influence on gender roles in society. *Id.*

Your paragraph-thesis sentence works. It tells the reader the point of the paragraph. The rest of the paragraph "proves" or "supports" the assertion made in the first sentence, which allows readers to see if you correctly represented the case.

Remember to use paragraph-thesis sentences in the application portion of your document as well. In that context, you might have a draft paragraph that reads like this:

> In *Mattel*, the defendant's photos were transformative because he used bits and pieces of Barbie and developed completely different associations with his use of the doll. Dash, on the other hand, failed to substantially transform Page's work in order to convey his message. The verse and chorus pattern in Dash's parody is the exact pattern used in Page's song. Dash did not take pieces of Page's lyrical organization, but instead copied the entire format. Additionally, Dash's work is not transformative because a substantial portion of the lyrics in Dash's song, including the majority of the chorus, is identical to Page's lyrics.

Putting the main point in a declarative sentence at the beginning—so starting with a paragraph-thesis sentence—you might revise that paragraph as follows:

> Under the first fair use factor, Dash's song is likely not "transformative" enough for that factor to weigh in his favor. Unlike the defendant's photos in *Mattel*, which were transformative because they used bits and pieces of Barbie to develop completely different associations than the company had created with the doll, Dash failed to substantially transform Page's work in order to convey his message. The verse and chorus pattern in Dash's song is the exact pattern used in Page's song. Dash did not take pieces of Page's lyrical organization, but instead copied the entire format. Additionally, a substantial portion of the lyrics in Dash's song, including the majority of the chorus, is identical to Page's lyrics.

This paragraph is stronger because the reader knows, just by reading the first sentence, what the paragraph will prove.

EXAMPLES

Review the following examples. For each example, there may be more than one correct answer. Explain to yourself why you have chosen that answer or those answers. Then read the explanations in the last section of this chapter to check your work.

EXAMPLES

Example 30-1

This question uses the copyright and fair use problem, which you can find in Appendix B.

> In *Mattel*, the court ruled that it is unlikely that the defendant's work could substitute for products that Mattel markets or licenses. *Mattel v. Walking Mountain Prods.*, 353 F.3d 792, 805 (9th Cir. 2003). The defendant's work portrayed Barbie in nude and sexualized positions, which serves a different market type than the one in which Mattel marketed the doll. *Id.* Furthermore, the court stated it was reasonable to assume that the defendant's work would not affect derivative works by Mattel because Mattel would not want to market products that are socially critical of themselves. *Id.*

The first sentence is . . .

- **A.** a paragraph-thesis sentence because it tells readers what the paragraph is about.
- **B.** a topic sentence, but not a paragraph-thesis sentence, because it doesn't make an assertion that tells the reader the main point this paragraph intends to make.
- **C.** not even a topic sentence.
- **D.** typical of good paragraph-thesis sentences because it starts by telling the reader what case it comes from.

EXAMPLES

Example 30-2

This question uses the copyright and fair use problem, which you can find in Appendix B.

> Here, Dash's lyrics are not entitled to fair use protection because it is likely that his song would serve as a substitute for Page's original. Unlike the defendant's work in *Mattel*, where viewers would have no question the defendant's photos were not produced by Mattel, Dash's work shares many similarities with Page's work that result in confusion by listeners and market harm to the copyright holder. Both songs are social commentaries that deliver similar messages. The market that Dash is catering to is precisely the same as Page's market: rock music fans who want political commentary.

The first sentence is . . .

A. a good paragraph-thesis sentence.
B. a topic sentence but not a paragraph-thesis sentence.
C. not a paragraph-thesis sentence because it's part of the application section, not the rule/rule explanation section.
D. not a good paragraph-thesis sentence because it's conclusory.

EXAMPLES

Example 30-3

This question uses the copyright and fair use problem, which you can find in Appendix B.

> Dash's song has many of the same lines and ideas as Page's song, but puts a positive spin on it. Unlike the songs in *Campbell* and *Fisher*, which were of different genres, here the allegedly infringing song is in the same rock genre as the original and contains the same subject matter. Dash's song could easily replace the original as a sort of anthem because society tends to like happy endings and thoughts of hope, especially in times of trouble. Because of its happy nature it is likely to "substitute the original" at many concerts and events, "fulfilling the same demand."

The first sentence is . . .

A. a good paragraph-thesis sentence because it includes facts.
B. a good paragraph-thesis sentence because it tells the reader where the author is going.
C. not a paragraph-thesis sentence.
D. not even a topic sentence.

EXAMPLES

Example 30-4

This question uses a hypothetical gift in contemplation of marriage problem.

> In *Priebe v. Sinclair*, 90 Cal. App. 2d 79, 84 (1949), the court examined the question of implied conditions in giving gifts. Gifts given after the acceptance of a marriage proposal do not have the same implied conditions as an engagement ring given at the time of acceptance of a proposal. *Id.* at 86. In *Priebe*, the donor gave the donee gifts of money and a gold brooch after the proposal had already been accepted. *Id.* at 81. The donor did not state that these gifts were conditional upon the marriage taking place. Because of this the court rejected the claim for recovery under section 1590 and allowed the donee to retain them. *Id.* at 86.

A. The first sentence is a good paragraph-thesis sentence except it shouldn't start with a case's name.
B. The first sentence is a topic sentence, but not a paragraph-thesis sentence.
C. The first sentence is not even a topic sentence.
D. It would be a good idea to eliminate the first sentence and use the second sentence as a paragraph-thesis sentence.

EXPLANATIONS

EXPLANATIONS

Explanation 30-1

A is incorrect. The sentence might be acceptable as a topic sentence, but it fails our test for a paragraph-thesis sentence because it doesn't make an assertion that the rest of the paragraph proves. **B** is correct. It does not state a thesis. **C** is incorrect. This sentence lets the reader know the paragraph is about the *Mattel* case, so it's a topic sentence. It's just not a paragraph-thesis sentence. **D** is incorrect. Most of the time paragraph-thesis sentences will be stronger if they don't begin with the preposition "in" and a case name.

EXPLANATIONS

Explanation 30-2

A is correct. This is a paragraph-thesis sentence because it makes an assertion about our facts that advances the argument. The rest of the paragraph supports the assertion with comparisons, or analogies, to a precedent case. **B** is incorrect. It's more than a topic sentence because it makes an assertion that advances the argument. **C** is incorrect. Paragraph-thesis sentences should appear at the beginning of all your paragraphs, including those in the application section of your memo or brief. **D** is incorrect. Remember that a paragraph-thesis sentence is often the conclusion you want the reader to draw after reading the paragraph. It's logical that a conclusion is "conclusory."

EXPLANATIONS

Explanation 30-3

A is incorrect. This is a statement of fact, not a paragraph-thesis sentence. The choice of facts announces the topic of the paragraph, but it's not an assertion that moves the argument forward. **B** is incorrect. This is not a paragraph-thesis sentence. It is not an assertion that the paragraph will explain and support. **C** is correct. It is not a topic sentence that acts as a thesis for the paragraph because it's simply a factual statement that doesn't make the reader ask "Why?"; connecting the factual statement to the legal conclusion would help solve this problem. **D** is incorrect. This sentence is not a paragraph-thesis sentence, but it is a topic sentence. The reader can understand the paragraph will be about the lines and ideas of Dash's and Page's songs, but she won't know why that matters.

EXPLANATIONS

Explanation 30-4

A is incorrect. This is not a paragraph-thesis sentence that states a thesis for the paragraph. It is true, however, that it's rarely effective to start a paragraph-thesis sentence with a case's name. **B** is correct. It does announce the topic of the paragraph, but only in the most general way. It does not make an assertion about the point of the paragraph. **C** is incorrect. The first sentence is a topic sentence, but not a paragraph-thesis sentence for the reasons stated in B. **D** is correct. The second sentence here would make a good paragraph-thesis sentence.

Checklist

Chapter 30: Starting Paragraphs Powerfully

✔	Start paragraphs with an assertion that advances your argument.
✔	Always put paragraph-thesis sentences at the beginning of the paragraph.
✔	Keep each paragraph focused only on the point announced in the paragraph-thesis sentence.

You will find all of the chapter checklists compiled in Appendix D.

Writing Concisely to Stay Within the Word Count or Page Limit

Uh-oh! You've been working hard on an assignment and you've finally finished a full draft. But you suddenly realize that you're over the word count—substantially over the word count! What now?

Terminology notes. If your professor calls your writing style "dense," "wordy," or "verbose," the tips in this chapter should help.

WHAT YOU NEED TO KNOW ABOUT WRITING CONCISELY

You can almost always cut down your document. Most law students feel they need every single word of their papers. But you can always find places to cut, and learning to cut with the least impact on the document's quality is an important skill. In fact, in practice you'll often need to make cuts. Sometimes you'll be part of a team of writers working on one document and the team will allot you only a little space because your issue is less important. Other times you'll be in charge of making decisions, but your draft will exceed the court's page limit. You'll learn that you can almost always make your point more economically.

You can prune a lot with stylistic cuts before you turn to substance. It takes going through the document sentence by sentence, line by line, but most students can find the extra words they need for arguments or analysis by deleting useless words. Here are four ways to cut out unnecessary words at the sentence level.

1. Make verbs carry the action; use passive voice rarely and only when you have a good reason for using it; use few nominalizations.
2. Look for clusters of small words; one way to do that is to look for unnecessary uses of the word *of*.
3. Avoid unnecessary "there is" and "it is" constructions.
4. Avoid throat-clearing; use concise introductory clauses; use signals; and use transitions.

Although you may repeat the same point in different sections of one document, avoid repetition within a single section of the document. Many times legal readers will have time to turn to only one section of the paper. Those hurried readers must be able to read a single section and understand what is going on. Therefore, you may need to repeat the same point in two different sections to make each section stand on its own for the reader. But within one section, ordinarily you should not repeat, unless you're repeating a thesis statement as a conclusion. Each sentence should move the reader forward.

Finally, when you must cut substance, you can shorten an argument or eliminate a weak argument. Sometimes shortening a point can make it stronger and more forceful; including weak arguments can make you seem desperate. At first, it's difficult to make good decisions about the relative strength of arguments and to know which arguments deserve the space needed to develop them. But cutting out the weak parts of your document is empowering! See Chapter 22 on Making Persuasive Arguments and Chapter 4 on Choosing Authorities for help on deciding what to cut.

HOW TO EDIT FOR A MORE CONCISE DOCUMENT

Using the copyright and fair use problem in Appendix B, we'll walk you through the process of writing more concisely. Although we suggest a step-by-step process, you can use these tips in any order that works for you.

PROBLEMS

Problem

Here is a quick overview of the copyright and fair use problem (for details, see Appendix B). Page is suing Dash for violating the Copyright Act when Dash wrote a song based on Page's song (which in copyright terms is called the "original"), "Red, White, and Blue." Dash's song uses the structure and many lyrics of the original but changes the original song's political message. The music of the two songs is not at issue, only the lyrics. Page expects that Dash will argue that his song is a parody that falls under the fair use exception to the Copyright Act. The court will consider the relevant factors set out in the fair use statute, 17 U.S.C. § 107: whether the copy was transformative and targeted the original; whether it took more than necessary of the original; and whether it will interfere with the original's market.

Here's a passage of dense text from an office memo.

The first factor also includes an examination by the court of whether there is a commercial aspect in the new work. *Campbell v. Acuff-Rose Music, Inc.*, 510 U.S. 569, 584 (1994). In cases from some circuits, it has been found that the derivative work's commercial purpose weighed against it. Plaintiffs in copyright infringement suits often present the commercial aspect of a derivative as a basis to rule against it. There are recent decisions, however, that have made clear the rule that the commercial character of a work does not automatically preclude a claim to fair use. The appeals court that ruled in the case of *Campbell v. Acuff-Rose* overruled an initial summary judgment that the new song was commercial, thus not able to claim fair use. Upon review the Supreme Court held that the decision was erroneous. The Supreme Court held that the song's commercial aspect is merely one point of consideration. *Campbell v. Acuff-Rose Music, Inc.*, 510 U.S. 569, 584 (1994). In the case of *Fisher v. Dees*, which was decided earlier, the court held likewise that the commercial purpose of the parody did not negate the claim of fair use. *Fisher v. Dees*, 794 F.2d 432, 437 (9th Cir. 1986). A parody may be commercial, but if it proves to be adequately transformative and if it comments on the original work then it will probably win more of the judges on the first factor.

Turning now to our case, it is possible that Billy Dash's song, "Red, White, and Blue Through and Through," will be found to be a parody. The lyrics mirror the original topically, but ironically reflect the opposite images. It is noteworthy that many listeners regard the original song, "Red, White, and Blue," as a cynical appraisal of the nation. Such listeners may therefore regard Dash's reworking as a mocking reflection, contrasting and correcting the original's pessimism and critique of economic inequality with a message praising the values in the United States and expressing hopefulness and pride in American traditions. It may be argued that Dash's derivative is not a parody. There are other interpretations of the original that find the message strangely supportive of the United States. The song is played at political rallies, where audiences chant "red, white, and blue" to the song's tune. In this sense the point of Dash's song is a mere appropriation of Page's vehicle, lacking the transformative quality necessary for parody.

These two paragraphs include 403 words. We'll explain how to reduce them. This isn't just an exercise in cutting words. When you tighten up the writing, you make it more powerful.

Step 1: Look for passive voice. Some students try to eliminate passive voice by looking for *is* or *was*, automatically getting rid of all forms of the verb *to be*, or by eliminating gerunds ("-ing" verbs). It is true that the verb *to be* often represents weak writing (see Step 4) and often you should replace it with an action verb. But looking for forms of *to be* and gerunds doesn't work to find passive voice in your writing because passive voice is not about verb tense or which verb one chooses. Instead, it occurs if the person or thing responsible for the action is either missing from the sentence or has become the object of the sentence.

The most effective method is to look at each sentence in isolation and ask yourself, "What is the action in this sentence and who is doing it?" Although the preceding sentence includes a form of *to be* three times, none of the three uses are in passive voice. Further, passive voice is not always bad. Sometimes you use passive voice because you want a different emphasis in the sentence. But eliminate passive voice wherever it obscures the action, weakens the writing, or adds too many words.

After you've identified the action, if you can't tell who's doing it, or the sentence uses the word *by* to identify the actor, then you have a passive voice problem. You'll solve it if you add an actor for the verb. When you're trying to cut words, you'll usually save words if you use active voice.

Find the passive voice in the previous two-paragraph example. There's one in the second sentence:

> In cases from some circuits, it has been found that the work's commercial purpose is weighed against it.
> *[18 words]*

This sentence includes two actions, "finding" and "weighing." In the phrase "it has been found," do we know who's finding? No. You know *where* it's found—in cases from the federal circuits—but the sentence doesn't tell you *who* found it. That's because the sentence is in passive voice. And who's weighing? Again, you don't know. If "finding" were the crucial action, you would need to supply a subject, such as "the courts within those circuits find." But here, weighing is the more important action, and the subject "circuits" works if we make "to weigh" the active verb. After recasting the sentence to save words, we get this:

> Some circuits weigh a work's commercial purpose against fair use.
> *[10 words]*

Step 2: Look for nominalizations. Nominalizations are words that could have been action verbs, but the writer instead has halted the action by turning the verb into a noun. For example, instead of saying "argue," you might be tempted to say "make an argument." There, "argument" would be a nominalization, the noun you've made out of the active verb "argue." Or instead of saying "the court interpreted" (*three words*) you might be tempted to say "the interpretation of the court was" (*six words, three of which are unnecessary*). Many nominalizations are "-tion" words. To cure nominalizations, find the action in the sentence and incorporate it into the verbs.

For example, find the nominalizations in the two-paragraph example at the beginning of this section. There's one in the first sentence:

> The first factor also includes an examination by the court of whether there is a commercial aspect in the new work.
> [*21 words*]

Looking for the action here, you can see that the court is really *examining*. As the sentence is written, however, "examination" is a nominalization that stores the action in a noun instead of a verb. You also see "includes," which is a verb but not a terribly active or necessary one. Rewrite the sentence so it focuses on action:

> Under the first factor, courts examine whether the new work is commercial.
> [*12 words*]

Notice that you also got rid of the word "of" and other words cluttering the sentence. That's the focus of the next step.

Step 3: Look for small-word clusters, especially those that include the word "of." These small-word clusters can occur in phrases or clauses that have no function other than to take up space. Often you can cut a lot in these situations. Sometimes the whole phrase can disappear without changing the meaning of the sentence. Other times, you can at least trim a few words. Remember that you were able to cut words in Step 2 by changing "of whether there is a"—a classic small-word cluster—to "whether." Here's another opportunity:

> There are other interpretations of the original that find the message supportive of the United States.
> [*16 words*]

Try cutting part of the "of" phrases and changing the nominalizations "interpretations" and "supportive" to the verbs "interpret," and "support" to get this:

> Others interpret the original's message to support the United States.
> [10 words]

We also eliminated the sentence's "there are" construction (the tip in Step 4).

Not every *of* is bad. Often you need to use it. But it's worth the time to check to see if you can save words by identifying small-word clusters.

Step 4: Avoid unnecessary "there is" and "it is" constructions. These often present opportunities to cut and to strengthen the writing at the same time. For instance, "there are many lawyers who believe that concise writing is important" (11 words) can become "many lawyers believe concise writing is important" (7 words, and stronger writing as well). This is from the two-paragraph example at the beginning of this section:

> There are recent decisions, however, that have made clear the rule that the commercial character of a work does not automatically preclude a claim to fair use.
> [27 words]

Changing the "there are" construction (and using some of the other steps) produces this:

> Recent decisions have clarified that a work's commercial character does not preclude claiming fair use.
> [15 words]

Step 5: Avoid throat-clearing, and instead use concise introductory clauses, signals, and transitions. Throat-clearing is an unnecessary introductory clause or phrase at or near the sentence's beginning. Often throat-clearing contains *metadiscourse*—writing that tells the reader how to think about the information in the sentence rather than simply providing that information. Examples of throat-clearing include "It is important to realize that," "Especially noteworthy is the fact that," or even something as simple as "It is clear."

Throat-clearing includes introducing a rule with something like "In the case of X, the court held . . . ." The citation tells the reader which court the rule comes from. Just state the rule, followed by a cite to the case.

Look for throat-clearing phrases or other long introductory clauses, signals, or transitions in the two-paragraph examples at the beginning of this section, where you'll find these sentences:

> It is noteworthy that many listeners regard the original song, "Red, White, and Blue," as a cynical appraisal of the nation.

> In the case of *Fisher v. Dees*, which was decided earlier, the court held likewise that the commercial purpose of the parody did not negate the claim of fair use. *Fisher v. Dees*, 794 F.2d 432, 437 (9th Cir. 1986).

> Turning now to our case, it is possible that Billy Dash's song, "Red, White, and Blue Through and Through," will be found to be a parody.

The first sentence here starts with a throat-clearing phrase. Just delete it and start the sentence "Many listeners regard . . ." (*saving four words*).

The second sentence uses the long, unnecessary introduction to the rule. You can delete the first 16 words and modify the rest of the sentence to frame the holding as a rule, leaving "The commercial purpose of a parody does not negate a fair use claim" (*saving 17 words*).

The third sentence uses a lengthy transition. You can trim it to "Here the court may decide Dash's song, "Red, White, and Blue Through and Through," is a parody" (*saving 9 words*).

Step 6: Check for repetition. The goal is for every sentence to move the reader forward. No marching in place! Look through the two-paragraph example at the beginning of this section. Do you see any repetition?

> The Supreme Court held that the song's commercial aspect is merely one point of consideration. *Campbell v. Acuff-Rose Music, Inc.*, 510 U.S. 569, 584 (1994). In the case of *Fisher v. Dees*, which was decided earlier, the court held likewise that the commercial purpose of the parody did not negate the claim of fair use. *Fisher v. Dees*, 794 F.2d 432, 437 (9th Cir. 1986).

The second sentence not only repeats the point, but repeats it with an older case from a lower court. Once you've cited the highest mandatory authority in your jurisdiction, there's no need to repeat the point with a lower court. You can cut the entire second sentence (*saving 30 words*).

Step 7: When you've cut all you can with style, shorten some arguments or evaluate which of your points are weakest and cut them. Look at the first of the two paragraphs in the example:

> The first factor also includes an examination by the court of whether there is a commercial aspect in the new work. *Campbell v. Acuff-Rose Music, Inc.*, 510 U.S. 569, 584 (1994). In cases from some circuits, it has been found that the derivative work's commercial purpose weighed against it. Plaintiffs in copyright infringement suits often present the commercial aspect of a derivative as a basis to rule against it. There are recent decisions, however, that have made clear the rule that the commercial character of a work does not automatically preclude a claim to fair use. The appeals court that ruled in the case of *Campbell v. Acuff-Rose* overruled an initial summary judgment that the new song was commercial, thus not able to claim fair use. Upon review the Supreme Court held that the decision was erroneous. The Supreme Court held that the song's commercial aspect is merely one point of consideration. *Campbell v. Acuff-Rose Music, Inc.*, 510 U.S. 569, 584 (1994). In the case of *Fisher v. Dees*, which was decided earlier, the court held likewise that the commercial purpose of the parody did not negate the claim of fair use. *Fisher v. Dees*, 794 F.2d 432, 437 (9th Cir. 1986).

> A parody may be commercial, but if it proves to be adequately transformative and if it comments on the original work then it will probably win more of the judges on the first factor.

In addition to all the stylistic problems, this paragraph uses many words to make a simple point: that a parody's commercial nature may weigh against it but won't automatically preclude fair use. And you have the best authority for that statement—the U.S. Supreme Court. For most readers, you need say no more. Other historical cases leading up to that point don't make it more convincing. The reader cares about the state of the law *today*, and unless a historical trend is part of your analysis, the reader cares little how you got to today's rule. Ordinarily you should avoid a one-sentence paragraph. Thus, when you revise the paragraph, although you could cut most of it, you may keep two sentences:

> A parody's commercial nature may weigh against it, but it will not automatically preclude fair use. *Campbell v. Acuff-Rose Music, Inc.*, 510 U.S. 569, 584 (1994). A song's commercial nature is merely one point of consideration. *Id.*

You've saved a whopping 199 words, which opens up a lot of space to develop your strongest arguments.

EXAMPLES

Review the following examples from an office memo's Discussion section. For each example, there may be more than one correct answer. Explain to yourself why you have chosen that answer or those answers. Then read the explanations in the last section of this chapter to check your work.

EXAMPLES

Example 31-1

This question uses the copyright and fair use problem, which you can find in Appendix B.

> On the other hand, one could make the argument that Dash's new work could be mistaken for Page's original, as was found in *Seuss*. Market confusion is not as likely as in *Seuss*, because in *Seuss* the amount of copying was extreme. In the case of *Seuss*, there were indications of seven recognizable features of the original. Further, the fact that the consumers of the work in *Seuss* are children who could easily mistake the gory parody for the original work of Dr. Seuss. This marketing to children foreseeably damages the market of the original. The facts support a conclusion that adult consumers would likely not mistake Dash's

pro-government copy for Page's cynical original. Thus the court is not likely to find Dash's copy interferes with Page's market.

A. The argument comparing children purchasing books to adults purchasing rock music is weak because it assumes that only children purchase children's books; in fact, adults purchase most children's books to give to children, so the comparison doesn't work.
B. This paragraph contains two instances of unnecessary passive voice.
C. The author used a grammatically incorrect "there were" construction in sentence three.
D. The phrase "in *Seuss* the amount of copying was extreme" in the second sentence uses passive voice.

EXAMPLES

Example 31-2

This question uses the copyright and fair use problem, which you can find in Appendix B.

> Here, because of the case-by-case analysis of parody "fair use" cases, Ms. Page might be able to bring a suit for infringement, but it is not likely that she would win. Ms. Page's chances of winning are slight. There is no doubt that the law favors parody as fair use if it meets the four statutory factors, and it appears in this case that Mr. Dash's parody of Ms. Page's original work would likely be found by the court to win if she can prove those factors are in her favor. The four factors are set out below.

A. The author could cut this entire paragraph and add a more effective introductory paragraph.
B. The hedging in the first sentence wastes words.
C. "There is no doubt that the law favors" is not just a throat-clearing phrase because it tells the reader how strong the chances are that Dash will win.
D. The author could cut the second sentence because it's repetitious.

EXAMPLES

Example 31-3

This question uses the copyright and fair use problem, which you can find in Appendix B.

> A parody may be an infringement if it causes a severe economic hardship regarding the work of the original artist. One way to make the determination of whether economic harm exists is the examination of whether the songs are targeting the same listeners. When the original song is of a completely different genre than the new song, it has been found that the new song is unlikely to be

in competition with the original. It is likely to be found that the competition to the original is limited because the group of listeners is different. When both songs are in the same genre the new piece may drown out the original and take its place, which indicates the creation of an economic hardship.

A. Every sentence in this paragraph contains either an unnecessary nominalization or passive voice.
B. The author should change the words "may drown out" in the last sentence because the author used passive voice.
C. The last sentence is a weak argument and the author should cut it.
D. Sometimes editing for a more concise style can show the author the strength of an argument because a dense writing style can hide errors in reasoning.

EXAMPLES

Example 31-4

This question uses the copyright and fair use problem, which you can find in Appendix B.

Review the following passage and decide which alternatives below are good edits. More than one answer may be correct. Note that citations are omitted.

The commercial nature of the work is a consideration when there is an examination of the purpose of the work. The fact that the work is commercial in nature does not mean that it negates consideration for fair use. If it is decided the work was created as more of a commentary than for profit, then an argument can be made for fair use. In order to prove that the song is more of a commentary or criticism, the defendant can try to show the new song does not unfairly interfere with the financial nature of the original. [98 *words*]

A. As a court examines a work, it considers whether the work's purpose is commercial. A work may be fair use and commercial if the defendant created it more for commentary than for profit. To show the work's nature is primarily to provide commentary, the defendant must demonstrate the new song does not unfairly interfere with the original's market. [58 *words*]
B. To prove fair use when there is a work commercial in nature, the courts examine whether the work interferes with the original's market. [23 *words*]
C. Courts consider the commercial nature of the work when there is an examination of the work's purpose. If the court decides the work was created for commentary and not for profit, then fair use is possible. The defendant can try to show the market of the original is not interfered with by the copy. [54 *words*]

D. Courts consider the commercial nature of a copy, although a commercial work can still be fair use. The defendant can demonstrate fair use by showing the new work is commentary that does not unfairly interfere with the original's market. [39 *words*]

EXPLANATIONS

EXPLANATIONS

Explanation 31-1

A is correct. This is a weak argument. Including it will weaken your other arguments. Cut it. ***B*** is also correct. The two instances are both in the first sentence: "could be mistaken" and "was found." **C** is incorrect. The grammar in sentence three is fine, although the style isn't concise or active. A good editor would delete the introductory phrase "In the case of *Seuss*" and make the verb active. Something similar to "the author copied seven recognizable features" would be a good solution. ***D*** is incorrect. That phrase uses the past tense ("the amount of copying was extreme"), but not passive voice. Students often confuse past tense or a verb gerund (-ing) for passive voice. Both of those types of verbs are fine. Remember to ask yourself whether you can identify who is doing the action in the sentence. If you can't tell who did it, or if it uses the word "by" to identify the actor, it's passive voice.

Here is one way to edit the paragraph. The paragraph starts with counterargument and then answers the counterargument with why Dash should ultimately win this factor:

> Conversely, just as the *Seuss* court found that book buyers could confuse the copy with the original book because the two were so similar and in the same genre, listeners could mistake Dash's copy for the original because they are similar and in the same genre. But here, Dash took far less of the original than the defendant in *Seuss*. Thus, consumers are far less likely to mistake the copy for the original and the court will probably not find Dash's copy interferes with Page's market.

Note that although this version adds words to strengthen the analogy, it still uses nearly 50 fewer words than the original.

EXPLANATIONS

Explanation 31-2

A is correct. An introductory paragraph is necessary for a well-organized, coherent document, but this particular introductory paragraph doesn't add much for the amount of words it uses. **B** is correct. A simpler thesis would be stronger: "Page is likely to lose her copyright infringement claim." **C** is incorrect. The phrase "there is no doubt that" adds little to the meaning of the sentence. Further, the sentence itself states the obvious because it essentially says "she will win if she can prove the case"—an obvious point that the author doesn't need to make. **D** is correct. The second sentence can be deleted entirely without a loss.

Here is one way to edit the paragraph:

> Page is unlikely to win a claim for copyright infringement because Dash can likely use the fair use defense. Courts examine the four factors for fair use below.

EXPLANATIONS

Explanation 31-3

A is correct. Here are the examples of the nominalizations or passive voice: "may be an infringement" (nominalization, "to infringe"); "make a determination" (nominalization, "to determine"); "it has been found" (passive voice, "courts have found"); "it is likely to be found" (passive voice, "a court will likely find" or just delete entirely); and "the creation of" (nominalization that the author can simply delete). **B** is incorrect. The phrase is not passive voice because we know who is doing the action: "*the new piece* may drown out." **C** is incorrect. The last sentence nicely sums up the argument that is the point of the paragraph. **D** is correct. Part of the magic of a good writing style is that it can show the author the strength of an argument because a dense writing style can cover up errors in reasoning. It's another reason to learn to write concisely.

Here is one way to edit the paragraph:

> A parody may infringe the copyright if it causes severe economic hardship by targeting the same listeners as the original. If the two songs are in different genres, they appeal to different listeners and are unlikely to compete for the same market.

This is a good edit of the passage, though it should include citations to authority.

Explanation 31-4

A is correct because this edit is a good improvement. It saves lots of words by changing nominalizations into active verbs. For example, "is a consideration" becomes "it considers" and "there is an examination" becomes "as a court examines." Further, it eliminates passive voice: "it is decided"; "was created"; and "an argument can be made." It saves 50 words and is easy to follow. **B** is incorrect. It is an extreme edit that probably doesn't preserve the meaning of the original passage. (Sometimes it's hard to tell the meaning of the original passage when the writing is particularly dense.) This edit eliminates the idea that courts consider whether the defendant created the copy as a commentary. It saves a lot of words, but unless you have decided the information about "more for commentary than for profit" is unimportant, the edit cuts too much. **C** is not correct. It saves words, but fails to minimize nominalizations and passive voice. You could shorten it by changing "when there is an examination of the work's purpose" to "when the court examines the work's purpose." The passage contains an example of passive voice in the third line: "was created." ***D*** is correct (it is an excellent edit) as long as the "created for commentary and not for profit" idea is clear enough. The verbs are active: "by showing" is not passive voice because we know who is doing it—the defendant. Depending on your goals for the passage, you might think carefully about whether you have cut needed emphasis. But you have saved 69 words that you can use to strengthen your argument in other ways.

Checklist:

Chapter 31: Writing Concisely to Stay Within the Word Count or Page Limit

✔	Comb the paper for stylistic cuts before cutting substance.
✔	Avoid repetition within one section of the document.
✔	If you must cut substance, shorten or eliminate weaker arguments.
✔	Minimize passive voice.
✔	Minimize nominalizations.
✔	Where appropriate, eliminate small clusters of words, often those that include "of."
✔	Avoid empty "there is" and "it is" constructions.
✔	Avoid throat-clearing phrases at the start of sentences or paragraphs.

You will find all of the chapter checklists compiled in Appendix D.

Bringing It Together: Transitions and Coherence

Imagine that after reading your memo or brief, the reader puts it down and thinks to himself or herself, "Now, that was good. I get it." As a writer, this is your goal. One of the key aspects of achieving readability is coherence, which you can improve by following the tips in this chapter.

WHAT YOU NEED TO KNOW ABOUT TRANSITIONS AND COHERENCE

Coherence is hard to pinpoint because it comes from both content and writing style. Words, and the ideas they convey, must be consistent, logical, and related to each other throughout the document so that the reader can easily follow the writer's flow of thought between sentences, paragraphs, and sections.

No short list of steps can help you achieve coherence in your writing. In that regard, coherence is more of a guiding principle or characteristic of good writing rather than a concrete section or component. It starts with your clarity of thought about the relevant law and facts and it doesn't end until you've completed the final polishing revisions. But you can do several things to significantly increase your document's coherence at both the large-scale (structural) level and the small-scale (paragraph and sentence) level.

TIPS ON TRANSITIONS AND COHERENCE

Use introductory paragraphs — also known as roadmap or umbrella sections — to give the reader a big-picture view of what you say next. If you have several steps of analysis, an introductory paragraph can make it much easier for your reader to use and understand your document. For help with introductory sections, see Chapter 13.

For a memo's Discussion or a brief's Argument, use the organizational pattern readers are familiar with. This is the pattern explained in Chapter 7 and known variously as IRAC, CRAC, CREAC, CRuPAC, or the "organizational paradigm." Be especially careful to keep the rule statement and explanation separate from the application.

Use signpost words or phrases to keep the reader aware of your analysis's sequence and main points. For instance, sometimes you can enumerate your points as a list up front ("Three exceptions exist for this requirement."). Then you can label each corresponding item in your analysis or argument as "First," "Second," and "Third." This works for various kinds of points—issues, elements, exceptions, questions, reasons, and so on. (Put the number before the noun: i.e., "The first issue," "The second element," "The third exception," "The fourth question," "The fifth reason.") Note that it is "first," "second," and "third," and not "firstly," "secondly," and "thirdly."

In a persuasive document, point headings and subheadings help the reader find a particular section of a document and understand the logical flow of your argument. For help with point headings and subheadings, see Chapter 21.

To begin a paragraph coherently, use a well-crafted paragraph-thesis sentence. See Chapter 30 for more help with this.

Keep each paragraph focused on supporting the paragraph-thesis sentence. Delete or move any extraneous statements. The paragraph should have just one purpose. Consider this paragraph:

> A parody may permissibly copy original works to some extent because the nature of parody necessitates using some distinctive or memorable features of the original work to communicate that it is the subject of parody. *Campbell*, 510 U.S. at 588. For example, in *Campbell* the Supreme Court determined that 2 Live Crew's verbatim use of the first line of Roy Orbison's song "Oh, Pretty Woman" was permissible because it was necessary for the listener to "conjure up" the original. *Id.* Further, courts do not require parodies to take the minimum amount of copyrighted works needed for identification. *See Mattel*, 353 F.3d at 804. In *Mattel*, although the artist arguably could have used a smaller

> portion of the Barbie doll in his photography, the Ninth Circuit concluded that the artist's purpose and artistic medium justified the extent of copying. *Id.* Moreover, the court considered that the artist's photography was transformative because the context in which the artist put the doll illuminated his view of Barbie's influence on societal gender roles. *Id.* at 802.

This paragraph is nicely unified on the point of the permissible amount of copying for a parody until the last line that begins "Moreover, . . ." At that point, the writer has put in an idea that goes to the first statutory fair use factor, the "purpose and character" of the work. This is a related point, but it is extraneous to this paragraph, which is focused on the third statutory fair use factor. It would be better to delete the last sentence or move it elsewhere.

Sequence your sentences in a logical order. A common sequence in legal writing is like a triangle that goes from a broad statement and narrows to specific support. A variation on this is to include a broader, general conclusion again at the end of the paragraph.

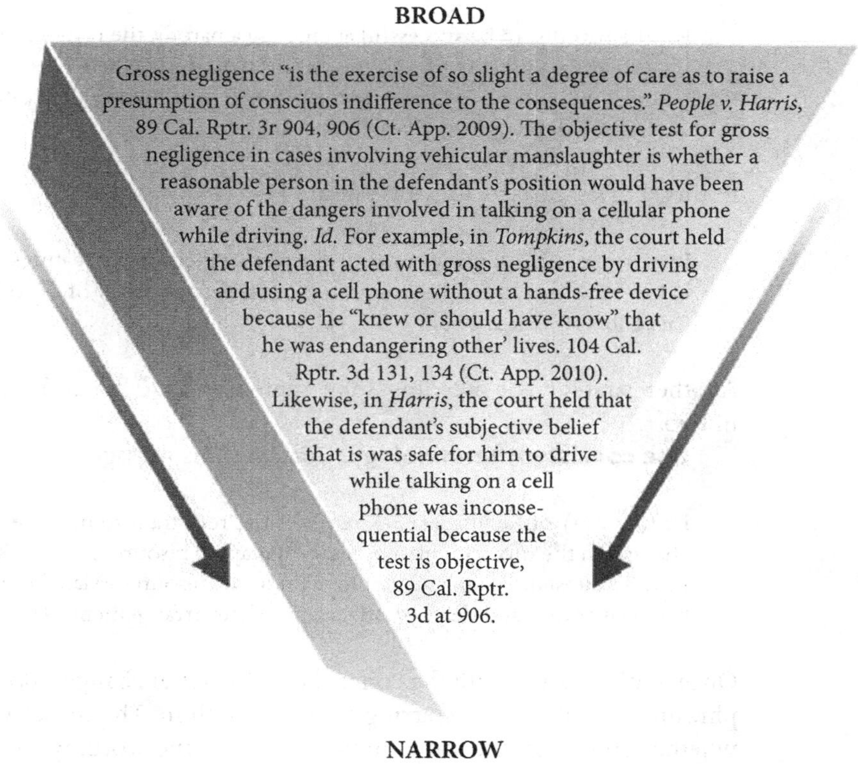

BROAD

Gross negligence "is the exercise of so slight a degree of care as to raise a presumption of consciuos indifference to the consequences." *People v. Harris*, 89 Cal. Rptr. 3r 904, 906 (Ct. App. 2009). The objective test for gross negligence in cases involving vehicular manslaughter is whether a reasonable person in the defendant's position would have been aware of the dangers involved in talking on a cellular phone while driving. *Id.* For example, in *Tompkins*, the court held the defendant acted with gross negligence by driving and using a cell phone without a hands-free device because he "knew or should have know" that he was endangering other' lives. 104 Cal. Rptr. 3d 131, 134 (Ct. App. 2010). Likewise, in *Harris*, the court held that the defendant's subjective belief that is was safe for him to drive while talking on a cell phone was inconsequential because the test is objective, 89 Cal. Rptr. 3d at 906.

NARROW

Avoid long sentences, particularly lots of them in a row. Chapter 31 can help. As a general rule of thumb, a long sentence is 25 or more words or three to four lines of type. For instance, this sentence of 41 words is long and a bit hard to follow:

> The amount of the work used in copying, whether that is large or small, is deemed permissible by the extent of its purpose and character, such as to parody the original work without becoming a market substitute for the original work. *Campbell*, 510 U.S. at 587.

You could edit this to a sentence of 24 words that's much easier to read:

> The extent of permissible copying depends on its purpose and character, such as to parody without becoming a market substitute for the original work. *Campbell*, 510 U.S. at 587.

Here's another illustration of revising long sentences, reducing this long one:

> For the parodist to be successful at creating a parody, the reader must be able to identify the original work and this means that, due to the nature of parody, the parodist will often need to use some distinctive or memorable features that the audience will recognize. *Campbell*, 510 U.S. at 588.

to this shorter, easier-to-read version:

> Parody necessitates using some distinctive or memorable features of the original work so that the audience can recognize it as a parody of the original work. *Campbell*, 510 U.S. at 588.

Another strategy for avoiding long sentences is to break long sentences in two.

Use consistent terminology. Consider this passage:

> Item 303(a) of Regulation S-K requires the registrant to disclose any material changes in the mix and relative cost of its capital resources. 17 C.F.R. § 229.303 (2023). Substantial changes could include any resource-related trends, changes between equity and debt, or off-balance sheet arrangements. *Id.*

Once you've started with the concept of a "material change," don't vary this phrasing later if you're referring to the same thing. The reader won't know whether you mean the same thing if you vary the wording to "substantial change." Moreover, the phrase "material change" could be a legal term of art with a precise meaning (and if so, you should use quotation marks at least the first time you discuss it).

You can fix many sentence-level problems by keeping the subject and verb close together and using active voice. For help with sentence structure, refer to Chapter 29.

Keep paragraphs to a moderate length. As a rough benchmark, a paragraph that is three-quarters of a double-spaced page or less is typically a moderate length.

Use transitional words or phrases to connect your ideas between sentences and from paragraph to paragraph. Transitions signal to the reader how your ideas are connected and where your analysis is headed. Transitions might be as simple as a word like "Nevertheless," or "Furthermore," but you must carefully choose them and where you put them to properly convey your meaning. Here are some useful transitional words.

new or additional info:	*additionally, furthermore, further, in addition, and*
a list of coordinated ideas:	*first, second, third*
when giving examples:	*for instance, for example, such as, to illustrate, specifically*
time relationships:	*before, after, previously, at the same time, later, then, subsequently*
to show similarities:	*likewise, analogously, similarly*
for causation:	*therefore, thus, consequently, accordingly, because*
for contrasts:	*although, but, even though, despite, even if, nevertheless, in contrast*
for emphasis:	*moreover, above all, indeed*
to concede a point:	*although, granted, to be sure*
more or less abstraction:	*more generally, as a general matter, in general, specifically, more specifically, namely, in fact*

You can also use a substantive transition or "dovetailing." To do this, begin a sentence with information you've already introduced to the reader and then add new information. This overlapping or dovetailing of key words or ideas adds coherence and makes it easier for the reader to digest your writing. In this example, we bolded certain words and phrases to illustrate dovetailing. (The bold should not appear in your work.)

> Item 303(a) of Regulation S-K requires the registrant to disclose **any material changes** in the mix and relative cost of its capital resources. 17 C.F.R. § 229.303 (2023). **Material changes** could include any resource-related trends, changes between equity and debt, off-balance sheet arrangements, or **financial condition**. *Id.* Whereas section 303 concerns **material changes** to **financial condition** and the like, the comparable European Transparency Directive refers to principal risks more generally.

Remember, though, that you must have coherence in substance as well as style. No amount of transitions or dovetails will help you achieve coherence if your analysis doesn't make sense. Consider the following passage:

> The suspect killed the victim with a **gun**. **Guns** are often banned in states or are subject to waiting periods and permit requirements to reduce **crime**. Indeed, **crimes** like murder and robbery often involve **weapons**. **Weapons** are **dangerous**. Of course, **danger** comes from many sources; it could come from natural disasters or **extreme weather**. Such **weather** may be responsible for **death**. This kind of **death** is a tragedy.

EXAMPLES

Review the following examples. For each example, there may be more than one correct answer, but try to choose the *best* answer. Explain to yourself why you have chosen that answer. Then read the explanations in the last section of this chapter to check your work.

Example 32-1

This question uses the cell phone manslaughter problem, which you can find in Appendix A.

Choose the best answer about the effectiveness of the transition word bolded in this passage:

> For a call to be made for "emergency purposes" and constitute a valid exception, there must be a risk of "imminent danger" threatening the driver or other individuals. *People v. Tompkins*, 104 Cal. Rptr. 3d 131, 136 (Ct. App. 2010); *People v. Newton*, 104 Cal. Rptr. 3d 138, 141 (Ct. App. 2010). **However**, in *Tompkins*, the court held that the defendant's call was not for "emergency purposes" when he called his family after learning that an earthquake had struck in their vicinity, because any potential danger to the defendant's family had passed by the time the defendant made the call. 104 Cal. Rptr. 3d at 136.

The choice of "However" is . . .

- **A.** effective.
- **B.** not effective and "Similarly," would be a good replacement.
- **C.** not effective and "For example," would be a good replacement.
- **D.** not effective and "Likewise," would be a good replacement.

EXAMPLES

Example 32-2

This question uses the copyright and fair use problem, which you can find in Appendix B.

The four sentences in this paragraph aren't in a logical order. Rearrange them so that they make better sense.

> Like the *Campbell* defendants, who copied some lyrics from Roy Orbison's "Oh, Pretty Woman" to conjure up the original for purposes of parody, Dash accomplished the same with his song's refrain "red, white, and blue through and through," which mirrors Page's phrasing. Although Dash used some of Page's lyrics, he did so to invoke and parody the original. Furthermore, as with the *Campbell* defendants, who transformed Roy Orbison's saccharine lyrics into a commentary on the harsh reality of street life, Dash has entirely reversed the anti-establishment message in Page's original song. Here, Dash targeted the anti-establishment message of Page's original song and transformed it into a social commentary about patriotism.

EXAMPLES

Example 32-3

This question uses the copyright and fair use problem, which you can find in Appendix B.

Identify the inconsistent terminology in this example. Replace with consistent terminology.

> Use of copyrighted material in a parody may fall under the fair use exception to the Copyright Act. *See* 17 U.S.C. § 107. To qualify for allowable use, parodists' work must fulfill the four factors of the permissibility test. *Id.* These factors include: "the purpose and character of the use, including whether such use is of a commercial nature or is for nonprofit educational purposes; the nature of the copyrighted work; the amount and substantiality of the portion used in relation to the copyrighted work as a whole; and the effect of the use upon the potential market for or value of the copyrighted work." *Id.*

EXAMPLES

Example 32-4

This question uses the cell phone manslaughter problem, which you can find in Appendix A.

This paragraph for a draft objective memo is too long and is not unified around the paragraph-thesis sentence. Try to break this paragraph into two paragraphs in a logical way and write a paragraph-thesis sentence for the second paragraph.

> For a call to be made for "emergency purposes" and constitute a valid exception to section 23123 of the California Vehicle Code, there must be "imminent danger" threatening the driver or other individuals. *People v. Tompkins*, 104 Cal. Rptr. 3d 131, 136 (Ct. App. 2010). For example, in *People v. Newton*, the court held that a call was for emergency purposes when the defendant's wife began going into labor during a complicated pregnancy. 104 Cal. Rptr. 3d 138, 141 (Ct. App. 2010). Accordingly, the defendant had no obligation to pull over while driving when calling his wife's obstetrician. *Id.* By contrast, in *People v. Harris*, the court held that the call was not made for emergency purposes where a driver used his phone without a hands-free device to call a wedding party to inform them that he, the best man, would be late. 89 Cal. Rptr. 3d 904, 907 (Ct. App. 2009). Likewise in *People v. Tompkins*, the court held that the defendant's call was not for "emergency purposes" when he called his family after learning that an earthquake had struck in their vicinity, because any potential danger to himself and his family had passed by the time the defendant made the call. 104 Cal. Rptr. 3d at 136. Unlike in *Harris*, here there was real danger: the hazardous conditions of the road posed a threat to travelers. Our client, Ms. King, was calling to warn her friends of future danger, not simply checking in, like the defendant in *Tompkins*, to see how his family fared against a past threat. As in *Newton*, where the expecting father called his wife's obstetrician when his wife went into labor, King's cell phone use concerned a present emergency her friends were facing. King's friends were going to drive into the same perilous conditions that she was encountering, and warning them of the imminent danger constituted a justified emergency purpose.

EXPLANATIONS

Explanation 32-1

A is incorrect. "However" doesn't work well here because the sentence isn't a countervailing point, but rather an explanation or illustration of the rule. **B** is incorrect. Although in a sense there's a similarity between the statement of the rule and an explanation of how a court applied the rule in a precedent case, "Similarly," is not a precise word choice. The rule explanation is more explanatory than similar. **C** is correct. "For example," would be a good replacement because it expresses the relationship between the sentence and the preceding sentence. The rule explanation provides an example of how a court applied the rule. **D** is incorrect for the same reason B is incorrect.

Explanation 32-2

The following sentence order is more logical:

> Here, Dash targeted the anti-establishment message of Page's original song and transformed it into a social commentary about patriotism. Although Dash used some of Page's lyrics, he did so to invoke and parody the original. Like the *Campbell* defendants, who copied some lyrics from Roy Orbison's "Oh, Pretty Woman" to conjure up the original for purposes of parody, Dash accomplished the same with his song's refrain "red, white, and blue through and through," which mirrors Page's phrasing. Furthermore, as with the *Campbell* defendants, who transformed Roy Orbison's saccharine lyrics into a commentary on the harsh reality of street life, Dash has entirely reversed the anti-establishment message in Page's original song.

This revised sequencing puts the broad thesis sentence at the start of the paragraph. That is the point that the other sentences in the paragraph go toward proving or supporting. Following the paragraph-thesis sentence are points of support, including analogical reasoning to precedent cases. The paragraph also includes a logical transition ("Furthermore"), which leads into a sentence making an additional point on the same topic.

EXPLANATIONS

Explanation 32-3

The words in bold are unnecessary variations on the phrase "fair use." It would be better to keep "fair use" in those spots to avoid confusion about whether the writer is referring to the same thing or something different.

> Use of copyrighted material in a parody may fall under the fair use exception to the Copyright Act. *See* 17 U.S.C. § 107. To qualify for **allowable use**, parodists' work must fulfill the four factors of the **permissibility** test. *Id.* These factors include: "the purpose and character of the use, including whether such use is of a commercial nature or is for nonprofit educational purposes; the nature of the copyrighted work; the amount and substantiality of the portion used in relation to the copyrighted work as a whole; and the effect of the use upon the potential market for or value of the copyrighted work." *Id.*

EXPLANATIONS

Explanation 32-4

The example paragraph contains both rule statement and explanation about the applicable legal rules as well as rule application about how those rules will likely apply in a particular case at hand. A logical place to break this excessively long paragraph is where the switch to rule application occurs. In this example, that is at the sentence beginning "Unlike in *Harris*, here there was real danger present . . . ." The word "here" is a tip that the writer is talking about the instant case, namely Allison King's case in this example.

Once you break the paragraph in two, remember to review the new paragraphs to check that they each have well-crafted paragraph-thesis sentences and that the sentences in each paragraph are unified on the topic contained in the paragraph-thesis sentence and ordered in a logical sequence.

With this example, the paragraph-thesis sentence in the second paragraph can be revised in several ways. A simple solution would be to delete the lead-in "Unlike in *Harris*," because the paragraph does not go toward proving that narrow point of distinguishing King's case from *Harris*. Another improvement would be to more precisely echo the rule's language in the sentence so that the application paragraph is clearly applying the rule established. We could change "real danger" to "imminent danger" and include the idea of this constituting an "emergency purpose." Here's what it might look like once we break the paragraph in two where the application begins and we revise the paragraph-thesis sentence for that paragraph:

> For a call to be for "emergency purposes" and constitute a valid exception to section 23123 of the California Vehicle Code, there must be "imminent danger" threatening the driver or other individuals. *People v. Tompkins*, 104 Cal. Rptr. 3d 131, 136 (Ct. App. 2010). For example, in *People v. Newton*, the court held

that a call was for emergency purposes when the defendant's wife began going into labor during a complicated pregnancy. 104 Cal. Rptr. 3d 138, 141 (Ct. App. 2010). Accordingly, the defendant had no obligation to pull over while driving when calling the hospital. *Id.* By contrast, in *People v. Harris*, the court held that the call was not made for emergency purposes where a driver used his phone without a hands-free device to call a wedding party to inform them that he, the best man, would be late. 89 Cal. Rptr. 3d 904, 907 (Ct. App. 2009). Likewise in *People v. Tompkins*, the court held that the defendant's call was not for emergency purposes when he called his family after learning that an earthquake had struck in their vicinity, because any potential danger to himself and his family had passed by the time the defendant made the call. 104 Cal. Rptr. 3d at 136.

Here, there was imminent danger constituting an emergency purpose: the hazardous conditions of the road posed a threat to travelers. Our client, Ms. King, was calling to warn her friends of future danger, not simply checking in, like the defendant in *Tompkins*, to see how his family fared against a past threat. As in *Newton*, where the expecting father called his wife's obstetrician when his wife went into labor, King's cell phone use concerned a present emergency her friends were facing. King's friends were going to drive into the same perilous conditions that she was encountering, and warning them of the imminent danger constituted a justified emergency purpose.

Checklist:

Chapter 32: Bringing It Together: Transitions and Coherence

✔	Use introductory paragraphs (umbrella sections and roadmaps) to give the big-picture view of what comes next.
✔	In a Discussion or Argument section, use the organizational pattern readers are familiar with (e.g., CRAC).
✔	Use signpost words or phrases to tell the reader the sequence of analysis and main points.
✔	Use headings and subheadings.
✔	Use paragraph-thesis sentences at the start of paragraphs and keep each paragraph a moderate length, focused on supporting its paragraph-thesis sentence.
✔	Use a logical order, usually moving from broad to narrow.
✔	Avoid long sentences, especially several long sentences in a row.
✔	Use consistent terminology.
✔	For sentences, keep the subject and the verb close together and use active voice.
✔	Use transitions to connect ideas between sentences and paragraphs.

You will find all of the chapter checklists compiled in Appendix D.

The Writer's Life: Where to Go From Here

The old cliché that "in every ending is a new beginning" is especially true for students finishing the basic courses in Legal Writing. Completing your basic legal writing training is an important milestone, but it is just the beginning of your life as a legal writer. There is still much to do to become that valuable commodity—the lawyer to whom others turn when they need an important document or for help in making their own writing better. To that end, we'll use this chapter to describe habits you can develop to continue the quest to become a great legal writer.

WHAT YOU NEED TO KNOW ABOUT BECOMING A GREAT LEGAL WRITER

"How do you get to Carnegie Hall? Practice, practice, practice!" This old joke makes a great point: with any task, you'll get better with practice. Take advantage of every chance you have to write in law school—especially those opportunities that include feedback. Whether it's an advanced legal writing class, a seminar paper, a student competition, working for a professor as a research or teaching assistant, or an experiential learning course like an externship or clinic: write, write, write!

You can also create your own opportunities to write and get feedback by creating a "writers' group." Choose a group of peers who, like you, are determined to become excellent writers. When the group meets, members can share drafts and respond to each other's writing. Make the experience more than simple line editing by attempting to articulate your reactions evoked by the logic, emotion, tone, and style of your partners' works. As you gain practice responding to another's work, you will not only develop a richer vocabulary with which to talk about writing, but your own writing will improve.

Pay attention and find heroes. As a law student and as a lawyer, you read constantly. As you read, be on the lookout for what makes a document effective. Collect examples of good writing and keep your own list of legal writing heroes. To get you started, here is a list of legal writers that many readers find admirable. On the current U.S. Supreme Court, many have praised the writing skill of Chief Justice John Roberts, Justice Elena Kagan, and Justice Sonia Sotomayor. Former Justice Antonin Scalia is regarded as an excellent writer but is sometimes criticized for a disrespectful tone. Historical figures and other current judges, scholars, and attorneys who many find praiseworthy include Louis Brandeis, Benjamin Cardozo, Paul Clement, Walter Dellinger, Andrew Frey, Ruth Bader Ginsburg, Learned Hand, Oliver Wendell Holmes, Robert Jackson, Karen Nelson Moore, Theodore Olsen, Richard Posner, and Kathleen Sullivan.

You've probably noticed that many of the people on this list are influential legal giants who rose to the top of their field, whether as a judge, an attorney, or in the legal academy. Are they great writers because they are great thinkers, or are they great thinkers because they are great writers? We've tried to show you that the two—good thinking and good writing—are inextricably intertwined. Paying attention and collecting your own examples of writing that makes a difference in the world is an important step to developing excellence in your own writing.

Break the rules. Innovative dancer Twyla Tharp tells dance students who are eager to break with tradition, "Before you can think outside the box, you have to have a box." Just as some dancers chafe at the restriction and discipline of "learning the box" first, many students feel that a first-year writing class has put them in a box that requires strict adherence to organizational paradigms, traditional forms of argument, and a sparse writing style. But, like the dancers, once you have internalized the basic box you can begin to move outside it. As you gain experience in the law and in legal writing, you will have the knowledge you need to decide when and how to break the rules.

As you move on, perhaps your document doesn't need to follow CRAC, or to put "all the explanation before the application." Maybe you find starting with persuasive authority rather than binding authority makes for a brilliant introduction to an issue in your particular case. Whatever the decision, though, it is important at first that you make a conscious choice, with articulable reasons for thinking outside our box of fundamentals. Later, with years of experience, you will develop an expertise that feels like intuition about when to be more experimental. The old adage that "rules are made to be broken" is true sometimes for experienced writers.

Read legal writing scholarship. Every first-year legal writing class makes time for the basics. There is a lot more, however, to legal writing than anyone can address in beginning classes. Professional journals dedicated to legal writing include: *Legal Writing: The Journal of the Legal Writing Institute; Legal Communication and Rhetoric: JALWD; The Scribes Journal of Legal Writing;* and *The Journal of Appellate Practice and Process.*

Several current areas of study in legal writing are providing practical insight for making arguments and writing more effectively. Three of the most interesting areas are classic and modern rhetoric theory, narrative theory, and cognitive science.

The traditional definition of classic rhetoric is the science of persuasion, surely a worthy topic for any lawyer. Concepts of classic rhetoric such as repetition, parallelism, alliteration, comparison, and classic figures of speech like metaphor, simile, analogy, and euphemism will give you tools to become a better writer. Further, the modern view on rhetoric is very broad and includes the use of symbols, whether words or other symbols, to effect a change. Sometimes the change the speaker seeks is as simple as adding to the listeners' information; other times the speaker is overtly looking to persuade. But how such change happens is rarely simple and always important for lawyers to understand. Deepening your understanding of how law and language work can make your communication more powerful.

Narrative theory has captured the imagination of many legal writing experts. Narrative theorists maintain that human beings understand all communication in the form of stories. Some scholars have identified the ways in which archetypal characters and plots weave through our understanding of law. As you become more sophisticated in your understanding of law and legal writing, consider becoming more aware of using stories to make meaningful arguments that will persuade the reader.

Advances in cognitive science have also piqued the interest of those interested in legal writing. Some scholars have explored biases in decision making such as framing, priming, anchoring, optimism biases, and more. Others look at how memory works, or the interplay between the conscious and unconscious minds. The area is exploding with research and new developments. Regardless of the specific research area, advances in cognitive science are providing fertile ground for those interested in legal writing.

These topics are rich and complicated, making it difficult for a simple summary here. But they are well worth your time. Conferences devoted to each of these areas often welcome advanced students or practitioners. As for books and articles, any list we provided of interesting articles or authors would perforce be incomplete. Following up on articles in the legal writing journals or even a simple Internet search, though, will uncover a wealth of material that will help you take your writing to a more sophisticated level.

Read practitioners' blogs, bar journal articles, and books. It doesn't take long in practice to realize that writing is at the heart of a lawyer's work. Thus, in addition to scholarly journals and publications, many practitioners publish blogs, bar journal articles, and books aimed at practicing attorneys. Bar associations usually offer members the chance to exchange ideas within certain practice areas and some of those sections or areas are explicitly tied to writing, such as appellate work or contract drafting. Some practitioners have built a reputation as writing specialists and maintain blogs and work as writing consultants to other attorneys. Also, bar associations and consulting companies offer continuing education classes in writing. If you are on the lookout, you will find plenty of ways to expand your skills, even after leaving your formal training in law school.

Resolve to stay current on changes in technology that may impact your writing. Changes in technology lawyers can use to generate content or improve a document are a reality in today's world. Programs or applications that use artificial intelligence may create documents that jumpstart the writing process or change the way you work. Revising and editing may become even more important. Understanding how new technology works in general will help you spot the pitfalls and ethical risks involved in using it. And ethical obligations can, at some point, mean you must use new technology in order to best serve your client. The changes come quickly now, and it's your job to stay on top of these changes that can improve your writing.

It all boils down to continuing to care about writing. It might sound melodramatic, but caring about continuing to improve as a legal writer is another way to care about your clients and to care about justice. Further, in your own self-interest, lawyers who take pride in their work are happier in their professional lives than those who simply put in the hours and collect a paycheck. Continuing the pursuit of excellence in writing will advance your career and enhance your enjoyment of being a lawyer. We wish you good luck!

Checklist

Chapter 33: The Writer's Life: Where to Go From Here

✔	Take every opportunity to practice writing in law school, especially those where you will get feedback.
✔	Keep a personal list of legal writers you find effective and inspiring.
✔	As you read for other purposes, when you find an effective document, analyze what makes it good.
✔	As you gain experience and nuance, know that you can sometimes innovate by ignoring some of the fundamentals you have learned.
✔	Read articles and books about writing by legal writing scholars and practitioners.
✔	Stay aware of the trends in legal writing theory like rhetoric theory, narrative theory, and cognitive science advances.
✔	Be aware of continued technological changes that can improve your writing.
✔	Continue to think about and care about your writing.

You will find all of the chapter checklists compiled in Appendix D.

APPENDIX A

The "Cell Phone Manslaughter" Problem

Allison King has been charged with vehicular manslaughter in California. The facts that form the basis of the allegation are below.

King was driving from Jenner to Gualala on State Highway 1. This road is well known for being a winding two-lane highway on the edge of a cliff with the sea below. The highway offers very few places to pull over. King planned to meet several friends from San Francisco for a weekend vacation on the coast near Gualala. The night King was driving, the fog was rolling in from the ocean and driving conditions were even more hazardous than usual. King was terrified and kept her bearings in near-whiteout conditions by hugging the road on the side of the cliff. She also became concerned that the fog presented such dangerous driving conditions that she should warn her friends and suggest that they refrain from driving until road conditions improved. King pulled out her cell phone and, while driving slowly along the cliff, she dialed one of her friends, June Coughlin, to give the warning. Her phone was not designed and configured to allow hands-free listening and talking. Suddenly a bicyclist appeared from out of the fog. King's car struck the cyclist, and he slipped across the road and over the cliff. The fall killed him. King has been charged with vehicular manslaughter. The following California authorities may apply to this problem. (Note: the cases are fictional and internal citations to other cases are omitted.)

Cal. Penal Code § 192. Manslaughter; voluntary, involuntary, and vehicular

Manslaughter is the unlawful killing of a human being without malice. It is of three kinds:

(a) Voluntary—upon a sudden quarrel or heat of passion.

(b) Involuntary—in the commission of an unlawful act, not amounting to felony; or in the commission of a lawful act which might produce death, in an unlawful manner, or without due caution and circumspection. This subdivision shall not apply to acts committed in the driving of a vehicle.

(c) Vehicular —

(1) Except as provided in subdivision (a) of Section 191.5, driving a vehicle in the commission of an unlawful act, not amounting to felony, and with gross negligence; or driving a vehicle in the commission of a lawful act which might produce death, in an unlawful manner, and with gross negligence . . . .

Cal. Penal Code § 191.5. Gross vehicular manslaughter while intoxicated

(a) Gross vehicular manslaughter while intoxicated is the unlawful killing of a human being without malice aforethought, in the driving of a vehicle, where the driving was in violation of Section 23140, 23152, or 23153 of the Vehicle Code, and the killing was either the proximate result of the commission of an unlawful act, not amounting to a felony, and with gross negligence, or the proximate result of the commission of a lawful act that might produce death, in an unlawful manner, and with gross negligence . . . .

Cal. Vehicle Code § 23123. Driving motor vehicle while using wireless telephone; penalty; exceptions

(a) A person shall not drive a motor vehicle while using a wireless telephone unless that telephone is specifically designed and configured to allow hands-free listening and talking, and is used in that manner while driving.

(b) A violation of this section is an infraction punishable by a base fine of twenty dollars ($20) for a first offense and fifty dollars ($50) for each subsequent offense.

(c) This section does not apply to a person using a wireless telephone for emergency purposes, including, but not limited to, an emergency call to a law enforcement agency, health care provider, fire department, or other emergency services agency or entity.

People v. Harris, 89 Cal. Rptr. 3d 904 (Ct. App. 2009)

The Defendant, Mark Harris, challenges his conviction for vehicular manslaughter in violation of Cal. Penal Code § 192(c) (West 2008). A jury convicted him of the sole count in the indictment. Harris contends that his conviction should be reversed because his actions met the "emergency purposes" exception to California's prohibition on driving a motor vehicle while using a wireless telephone and because he did not act with "gross negligence" as required by California's vehicular manslaughter statute. For the following reasons, we affirm.

The facts of the incident are as follows. Harris was driving his car at approximately the speed limit, which was 45 miles per hour. Harris was on his way to his best friend's wedding and Harris was the best man. Harris ran into delays earlier that day when picking up his tuxedo, so he ended up leaving for the wedding almost 45 minutes later than he had planned.

It was the middle of the day and the driving conditions were normal. In front of Harris' vehicle was a car being driven by Bernard Colter. Colter was preparing to turn right at an intersection and his turn signal was on. A pedestrian was crossing in the crosswalk, however, and Colter therefore had to stop before he could turn. Harris's vehicle struck the back of Colter's car. Colter was taken by ambulance from the scene of the accident and pronounced dead at the hospital approximately one hour later. The cause of death was severe head trauma resulting from the collision. Skid marks at the scene revealed that Harris did not apply his brakes until his vehicle was only three feet from Colter's car.

At the time of the accident, Harris was talking on his cell phone. Harris had decided that he should call another friend in the wedding party to inform him that he would be late. Harris admitted that although he was from Nevada, he was aware it was a violation of California law to use a wireless telephone while driving. Harris' wireless telephone was not configured for "hands-free" listening and talking.

First, we hold that calling to inform a wedding party that the best man would be late does not meet the "emergency purposes" exception within Cal. Vehicle Code § 23123(c) (West Supp. 2008). The statute includes examples of the types of calls that the legislature considered as emergencies, including calls to law enforcement agencies, health care providers, fire departments, and other emergency services providers. Even though the bride and groom might think of their wedding as the most significant moment in their lives, being late for that event, even for the best man, is not a true "emergency" as contemplated by the statute. Furthermore, Harris' contention that pulling over to call would make him even later does not elevate the nature of the call to emergency status. If it did, every call made to inform someone that the caller was late would qualify as an "emergency," and that is clearly beyond the scope of the statute's exception.

Second, as for whether Harris acted with "gross negligence" under Cal. Penal Code § 192(c)(1) (West 2008), a reasonable person in Harris' position would have realized the risk involved in making the phone call while driving. "Gross negligence" is the exercise of so slight a degree of care as to raise a presumption of conscious indifference to the consequences. The test is objective: whether a reasonable person in the defendant's position would have been aware of the risk involved. If a *reasonable person* in the defendant's position would have been aware of the risk involved, then the defendant is presumed to have had such an awareness. The defendant's *lack* of such awareness does not preclude a finding of gross negligence if a reasonable person would have been so aware. The fact that Harris was from Nevada and that the state of Nevada allows drivers to use cell phones while driving does not mitigate the risk. Harris' subjective belief in the safety of his act does not mitigate the fact that he should have known the danger involved.

For the foregoing reasons, we affirm Harris' vehicular manslaughter conviction.

People v. Tompkins, 104 Cal. Rptr. 3d 131 (Ct. App. 2010)

In the case before us today, Samuel Tompkins was convicted of vehicular manslaughter for causing the death of Jordan Smith while driving and simultaneously talking on his cell phone. To be guilty of vehicular manslaughter the state must show the defendant was "driving a vehicle in the commission of an unlawful act, not amounting to felony, and with gross negligence." Cal. Penal Code § 192(c)(1) (West 2008). In this case, the unlawful act was the violation of Cal. Vehicle Code § 23123(a) (West Supp. 2008), driving "a motor vehicle while using a wireless telephone" that is not "configured to allow hands-free listening and talking."

It is undisputed that Tompkins was driving and simultaneously using his cell phone without a hands-free device when he struck and killed Smith. Tompkins contends, however, that he did not act with "gross negligence" as required by the vehicular manslaughter statute, Cal. Penal Code § 192(c), and that the exception in the vehicle code that permits using a cell phone in case of an emergency under Cal. Vehicle Code § 23123(c) applies.

Tompkins was driving from his home in San Francisco to Los Angeles for a conference when he learned from a radio newscast that an earthquake measuring 6.9 on the Richter scale had struck the Bay Area. At the time he heard the broadcast, Tompkins was driving south on Interstate 5 just past exit 263 near Buttonwillow. Concerned about his family, he called home to reassure himself that his wife and children were safe. As Tompkins was dialing, he failed to notice a piece of tire in the road. When he looked up, he swerved to avoid the obstacle and his vehicle struck the side of a motorcycle being driven by Mr. Smith. Smith was thrown from the motorcycle and died immediately.

Tompkins' first claim, that he did not act with "gross negligence," is without merit. Cal. Penal Code § 192(c). "Gross negligence" is determined using an objective test; if a reasonable person in the defendant's position would have been aware of the risk involved in his behavior, then the defendant is considered to have acted with gross negligence. Under the circumstances presented in this case, driving on a freeway at high speeds where debris is occasionally left and other drivers are often present, Tompkins either knew or should have known that using his cell phone while driving was endangering the lives of others.

We also hold that under these facts, Tompkins does not meet the "emergency purposes" exception. Cal. Vehicle Code § 23123(a). "Emergency" implies imminent danger. It implies the need to react quickly to avoid harm, such as when there is a fire or when being attacked at a stop light by a potential carjacker. Those are emergencies, and calls made to prevent that imminent danger are calls made for "emergency purposes." But the earthquake in this case had already happened in northern California, and any danger to Tompkins' family had passed before the time of Tompkins' phone call. It is understandable that a husband and father would want to reassure himself that his family was safe. But the law requires that to do so, he not endanger the lives of others. He could have waited until it was safe to pull over or exit the freeway and make his call then. The situation was no longer an emergency and his call was not for "emergency purposes" as required by the statute's exception.

Therefore, we affirm the trial court's decision finding the defendant guilty of vehicular manslaughter.

People v. Newton, 104 Cal. Rptr. 3d 138 (Ct. App. 2010)

Roger Newton was driving to the mall just outside of San Bernardino, California on a typical Saturday afternoon. The road was in a predominantly commercial area, and the speed limit was 40 mph. Newton was driving within the speed limit and the road was slightly wet from an earlier rain but otherwise, conditions were normal. Newton was accompanied by his wife, Annette, who was seven months pregnant. Annette Newton had experienced several problems in the pregnancy, but had been free of problems for the previous three weeks. Suddenly, Mrs. Newton moaned in pain and announced she could "feel the baby coming."

Mr. Newton immediately altered his course to head to St. Thomas Hospital in San Bernardino, which was approximately 15 minutes away and where the couple had been taking birthing classes. He also used his wireless telephone to call Mrs. Newton's obstetrician, hoping the doctor would meet the couple at the hospital. While on the phone, Newton did not see Julie

Wolfe, who was jogging on the side of the road. The Newtons' car struck Ms. Wolfe and she died from injuries suffered in the accident. The Newtons' baby was born at the site of the accident.

Roger Newton was charged with vehicular manslaughter under Cal. Penal Code § 192(c) and convicted. At trial, Newton made two claims; first, he argued that calling his wife's doctor was a call made for "emergency purposes," and hence, he was entitled to the exception in the statute that generally prohibits making wireless telephone calls while driving. Second, Newton argued that under the circumstances, it was impossible for him to be aware of any risks inherent in his actions because of the urgency of his wife's medical condition. The trial court rejected both arguments. On Newton's first claim, the court stated that he could have pulled over to make the call and although the statute contemplates calls for emergency medical help, Newton was not calling doctors to the scene of an emergency. The trial court also noted that there would be doctors at the hospital when the couple arrived. On his second claim, the court relied on People v. Harris to conclude that "a reasonable person in [his] position would have realized the risk involved in making the phone call while driving." *People v. Harris*, 89 Cal. Rptr. 3d 904, 908 (Ct. App. 2009). Newton appeals his conviction.

We hold that Newton's call meets the statute's "emergency purposes" exception. Cal. Vehicle Code § 23123(c) (West Supp. 2008). The trial court concluded that Newton could have pulled over to call the doctor, but that reasoning fails to acknowledge the severity of the situation: Newton's wife was in labor and it was two months before her due date. She had already experienced difficulties in the pregnancy, and Newton was no doubt aware of the dangers to his wife and child of any delivery, much less an early one. Furthermore, even though the call was not made to the scene of the emergency, the call was made *in* an emergency and to *address* that emergency—his wife and child were far more likely to survive if Newton drove to the hospital and met his wife's obstetrician there than if he waited where he was for an ambulance and an EMT to deliver the baby roadside. This life-and-death situation is the epitome of an emergency. And even though there would be doctors at the hospital when the couple arrived, Newton's wife's obstetrician was familiar with her medical history and would be best equipped to deliver the baby safely. A genuine emergency existed and a reasonable person in Newton's shoes would have wanted the physician most familiar with his wife's pregnancy to meet the couple at the hospital. Under all these circumstances, the wireless telephone call in this case qualifies as a call for "emergency purposes."

In addition, "gross negligence" depends on the nature of the circumstances and was not present here. This court has defined "gross negligence" as "the exercise of so slight a degree of care as to raise a presumption of conscious indifference to the consequences." *People v. Harris*, 89 Cal. Rptr. 3d 904, 906 (Ct. App. 2009). It is an objective test, but the test is not whether any person would be aware of the risks of making a cell phone call while driving under any circumstances—the test is whether "a reasonable person *in the defendant's position* would have been aware of the risk involved." *Id.* (emphasis added). A reasonable person in the Defendant's position would not likely have been aware of the risks of making such a call because of the emergency he was trying to address. The cell phone call, even though made while driving, was in this case the lesser of two evils and this court could not have expected Mr. Newton to appreciate the risks inherent in making that call.

This case also differs substantially from the other case on this issue that we decide today, *People v. Tompkins*. There, we held that "[u]nder the circumstances presented in this case, driving on a freeway at high speeds where debris is occasionally left and other drivers are often present, Tompkins either knew or should have known that using his cell phone while driving was endangering the lives of others." *People v. Tompkins*, 104 Cal. Rptr. 3d 131, 134 (Ct. App. 2010). Tompkins was not facing an emergency, and he was driving on a freeway at high speeds with other vehicles, including a motorcycle, nearby. Newton was making the best decision he could under difficult and obviously emotional circumstances. He had to act quickly and this court finds that in doing so, he did not act with gross negligence.

We therefore reverse Newton's vehicular manslaughter conviction.

APPENDIX B

The "Copyright and Fair Use" Problem

Note: To help you keep the parties straight, we have named the Plaintiff "Page" because both words start with the letter P. Similarly, we have named the Defendant "Dash" because both words start with the letter D.

Jenna Page is a rock musician who is most famous for a song she wrote and recorded, "Red, White, and Blue." Page holds the copyright to the song's lyrics. The song's refrain repeats the colors of the flag, "Red, White, and Blue," and then makes the song's true point: "Red, White, and Through with Blue." The song is critical of the United States and has become an anthem among those in the anti-establishment movement.

Within a few years of the song becoming popular, the song's refrain also became a popular chant at patriotic rallies, where audience members would dance and sing, "Red, White, and Blue; Red, White, and Blue" to the song's tune.

The lyrics of Page's song complain of economic inequality and politicians' failure to remedy the country's problems. The song received extensive radio play when it was first released and still enjoys a fair amount of notoriety.

Page just discovered that Billy Dash, a relatively unknown young singer, has produced and is successfully marketing a rock song entitled "Red, White, and Blue Through and Through." Dash's patriotic song celebrates America's freedom and traditions.

The music appears to be identical to the original, but the words are different. Following is a comparison of the lyrics of the two songs. Dash's song champions pride in America without the critical element Page's song emphasizes. Dash's song parallels the lyrics and structure of Page's song.

Page wants to know how to stop Dash from using her lyrics. (The copyright on the musical composition, as opposed to the lyrics, is held jointly with members of Page's band; we will concentrate only on the lyrics, not on the music.) Dash is likely to claim his use of Page's song is protected as "fair use."

Assume that a legal challenge would be filed in the Northern District of California.

"Red, White, and Blue" **by Jenna Page**	**"Red, White, and Blue Through and Through"** **by Billy Dash**
The bankers fought for their mountains of cash	The heroes fought for our land of the free
And the elites added to their stash	And they gave a lot, so we can be
They got their fancy gems and their private jets	They paved the way for us free, proud, and brave
There's no work to be had and no safety nets	This country great, the traditions we save
Red, white, and blue	Red, white, and blue
Red, white, and blue	Red, white, and blue
Red, white, and through with being blue	Red, white, and blue through and through
We got houses abandoned, lives torn apart	We got flags a-wavin', America the best
And we got mamas on food stamps, babies in the cart	And we got proud mamas cheering, babies held to chest
Factories closed and laughs turn to sobs	Fireworks, apple pie, stripes and stars,
There's hungry mouths, but no jobs, no jobs	There's love of country, rock n' roll, fast cars
Red, white, and blue	Red, white, and blue
Red, white, and blue	Red, white, and blue
Red, white, and through with being blue	Red, white, and blue through and through
We were told there was hope, to vote, just vote	We were raised with hope and with pride
And the prospect for change, it grows more remote	And from what's right, we never, we never hide
They're lining their pockets, a capital of gold	They're shining, the colors of our crew
And they're fighting like children, while our future is sold	And they're fighting, showing what we know is true
Red, white, and blue	Red, white, and blue
Red, white, and blue	Red, white, and blue
Red, white, and through with being blue	Red, white, and blue through and through

The following statutes and cases may apply to this problem. Cases have been altered for convenience and brevity.

17 U.S.C. § 106. Exclusive rights in copyrighted works

Subject to sections 107 through 122, the owner of copyright under this title has the exclusive rights to do and to authorize any of the following:

(1) to reproduce the copyrighted work in copies or phonorecords;
(2) . . .
(3) to distribute copies or phonorecords of the copyrighted work to the public by sale or other transfer of ownership, or by rental, lease, or lending;
(4) in the case of literary, musical, dramatic, and choreographic works, pantomimes, and motion pictures and other audiovisual works, to perform the copyrighted work publicly; . . .

17 U.S.C. § 107. Limitations on exclusive rights: Fair use

Notwithstanding the provisions of section 106 . . . , the fair use of a copyrighted work, including such use by reproduction in copies or phonorecords or by any other means specified by that section, for purposes such as criticism, comment, news reporting, teaching (including multiple copies for classroom use), scholarship, or research, is not an infringement of copyright. In determining whether the use made of a work in any particular case is a fair use the factors to be considered shall include:

(1) the purpose and character of the use, including whether such use is of a commercial nature or is for nonprofit educational purposes;
(2) the nature of the copyrighted work;
(3) the amount and substantiality of the portion used in relation to the copyrighted work as a whole; and
(4) the effect of the use upon the potential market for or value of the copyrighted work. . . .

Campbell v. Acuff-Rose Music, Inc., 510 U.S. 569 (1994)

In 1964, Roy Orbison and William Dees wrote a rock ballad called "Oh, Pretty Woman" and assigned their rights to Acuff-Rose Music. Campbell and his popular rap music group, 2 Live Crew, wrote a rap song in 1989 entitled "Pretty Woman." After nearly a quarter of a million copies of the rap recording had been sold, Acuff-Rose Music sued to enforce their copyright. 2 Live Crew claims their commercial parody is a "fair use" within the meaning of the Copyright Act, 17 U.S.C. § 107. 2 Live Crew does not dispute that the song would infringe on the copyright absent a finding of fair use.

The fair use doctrine "permits [and requires] courts to avoid rigid application of the copyright statute when, on occasion, it would stifle the very creativity which that law is designed to foster." *Stewart v. Abend*, 495 U.S. 207, 236 (1990) (internal quotation marks and citation omitted). There are no bright-line rules, and the statute calls for case-by-case analysis. Similarly, nor may the four statutory factors be treated in isolation, one from another. The results must be weighed together, in light of the purposes of copyright.

1

The first factor, "the purpose and character of the use, including whether such use is of a commercial nature or is for nonprofit educational purposes," considers whether the use is for criticism, comment, or the like. The question is whether the new work "merely supersede[s] the objects" of the original creation, or instead "adds something new, with a further purpose or different character, altering the first with new expression, meaning, or message; it asks, in other words, whether and to what extent the new work is 'transformative.'" (Citations omitted.) Such transformative use is not absolutely necessary for a finding of fair use, but the goal of copyright, to promote science and the arts, is generally furthered by the creation of transformative works.

Parody has an obvious claim to transformative value. It can provide social benefit, by shedding light on an earlier work, and, in the process, creating a new one. Parody may or may not be fair use under § 107; parody, like any other use, has to work its way through the relevant factor, and be judged case by case.

Parody is transformative when it has "critical bearing on the substance or style of the original composition." The threshold question is whether a parodic character may reasonably be perceived.

2 Live Crew's song is transformative. The song could reasonably be perceived as commenting on the original or criticizing it. 2 Live Crew juxtaposes the romantic musings of a man whose fantasy comes true (with a prostitute), on the one hand, with degrading taunts, a bawdy demand for sex, and a sigh of relief from paternal responsibility on the other. The later words can be taken as a comment on the naivete of the original of an earlier day, as a rejection of its sentiment that ignores the ugliness of street life and the debasement that it signifies.

Furthermore, contrary to the court of appeals' ruling, which held that the commercial or nonprofit educational purpose of a work precluded a fair use finding, this is only one element of the first factor. Section 107(1) speaks of a broader investigation into "purpose and character."

2

The second statutory factor, "the nature of the copyrighted work," is generally disregarded in parody cases. It is not much help in this case, or in any parody case, since parodies almost invariably copy publicly known, expressive works.

3

The third factor asks whether "the amount and substantiality of the portion used in relation to the copyrighted work as a whole" is reasonable in relation to the purpose of the copying. The persuasiveness of a parodist's justification for the particular copying is significant, for we recognize that the extent of permissible copying varies with the purpose and character of the use.

When parody takes aim at a particular original work, the parody must be able to "conjure up" at least enough of that original to make the object of its critical wit recognizable. Hence, using some of the original's most distinctive or memorable features is common, as the audience will recognize them. Once enough has been taken to assure identification, how much more is reasonable will depend on the extent to which the song's overriding purpose and character is to parody the original or, in contrast, the likelihood that the parody may serve as a market substitute for the original. But using some characteristic features cannot be avoided.

Here, 2 Live Crew copied the characteristic opening bass riff (or musical phrase) of the original and the words of the first line copy the Orbison lyrics, arguably the "heart" of the original. But the question of fairness asks what else the parodist did besides go to the heart of the original. 2 Live Crew copied the bass riff and repeated it, but also produced otherwise distinctive sounds, interposing "scraper" noise, overlaying the music with solos in different keys, and altering the drum beat, changing the structure of the original song. The parody is not so insubstantial, as compared to the copying, that the third factor must be resolved as a matter of law against the parodists.

4

The fourth factor, "the effect of the use upon the potential market for or value of the copyrighted work," requires courts to consider not only the extent of market harm caused by the particular actions of the alleged infringer, but also "whether unrestricted and widespread conduct of the sort engaged in by the defendant . . . would result in a substantially adverse impact on the potential market" for the original. (Citations omitted.)

As to parody, it is more likely that the new work will not affect the market for the original because the parody and the original usually serve different market functions. We do not, of course, suggest that a parody may not harm the market at all, but when a lethal parody, like a scathing theater review, kills demand for the original, it does not produce a harm cognizable under the Copyright Act.

Since fair use is an affirmative defense, however, 2 Live Crew should have addressed the effect on the market for rap derivatives, not just demonstrated that there was no likely effect on the market for the original. Affidavits addressing the likely effect of 2 Live Crew's parodic rap song on the market for a non-parody, rap version of "Oh, Pretty Woman" should also have been submitted. This evidentiary hole can be plugged on remand.

In conclusion, it was error for the Court of Appeals to conclude that the commercial nature of 2 Live Crew's parody of "Oh, Pretty Woman" rendered it presumptively unfair. The court also erred in holding that 2 Live Crew had necessarily copied excessively from the Orbison original, considering the parodic purpose of the use. We therefore reverse the judgment of the Court of Appeals and remand the case for further proceedings consistent with this opinion.

Appendix A to
Opinion of the Court

"Oh, Pretty Woman"
by Roy Orbison and William Dees

Pretty Woman, walking down the street
Pretty Woman, the kind I like to meet

Pretty Woman, I don't believe you,

you're not the truth
No one could look as good as you
Mercy
Pretty Woman, won't you pardon me
Pretty Woman, I couldn't help but see
Pretty Woman, that you look lovely as can be

Are you lonely just like me?

Pretty Woman, stop a while

Pretty Woman, talk a while
Pretty Woman give your smile to me

Pretty Woman, yeah, yeah, yeah
Pretty Woman, look my way

Pretty Woman, say you'll stay with me

'Cause I need you, I'll treat you right
Come to me baby, Be mine tonight
Pretty Woman, don't walk on by
Pretty Woman, don't make me cry
Pretty Woman, don't walk away

Appendix B to
Opinion to the Court

"Pretty Woman"
as recorded by 2 Live Crew

Pretty woman walkin' down the street
Pretty woman girl you look so sweet
Pretty woman you bring me down to that knee
Pretty woman you make me wanna beg please
Oh, pretty woman
Big hairy woman you need to shave that stuff
Big hairy woman you know I bet it's tough
Big hairy woman all that hair it ain't legit
'Cause you look like 'Cousin It'
Big hairy woman
Bald headed woman girl your hair won't grow
Bald headed woman you got a teeny weeny afro
Bald headed woman you know your hair could look nice
Bald headed woman first you got to roll it with rice
Bald headed woman here, let me get this hunk of biz for ya
Ya know what I'm saying you look better than rice a roni
Oh bald headed woman
Big hairy woman come on in
And don't forget your bald headed friend
Hey pretty woman let the boys

Appendix A to Opinion of the Court	*Appendix B to Opinion to the Court*
Hey, O.K. If that's the way it must be, O.K. I guess I'll go on home, it's late There'll be tomorrow night, but wait! What do I see? Is she walking back to me? Yeah, she's walking back to me! Oh, Pretty Woman	Jump in Two timin' woman girl you know you ain't right Two timin' woman you's out with my boy last night Two timin' woman that takes a load off my mind Two timin' woman now I know the baby ain't mine Oh, two timin' woman Oh pretty woman

Dr. Seuss Enters., L.P. v. Penguin Books USA, Inc., 109 F.3d 1394 (9th Cir. 1997)

We must decide whether a poetic account of the O.J. Simpson double murder trial entitled *The Cat NOT in the Hat! A Parody by Dr. Juice*, presents a sufficient showing of copyright and trademark infringement of the well-known *The Cat in the Hat* by Dr. Seuss.

Under the pseudonym "Dr. Seuss," at least 47 books were published over 60 years, with approximately 35 million copies currently in print worldwide. The books use simple, rhyming, repetitive language, accompanied by characters that are recognizable by and appealing to children.

The Cat in the Hat involves a mischievous but well-meaning character, the Cat, who continues to be among the most famous and well recognized of the Dr. Seuss creations. The Cat is almost always depicted with his distinctive scrunched and somewhat shabby red and white stovepipe hat. Almost 40 years later, Penguin Books published *The Cat NOT in the Hat!* satirizing the O.J. Simpson double murder trial. Seuss sued for copyright infringement, and Penguin Books claimed fair use for a parody. The court therefore applied the four factors stated in § 107 of the Copyright Act.

1

Under the first factor, "the purpose and character of the use, including whether such use is of a commercial nature or is for nonprofit educational purposes," the inquiry is whether *The Cat NOT in the Hat!* merely supersedes the Dr. Seuss creations, or whether and to what extent the new work is "transformative," i.e., altering *The Cat in the Hat* with new expression, meaning or message. Looking at *The Cat NOT in the Hat!* itself, the first two pages present a view of Los Angeles, with particular emphasis on the connection with Brentwood, given the depiction of the news camera lights. The story begins as follows:

A happy town
Inside L.A.
Where rich folks play
The day away.
But under the moon
The 12th of June.
Two victims flail
Assault! Assail!
Somebody will go to jail!
Who will it be?
Oh my! Oh me!

The third page reads: "One Knife?/Two Knife?/Red Knife/Dead Wife." This stanza no doubt mimics the first poem in Dr. Seuss' *One Fish Two Fish Red Fish Blue Fish*: "One fish/two fish/red fish/blue fish. Black fish/blue fish/old fish/new fish." Throughout the book, these stanzas and the illustrations simply retell the Simpson tale. Although *The Cat NOT in the Hat!* does broadly mimic Dr. Seuss' characteristic style, it does not hold his style up to ridicule. The book merely uses the Cat's stovepipe hat, the narrator ("Dr. Juice"), and the title (*The Cat NOT in the Hat!*) "to get attention" or maybe even "to avoid the drudgery in working up something fresh." *Campbell*, 510 U.S. at 580. Because there is no effort to create a transformative work with "new expression, meaning, or message," the infringing work's commercial use further cuts against the fair use defense. *Id.* at 579.

2

While the second statutory factor, "the nature of the copyrighted work," has not been terribly significant in the overall fair use balancing, the creativity, imagination and originality embodied in *The Cat in the Hat* and its central character tilts the scale against fair use.

3

The third factor, "the amount and substantiality of the portion used in relation to the copyrighted work as a whole," raises the question of substantial similarity. "The Cat in the Hat" is the central character. We have no doubt that the Cat's image is the highly expressive core of Dr. Seuss' work. Penguin Books insists that The Cat in the Hat is the vehicle for their parody because of the similarities between the two stories: Nicole Brown and Ronald Goldman were surprised by a "Cat" (O.J. Simpson) who committed acts contrary to moral and legal authority. The prosecution of Simpson created a horrible mess, in which the defense team seemed to impose "tricks" on an unwilling public, resulting in a verdict that a substantial segment of the public regarded as astonishing. Just as *The Cat in the Hat* ends with the moral dilemma of whether the children should tell their mother about their visitor that afternoon, *The Cat NOT in the Hat!* ends with a similar moral dilemma:

JUICE
+ST
JUSTICE
Hmm . . . take the word JUICE.
Then add ST.
Between the U and I, you see.
And then you have JUSTICE.
Or maybe you don't.
Maybe we will.
And maybe we won't.
'Cause if the Cat didn't do it?
Then who? Then who?
Was it him?
Was it her?
Was it me?
Was it you?
Oh me! Oh my!
Oh my! Oh me!
The murderer is running free.

We agree with the district court that Penguin's fair use defense is "completely unconvincing."

4

The fourth factor is "the effect of the use upon the potential market for or value of the copyrighted work." The good will and reputation associated with Dr. Seuss' work is substantial. Because, on the facts presented, Penguin's use of *The Cat in the Hat* original was non-transformative, and admittedly commercial, we conclude that market substitution is at least more certain, and market harm may be more readily inferred. Especially because the market was children, who could easily mistake the copy for the original, a negative effect is likely.

Since fair use is an affirmative defense, Penguin must present favorable evidence about relevant markets. Given their failure to submit evidence on this point, Penguin is not entitled to relief.

Affirmed.

Mattel Inc. v. Walking Mountain Prods., 353 F.3d 792 (9th Cir. 2003)

Mattel asks us to prohibit artist Thomas Forsythe from producing and selling photographs containing Mattel's "Barbie" doll. Forsythe, aka "Walking Mountain Productions," is a photographer who produces photographs with social and political overtones. In 1997, Forsythe developed a series of 78 photographs entitled "Food Chain Barbie," in which he depicted Barbie in various absurd and often sexualized positions. Forsythe generally depicts one or more nude Barbie dolls juxtaposed with vintage kitchen appliances.

Forsythe chose to parody Barbie in his photographs because he believes that "Barbie is the most enduring of those products that feed on the insecurities of our beauty and perfection-obsessed consumer culture." His photos critique the objectification of women associated with Barbie and "the societal acceptance of women as objects." Forsythe's market success was limited, earning him a total of $3,659.

The Copyright Act seeks to promote the progress of science and art by protecting artistic and scientific works while encouraging the development and evolution of new works. *See Campbell v. Acuff-Rose Music, Inc.*, 510 U.S. 569, 575-76 (1994). The fair use exception excludes from copyright restrictions certain works, such as those that criticize and comment on another work. 17 U.S.C. § 107. The primary intent of fair use is to weigh the rights of the original owner against the benefit that the secondary use provides to society.

To determine whether a work constitutes fair use, we engage in a case-by-case analysis and a flexible balancing of relevant factors. *Campbell*, 510 U.S. at 577-78. The factors are "to be explored, and the results weighed together, in light of the purposes of copyright." *Id.* at 578.

The district court granted Forsythe's motion for summary judgment on Mattel's claim of copyright infringement. We review de novo a grant of summary judgment. *See Oliver v. Keller*, 289 F.3d 623, 626 (9th Cir. 2002). We also review the district court's finding of fair use under the Copyright Act, a mixed question of law and fact, by the same de novo standard. *Kelly v. Arriba Soft Corp.*, 336 F.3d 811, 817 (9th Cir. 2003).

A. Purpose and character of use

The first factor asks "to what extent the new work is transformative." *Campbell*, 510 U.S. at 579. A work must add "something new, with a further purpose or different character, altering the first with new expression, meaning, or message." *Id.* Parodic works, like other works that comment and criticize, are by their nature often sufficiently transformative to fit clearly under the fair use exception. *Id.*

In assessing whether Forsythe's photographs parody Barbie, Mattel urges us to ignore context—both the social context of Forsythe's work and the actual context in which Mattel's copyrighted works are placed in Forsythe's photographs. However, "in parody, as in news reporting, context is everything." *Id.* at 588 (citations omitted). We conclude that Forsythe's work may reasonably be perceived as a parody of Barbie.

Mattel has established Barbie as "the ideal American woman." Mattel's advertisements show these plastic dolls dressed in various outfits, leading glamorous lifestyles and engaged in exciting activities, representing women's traditional role positively. To sell its product, Mattel uses associations of beauty, wealth, and glamour.

Forsythe turns this image on its head with his photographs of Barbies in often ridiculous and apparently dangerous situations. In some of Forsythe's photos, Barbie is about to be destroyed or harmed by domestic life in the form of kitchen appliances. In other photographs, Forsythe conveys a sexualized perspective of Barbie by showing the nude doll in sexually suggestive contexts. It is not difficult to see the commentary that Forsythe intended or the harm that he perceived in Barbie's influence on gender roles and the position of women in society.

Another element of the first factor analysis is whether the work's "purpose" was commercial or had a non-profit aim. *Campbell*, 510 U.S. at 584. Clearly, Forsythe had a commercial expectation and presumably hoped to find a market for his art. However, given the extremely transformative nature and parodic quality of Forsythe's work, its commercial qualities become less important. However one may feel about his message, his photographs parody Barbie and everything Mattel's doll has come to signify. We find that this factor weighs heavily in favor of Forsythe.

B. *Nature of the copyrighted work*

The second factor typically has not been terribly useful in the overall fair use balancing. In any event, it may weigh slightly against Forsythe.

C. *Amount and substantiality of the portion used*

Under the third factor, the "extent of permissible copying varies with the purpose and character of the use." *Campbell*, 510 U.S. at 586-87. Mattel argues that Forsythe used the entirety of its copyrighted work and that this factor weighs against him. Mattel contends that Forsythe could have used less of the Barbie figure by, for example, limiting his photos to the Barbie heads.

First, Forsythe did not simply copy the work "verbatim" with "little added or changed." *Id.* at 587-88. Forsythe did not display the entire Barbie head and body in his photographs. Second, Mattel attempts to benefit from the somewhat unique nature of the copyrighted work in this case. Copyright infringement actions generally involve songs, video, or written works, which are naturally severable. Here, short of severing the doll, Forsythe must add to it by creating a context around it and capturing that context in a photograph. Forsythe's use of the entire doll and his use of dismembered parts of the doll are incorporated into the new work but emerge imbued with a different character.

Moreover, Forsythe was justified in the amount of Mattel's copyrighted work that he used in his photographs. We do not require parodic works to take the absolute minimum amount of the copyrighted work possible. As the Supreme Court stated in *Campbell*, "once enough has been taken to assure identification, how much more is reasonable will depend, say, on the extent to which the [work's] overriding purpose and character is to parody the original or, in contrast, the likelihood that the parody may serve as a market substitute for the original." *Id.* at 587. We conclude that the extent of Forsythe's copying of the Barbie figure and head was justifiable in light of his parodic purpose of criticizing stereotypical feminine roles in society and the medium used. This factor weighs in his favor.

D. Effect of the use upon potential market

The fourth factor considers whether actual market harm resulted from the defendant's use of plaintiff's protected material. Because of the parodic nature of Forsythe's work, it is highly unlikely that it will substitute for products in Mattel's markets or licenses. In *Campbell*, the Court clearly stated, "as to parody pure and simple, it is more likely that the new work will not affect the market for the original in a way cognizable under this factor." 510 U.S. at 591. Forsythe's work could only reasonably substitute for a work in the market for adult-oriented artistic photographs of Barbie. We think it safe to assume that Mattel will not enter such a market. Nor is it likely that Mattel would license an artist to create a work that is so critical of Barbie. Hence, Forsythe's works do not negatively affect any derivative work by Mattel.

Furthermore, this factor does not recognize a decrease in value of a copyrighted work that may result from a particularly powerful critical work. *Id.* at 593 ("The fact that a parody may impair the market for derivative uses by the very effectiveness of its critical commentary is no more relevant under copyright than the like threat to the original market . . .").

Having balanced the four § 107 fair use factors, we hold that Forsythe's work constitutes fair use.

Fisher v. Dees, 794 F.2d 432 (9th Cir. 1986)

FACTUAL AND PROCEDURAL BACKGROUND

The plaintiffs-appellants, Marvin Fisher and Jack Segal (the composers), composed and own the copyright to the '50s standard "When Sunny Gets Blue" (the song). In late 1984, a law firm representing the defendants-appellees contacted Fisher and requested permission to use part or all of the music to "When Sunny Gets Blue" in order to create a comedic and inoffensive version of the song. Fisher refused the request.

A few months later, Dees released a comedy record album called *Put It Where the Moon Don't Shine*. One cut on the album, entitled "When Sonny Sniffs Glue" (the parody), is an obvious take-off on the composers' song. The parody copies the first six of the song's 38 bars of music—its recognizable main theme. In addition, it changes the original's opening lyrics—"When

Sunny gets blue, her eyes get gray and cloudy, then the rain begins to fall" to "When Sonny sniffs glue, her eyes get red and bulgy, then her hair begins to fall." The parody runs for 29 seconds of the approximately 40 minutes of material on Dees's album.

DISCUSSION

Dees claims copying of the song for purposes of parody constituted a fair use. We agree.

Overview of the fair-use doctrine

The fair-use doctrine was initially developed by courts as an equitable defense to copyright infringement. In effect, the doctrine creates a limited privilege in those other than the owner of a copyright to use the copyrighted material in a reasonable manner without the owner's consent. (Citations omitted.) In restating the fair-use doctrine Congress enumerated four nonexclusive factors for courts to consider:

(1) the purpose and character of the use, including whether such use is of a commercial nature or is for nonprofit educational purposes;
(2) the nature of the copyrighted work;
(3) the amount and substantiality of the portion used in relation to the copyrighted work as a whole; and
(4) the effect of the use upon the potential market for or value of the copyrighted work.

17 U.S.C. § 107 (1982). In addition, in the legislative notes accompanying the provision, Congress listed examples "of the sort of activities the courts might regard as fair use under the circumstances." *Id.* § 107 historical and revision notes (1982). Congress named parody as one of these activities. Nonetheless, parody was not classified as a *presumptively* fair use. Each assertion of the "parody defense" must be considered individually, in light of the statutory factors, reason, experience, and, of course, the general principles developed in past cases. (Citations omitted.)

Applying the fair-use test

The subject of the parody

The composers assert that the parody, although it borrows from the original work, was not "directed" at the original. That is, a humorous or satiric work deserves protection under the fair-use doctrine only if the copied work is at least partly the target of the work in question. Otherwise, there is no need to "conjure up" the original in the audience's mind and no justification for borrowing from it. (Citations omitted.)

We requested counsel to provide us with tapes of both Dees's parody and the original (as sung by Johnny Mathis). Although we have no illusions of musical expertise, it was clear to us that Dees's version was intended to poke fun at the composers' song, and at Mr. Mathis's rather singular vocal range. We reject the notion that the song was used merely as a vehicle to achieve a comedic objective unrelated to the song, its place and time.

The economic effect of the use

Thus, we must turn our attention to the fourth factor in the fair-use analysis—"the effect of the use upon the potential market for or value of the copyrighted work," 17 U.S.C. § 107(4). This factor, not surprisingly, "is undoubtedly the single most important element of fair use." In assessing the economic effect of the parody, the parody's critical impact must be excluded. Through its critical function, a parody may quite legitimately aim at garroting the original, destroying it commercially as well as artistically. (Citation and quotation marks omitted.)

Copyright law is not designed to stifle critics. "Destructive parodies play an important role in social and literary criticism and thus merit protection even though they may discourage or discredit an original author." Accordingly, the economic effect of a parody with which we are concerned is not its potential to destroy or diminish the market for the original—any bad review can have that effect—but rather whether it *fulfills the demand* for the original. Biting criticism suppresses demand; copyright infringement usurps it. Thus, infringement occurs when a parody supplants the original in markets the original is aimed at, or in which the original is, or has reasonable potential to become, commercially valuable. (Citations omitted.)

This is not a case in which commercial substitution is likely. "When Sunny Gets Blue" is "a lyrical song concerning or relating to a woman's feelings about lost love and her chance for . . . happiness again." Appellants' Opening Brief at 3. By contrast, the parody is a 29-second recording concerning a woman who sniffs glue, which "ends with noise and laughter mixed into the song." We do not believe that consumers desirous of hearing a romantic and nostalgic ballad such as the composers' song would be satisfied to purchase the parody instead. Nor are those fond of parody likely to consider "When Sunny Gets Blue" a source of satisfaction. The two works do not fulfill the same demand. Consequently, the parody has no cognizable economic effect on the original.

The amount and substantiality of the taking

This court has also consistently focused on the third fair-use factor—the amount and substantiality of the taking, 17 U.S.C. § 107(3). Thus far, however, we have provided few concrete guidelines; we have merely sketched the outer boundaries of the inquiry. On the one hand, "substantial copying by a defendant, combined with the fact that the portion copied constituted a substantial part of the defendant's work," does not automatically preclude the fair use defense. On the other hand, "copying that is virtually complete or almost verbatim" will not be protected. (Citations omitted.)

Like a speech, a song is difficult to parody effectively without exact or near-exact copying. If the would-be parodist varies the music or meter of the original substantially, it simply will not be recognizable to the general audience. This "special need for accuracy" provides some license for "closer" parody. To be sure, that license is not limitless: the parodist's desire to make the best parody must be balanced against the rights of the copyright owner in his original expressions. (Citation and quotation marks omitted.) We think the balance tips in the parodists' favor here. In view of the parody's medium, its purposes, and its brevity, it takes no more from the original than is necessary to accomplish reasonably its parodic purpose.

Summation

We conclude that "When Sonny Sniffs Glue" is a parody deserving of fair-use protection as a matter of law. Thus, we affirm the district court's grant of summary judgment on the copyright claim.

[illegible] constant, combined with the fact that the portion copied constituted a substantial part of the defendant's work, does not automatically preclude the fair use defense. On the other hand, copying that is virtually complete or almost verbatim will not be protected. (Citations omitted.)

Just as [illegible] a song is difficult to parody effectively without exact or near-exact copying. If the would-be parodist varies the music or meter of the original substantially, it simply will not be recognizable to the general audience. This "special need for accuracy," provides some license for "closer" parody. [illegible] to make the best parody must be balanced against the rights of the copyright owner in his original expressions. (Citations and quotation marks omitted.) We think the balance tips in the parodists' favor here. In view of the parody's brevity and its purposes, and [illegible] that is necessary to accomplish reasonably its parodic purpose.

Conclusion

We conclude that "When Sonny Sniffs Glue" is a parody deserving of fair use protection as a matter of law. Thus, we affirm the district court's grant of summary judgment on the copyright claims.

The "Negligent Infliction of Emotional Distress" Problem

Note: To help you keep the parties straight, we have named the Plaintiff "Poe" because both words start with the letter P. Similarly, we have named the Defendant "Defoe" because both words start with the letter D, and we have named the victim "Valenzuela" because both words start with the letter V.

Our client, Jane Poe, was gardening in her front yard with her fiancé, John Valenzuela, when Dan Defoe was texting while driving and veered off the road, hitting Valenzuela. Poe was listening to music on her earbuds and tending to her flowers with her back to the road at the time of the accident. Valenzuela was mowing the lawn behind her and did not hear or see Defoe's vehicle coming toward him until it was too late.

Poe heard the impact but was not immediately sure what had happened. When she turned, she saw the lawnmower, without Valenzuela operating it, coming toward her. Poe was able to jump out of the way and was not hit. She then saw Valenzuela, who was about ten feet away, lying on the ground with Defoe's vehicle just a few feet from him. Poe rushed over to Valenzuela, who was covered in blood and not making a sound, to see if he was breathing. Poe found a weak pulse and tried to get Valenzuela to respond. A neighbor who saw the commotion called 911. An ambulance took Valenzuela to the hospital, with Poe riding along. Poe stayed at the hospital as Valenzuela underwent surgery for a punctured lung and internal bleeding. Valenzuela remained in the hospital for three weeks until it was safe for him to return home for the rest of his recovery.

After this incident, Poe experienced frequent anxiety attacks. She did not return to work while Valenzuela remained in the hospital because she feared leaving him alone. Once Valenzuela was released from the hospital, she sought help from a psychiatrist. She was diagnosed with an anxiety disorder and prescribed medication. She continues to see her psychiatrist on a regular basis.

At the time of the accident, Poe and Valenzuela had been dating for five years and were recently engaged. They had not yet set a date, but planned to marry within the next two years. They did not live together, but Valenzuela stayed at Poe's house four to five nights a week and Poe stayed at Valenzuela's house most other nights. Once they got engaged, they decided they should live together to start saving money for the wedding and Valenzuela planned to move into Poe's home in the next few months. They had recently purchased a car together when Valenzuela needed a new vehicle, but otherwise their finances were separate.

Ms. Poe would like to sue Dan Defoe. Mr. Valenzuela's case is being handled separately. I believe Ms. Poe may have a case for negligent infliction of emotional distress as a bystander who witnessed her fiancé's injuries.

You may assume we can establish that Mr. Defoe was negligent and that Ms. Poe has suffered severe emotional distress as a result of his negligence.

The following cases may apply to this problem. Cases have been modified from New Jersey cases for convenience, brevity, and educational purposes. Within the parentheticals after each case citation, "N.F." stands for the New Fornia Supreme Court, and that is followed by the year of the decision. "N.F. App." stands for the New Fornia Court of Appeals.

Portee v. Jaffee, 417 A.2d 521 (N.F. 1980)

We are asked to determine whether a parent can recover damages for the emotional anguish of watching her young child suffer and die in an accident caused by defendant's negligence. In *Falzone v. Busch*, 278 A.2d 559 (N.F. 1965), this Court imposed liability for such infliction of mental or emotional distress when negligence created the potential, but not the occurrence, for physical harm to the traumatized individual. The question presented here is whether liability should exist where there was no potential for personal injury, but distress resulted from perceiving the negligently inflicted injuries of another.

Relying on *Falzone*, the trial court rejected liability and granted summary judgment for defendants on this issue. After the Appellate Division granted plaintiff's motion for leave to appeal, we directly certified the case, R. 2:12-1. 82 N.F. 295 (1980). We now reversed the trial court and remand the matter for further proceedings.

Plaintiff's seven-year-old son, Guy Portee, resided with his mother in a Newark apartment building. Defendants Edith Jaffee and Nathan Jaffee owned and operated the building. On the afternoon of May 22, 1976, the youngster became trapped in the building's elevator between its outer door and the wall of the elevator shaft. The elevator was activated and the boy was dragged up to the third floor. Another child who was racing up a nearby stairway to beat the elevator opened it, saw the victim wedged within it, and ran to seek help. Soon afterwards, plaintiff and officers of the Fornia Police Department arrived. The officers worked for four and one-half hours to free the child. While their efforts continued, the plaintiff watched as her son moaned, cried out and flailed his arms. Much of the time she was restrained from touching him, apparently to prevent interference with the attempted rescue. The child suffered multiple bone fractures and massive internal hemorrhaging. He died while still trapped, his mother a helpless observer.

After her son's death plaintiff became severely depressed and seriously self-destructive. On March 24, 1979, she attempted to take her own life. She survived and has received extensive counseling and psychotherapy to help overcome the mental and emotional problems caused by her son's death.

On December 2, 1976, plaintiff brought suit against the Jaffees premised on defendants' negligence in failing to provide a safe elevator. Plaintiff sought damages for her mental and emotional distress caused by observing her son's anguish and death.

Defendants Edith and Nathan Jaffee moved for summary judgment as to plaintiff's claims for mental and emotional distress on June 27, 1979. After a hearing the trial court granted the motion. In an oral opinion the court stated that *Falzone v. Busch* set the outer limits of liability for the negligent infliction of mental and emotional distress. Since plaintiff had concededly not been subjected to any risk of physical harm caused by defendants' alleged negligence, the trial court found that plaintiff's claims for psychological injury did not meet the requirements of *Falzone*.

Since *Falzone*, this Court's decisions have shown no hostility to the imposition of liability for negligently caused mental or emotional distress even without an attendant risk of physical harm. *Berman v. Allen*, 402 A.2d 421, 426 (N.F. 1979); *Heavner v. Uniroyal, Inc.*, 362 A.2d 130, 133 (N.F. 1973).

Courts in other jurisdictions have found liability in the circumstances before us. In *Dillon v. Legg*, 68 Cal.2d 728, 441 (1968), the California Supreme Court permitted recovery when the emotional injury was foreseeable, and concluded that foreseeability existed when the plaintiff was at the scene of the accident and directly observed the accident (as contrasted with learning of the accident from others after its occurrence) and when the plaintiff and the victim were closely related. *Id.* at 740.

Those courts which have permitted actions for negligent infliction of emotional injuries unaccompanied by the risk of physical harm have adopted or followed these guidelines. *See D'Amicol v. Alvarez Shipping Co., Inc.*, 326 A.2d 129 (Conn. 1973); *Kelley v. Kokua Sales Supply, Ltd.*, 532 P.2d 673 (Hawaii 1975); *Dziokonski v. Babineau*, 380 N.E.2d 1295 (Mass. 1978); *Toms v. McConnell*, 207 N.W.2d 140 (Mich. 1973); *Sinn v. Burd*, 404 A.2d 672 (Pa. 1979).

We agree with the court in *Dillon* that these emotional injuries are foreseeable. The cause of action we approve today for the negligent infliction of emotional distress by a bystander requires proof of the following elements: (1) the death or serious physical injury of another caused by defendant's negligence; (2) a marital or close blood relationship between the plaintiff and the injured person; (3) the plaintiff's direct observation of the death or injury at the scene of the accident; and (4) resulting severe emotional distress in the plaintiff. We find that a defendant's duty of reasonable care to avoid physical harm to others extends to the avoidance of this type of mental and emotional harm.

For the foregoing reasons, the judgment of the trial court is reversed.

Dunphy v. Gregor, 642 A.2d 372 (N.F. 2013)

Plaintiff Dunphy brought a claim for negligent infliction of emotional distress as a bystander. Dunphy prevailed at trial, and Gregor appealed. The Appellate Division affirmed, and the defendant appealed.

I

Eileen Dunphy and Michael Burwell began dating in 2002. They became engaged to marry in April 2007 and, at that point, began cohabitating. They were to be married in February 2011. In September 2009, a friend called the couple to help her change her car tire. As Michael changed the left rear tire of the friend's car on the shoulder of the roadway, he was struck by a car driven by defendant, James Gregor. After being struck by the vehicle, his body was propelled 240 feet.

Dunphy, who had been standing approximately five feet from Burwell, witnessed the impact and ran to him immediately. Realizing that he was still alive, she cleared pebbles and blood from his mouth to ease his breathing. She attempted to subdue his hands and feet as they thrashed about, all the while talking to him in an effort to comfort him.

The following day, Burwell died as a result of his injuries. Since the accident, Dunphy has undergone psychiatric and psychological treatment for depression and anxiety. She instituted an action seeking to recover damages for the "mental anguish, pain and suffering" experienced as a result of witnessing the events that led to the death of her fiancé.

Dunphy testified that both she and Burwell had taken out life-insurance policies making each other beneficiaries. They had maintained a joint checking account from which they paid their bills, and they had jointly purchased an automobile. In addition, Burwell had asked her several times to elope with him, and he had introduced her in public as his wife.

II

To prevail on a claim of negligent infliction of emotional distress as a bystander, four elements must be proved. *Portee v. Jaffee*, 417 A.2d 521, 526 (N.F. 1980). Those elements are: (1) the death or serious physical injury of another caused by defendant's negligence; (2) a marital or close blood relationship between the plaintiff and the injured person; (3) the plaintiff's direct observation of the death or injury at the scene of the accident; and (4) resulting severe emotional distress in the plaintiff. *Id.*

At trial, the defendant conceded his negligence and the plaintiff's severe emotional distress. We therefore will not address those elements here. Furthermore, there is no question based on the evidence that the plaintiff directly observed the accident and her fiancé's resulting injury.

The defendant argues, however, that the relationship between the plaintiff and the deceased was insufficient to establish liability. We therefore consider whether bystander liability allows recovery by a person who was not legally married to a deceased victim but who cohabitated with and was engaged to marry the decedent.

Although novel, affording an unmarried cohabitant such as Eileen Dunphy the protections of bystander liability is hardly unfair. She represents an eminently foreseeable but clearly discrete class of potential plaintiffs. One can reasonably foresee that people who enjoy an intimate, familial relationship with one another will be especially vulnerable to emotional injury resulting from a tragedy befalling one of them. Foreseeability based on that standard, as recognized by the Appellate Division majority, preserves the distinction that must be made between ordinary emotional injuries that would be experienced by friends and relatives in general and those indelibly stunning emotional injuries suffered by one whose relationship with the victim at the time of the injury is deep, lasting, and genuinely intimate.

Persons engaged to be married and living together may foreseeably fall into that category of relationship. Given the widespread reality and acceptance of unmarried cohabitation, a reasonable person would not find the plaintiff's emotional trauma to be remote and unexpected.

Nor can we discern any additional, unfair burden that would be placed on potential wrongdoers in general, or, as in this case, negligent drivers. The identical acts of reasonable care that would have prevented the fatal accident that claimed the life of Michael Burwell would have preserved the emotional security of Eileen Dunphy. Certainly, the extension of such a duty of care to an engaged cohabitant as a foreseeable and protectable person does not increase the burden of care or extend it beyond what is ordinarily expected and appropriate for reasonable drivers. Those in an intimate and familial relationship are foreseeably and genuinely injured by a negligent defendant's acts. Allowing for their recovery both advances a key goal of tort compensation—to encourage acting with reasonable care—and maintains fairness for potential defendants by limiting liability to those who can demonstrate this relationship.

We acknowledge that this critical determination must be guided as much as possible by a standard that focuses on those factors that identify and define the intimacy and familial nature of such a relationship. That standard must take into account the duration of the relationship; the type of relationship (dating, engaged, cohabitating, etc.); the degree of financial intermingling; and the extent and quality of shared experiences.

We are unpersuaded by the concerns that without a "bright line" definition of the bystander-victim relationship, courts will not be able to counteract fraudulent claims. That consideration does not outweigh the need to recognize claims that are legitimate and just.

III

We conclude that under the circumstances of this case an unmarried cohabitant should be afforded the protections of bystander liability for the negligent infliction of emotional distress. The basis for that protection is the existence of an intimate, familial relationship with the victim of the defendant's negligence.

When that emotional security is devastated because one witnesses, in close and direct proximity, an accident resulting in the wrongful death or grievous bodily injury of a person with whom one shares an intimate, familial relationship, the infliction of that severe emotional injury may be the basis of recovery against the wrongdoer.

The judgment of the Appellate Division is affirmed.

Ortiz v. JDP Builders, Inc., 689 A.2d 1135 (N.F. 2015)

The plaintiffs Ortiz and Cruz brought a claim for negligent infliction of emotional distress after a January 2012 house fire which killed five-year-old Jasmine Ortiz and seriously burned Cruz, Jasmine's maternal grandmother.

The plaintiffs prevailed in the trial court. The defendant appealed, and the Appellate Division affirmed. The issue before us is whether a bystander's emotional distress claim is actionable when the bystander does not directly observe the actual death of a relative. For the reasons below, this court concludes that such a claim is viable even without actually seeing a relative ablaze, so long as the bystander is sensorially aware of the relative burning to death.

I

In January 2012, plaintiff Adelaida Ortiz resided with her mother, plaintiff Maria Cruz, and Ortiz's three children in an apartment owned by the defendant. At approximately 3:00 a.m., Cruz awoke when she felt heat on her face. When Cruz saw the curtains in her bedroom on fire, she picked up her infant grandson, James, and awoke her five-year-old granddaughter, Jasmine, who were both sleeping in Cruz's ground floor bedroom. As Cruz was carrying her grandson in her arms and holding Jasmine by the hand, the windows exploded. The explosion startled Jasmine, who broke away from Cruz's grasp and disappeared into the smoke and flames. All during this horrifying experience Cruz was screaming "Fire!"

Cruz's warnings awoke Ortiz, who saw flames at her second-story window. Ortiz wrapped herself in a blanket and ran to wake her daughter, Lakiesha, whose bedroom was also on the second floor.

When Ortiz reached the kitchen, she met her mother, who handed the infant to Ortiz. Cruz kept screaming, "Jasmine let's go, Jasmine let's go!" Cruz then ran back into the burning house searching for Jasmine. Once Ortiz had James and Lakiesha outside, she attempted to break the back window to create an escape route for her mother and Jasmine.

After several unsuccessful attempts to break the window, she returned to the front of the house. Ortiz then witnessed her mother, on fire, running out of the house. As Ortiz patted out the flames on her mother, Cruz screamed hysterically, "I can't find her, I can't find her." Ortiz knew Cruz was referring to her daughter, Jasmine.

When police arrived, Ortiz screamed that Jasmine was still inside the burning building. Although an ambulance transported Cruz, James, and Lakiesha to the hospital, Ortiz remained at the scene hoping that rescuers would find Jasmine alive. Ortiz remained at the scene until rescue workers ordered her to go to the hospital. The day after the fire, Ortiz learned that Jasmine burned to death.

Dr. Smith, a psychiatrist who examined Ortiz months after the fire, noted that Ortiz cries every day, isolates herself, has flashbacks and nightmares about the fire, has difficulty sleeping, gets chills when she is close to the location of the fire, and is reluctant to talk about the loss of her daughter Jasmine. Smith opined that as a direct result of the fire, Ortiz suffers from "Chronic Posttraumatic Stress Disorder." Smith also opined that Ortiz's "psychiatric problem is a direct result of the consequences of the fire as described and will continue to have a very significant emotional effect on Ms. Ortiz."

II

To prevail on a claim for the negligent infliction of emotional distress by a bystander, the plaintiff must demonstrate "(1) the death or serious physical injury of another caused by defendant's negligence; (2) a marital or close blood relationship," or an "intimate, familial relationship," between "the plaintiff and the injured person; (3) the plaintiff's direct observation of the death or injury at the scene of the accident; and (4) resulting severe emotional distress in the plaintiff." *Dunphy v. Gregor*, 642 A.2d 372, 373, 376 (N.F. 2013).

Although the defendant concedes the plaintiffs meet the other elements necessary for a bystander's successful negligent infliction of emotional distress claim, this appeal rests on the sole argument that the plaintiffs did not directly observe the death of the deceased at the scene of the accident.

Recovery for the negligent infliction of emotional distress by a bystander is meant to cover the observation of shocking events that do not occur in the daily lives of most people. Although this court has never squarely addressed this issue, courts outside New Fornia have extended this "observation requirement" to permit bystanders to recover for emotional distress even if they do not witness, with their own eyes, the actual injuries or death of a loved one. In *Wilks v. Hom*, 3 Cal. Rptr. 2d 803, 805 (Ct. App. 2008), an explosion in the plaintiff's home killed one child, severely burned another, and propelled the mother out of the house. Although the plaintiff mother was aware that the explosion and fire likely harmed her two daughters, she did not visually witness the injuries being inflicted. The court concluded that it "is not necessary that a plaintiff bystander actually have witnessed the infliction of injury to her child, provided that the plaintiff was at the scene of the accident and was sensorially aware, in some important way, of the accident and the necessarily inflicted injury to her child." *Id.* at 807.

This court recognizes that some circumstances, like fire cases, are unique because "the flames are likely to hide the victims from the view of those present at the scene. To disallow recovery to plaintiffs in such cases merely because they did not actually view the injury being inflicted on the bodies of the victims defies reason and common sense." *Stump v. Ashland*, 201 S.E.2d 541, 545 (W.Va. 2003).

Similarly, in the instant matter, there could be very little doubt in plaintiffs' minds that Jasmine was in the house that they saw engulfed in flames. Ortiz was aware of who was in the house when her mother's screams awakened her. Ortiz knew that Cruz, at one point, had Jasmine in her grasp, that Jasmine had broken free of her grandmother, and that Cruz raced back into the burning house to search for Jasmine. When Ortiz's mother reappeared from the burning house, Jasmine was not with her. Both Ortiz and Cruz were "sensorially aware, in some important way, of the fire and the necessarily inflicted injury to their child." *Wilks*, 2 Cal. Rptr. 2d at 807. Both Ortiz and Cruz observed "shocking events that do not occur in the daily lives of most people."

For the foregoing reasons, this court adopts the modern view where direct observation of the accident is not required if there is, as here, otherwise an experiential perception of it. In doing so, this court extends the requirement of direct observation to include being "sensorially aware" of a family member being injured or killed. Whether or not plaintiffs actually saw the fire incinerating Jasmine does not prevent them from meeting this requirement. To deny the plaintiffs the right to recover for emotional distress resulting from observing the fire burning Jasmine to death merely because they did not actually view the injury being inflicted on Jasmine defies reason and common sense.

III

This court concludes that that plaintiffs' negligent infliction of emotional distress bystander claims are viable because the plaintiffs sensorially experienced the burning death of their five-year-old relative. The judgment of the Appellate Division is affirmed.

Miller v. Davidson, 794 A.2d 175 (N.F. App. 2017)

Plaintiff Patricia Miller appeals from a summary judgment order dismissing her complaint. Miller sought to recover for the emotional damage that she claimed to have sustained as the result of a fatal attack by a circus leopard upon her long-term boyfriend, Edward Ferguson, at a circus performance.

For summary judgment purposes, the defendant conceded his negligence and the plaintiff's severe emotional distress. The two issues before us, therefore, are whether Miller and Ferguson meet the intimate, familial relationship element required for Miller to recover and whether Miller directly observed Ferguson's death at the scene of the accident.

I

In June 2013, when this incident occurred, plaintiff Miller and her boyfriend Ferguson had been dating for three years. They did not live together but stayed over at each others' apartments two or three nights a week. They discussed getting married in the future but there were no formal plans or timeline for when they might become engaged to be married. They shared one bank account that they each put money into every month; they used the account to pay for eating out and entertainment so they would not need to figure out who was paying each time. Otherwise, all their finances were separate.

On the night of the incident, Miller and Ferguson arrived for an 8:00 p.m. circus performance and seated themselves in the bleachers erected around the circus' three rings. The defendant Davidson's animal act was first on the program. Just after it started, Ferguson had to use the bathroom, necessitating a trip out of the tent and into another building. When Ferguson returned, Davidson was working with the jaguar, and the two leopards were on stools. As Miller saw Ferguson return to the tent, she received a phone call from her boss. Miller then moved to the end of the aisle, went up several stairs to a less crowded part of the bleachers, and turned her back to the performance so she could hear her boss and participate in the phone conversation. Miller covered her other ear and could only hear vague circus sounds in the background while she was conversing with her boss.

After Ferguson entered the tent, in order to return to his bleacher seats, Ferguson had to walk close to the center ring where the animals were performing. As he passed, one of the leopards leaped off its stool, pounced on Ferguson, and dragged him under an empty transport cage.

Miller was not aware that the leopard had dragged Ferguson away until her phone call concluded several minutes later. At the conclusion of her call, as Miller started to return to her original bleacher seat, Miller realized Ferguson was not there and saw a crowd near the ring. Miller rushed toward the ring. By the time she reached Ferguson, others had already freed him from the leopard's jaw and he had bled to death.

The psychological aftermath of the tragedy has been devastating for Miller. A year-and-a-half after the event, Miller was diagnosed as suffering from depressive neurosis, characterized as a "significant disorder for which the prognosis is poor without continued psychotherapy." Miller was psychologically unable to continue her employment at a local nursery school and resigned from that job. She is chronically depressed and is aware of the deterioration of her personal relationships. Clearly, Miller has suffered serious and permanent psychological damage which significantly affects her ability to function normally in her daily life and relationships.

New Fornia extends compensability to the emotional stress suffered by a bystander who witnesses the negligently inflicted personal injury or death of another even if he himself is not in any physical danger. *Portee v. Jaffee*, 417 A.2d 521, 530 (N.F. 1980). To succeed on her claim, the plaintiff must demonstrate four elements: her boyfriend's death was caused by the defendant's negligence; the plaintiff and her boyfriend shared an "intimate, familial relationship"; she directly observed or was "sensorially aware" of her boyfriend's injury and death; and she suffered severe emotional distress as a result. *Dunphy v. Gregor*, 642 A.2d 372, 373, 376 (N.F. 2013); *Ortiz v. JDP Builders, Inc.*, 689 A.2d 1135, 1139 (N.F. 2015).

II

The first legal issue is whether Miller and Ferguson meet the intimate, familial relationship requirement required for her psychological damage to be compensable. It is clear that they were not married and were not blood relatives. The trial judge concluded that the relationship was not sufficient and granted the defendant's motion for summary judgment dismissing the complaint. Plaintiff appeals.

In *Dunphy*, the court held that in order for unmarried non-relatives to meet this requirement, the bystander and the victim must be in an "intimate, familial relationship" such as that of an engaged cohabitating couple. 642 A.2d at 376. The court considered "the duration of the relationship;

the type of relationship (dating, engaged, cohabitating, etc.); the degree of financial intermingling; and the extent and quality of shared experiences." *Id.* The New Fornia Supreme Court held that a woman who suffered severe emotional distress after witnessing her fiancé fatally hit and propelled by a car could recover. *Id.* The court found their relationship to meet the requirement because they lived together, were engaged to be married, shared finances, and owned a vehicle together. *Id.* at 375.

This case, however, is distinguishable. In *Dunphy*, the plaintiff and deceased dated for seven years, had a wedding date set, had been cohabitating for two years, had a bank account together to pay for their bills, and had each other named as beneficiaries on life insurance policies. Their relationship was mutually dependent in that they lived with each other and paid joint bills together. They were further emotionally reliant on each other and had plans to get married. Based on their day-to-day lives, they were effectively married. Here, the plaintiff and deceased had been dating three years and only stayed at each other's apartments occasionally, with no explicit plans to become engaged to be married. Even though they shared a bank account to pay for eating out and entertainment, their financial lives were otherwise separate. This does not meet the level of dependency that is required to meet the intimate, familial relationship requirement.

III

The second issue is whether Miller directly observed or was sensorially aware of the accident and Ferguson's resulting injury. *Dunphy v. Gregor*, 642 A.2d 372, 372 (N.F. 2013); *Ortiz v. JDP Builders, Inc.*, 689 A.2d 1135, 1139 (N.F. 2015).

Recovery for negligence is permitted not just by the injured party, but also by certain bystanders. In those instances, observing a shocking event causing severe injury or death to a loved one can itself cause foreseeable harm. When a plaintiff is present at the scene and observes a spouse or other family member suffering a horrific injury, denying recovery furthers no legitimate purpose. *Dunphy*, 642 A.2d at 375. This is true even when the plaintiff cannot actually see the injury and death, as when a fire obstructs the view but the plaintiff is still "sensorially aware" of the injury and death. *Ortiz*, 689 A.2d at 1139.

However, when the plaintiff does not directly observe the accident which causes injury or death, the sphere of potential claims is limitless. To allow all persons, even limited to those in intimate familial relationships, to recover whenever a loved one is injured or killed—without requiring the plaintiff observe that injury—would extend negligence liability beyond its reasonable boundaries.

In this case, Miller did not observe the injury to Ferguson. She was completely unaware that he had been mauled by the leopard until she had finished her phone call, realized Ferguson had not returned, realized a crowd had formed near the ring, and ran down and discovered Ferguson had just bled to death. He had already been freed by others and an ambulance was on the way to the scene, although its arrival was too late to help Ferguson.

Furthermore, Miller was not sensorially aware of his injury and death. Unlike the fire in *Ortiz*, the only thing that prevented Miller from directly observing Ferguson's injury and death was her own inattention. Although she was present at the scene where Ferguson was mauled, she was not in any way aware of his injury and death until after the fact.

Although this court does not dispute the significant emotional injury Miller suffered, it is not compensable because she did not directly observe and was not sensorially aware of Ferguson's injury and death.

IV

This court concludes that plaintiff's bystander negligent infliction of emotional distress claim is not viable for two reasons. First, plaintiff and victim fail to meet the intimate, familial relationship requirement. Second, the plaintiff did not directly observe and was not sensorially aware of the events that resulted in Ferguson's death. This court therefore affirms the trial court's dismissal of the claim.

***Vargas v. Quinones*,** 801 A.2d 1440 (N.F. App. 2018)

In March 2015, plaintiff Paula Vargas's car collided at an intersection with a car operated by defendant Mildred Quinones. Mrs. Vargas was eight months pregnant at the time. After the accident, paramedics removed Mrs. Vargas from her car and placed her in an ambulance.

Mrs. Vargas's husband, plaintiff Luis Vargas, was at home when the accident occurred. His sister informed Mr. Vargas of the accident by telephone and he drove to the scene. Mrs. Vargas was already in the ambulance, waiting to be driven to the hospital, when he arrived. Mr. Vargas observed his wife in the ambulance bleeding, crying hysterically, and holding her stomach. According to Mr. Vargas, he also "noticed what appeared to be a wet stain on [his wife's] clothing making me think that her water was caused to break." He then followed the ambulance to the hospital, where it was determined the fetus had died in utero in the accident. A doctor performed a caesarian section to remove the fetus. Mr. Vargas did not observe this procedure.

Plaintiffs subsequently brought this negligence action against Mildred Quinones and Jose Quinones, the owner of the car Mildred was driving at the time of the accident. In addition to Mrs. Vargas's own personal injury claim, both Mr. and Mrs. Vargas asserted claims for negligent infliction of emotional distress based on the death of the fetus.

The trial court granted defendants' motion for summary judgment dismissing Mr. Vargas's claim for his emotional distress caused by the death of the fetus. Plaintiff Mr. Vargas appeals.

Mr. Vargas's claim is a bystander claim for negligent infliction of emotional distress. The trial court granted defendants' motion because Mr. Vargas did not directly observe the accident or the death of the fetus at the scene of the accident. Since he was not near the accident when it had occurred, he could not have been sensorially aware of it.

Ordinarily, only a witness at the scene of the accident causing death or serious injury can recover on a negligent infliction of emotional distress bystander claim. *Dunphy v. Gregor*, 642 A.2d 372 (N.F. 2013). Witnessing the accident and resulting injury or death is likely to create a traumatic sense of loss, destroying the plaintiff's sense of security and causing severe emotional distress. Without such perception, the threat of emotional injury is lessened and the justification for liability is fatally weakened. The law of negligence, while it redresses suffering wrongfully caused by others, must not itself inflict undue harm by imposing an unreasonably excessive measure of liability. Directly observing the death or serious injury of another while it occurs is an essential element of a cause of action for a bystander claiming negligent infliction of emotional distress.

It is clear that Mr. Vargas did not "directly observe" either his wife's car accident or the death in utero of the fetus she was carrying. Mr. Vargas was at home when the accident occurred. He did not arrive on the scene until ten to thirty minutes later, after Mrs. Vargas had been removed from the car and placed in an ambulance, and his observations were not significantly different from what they would have been if he had first observed her when she arrived at the hospital.

Moreover, the death of the fetus was not immediately apparent upon Mr. Vargas's arrival at the accident scene. It was only after tests were performed at the hospital that the attending doctors concluded the fetus was probably not viable, and this conclusion was not confirmed until the fetus was delivered by a caesarian section performed hours after the accident.

Plaintiff relies upon bystander cases where plaintiffs have been allowed to proceed when they suffered emotional distress from observing fires that resulted in the death of a close relative, even though the smoke and flames from the fire prevented them from actually seeing the victims. *See, e.g., Ortiz v. JDP Builders, Inc.*, 689 A.2d 1135 (N.F. 2015). However, this line of case rests on the recognition that "some instances, like fire cases, are unique because 'the flames are likely to hide the victims from the view of those present at the scene.'" *Id.* Denying recovery in these cases solely because plaintiffs did not directly observe "the injury being inflicted on the bodies of the victims defies reason and common sense." *Id.* (internal citations omitted). In *Ortiz*, the court held that the "direct observation of the accident" requirement was met when the plaintiff was "'sensorially aware' of a family member being injured or killed." *Id.*

Here, in contrast, Mr. Vargas was at home when the accident occurred some distance away. He was not present at the scene and did not see or hear the accident. In short, he was not "sensorially aware" in any way of Mrs. Vargas's car accident and the resulting harm to the fetus until later. His distress from this incident is understandable, but without being "a witness at the scene of the accident causing death or serious injury," his emotional distress is not compensable.

For the reasons above, we affirm the dismissal of Mr. Vargas's claim for negligent infliction of emotional distress.

Checklists

Chapter 1: How to Use This Book

✔	Write for your reader: your professor's advice trumps this book and you should always keep in mind who your audience is when writing.
✔	Observe, evaluate, and reflect as you work through this book.
✔	Actively engage with the examples by explaining to yourself why you made the choices you made.
✔	Think about whether the example fits your assignment before you imitate it.
✔	Practice "interleaving" by skipping around the text and returning to previous examples to improve your understanding.

Chapter 2: Transitioning to Legal Writing

✔	Start working on your assignment early and plan for writing to take longer than usual and to work through many drafts.
✔	Be concise.

✔	Use a formal tone without first person or contractions but with last names and using articles.
✔	Quote key statutory language, but generally paraphrase cases.
✔	Avoid "elegant variation," unnecessary legalese, and other distracting stylistic choices.
✔	Use past tense to discuss the client's facts as well as the facts and holdings of other cases, but use present tense when stating a rule of law.
✔	A court doesn't "feel," "think," or "believe," and a court is an "it" not a "they."

Chapter 3: Overview: Office Memos

✔	Evaluate each question presented with objective, thorough, and accurate analysis.
✔	Determine if your audience wants a full formal memo and include the appropriate components (e.g., Heading, Question Presented, Brief Answer, Facts, Discussion, and Conclusion).
✔	Even if the assignment calls for handing in a "first draft," plan to revise your work so that you hand in the best draft you can.
✔	Budget time for reading the relevant authorities carefully.
✔	Avoid the pitfall of organizing by authorities rather than substantive points.
✔	Use an objective tone for memos, rather than a persuasive tone.
✔	Avoid waffling language to the extent you can while maintaining accuracy.
✔	Include thorough analysis regarding how the law will likely apply to the facts ("show your work").

Chapter 4: Choosing Authority

✔	Make a list of all your research and organize the sources according to weight of authority principles, starting with rules from governing statutes and regulations and then moving to cases.

✔	Plan to use mandatory authority before persuasive authority.
✔	Plan to use primary sources before secondary sources (use secondary sources to inform yourself, but they are often not important enough to cite).
✔	If your case is governed by a statute, start the discussion by quoting its relevant parts.

Chapter 5: Interpreting Statutes

✔	Closely read the statute to figure out exactly what parts are relevant for the problem at hand.
✔	Quote the relevant parts of the statute early in the memo's Discussion section or the brief's Argument section.
✔	Notice whether any canons or rules of construction apply.
✔	Discuss the cases interpreting the statute and use weight of authority to order those cases.
✔	If a plain language argument applies, analyze or make it first.

Chapter 6: Interpreting the Common Law

✔	Use precedent that has applied and interpreted the applicable rule—whether that comes from common law or a statute—to analyze your issue.
✔	For each case, identify the relevant facts, issue, holding (including the outcome), and rationale so you can deduce the rule.
✔	Pay special attention to the *most recent* formulation of the rule from the highest court or courts because the common law evolves.
✔	Make sure to rely on holdings rather than dicta.
✔	Outline the complete, synthesized rule, and using a chart for the key case facts and outcomes might help.
✔	Articulate the current, complete, synthesized rule.

Chapter 7: Organizing the Discussion

✔	Use IRAC, CRAC, or the organizational paradigm that your professor uses to organize each issue and sub-issue in the assignment.
✔	Start and end each CRAC with a conclusion statement for that issue or sub-issue, generally signaling this with a heading at the beginning of each issue or sub-issue.
✔	State the rule for that issue or sub-issue.
✔	Explain the rule with citations to authority and a discussion of the facts, outcomes, and rationales in the precedent cases for that issue or sub-issue.
✔	Apply the law in the rule and rule explanation to your assignment facts for each issue or sub-issue.

Chapter 8: Constructing a Rule

✔	Pay attention to rule construction: whether the rule is structured as a conjunctive, disjunctive, defeasible, factors, or balancing test.
✔	Decide whether the rule is completely stated in one source or whether you need to synthesize multiple sources to state the rule.
✔	If you need to synthesize multiple sources, identify the relevant authorities and think about how they relate to each other in terms of weight of authority, when enacted or decided, and how various courts have framed the rule.
✔	Consider sorting out the synthesized rule by making a chart of the relevant authorities.

Chapter 9: Stating and Explaining the Rule

✔	Clearly state the rule (quote key statutory language and generally quote sparingly from cases).
✔	Add citations to support each component of the rule stated.
✔	Discuss the authorities that support the rule—for example, illustrate the way courts have interpreted and applied the rule by explaining the precedents' facts, outcomes, and rationales.

✔	Consider the types of relevant authorities and put mandatory authority first or give it more space in the rule explanation.
✔	When the precedent is central to the analysis, feature it more prominently or give it more space in rule explanation.
✔	If there are alternative formulations of the rule, explain both.
✔	When the rule is unsettled or controversial, provide detailed explanation of relevant cases.
✔	When the precedent is less central or weighty for the analysis, give it less space and consider simply using a parenthetical.

Chapter 10: Applying the Law: Fact-Based Analysis

✔	Sort the facts, deciding which facts and inferences support each side.
✔	Review the fact-based inferences you have generated and choose the strongest one or two.
✔	Write sentences that tie together the fact and the legal rule.

Chapter 11: Applying the Law: Analogical Analysis

✔	Read the precedent cases and consider the facts that are relevant to the applicable legal test.
✔	Choose the facts from the assignment that are relevant to the applicable legal test.
✔	Articulate exactly how and why the facts from a precedent and from the assignment are similar or different.
✔	Compare apples to apples: make sure the facts compared or contrasted are actually parallel to the facts from precedents and the connections are explicit.

Chapter 12: Applying the Law: Policy Analysis

✔	Consider the audience and whether the analysis or arguments will be stronger if you add policy rationales.

✔	If appropriate, specifically articulate or craft an argument about how an outcome in the case will benefit or disadvantage society.
✔	Support policy analysis or arguments with cites to authority, especially mandatory primary authority if available.

Chapter 13: Writing the Introduction to the Discussion or Argument

✔	Plan for the components of a good introduction: a thesis, the main rule that applies to the issue, a statement about any parts of the rule that will not be at issue and a very brief explanation of why not, and a roadmap.
✔	Include a thesis statement.
✔	Include the main rule that applies to the issue.
✔	If any parts of the rule will be undisputed by the parties, briefly state and explain that.
✔	Include an explicit roadmap when the rule does not roadmap your paper.
✔	Include any other important statements that apply to the issue generally.
✔	Edit the introduction to include an appropriate amount of detail by giving legal readers enough to understand what the memo or brief addresses without including more detailed information that would be better addressed in the body of the Discussion or Argument.

Chapter 14: Writing the Question Presented (Objective)

✔	Use a format your professor recommends, "under, does, when" or "whether, when."
✔	State the applicable law (the "under" component).
✔	State the specific legal question (the "does" component).
✔	State the determinative facts (the "when" component).

✔	Put the components together.
✔	Usually make the Question Presented one complete sentence.
✔	Phrase the Question Presented as a question so the answer would be either "yes" or "no" or a qualified "yes" or "no" (such as "likely yes" or "probably no").
✔	Include only the main issue in the QP.
✔	If you have more than one QP, use numbers to separate them and use that same scheme for later parts of the memo.

Chapter 15: Writing the Brief Answer

✔	Aim to indicate an accurate degree of certainty about your answer to the Question Presented.
✔	Start with "Yes" or "No" and if it is really a close call, add "Probably" or "Likely" before the "yes" or "no."
✔	Briefly summarize the key reasons for the answer, melding law and fact.
✔	Be conclusory without discussing or evaluating authorities and arguments.
✔	Usually do not include citations.
✔	Keep it short—typically about two or three sentences.
✔	Have a Brief Answer for each Question Presented and if there is more than one, make the numbers match.

Chapter 16: Writing the Facts

✔	Gather and read all the facts, whether in a case file, a memo from the assigning attorney, or some other source your professor has provided.
✔	Decide which facts are relevant by asking if removing the fact would change the analysis.
✔	Include all relevant facts.
✔	Include background and procedural facts necessary for context.

✔	Write in a regular paragraph format, usually without numbered lines.
✔	Frame facts objectively and do not include opinion or argument.
✔	Usually organize facts in chronological order and use past tense.
✔	For lengthy Facts sections, consider using subheadings to break it into logical chunks so it's easier to read and understand.
✔	After completing the Discussion section, go back to check that all the facts you use in the analysis are stated in the Facts section.

Chapter 17: Writing the Conclusion Section (Objective)

✔	Conclusion sections usually include a paragraph or two for each main section of the memo.
✔	A memo's Conclusion is generally longer than the Brief Answer and shorter than the Discussion, but be sure to consider your audience's preferences.
✔	Conclusions are usually organized around the structure of the rule, just like your memo.

Chapter 18: Overview: Motions and Briefs

✔	Plan time for multiple drafts and polishing.
✔	Include relevant, unfavorable facts and binding authorities.
✔	Make your own affirmative argument and do not just respond to your opponent's arguments.
✔	Support factual assertions with citations to the record.
✔	Read local rules and/or the assignment and include what the rules require.
✔	Do not go overboard with exaggerated attempts at persuasion.

Chapter 19: Handling Standards of Review

✔	Understand what a standard of review is and how it can affect the case.
✔	Identify the issue or issues on appeal.
✔	Conduct research to figure out the standard or standards of review that apply in the case.
✔	Consider whether the standard of review itself might be at issue.
✔	Check and follow the court rules about where to address standard of review in the brief.
✔	State the applicable standard of review for each issue on appeal and cite authority.
✔	If the standard of review favors your client's case, emphasize it where you can to strengthen the arguments.

Chapter 20: Developing a Theory of the Case and Themes

✔	Consider each side's strengths and weaknesses, thinking about the evidence and weight of authority supporting each side's arguments.
✔	Create an overarching narrative or idea that explains the key issues and why your client should win—the theory of the case and core themes.
✔	Weave the theory of the case and core themes through the brief, while not overpowering the reader.

Chapter 21: Writing Point Headings and Subheadings

✔	Point headings meld the legal issue with key facts and are phrased as the conclusion you want the court to reach or the action you want it to take.
✔	Use a point heading for each dispositive argument.
✔	Use subheadings to set out the steps of logic or conclusions that prove your point heading or headings.

✔	Follow conventions of using different formatting and numbering for different levels of headings.
✔	Point headings and subheadings set out a complete and persuasive outline of the argument.

Chapter 22: Making Persuasive Arguments

✔	The substance of the argument is most important so concentrate on that first.
✔	Be subtle when using persuasive techniques so the reader does not notice the technique but is persuaded.
✔	Usually put strongest arguments first and also end on a strong note.
✔	Structure the argument to persuade by using thesis statements at the start of every section, argument, and paragraph.
✔	Structure the argument to persuade by putting the most important information at the beginning or the end of units of information.
✔	Use headings and transitions to persuade.
✔	Use a forceful writing style with thoughtful stylistic choices (e.g., active vs. passive voice, word choice, etc.) to persuade.

Chapter 23: Making Persuasive Counterarguments

✔	Put yourself in the other side's shoes and identify the other side's arguments.
✔	Evaluate whether your adversary is likely to raise the arguments identified, whether a court would be concerned with them, and whether your response lessens their sting.
✔	Do not nitpick or create weak arguments just to shoot them down; only address opposing counsel's argument if the court is likely to be concerned with it.
✔	Phrase counterarguments as an affirmative argument rather than a response to your opponent's arguments.
✔	Put your best arguments first, and then address counterarguments.
✔	Give more space to your arguments than to your counterarguments.

✔	Anticipate your opponent's argument but do not score points for the other side.

Chapter 24: Writing the Summary of the Argument

✔	Begin the Summary of the Argument with an introductory paragraph that sets out a thesis statement and the rules that apply to the whole argument.
✔	Write only one or two paragraphs for each main issue in the brief.
✔	Use a topic thesis sentence to start each paragraph in the Summary of the Argument.
✔	State a rule, choose the strongest argument about this issue or sub-issue, and make the argument succinctly in a sentence or two.
✔	End the Summary of the Argument on a strong note for your side.
✔	Check the Summary of the Argument when you've finished writing the Argument section to make sure it's complete.

Chapter 25: Writing a Persuasive Fact Statement

✔	Use your client's point of view.
✔	Tell the whole story to be credible and so the reader can understand what happened.
✔	Don't analyze or argue in the Fact Statement and avoid an argumentative tone.
✔	Pay attention to organization, positions of emphasis, sentence construction, detail, and word choice for nonobvious persuasion in the Fact Statement.
✔	Don't make statements your opponent could justifiably claim are inaccurate.
✔	Follow local rules or professor's rules on whether to include procedure in the Fact Statement.
✔	Include every fact you use in the Argument section.
✔	Include a cite to the record for every fact.

✔	Use storytelling techniques to tell a persuasive story.

Chapter 26: Writing the Question Presented (Persuasive)

✔	Phrase the Question Presented to invite a "yes" answer that would result in your client prevailing.
✔	Include the applicable law, the precise legal question, and the facts most significant to your theory of the case.
✔	Make the Question Presented persuasive by using the techniques used elsewhere in the brief to persuade: emphasis, word choice, level of detail, and storytelling.
✔	Rewrite several times to make sure the Question Presented is as strong as possible.

Chapter 27: Writing the Conclusion Section (Persuasive)

✔	Conclusions in motions and briefs tend to be very short—one to two sentences (a short paragraph at most).
✔	Persuasive conclusions often begin with the words "For the foregoing reasons" and then state, in one short phrase, the relief the party requests.
✔	In stating the relief requested, be aware of the procedural posture of the case.
✔	As with all writing to a court, follow court rules or court expectations regarding Conclusions.

Chapter 28: Overview: Revising and Rewriting

✔	Plan your revision and rewriting strategy.
✔	Revise in several sessions and focus each session on just one or two types of edits.

✔	Revise in layers from big to small.
✔	Don't hesitate to make changes—even big changes.
✔	Appearance and visual presentation matter.
✔	Proofreading is critical because even small errors chip away at your credibility.

Chapter 29: Fixing Awkward Sentence Structure

✔	Use a subject–verb–object sentence structure.
✔	Keep the subject and the verb close together.
✔	Keep sentence length to no more than three to four lines of type.

Chapter 30: Starting Paragraphs Powerfully

✔	Start paragraphs with an assertion that advances your argument.
✔	Always put paragraph-thesis sentences at the beginning of the paragraph.
✔	Keep each paragraph focused only on the point announced in the paragraph-thesis sentence.

Chapter 31: Writing Concisely to Stay Within the Word Count or Page Limit

✔	Comb the paper for stylistic cuts before cutting substance.
✔	Avoid repetition within one section of the document.
✔	If you must cut substance, shorten or eliminate weaker arguments.
✔	Minimize passive voice.
✔	Minimize nominalizations.
✔	Where appropriate, eliminate small clusters of words, often those that include "of."

✔	Avoid empty "there is" and "it is" constructions.
✔	Avoid throat-clearing phrases at the start of sentences or paragraphs.

Chapter 32: Bringing It Together: Transitions and Coherence

✔	Use introductory paragraphs (umbrella sections and roadmaps) to give the big-picture view of what comes next.
✔	In a Discussion or Argument section, use the organizational pattern readers are familiar with (e.g., CRAC).
✔	Use signpost words or phrases to tell the reader the sequence of analysis and main points.
✔	Use headings and subheadings.
✔	Use paragraph-thesis sentences at the start of paragraphs and keep each paragraph a moderate length, focused on supporting its paragraph-thesis sentence.
✔	Use a logical order, usually moving from broad to narrow.
✔	Avoid long sentences, especially several long sentences in a row.
✔	Use consistent terminology.
✔	For sentences, keep the subject and the verb close together and use active voice.
✔	Use transitions to connect ideas between sentences and paragraphs.

Chapter 33: The Writer's Life: Where to Go From Here

✔	Take every opportunity to practice writing in law school, especially those where you will get feedback.
✔	Keep a personal list of legal writers you find effective and inspiring.
✔	As you read for other purposes, when you find an effective document, analyze what makes it good.
✔	As you gain experience and nuance, know that you can sometimes innovate by ignoring some of the fundamentals you have learned.

✔	Read articles and books about writing by legal writing scholars and practitioners.
✔	Stay aware of the trends in legal writing theory like rhetoric theory, narrative theory, and cognitive science advances.
✔	Be aware of continued technological changes that can improve your writing.
✔	Continue to think about and care about your writing.

Index